Identity and Power

Puerto Rican Politics and the
Challenge of Ethnicity

To Louis Núñez,
with best
wishes,

Jose

Albany, NY
June 2004

Identity
and Power

*Puerto Rican Politics and the
Challenge of Ethnicity*

JOSÉ E. CRUZ

TEMPLE UNIVERSITY PRESS
Philadelphia

Temple University Press, Philadelphia 19122
Copyright © 1998 by Temple University. All rights reserved
Published 1998
Printed in the United States of America

Library of Congress Cataloging-in-Publication Data

Cruz, José E., 1953–
    Identity and power : Puerto Rican politics and the challenge of ethnicity / José E. Cruz.
        p.   cm.
    Includes bibliographical references (p.   ) and index.
    ISBN 1-56639-604-2 (cl. : alk. paper). — ISBN 1-56639-605-0 (pbk. : alk. paper)
        1. Puerto Ricans—Connecticut—Hartford—Politics and government.   2. Puerto Ricans—Connecticut—Hartford—Ethnic identity.   3. Hartford (Conn.)—Ethnic relations.   I. Title.
    F104.H3C78   1998
    324′.089′678729507463—dc21   97–45555
                                                                                CIP

For my extended family
and
in memory of my brother,
José Miguel Cruz Figueroa
(1958–1984)

Contents

Maps, Tables, and Photos   ix

Preface   xi

1   Introduction   1

2   Hartford: The City and Its Politics   20

3   Puerto Ricans in Hartford: From Settlement to
    Collective Behavior   37

4   From Collective Behavior to Brokered Representation   67

5   From Brokered Representation to Political Mobilization   99

6   Identity Politics: The Puerto Rican Political Action
    Committee of Connecticut   124

7   Identity and Power   155

8   Puerto Rican Politics and the Challenge of Ethnicity   201

    Notes   217

    Select Bibliography   255

    Index   273

Maps, Tables, and Photos

MAPS

1 Patterns of Puerto Rican Migration to Hartford, Connecticut   38
2 Hartford, Connecticut, 1969 Riots   59

TABLES

1 U.S. Cities with Large Concentrations of Puerto
Ricans, 1990   5
2 Total, White, Puerto Rican, and African American
Population in Hartford, 1950–1990   26
3 Selected Nonagricultural Employment in Hartford,
1965–1980   29
4 Selected Nonagricultural Employment in Hartford,
1980–1990   30
5 Resident/Commuter Employment and Unemployment Rate,
Hartford, 1960–1993   33
6 Estimated Population Growth of Puerto Ricans in Hartford,
1954–1970   75
7 Estimated Voter Turnout in Districts with High Concentrations
of Puerto Ricans, 1971–1991   150
8 Electoral Support for Puerto Rican Candidates, 1971–1991   164
9 Changes in Manufacturing and Financial, Insurance, and Real
Estate (FIRE) Jobs in Hartford in Comparative Perspective,
1980–1990   173
10 Hartford Labor Force Participation Rates in Comparative
Perspective, 1980–1990   174
11 Characteristics of Hartford's Puerto Rican
Neighborhoods, 1990   214

PHOTOS

1 Family of Venan Rodríguez   38
2 Unidentified Puerto Rican farmworker   39
3 Mrs. Joaquín Vargas, an employee at Hartford Live Poultry   40

4   Antonio Gómez, a Puerto Rican worker at Royal Typewriter   41
5   Julián Vargas at La Popular, Bodega Hispana   42
6   Officers of the Liga Cívica Puertorriqueña de Hartford   46
7   María Sánchez at a community meeting during the 1969 riots   57
8   María Sánchez and Alejandro La Luz   61
9   Connecticut palm trees   63
10 Roger W. Lindgren, Gilberto Camacho, and
      Wallace A. Curtis   69
11 Mildred Torres, Sarah Romany, Olga Mele, and
      Diana Alverio   77
12 Julián Vargas and members of the Juana Díaz
      baseball team   78
13 Yasha Escalera, the first Puerto Rican director of
      the San Juan Center   79
14 Edna Negrón Smith testifying in support of bilingual
      education   80
15 José Claudio and Eugenio Caro marching into Hartford
      City Hall   85
16 Puerto Rican rally outside Hartford City Hall   86
17 William Pérez and Wallace Barnes   91
18 José La Luz, Yolanda Carrera, Edwin Vargas, Jr., and
      Esther Vargas   110
19 Andrés Vázquez, Mildred Torres, Eugenio Caro, and
      Edwin Vargas, Jr.   120
20 Mildred Torres campaigning in 1979   128
21 Antonio González, the first Puerto Rican elected to
      the city council   129
22 Edwin Vargas, Jr., and Thirman Milner   131
23 Nancy Meléndez   137
24 Américo Santiago, Carrie Saxon Perry, and Juan
      Figueroa   143
25 Edwin Vargas, Jr., and Frances Sánchez   144
26 Carrie Saxon Perry, Henrietta Milward, Wilbur Smith, Edwin
      Vargas, Jr., Shawn Wooden, and Danny Pérez   147
27 Fernando Comulada, Carmen Rodríguez, Edwin Vargas, Jr.,
      Yolanda Castillo, and Juan Figueroa   148
28 Edwin García greeting Bill Clinton during the 1992
      presidential campaign   210

Preface

OF THE hundreds of newspaper articles I read while doing the research for this book, two stand out. The first, written in 1957, tells the story of Zoilo Caraballo, one of Hartford's earliest Puerto Rican residents. A photograph of a cheerful Caraballo coming home to his children illustrates the article. The headline encapsulates the profile: PUERTO RICANS LIKE LIFE HERE, THEY'RE CROWDED BUT OPTIMISTIC. The second, published in 1970, also chronicles difficulties and hope. Titled ETHNIC NEED: POLITICAL MUSCLE, it summed up what some felt was necessary to achieve progress. According to Alejandro La Luz, a community organizer, Puerto Ricans needed better leadership. Most important, they needed to develop their own groups to mobilize along ethnic lines.

These articles illustrate two key features of the Puerto Rican experience in Hartford: a long-standing mix of hardship and opportunity and the use of ethnicity to correlate ascriptive traits and status, to focus social capabilities, and to confront political reality. How Puerto Ricans used ethnicity to tackle adversity and exploit opportunities, to channel the energy created by the bonds of identity into the pursuit of political enfranchisement, is what this book is about.

The events recounted in this book intersect with aspects of my own experience in the United States. Like many early migrants to Hartford, I came from Puerto Rico not speaking much English and seeking opportunities that were unavailable to me on the island. I too moved to a Connecticut city and was challenged by my new circumstances. Once on the mainland, I realized I was an "ethnic," a discovery that baffled me. I was psychologically and culturally stricken upon arrival, but I adjusted quickly and looked forward to a new chapter in my life.

During my eighteen years in the United States, ethnicity has structured my experience in both positive and negative ways. Otherness has been my ticket to the mainstream of society. But it has been the source of much misunderstanding and conflict as well. Once, while visiting Milwaukee, a fellow called me "foreigner." I am a U.S. citizen by birth, but I am not blond and blue-eyed as he was. I cannot forget the old man who, alarmed at the sound of salsa coming from my apartment, angrily told me that "bongo music" was not welcome in "his" neighborhood because "this is Little Italy!" I kept playing my music but not as loudly as before. And then there was the cab driver who expressed his dissatisfaction with my tip by calling me a "fucking spic." That insult left me speechless, but it drove my wife to threaten him with bodily harm. Fortunately, my run-ins with prejudice have been infrequent, partly because of the struggle of people like Zoilo Caraballo and Alejandro La Luz to gain acceptance and respect for themselves and for others like them.

Just as I find echoes of my personal experience in the collective history of Puerto Ricans in Hartford, their story resonates in other cities, big and small. Hartford is not the only place where ethnicity has been an important mobilizing factor in key social and political battles. Elsewhere, Puerto Ricans and Latinos have used ethnicity to define their needs, and ethnicity in turn has structured their positions and their choices. The claim that the political significance of ethnicity is bound to decline is by now several generations old, yet this has not happened.

In 1996, when Mayor Rudolph Giuliani marched up Fifth Avenue during the Puerto Rican Day Parade, thousands jeered him for his neglect of Puerto Rican concerns. At Columbia University students demanded a program of ethnic studies. At Cornell they protested the elimination of ethnic dormitories. In Chicago, after a long struggle against discrimination in housing, Latinos won an agreement from the Housing Authority to print bilingual forms and give priority to Hispanic families on the waiting lists for apartments. Also in 1996, Bronx congressman José Serrano maintained his stronghold on the sixteenth district with 96 percent of the mostly Puerto Rican vote. In the twelfth congressional district, encompassing parts of Brooklyn and Manhattan, Nydia Velázquez won handily with 84 percent of the ballots. Meanwhile, elected officials in Hartford struggled with budget cuts that many thought would have a disproportionate effect on Puerto Rican residents. As a result, community leaders prepared for yet another battle. There is no doubt in my mind: ethnicity will continue to be an important ingredient in the American quest for unity, diversity, democratic participation, and equality.

CHAPTER I of the book, the Introduction, treats the subject topically and theoretically. It describes the object of study, its significance, and the conceptual framework underlying the narrative. Chapter 2 reviews Hartford's political history and the place of Puerto Ricans in the city's political system during the post–World War II period. Chapters 3 and 4 describe and analyze Puerto Rican political development in the city. Despite transient elements and travel back and forth between island and mainland, over the years Puerto Ricans have carved a permanent space for themselves in Hartford. To better understand the process of incorporation, I explain how it developed over time. Chapter 5 analyzes a set of events during the 1970s that illustrate the tension between brokered representation and political mobilization. Chapter 6 expands this analysis by focusing on the Puerto Rican Political Action Committee of Connecticut. The origins and development of this group illustrate the connection between ethnicity, organization, and power. Chapter 7 focuses on the relationship between identity and power, beginning with an analysis of the city as the context for political action and then examining the nature and expressions of identity politics. An examination of the link between access to power and its exercise follows. The final section of chapter 7 outlines issues for future research. Chapter 8 concludes the book by reflecting on the challenge of ethnicity and the role it ought to play in the political process.

WRITING MY doctoral dissertation and then transforming it into this book required more time and energy than I ever dreamed would be necessary. Luckily, many people helped me, and I owe them an enormous debt of gratitude. I received intellectual direction, practical advice, encouragement, and support from John Mollenkopf and Marshall Berman. Their empathy during a period of personal crisis kept me "keeping on." Early guidance also came from Krista Alstentetter, Frank Bonilla, Bernard Brown, Marilyn Gittell, Olga Jiménez-Wagenheim, William Kornblum, Howard Lentner, Frances Fox Piven, Stanley Renshon, Melvin Richter, and the late Richard Styskal. The cooperation of Pedro Juan Hernández, former director of the archives of the Commonwealth of Puerto Rico's Department of Puerto Rican Community Affairs in the United States (now located at the Center for Puerto Rican Studies at Hunter College), was crucial to my research. His staff, Carlos Bruno, Felipe Morales Millán, and Catrize Ortiz, kindly guided me through seventy boxes of documents containing information on Puerto Ricans in Hartford. Marisol Ramos-Aponte and María Cecilia Onetti, both graduate students at SUNY-Albany, were efficient research assistants.

In the city, I received help from Benjamin B. Barnes and Crucita D. Soto, from Hartford's Planning Department; Juliann Butler, from the city's Office of Management and Budget; Henry Bissonnette, from the United Way of the Hartford Capital Area; Nick Nyhart, executive director of the Legislative Electoral Action Program (LEAP); Susan Pennybacker and Eddie Pérez, from Trinity College; and John Rogan, area director of the New England Farmworkers Council (NEFC). Penny Rusnak and Janice Mathews, from the Hartford Public Library, gave me access to photographs from the library's Hartford collection, and Juan Fuentes graciously allowed me to publish some from his. The owners of the Chester

Bulkley House in nearby Wethersfield, Frank and Sophie Bottaro, were accommodating beyond their commercial interest. Their hospitality made the fieldwork experience all the better.

My colleagues at SUNY-Albany, Edna Acosta-Belén, Richard Alba, Anne Hildreth, Richard Nathan, Colbert Nepaulsingh, Carlos A. Santiago, and Todd Swanstrom, read parts of the manuscript and offered pointed comments and criticism. I also received helpful suggestions from Pedro Cabán and Steve Valocchi. Recommendations from two anonymous reviewers for Temple University Press were crucial in the transformation of the manuscript from first to final draft. At the Press, Doris Braendel offered smart and substantive editorial advice. It was a pleasure and a privilege to work with her. Charles Ault, of Temple University Press, and Fred Thompson, of Book Production Resources, succeeded in making the production process author-friendly. My sincere thanks also go to Erica Fox for a careful and thorough job of copy editing.

It is wonderful to finally be able to acknowledge people who contributed in their own special ways: Ramón Daubón, Benedetto Fontana, Jeffrey Gerson, Jennifer Kaylin, Louis Núñez, Felipe Pimentel, Lucy Potter, Doris Suarez, and Stephanie Wiles.

My profound appreciation goes to all the individuals who consented to share their knowledge about Puerto Rican and Hartford politics with me. I thank especially Juan Brito for lending me his collection of newspapers, and Edwin Vargas, Jr., and Louise Simmons for always being ready to provide information and analysis.

My wife, Elizabeth Allen, read more versions of this study than she cares to remember. If I have enjoyed my work, it is in part because of the intellectual and professional partnership we have forged over time. But she and the members of my extended family were special to this project in a deeper sense. Elizabeth, her parents and brothers gave me emotional and material support without which I could not have completed this book. Equally important in this regard were my mother, Gloria Figueroa, my grandmother Josefa Sánchez, God bless her soul; my sister, Vilma; my aunts Palmira, Elsie, and Rosa Julia; and my children, Víctor, Gabriel, and Elena. They sustained me with more than a fair share of love. So did my brother José Miguel during his short life. I dedicate this book to them and to the enduring memory of Miguelito.

Identity and Power

Puerto Rican Politics and the Challenge of Ethnicity

1   Introduction

ONE NOVEMBER night in 1992, while sitting at his kitchen table with a reporter from the *Hartford Advocate*, Edwin Vargas, Jr., then chairman of the Hartford Democratic Town Committee and leading light of the Puerto Rican Political Action Committee of Connecticut (PRPAC), reviewed his twenty years of political activism. "I really don't like politics," he said. The reporter, after nearly choking on a mouthful of food, exclaimed, "That's the most ridiculous thing I ever heard. Everything you do, everything you say, screams politics! Your pores sweat politics. How can you tell me something like that?" Vargas offered a simple explanation: altruism. Puerto Ricans were poor, disfranchised, ignored by the power structure, and they needed him. He was in politics not for his sake but to do something for the community. Vargas allowed that this explanation was corny but true. The journalist later wrote that it was not believable.[1]

When I read the story, I too was puzzled by Vargas's admission. I was sure that his explanation was sincere, although I also understood how it could come across as self-serving. Still, this professed dislike of politics did not make sense. I remembered the afternoon in August 1991 when, with a broad smile and shining eyes, Vargas told me that PRPAC was risking its political future in an all-out challenge against six Democratic incumbents. The more he talked, the more I realized how significant the risk was. Yet his voice and his demeanor exuded only confidence and excitement. Likewise, when he shared the story behind his election as the Democratic party's town chair—a truly Machiavellian tale of wily maneuvers and unsavory alliances—his sense of satisfaction and exultant tone were nearly palpable. These recollections did not jibe with the image of a reluctant player. How could he say that he hated politics when his behavior indicated that to him politics was what the hunt is to the predator?

The answer to this question echoes in the story this book tells. Vargas did not really hate politics; he hated its messiness, its burdensome demands, and its mixed outcomes. During his term as president of PRPAC Vargas and his allies devised a strategy that focused the energy drawn from Puerto Rican identity on achieving political power. By 1991, the results were dramatic: two state representatives were Puerto Rican, as well as a department head, several members of commissions, the corporation counsel, a deputy city manager, and three members of the city council.

True, almost one-third of Hartford's population was Puerto Rican, but the community also was barely two generations old. Yet, although the accomplishments had been significant, important campaigns had not turned out as expected, substantial agendas remained unfinished, and a trail of friends had turned bitter enemies.

Six months after the interview with the reporter for the *Advocate*, Vargas shared his mixed feelings about politics with me as he talked about Hartford's 1993 budget. Proposed cuts included a $27 million reduction in the allocation for education, just when the majority of students were Puerto Rican and black. "Politically, we have arrived," he said, "at a time in which, instead of deciding who gets what, we have to decide who will be left out."[2]

THIS BOOK is about political mobilization and political change from below. It is about identity politics and urban power, about how ethnicity contributes to political action and how previously excluded actors access power. The focus is on Puerto Ricans and how they organized and mobilized to demand accountability from Hartford's political stratum. It chronicles and analyzes a process of empowerment—a process entailing incorporation and responsiveness—in which ethnicity played a major role. In fact, ethnicity played a *positive* role, thus casting the relationship between identity and power in a favorable light. For reasons related to the context and character of political action, however, success was only partial. Rewards were limited and costs substantial, accruing over an extended period of time.

Fueling this political mobilization were demographic growth, leadership development, and a relentless organizational drive. Puerto Ricans used ethnicity for political purposes in ways that represented a challenge both to the city and to themselves. To satisfy their social and political needs, they sought power. In this they succeeded, but access to power became only a threshold beyond which new difficulties lay. Ethnicity prompted expressions of cooperation and solidarity, but conflict was often the result as well. Finally, the relationship between political representation and socioeconomic gains was problematic.

The struggles of PRPAC from 1983 to 1991 epitomized this effort. Its leaders demanded accountability and respect for the Puerto Rican community. Before the creation of PRPAC, Puerto Ricans directed many of their claims to Nicholas Carbone, the city's deputy mayor from 1970 to 1979. Puerto Ricans focused on him after realizing that his obligation to them, and more generally, to the neighborhoods in which they lived, could not be taken for granted. For this reason, the generally cooperative relationship they had with Carbone and with the Democratic party was punctuated by challenges that sought to address the imbalance between political rhetoric and political reality. That these challenges occurred was not surprising. But the Puerto Rican case added issues of identity to the mix of change and continuity that characterized the dynamics of power in Hartford.

PUERTO RICAN MIGRATION TO THE UNITED STATES

The story of Puerto Rican migration to the United States is a familiar one and need not be retold here except in its barest outline.[3] The presence of Puerto Ricans in Connecticut goes back to the antebellum period,[4] and, according to popular lore, the nexus between New England and Puerto Rico has not only been long-standing but culturally significant. The origin of the fritter known as *bacalaíto*—which consists of chunks of cod deep fried in flour batter—is related to trade between Massachusetts and Puerto Rico in the nineteenth century. Similarly, the machete, which in Puerto Rican culture alternates between agricultural implement and national symbol, is said to have come from the U.S. Northeast as a result of nineteenth-century trade.[5]

The larger forces behind Puerto Rican migration to the United States were colonialism and capitalism. The so-called change of sovereignty, a euphemistic way to refer to the substitution of U.S. for Spanish colonial rule in 1898, opened the door for systematic population movements between the island and the mainland. By 1910, stateside Puerto Ricans numbered three thousand. By 1920, three years after the Jones Act granted them American citizenship, that number had increased sixfold.[6] Colonialism gave Puerto Ricans freedom of movement between island and mainland. Capitalism gave them incentives to move, and easy access to steamship and air travel made the trek possible. Citizenship made them eligible for military service in World War I. Through their experience in the service, Puerto Ricans became acquainted with life in the United States and this prompted many to stay.

In 1921, Congress passed the Johnson Act to curtail European immigration, and this contributed to the opening of job opportunities for Puerto Ricans, to whom alien restrictions did not apply. Furthermore, top government officials in San Juan and Washington, D.C., promoted the importation of Puerto Rican labor, arguing that as U.S. citizens they ought to be considered before foreigners.[7]

From the migrants' point of view, the fundamental motive for leaving the island was economic. In their study of Puerto Rican migration, C. Wright Mills, Clarence Senior, and Rose Goldsen suggested that "economic pull could not operate unless there were sources of favorable information about

New York City on the island."[8] They failed to note, however, that economic pull was matched not just by sources of information but by a favorable legal and political context created by the state.

Colonialism and capitalism and economics and politics provided the conditions that made migration possible, but individual Puerto Ricans, with help from institutional actors, such as Puerto Rico's Department of Labor, the U.S. Employment Service, and representatives of interested corporations, made the decision to come. What Senior and Donald Watkins called the "family intelligence service" also played a role, as spouses and relatives rejoined on the mainland and acquaintances lured others to make the move.[9] All took the promise of American citizenship seriously, hoping that Americans on the mainland would welcome them as equals.

Since Puerto Ricans arrived on the mainland, people have been studying them, but the focus of this research has been New York City, where before 1980 the majority of Puerto Ricans lived. By 1980, however, although New York still had the largest single community on the mainland (43 percent), the majority of mainland Puerto Ricans lived elsewhere,[10] and by 1990, only one-third lived in New York. During this period the growth was most pronounced in medium-sized cities, that is, jurisdictions with populations of between 150,000 and 250,000, such as Hartford.

In 1990, 27 percent of Hartford's total population was Puerto Rican. Nowhere else were they as concentrated (see Table 1). The reasons will not be explored here, but the implications for ethnic politics are crucial to my analysis.[11] Demographic concentration facilitated ethnic political mobilization, promoting the development of leaders and organizational efforts and acting as a counterweight to the forces of poverty and marginality. Context, as the reader shall see, was not everything, but its importance was cardinal.

Puerto Ricans came to Hartford propelled by the force of circumstance but motivated by desire and ambition. Some followed their American spouses, others wanted a better life, a few came just for the excitement of discovering what lay beyond island boundaries. Unemployed farmworkers and impoverished *arrimaos* (sharecroppers) were part of the mix, but skilled workers and a few professionals also made it, lured, respectively, by the prospect of work in tobacco farms, the possibility of industrial employment, or simply the desire to rejoin family members. Not all were poor, but poverty and marginalization became the defining elements of life, even for those to whom Hartford appeared "a perfect city."

The Puerto Rican settlement in the insurance city coalesced during the 1950s. The review of the political development of the community shows the protracted nature of interest articulation and how it responds to both endogenous and exogenous factors. This micro-history is useful because

Table 1. U.S. Cities with Large Puerto Rican Concentrations, 1990

State and City	Total Population	Puerto Ricans	% of Total
California			
Los Angeles	3,485,398	14,367	0.4
Connecticut			
Bridgeport	141,686	30,250	21
Hartford	*139,739*	*38,176*	*27*
New Haven	130,474	13,866	11
New Britain	75,491	10,325	14
New York			
New York City	7,322,564	896,763	12
Rochester	231,636	16,383	7
Yonkers	188,082	14,420	8
New Jersey			
Camden	87,492	22,984	26
Elizabeth	110,002	12,062	11
Jersey City	228,537	30,950	14
Newark	275,221	41,545	15
Paterson	140,891	27,580	20
Massachusetts			
Boston	574,283	25,767	4
Lawrence	70,207	14,661	21
Springfield	156,983	23,729	15
Ohio			
Cleveland	505,616	17,829	4
Pennsylvania			
Philadelphia	1,585,577	67,857	4
Reading	78,380	11,612	15
Florida			
Miami	358,548	12,004	3
Illinois			
Chicago	2,783,726	119,866	4

SOURCE: U.S. Department of Commerce, 1990 Census of Population.

it reveals that Puerto Rican politics in Hartford is not New York City politics writ small. New York City was important to Hartford—intercity migration did take place, and Puerto Rican politics was not disconnected from developments elsewhere. But if one assumes that point of origin determines the character of politics in the receiving society, Puerto Rican politics in Hartford should be a mixture of island, mainland, and local influences rather than a small-scale version of Puerto Rican politics in New York. This is indeed the case.

This review also shows how the story of Puerto Ricans fits within broader developments. For example, it is inappropriate to see their ethnic-based mobilization as an epiphenomenon of the struggle of African Americans. Was ethnicity "quickly taken up" by Puerto Ricans after its expression was legitimized by blacks?[12] To be sure, the black movement caught the attention of intellectuals, publishers, the media, and government, and, assuming that it is reasonable to label their movement as "ethnic," it gave visibility to ethnic politics. But this says nothing about why there was a resurgence of ethnicity during the 1970s and even less about the Puerto Rican case. Puerto Rican identity politics in Hartford dates from the 1950s, before black militancy became widespread. Puerto Ricans were not impervious to contextual influences, but their history reveals that identity politics preceded not just the civil rights movement but its corollaries and the so-called ethnic revival of the 1970s as well. In their case, ethnic awareness was shaped by life in the United States but rooted in their island experience.

To be sure, the decline of Americanism brought about by racial conflict and the Vietnam War made ethnicity more acceptable during the 1970s than it was during World War II, when it was associated with fascist sympathies and betrayal. But the changed context alone does not explain why Puerto Ricans engaged in identity politics. It is by reviewing their political history that one realizes that their ethnic identity was strong before these conditions set in and that identity politics was a way of achieving representation and a means to negotiate individual and group benefits. To some, ethnicity meant a rejection of Americanism—to the extent that embracing the United States meant sanctioning colonialism in Puerto Rico—but to the majority, ethnicity was a code that structured their entrance into mainstream society and politics.

THE PUERTO RICAN POLITICAL ACTION COMMITTEE OF CONNECTICUT

In 1989, when this study began, there were signs of a political emergence among Puerto Ricans in Hartford that contrasted with the traditional and better-known New York experience. PRPAC was emblematic of this process. As I began to gather information on the community, it quickly became apparent that PRPAC was the leading political force among Puerto Ricans in the city. Its importance as object of study was clear. The contrast of Hartford with New York City, where, despite being the oldest and largest settlement, Puerto Ricans had no representation, was notable, and the saliency of PRPAC was a departure from situations of nearly complete political invisibility. Elsewhere, Puerto Ricans were excluded from political parties, policy-making bodies, and even from the antipoverty programs that other groups used to promote political mobilization and political access.[13]

I was fortunate to chance upon a group that provided an opportunity to fill a gap in the literature on Latino studies and that also fit within broader political science themes.[14] A focus on PRPAC enabled a look at community organization primarily as political action instead of as an expression of cultural patterns of behavior.[15] To be sure, culture and politics turned out to be interrelated in Hartford, but PRPAC represented an instance of ethnic-based mobilization that raised questions about how identity affected politics rather than the other way around.[16] And although this relationship was not entirely neglected in the literature, PRPAC provided an opportunity to examine ethnic awareness as an ingredient of power awareness as opposed to an epiphenomenon of structural factors.

That PRPAC was an example of the specificity of Puerto Rican politics on the mainland enticed me to document its story. But in the context of examining the relationship between ethnicity and politics, I also sought to explore the relationship between mainland and island politics within the Puerto Rican community to see if, as others had claimed, Puerto Rican politics on the mainland was a replica of colonial relations between Puerto Rico and the United States.[17]

The focus on PRPAC also provided an opportunity to answer a set of key questions: Puerto Rican access to power occurred relatively quickly—how did this happen? Did identity politics facilitate this access? Once ethnicity finds it way into the structure of representation, what are the consequences?

By the time PRPAC began its heady ascent to power in 1985, Puerto Ricans had been a presence in Hartford for nearly half a century. By then they constituted a largely poor and segmented community. Yet the most powerful trigger of political mobilization was ethnicity rather than class, although at times the line separating these categories was significantly blurred.

The account of Puerto Rican political development in Hartford begins during the 1950s because until then the community was negligible. The cut-off date of the study is 1993. In 1991, PRPAC became the most significant force of its kind in Hartford's electoral politics. By 1993, PRPAC had missed opportunities to consolidate its gains and failed to meet the challenges posed by new circumstances.

HARTFORD

Although Puerto Rican politics represents a new chapter in Hartford's political development, there are elements of continuity in this experience. Understanding the city's earliest political history helps explain current phenomena—such as identity politics, with its emphasis on group rather than individual claims. The point is not to tell Hartford's history but to highlight key features to place the Puerto Rican story in context.

In its three hundred–year history, Hartford has experienced many transformations.[18] One of the most important took place in 1639, when Hartford joined Windsor and Wethersfield to form the state of Connecticut. The union was cemented by the Fundamental Orders of Connecticut, the New World's first written constitution, which articulated a set of principles outlined a year earlier by Hartford's founder, Thomas Hooker. In a notable sermon, Hooker emphasized three points: the divine right of the people to choose their rulers; the right to exercise this choice through elections; and the power of the people to set limitations on the prerogatives of their representatives.

These principles formed the framework for a system of theocratic rule based on popular consent. Its key feature was an emphasis on the accountability of elected officials to the people, who remained the ultimate source of authority. This was not an exceptional development, but in the context of the Puritan value of submission to power and the concomitant notion of the absolute sovereignty of ruling magistrates, it was remarkable.

Over time, Hartford's political culture was organized around three distinct but related orientations—religious, secular, and business—that correlated with three distinct political societies. The historical record shows how agents of change were invariably greeted with suspicion and even hostility. The economic notables that sought to incorporate Hartford town in 1784 had to overcome the opposition of those who thought this move unnecessary and potentially disastrous.[19] Similarly, Republicans, by spearheading the transformation of Hartford into a business commonwealth at the turn of the nineteenth century, made themselves unpopular among machine politicians and immigrants alike.[20]

During the first decades of the twentieth century, the business-dominated political culture prospered.[21] But gradually, as elsewhere, the city became more liberal. This liberalism was abetted by the New Deal and the resurgence of the Democratic party. And despite a loss of ground after World War II, when business forces regained momentum, the Democrats flourished and Hartford became a one-party city.

The political history of Hartford is one in which the gap between promise and performance has been riddled with tension and discord. At times, social explosions disrupted civil discourse, but in most cases, tension, conflict, and even violence resulted in positive change. Herbert Janick's assessment of this dynamic for the state applies to the city:

> The history of Connecticut in the twentieth century has been marked by a series of clashes between the powerful and the powerless, always accompanied by intemperate demands and selfish resistance. As a result of this interaction, the range of economic, political, and social participation in the state

has been widened to include large numbers of European immigrants, organized labor, women, blacks, city dwellers, intellectuals, and young people.[22]

Historically, residents have quarreled over the meaning of democracy, the proper boundaries between church and state, the legitimacy of slavery, the place of immigrants in government and society, and the incorporation of women into the political process.[23] Each conflict produced a specific array of forces, often turning friends into adversaries and vice versa. Conflict brought progress to Hartford. But, more often than not, this change was slow in coming. Political accountability has always been problematic, even during the period when political and religious authority were synonymous and politics was considered a morally virtuous endeavor. Furthermore, to take advantage of the opportunities that propitiated progress, citizens frequently paid a high price.

When Puerto Ricans moved to Hartford during the second half of the twentieth century, they clearly encountered a city radically different from the original settlement or the city built by Republican Yankees and Democratic Irishmen during the nineteenth century. But the preceding account provides insights into the migrants' politics and situation. First, the principles outlined by Hooker in 1638 are relevant because they provided a standard for contemporary society. To be sure, those principles are enshrined in the U.S. Constitution and apply to all Americans. But in assessing Puerto Rican politics in Hartford, it is more useful to measure its contribution against *local* standards, of which Hooker's principles are one crucial example. The relevant question is, To what extent is Puerto Rican politics in conflict with the principles of participation, representation, and accountability outlined by Hartford's founding father? To put it in positive terms, one could argue that Puerto Rican politics is within the framework of what is best in Hartford's political heritage.

Second, the transformations outlined above were instances of clashes between the forces of tradition and the forces of change. This recurring element in the city's history helps us understand how Puerto Ricans were received by the city during the period after World War II. Should anyone be surprised that they were initially viewed with suspicion and even hostility? More important, even though this dialectic of resistance and innovation suggests a situation of simple polarization, the changes that occurred in the city over time actually developed in more complex ways, with politics making strange bedfellows more than just occasionally. Puerto Rican politics was not exempt in this regard. Puerto Ricans were thought by some to have a natural affinity with blacks, yet their relationship with African Americans was marked by conflict and subordination.

Puerto Ricans began to assert themselves politically during the period after World War II but most prominently during the 1970s. The events of this decade most directly shaped Puerto Rican politics, marking the interplay between identity politics and urban power that the remaining chapters describe and analyze.

How did issues of identity affect the quest for power? Developments in the United States during the post–civil rights period and in Europe after the dissolution of the Soviet Union have led to an array of simplistic assessments of the connection between these two variables. In this regard the Puerto Rican case is useful because it is both theoretically suggestive and politically reassuring.

IDENTITY POLITICS

In 1967, Kwame Ture, then known as Stokely Carmichael, and Charles Hamilton wrote: "The concept of Black Power rests on a fundamental premise: *Before a group can enter the open society, it must first close ranks.*"[24] That is, separation contributes to incorporation insofar as it helps the in-group marshal and consolidate its resources, thereby enhancing its bargaining power. As such, the concept of black power comes close to what identity politics is about. The experience of Puerto Ricans in Hartford, however, suggests a different proposition: *that the closing of ranks is not a precondition of incorporation but the precise way in which incorporation takes place.* In this analysis incorporation is understood as the process of entering society and politics and, as the reader will see, Puerto Ricans in Hartford did this at the very moment in which they asserted themselves as "the Other."[25] Thus, identity politics was not a *stage* in the process of incorporation, one to be left behind by integration.[26] It was instead both the medium for and *outcome* of political mobilization. In other words, incorporation was the result of the assertion of difference, but instead of being obliterated by it, difference gave meaning to, and was sustained by, incorporation.

This concept of identity politics relies on empirical data. It signifies the intersection of two transitional phenomena: the move from ethnic awareness to power awareness and from interests to interest group. The concept of interest group is defined broadly: although the Puerto Rican community in Hartford was not the same as a Washington, D.C., lobby, Puerto Rican groups developed a level of cohesiveness that made the pursuit of common political goals possible. In this sense, political mobilization signified the transition from interests to interest group.

The movement from ethnic to power awareness and from interests to interest group occurred when political claims encompassed concrete objectives that were pursued by actual organizations. Thus, identity was constant, but identity politics was subject to the ebb and flow of issues, agendas, and available resources.[27] According to this definition, identity politics is not just an attitude or an outlook but a sine wave-like process, cresting and dipping continuously, according to the fluctuations of focus, energy, resources, and circumstances that characterize political action.[28]

Ethnic awareness depended on the construction of a self-image in the context of place, an image that conveyed the following understanding: "I am a Puerto Rican in Hartford." The construction of this image was determined by personal and group background but also by social, economic, and political relationships in the city. In this sense, the resulting self-image was an "invention," although there is no evidence to indicate that it was a fictitious or purely symbolic category, as some have characterized ethnicity in the United States.[29] Instead, ethnic awareness was both a process and an outcome charged with deeply felt personal and historical meaning.

For Puerto Ricans in Hartford, ethnic awareness was the result of the clash between the psychological, cultural, and human capital characteristics associated with their nationality, the purposive action they conducted, and the reception accorded the group by the society, market, and state.[30] Felix Padilla relates Puerto Rican ethnic consciousness and behavior to the politics of place but also to Puerto Rico's colonial status. He argues that the Puerto Rican experience in Chicago is "a clear case of internal colonialism."[31] Yet, although colonialism explains the presence of Puerto Ricans in the United States, it does not fully account for their political behavior in Hartford.

Nathan Glazer and Daniel Moynihan distinguish rights that are derived from group identity from interests that are strategically advanced by exploiting the affective tie of ethnicity. In the former case, ethnic ends must be achieved through ethnic means (e.g., the maintenance of culture through bilingual education). In the latter case, ethnicity is a shell for other interest categories, such as class (e.g., when economic entrepreneurship is pursued through affirmative action set-asides). Puerto Ricans in Hartford exploited ethnicity in both ways, but their strategic use focused on political rights rather than on individual economic interests. Consequently, they insisted on the "significance of their group distinctiveness and identity,"[32] but the claims they articulated derived from power awareness as much as from their group character.

Power awareness was a sense of how political actors came to be favored by the polity.[33] This awareness was articulated as a proposition establishing a cause-and-effect relationship: "I am disadvantaged in Hartford because I am Puerto Rican." This was an objective realization insofar as it coincided with experiences of prejudice, discrimination, underrepresentation, and poverty.[34] But it was also a logical deduction based on the assumption that resources or characteristics (such as ethnicity) automatically translated into having or lacking influence or power.[35] In this sense, power awareness did not necessarily lead to political action because disadvantaged political actors often assumed that their relative deprivation would yield exclusion and disfranchisement. For this reason power awareness is different from empowerment; it is through the latter that citizens enter the political scene as knowledgeable and capable agents. In other words, empowerment begins when the perception or experience of social, economic, and political inequity leads citizens to organize and mobilize.

Although ethnic awareness was logically related to the notion of interests, once it became power awareness it set the stage for political action; action presupposed the existence of an interest group, that is, an organization ready and willing to mobilize. The notion of interests is based on the recognition of the existence of a distinct community with social, cultural, political, and economic needs. In addition to organization and willingness to mobilize, crucial to the notion of interest group is the idea that action will focus on the political process as the arena of mobilization and government as its target.

When these two phenomena—power awareness and interest group organization—intersected, the result was identity politics. In other words, erstwhile amorphous and passive interests acquired cohesion and were activated politically using as point of reference and rationale correlations between ethnicity and status. Because ethnic-based demands were pursued *in accordance with the rules of the political order*, this was not a destructive politics; instead, it was a complex politics in which integration was achieved through the mobilization of particularity. Identity politics highlighted inequity and disadvantage *to promote mobilization*.[36] For this reason, it did not reify victimization. Instead, it encouraged individuals to overcome passivity, which is the first step in moving beyond victim status.

Whereas the conventional understanding of identity politics alleges that its inevitable effect is separatism and instability, my narrative chronicles its structuring, stabilizing, and integrative role. Identity-based claims have been condemned as the whimpering of victims who exploit their victimization to demand rights without responsibilities. In the Puerto Rican case, identity was used not just to articulate redistributive claims but to construct a dignified self-image and demand equal access to positions of responsibility within the civil and political society.

Yet in the process of empowerment, identity politics was also problematic. Ethnic-based claims competed with and compounded other conflicts. Puerto Rican political agency was facilitated by ethnicity, but the extent to which public policy served as an instrument of power was limited. The limitations of ethnicity were not intrinsic, as is suggested by Rodney

Hero's criticism of the "Rainbow Myth" or by Andrés Torres's association of ethnic politics with unstable alliances and enduring conflict.[37] Instead, the experience of Puerto Ricans in Hartford suggests that specific rewards are obtained through discrete processes, each with its own logic.

To obtain ethnic representation, Puerto Ricans needed demographic concentration, organizational resources, and good leadership; but to benefit from public policy, they had to meet a different set of requirements. It was their inability to meet these demands that crippled their potential to exercise coalition power.[38] Nonethnic factors, such as the chosen mobilization strategy, the character of relations between groups, individuals, and institutions, the features of the policy process, and the disconnect between campaigning and governing, also played a part.

The story of Puerto Ricans in Hartford is about the ways in which a sense of self intertwined with a sense of power. Ethnicity was the substance of interest articulation. The specific ways in which ethnicity was politicized were determined by the strategy, focus, and structure of action, and action was structured in three major ways: as collective behavior, brokered representation, and political mobilization. As they moved from one form to the next, Puerto Rican leaders were faced with the challenge of finding a balance between *fortuna* and *virtù* that would enable them, as Machiavelli suggests in *The Prince*, to adapt their will to the demands of circumstances. To meet the challenge, they needed to adapt the instrumental qualities of ethnic politics to the constraints imposed by the context in which politics took place.

The problem was not that there were insurmountable barriers that only systemic changes could overcome, since the potency of structural factors did not originate in their structural quality per se. Instead, the dilemma these structures represented, in simultaneously being the products of human agency and forces beyond human power, was related to the discontinuities of time and space that characterized the emergence and reproduction of these arrangements.

Puerto Ricans in Hartford made their own history, but in the process they confronted plenty not of their choosing. For that reason, when they negotiated the terms of structural arrangements, much of what they confronted appeared to be beyond their grasp. The problem became one of matching will and circumstances. This was no easy task, in part because it required a seemingly opportunistic approach to action. Like the Machiavellian prince who must be both fox and lion as context demands, ethnic entrepreneurs had to emphasize or downplay ethnicity as necessary to pursue different kinds of alliances. This did not necessarily mean that, like Perseus, ethnic leaders had to draw magic caps over themselves to obscure their identity and their putative interests from the public or their rivals. Instead, it meant that a strategy for action had to be based on a careful reading of the situation, and the pursuit of goals had to focus as much as possible on the elusive middle point between a zero-sum game and Pareto optimality.

Notwithstanding the prediction of Herbert Gans that "in a few years the revival of ethnicity will also be forgotten," ethnicity did not disappear.[39] The impetus of the revival subsided, leaving behind a quieter but tenacious presence that ranged from the highly visible Irish, Puerto Rican, and West Indian parades in New York City to the more private *quinceañera* celebrations in Latino communities.[40] Whether public or private, ethnicity persisted: in Connecticut, Jews debated the legitimacy of interfaith marriages, while in New Jersey they built sukkahs in suburban backyards. In New York City, they conducted seders in rock clubs and broadcast them through the Internet.[41] In Miami, Cubans marched, stridently chanting "Pharaoh Clinton: Let My People Go!" while in Manhattan Boricuas opened "El Puerto Rican Embassy" on Broadway and 104th to issue fake passports that proclaimed a symbolic Puerto Rican citizenship.[42] And while Irish immigrants and Irish-Americans greeted cheerfully the first fund-raiser ever held in the United States by Sinn Fein, federal prosecutors smashed the Fukienese Flying Dragons, an ethnic organized-crime gang terrorizing Chinatown.[43] Such is the mix of American life. Questions tend to get raised about the role of ethnic identity, especially when it moves from society to politics.[44]

In the view of some, ethnicity distorts the political process by undermining policies that should focus on general interests.[45] By deviating from universalistic values, policies that focus on ethnic claims exacerbate conflict and promise only disharmony. In this view, ethnicity is nothing but an axis of domination and resistance.[46] This dimension is especially problematic in the context of nation building and is the most prominent on a global scale, threatening international stability and imposing enormous social and human costs.[47] In politically stable societies, however, ethnicity is thought to provide a criterion that sharpens the focus of public policy and thus allows the state to better serve a heterogenous population with diverse needs.[48] The state, of course, usually recognizes only what is brought to its attention and therefore it is only when groups politicize ethnicity that it becomes a resource to secure economic and political benefits.[49] Others have found that although ethnicity can provoke divisions, it also enriches liberal ideology and practice.[50]

What should ethnicity mean in the political process? The answer depends on how one sorts out these various assessments. Should it entail the self-conscious perpetuation of particularity or a voluntary emphasis on symbolic differences?[51] Should it be proscribed from the political process altogether, confined to the civic culture and kept there by an official stance of neutrality?[52] Or should it be a weapon in the struggle against the hegemony of Eurocentric values?[53]

Whatever stance one views as correct, ethnicity does play a role in politics.[54] It is also true that reports about the nefarious effects of identity politics have been greatly exaggerated. Whether grounded in class, race, gender, or ideology, conflict is inevitable. There is no substantive reason to single out identity politics. To be sure, ethnic-based claims can be unreasonable and ethnicity run amok has serious consequences. But these are extreme scenarios that no single variable can cause or explain.[55]

URBAN POWER

The experience of Puerto Ricans in Hartford also adds to our understanding of urban power. During the period from 1953 to 1992—the publication dates, respectively, of Floyd Hunter's *Community Power Structure* and John Mollenkopf's *A Phoenix in the Ashes*, the study of urban power completed a full cycle. The orbital points of this "revolution" are political approaches divorced from the economic context, a focus on the economy as a context and explanatory variable, and politics as the explanatory variable and the context in which decisions are made and processes take place.

Conceptually, politics was supreme in the 1960s. In the 1970s and '80s, politics became subordinate to the logic of capital; the 1990s, in contrast, has been the decade of the subject. Whether the focus is on class, race, ethnicity, or cities as a whole, the emphasis has shifted to political actors.

This broad outline does not deny the contested nature and deep roots of these frameworks.[56] Moreover, precedents for these approaches are found throughout the political science literature. For example, context and the role of systemic factors were already identified as important in some of the best work of the 1960s. Recall E. E. Schattschneider's wonderful Grand Central metaphor, in which the station is compared to party organization, as a system organized around a set of constraints (the timetables and the gates), where each party member is "organized by the system" through the limits placed on his choices.[57]

Nor is the emphasis on agency unique to the 1990s or to political science. In his 1941 critique of the materialist conception of history, for example, Rudolf Hilferding argued for the primacy of the subject: "It is the real human being, the thinking, willing and acting man, with his needs and interests, who constitutes the pre-condition for production relations."[58] The rediscovery of the subject in urban politics is important because it is meaningful and appropriate. To argue for a politics in which "social being determines consciousness" is like saying that the fertilizer determines the flower. Instead, theorizing has reached a point where even explanations of power that subordinate politics to the economy can be explained as political phenomena.

A key concern in the study of urban politics is with how previously excluded actors develop the wherewithal to access power. It would not be an exaggeration to say that for the most part this is the impetus of the Marxist, neo-Weberian, neo-Marxist, and post-Marxist response to pluralism. The animus behind this concern is varied: from the impulse to improve on the existing political order by rectifying its most glaring inequalities to the emphasis on the inadequacy of reform and the need for a fundamental challenge. There is another strand of criticism, which assumes both normative and formal overtones, that emphasizes, perhaps unfairly, the pluralist oversight of the existence and limits of preemptive power. But overall, the central concern, even of economic determinism, is empowerment. It is precisely along this dimension that the Puerto Rican experience in Hartford is relevant. In other words, *this case study illustrates how access to power takes place while identifying some of the elements that affect its exercise.*

None of the above intends to reduce urban power to a single logic but to highlight an underlying theme. This is an expedient that brings focus to the discussion and situates key theoretical approaches to the study of urban power. In fact, within the three orbital points noted above, five theoretical frameworks are relevant to the question of how interests are articulated and achieve access to power in urban settings. *Power elite* theories emphasize hierarchical arrangements in which command and control functions flow from the top and economic interests are paramount.[59] In the *pluralist* view, political processes are open-ended, interests are diffused, and no single interest holds a permanent monopoly on the command and control functions of power.[60] *Neocorporatism*, a 1970s development, suggests that the state can undercut the autonomy of interests by deliberately creating and institutionalizing groups. It grants them input prerogatives in exchange for surrender of control over their agenda.[61] *Structuralism* is an umbrella term that encompasses a variety of approaches whose theoretical coordinates are an emphasis on the distribution of economic resources as the fundamental measure of power, functionalist assumptions about the subservience of the state to dominant economic interests, and a market model of political transactions in which economic rationality drives political decision making.[62] Finally, the *dominant political coalition* approach is relevant to the question of interest articulation and interest representation through power. This approach, rather than denying the pluralist possibility of access, qualifies the process by specifying how the level of resource capability of political actors shapes and influences the rules that govern how coalitions become dominant, how they favor certain interests, and the conditions under which they persist or decay.[63]

Each framework is laden with assumptions that suggest how and which interests will access power. In power elite theory the game is rigged in favor of certain players. The pluralist model suggests a fair play among interests. Neocorporatism is a mixed-outcome model in which universal access to power is tainted by state control of both process and outcomes. Structuralist approaches also incorporate the notion of systemic bias, but here politics is subject to economic imperatives. The dominant political coalition approach sees a continuous structure of influence and power infrequently penetrated but not altogether impervious to challenge.

Insofar as hierarchical control, self-determination, co-optation, bias, stability, and change coexist within political systems, all theories have something to contribute. Paul Peterson made this point when he argued that the different approaches to the study of community power all "have captured one aspect of local politics." [64] In fact, these distinctions sometimes fail to hold in the work of the theorists in one or another camp. Clarence Stone argues, for example, that one can find elements of diffusion and instability in Floyd Hunter's concept of community power, and Stone's own work is not a total rejection of pluralism but an attempt to break the elitist-pluralist impasse.[65]

This book provides evidence to support a synthesis of these approaches to power. Throughout Hartford's history elites have played a prominent role in politics, and often their actions have been driven by economic interests. The Puerto Rican experience unmistakably demonstrates the pluralist proposition that all groups within the society can at some point be part of the political decision-making process and thereby have access to power. In 1978, Deputy Mayor Carbone organized the Citizens Lobby, a neocorporatist attempt at co-opting neighborhood discontent, which he used as a wedge in his running battle with the administration of Governor Ella Grasso. Even if the functionalist assumptions of structuralism are fundamentally wrong, its instrumentalist view is not altogether laughable. In Hartford, there were instances in which the level of affinity between city hall and the corporate sector was quite strong. Finally, the notion proposed by the dominant political coalition approach that political action is shaped by the configuration of systemic settings is also relevant.

Because none of these features fully describe the workings of the political process, I call the synthesis a contingency theory of power. Since its focus is on access to power rather than on its nature, the theory can be summarized with the following four propositions: (1) the building blocks of political action are the various sets of interests and interactions operating within state, society, and market. Power crystallizes in the intersection between public policy, organized interests, and the public at large, although expressions of power articulate these ingredients in random order and to varying degrees; (2) contrary to approaches that set these spheres of action in a fixed causal hierarchy, causality is contingent. In the Puerto Rican case, the economic and political context were important, but when ethnicity was the trigger to action, the crucial sphere was society; (3) whether a certain group will be able to access power at a given point in time depends on how it reconciles what it is capable of doing with what the systemic setting allows; (4) therefore, contingency is specified in the match between capability and feasibility. Capability is substantiated through interest articulation, and feasibility is measured by how interest articulation produces political effects. Ethnicity, for example, was an aspect of Puerto Rican capability. The effective exercise of power was contingent on the proper match between the use of ethnicity and the requirements of the situation. In campaigning, the match was positive and thus led to access; in governing, the match was not positive and therefore political gains were not secured.

NEXT STEPS

The Puerto Rican experience in Hartford raises substantive questions concerning political mobilization, the nature of the political process, the proper role of actors, and the relationship between the civil and political society. This book compresses those issues by looking at political mobilization as an expression of identity claims. In that sense, it is about Puerto Ricans as much as it is about the political process in general.

The conclusions presented are highly suggestive rather than universal statements. This is not because this is a case study of one group in one city but because even diachronic analyses of representative samples cannot possibly run the gamut of social and political experience. No single study, however representative its focus and comprehensive its range, is capable of considering the full extent of variables that influence and cause political action, and rarely, if ever, does analysis exhaust the possible interpretations of processes and outcomes.

Peterson has said that to have a complete theory of political causation is an achievement so remarkable that it is likely to elude the wit of social scientists for a long time.[66] Yet a complete theory is hardly necessary. What we need instead are persuasive arguments based on thick descriptions of specific experiences. The idea is to know what happened in order to sort out what it means—to figure out *what was* in order to project *what ought to be.*[67]

More than fifty years ago, V. O. Key warned against the pitfalls of particularism.[68] Many have echoed his admonitions since, and this book shares all the well-known reservations about the predominance of partiality: the fear that a vantage point might transform into an ideological fortress; that duty might be sacrificed on the altar of interest; that selfish regards might be substituted for empathy. Identity politics is not exempt from these and other aberrations, but these should be seen as cautionary rather than invalidating. After all, even the harshest critics of identity politics recognize that some of its defenders are moved by the desire to construct the "inclusive commonality" that hard-line separatists seek to destroy and ethnocentric liberals take for granted.[69]

What is crucial, however, is to show what actually happens when the mobilization of ethnicity—identity politics—translates into a quest for power in a particular context. If power is the intersection of public policy, organized interests, and the public at large, it is not only a legitimate but a necessary, useful, and inescapable relationship. In that sense, the view that identity politics balkanizes the political landscape and threatens the viability of the political order is more in tune with simplistic and misinformed apprehensions about the role of conflict in politics than with the more reasoned and well-established political science axiom that societal integration and political power are inextricably bound. As Philip Gourevitch suggests, the threat of conflict often lies in the inability of those who feel threatened to ascertain what the conflict is exactly about.[70] This is, in no small measure, true of identity politics and the feelings of distress that it causes among those who see only chaos and instability in its wake. Let us now specify what identity politics was about in Hartford by first analyzing the immediate urban and political context in which Puerto Ricans mobilized.

2   Hartford: The City and Its Politics

A MID-NINETEENTH-CENTURY assessment of Hartford's politics attributed its backwardness to the social character of its democracy. According to Samuel Goodrich, "The leading men were thrifty mechanics, with a few merchants, and many shopkeepers. . . . There were lawyers, judges, and public functionaries—men of mark—but their spirit did not govern the town."[1]

Writing at the turn of the century, James Welling noted how, instead of backward, Hartford was complex. Conservatism coexisted with liberalism and innovation, sometimes even conceding some of its privileged space. "Hartford is at once," he declared, " 'the birthplace of American Democracy' and the old historic stronghold of aristocratic politics in the United States."[2]

By the second half of the twentieth century, when Puerto Ricans began to settle in Hartford, the city no longer took its hue from "shopkeepers" and "thrifty mechanics." Aristocratic politics were all but dead, as the city was infused with progressivism, a form of elitism that focuses on broad-based interests and concerns. Yet, despite these changes, the city still reserved a place for businessmen among the highest social and political ranks.

BUSINESS HEGEMONY

During the teens and twenties, Connecticut was largely an industrial state. Bridgeport led in manufactured production, followed by Waterbury, New Haven, and then Hartford, which was already a national insurance center.

During this period Hartford's combination of a healthy economy and Republican hegemony had definite consequences. Among these was the belief that scientific management principles could be used to resolve all major economic problems. The *Hartford Courant* constantly called for "businesslike government," and its appeals for nonpartisanship and civil service were not just attacks against machine politics but against immigrants as well. Businessmen enjoyed considerable standing. They represented efficiency and rationality, and these became widespread values. Economic prosperity buttressed the resonance of these values as indicators of significance and worthiness.

It is no accident that the personal credo of J. Henry Roraback, Con-

20

necticut's Republican boss and the most influential power broker in the state and city during the first three decades of the century, was "good business is good politics; good politics is good business."[3] The preeminence of business in the city's political culture was the result of efficient organization, systematic lobbying, and the extensive links corporate officials cultivated with public officials.

Politically, business hegemony translated into antilabor efforts and propaganda. Campaigns for the open shop were central during this period, as were efforts to undermine unions. Yet the organizational style of nonbusiness institutions and the configuration of political conflict often failed to mirror the class cleavages embedded in their ideology. The clergy, for example, adopted a business style in its charitable operations and supported the business-oriented tenets of so-called good government. On specific issues, such as liberalizing Sabbath restrictions and the rejection of prohibition, the interests of business, lower-class migrants, and ethnic minorities sometimes coincided.

Hartford briefly deviated from the business credo in 1928, the year of Al Smith's presidential candidacy and his whistle-stop tour of Connecticut. Thousands cheered the Happy Warrior, especially in the city, where between 100,000 and 150,000 people gave him a warm welcome. After his visit, the *Courant* ran this headline: THOUSANDS ACCLAIM SMITH IN HARTFORD'S GREATEST OF OVATIONS.[4] Harding and Coolidge had won in Hartford by large margins in 1920 and 1924. But in 1928 the city belonged to Al Smith in what was interpreted as a triumph for Catholic working-class immigrants.

This exception notwithstanding, the business credo was widely held until the Great Depression. Beginning with the 1929 shutdown of the United States Rubber Company, economic dislocations were mostly felt by the manufacturing sector. By the winter of 1930, sixty-five hundred city residents were jobless, or 4 percent of the total population. In the manufacturing sector, however, the proportion of laborers that were out of work was 13 percent that year. As the Depression widened, more families went on public assistance. Between December 1931 and September 1932, this number increased by 28 percent.[5]

Governor John H. Trumbull and the Republican party adopted a policy of ignoring the plight of the cities. In response, the voters elected Wilbur Cross in 1930, making him the first Democrat elected governor in almost fifteen years. Cross won by a slim majority composed of a portion of the Republican rural and upper-class vote and the ethnic vote in the cities. He carried Hartford, New Haven, Waterbury, and Bridgeport by wide margins. For the first time since 1894, the Republicans were reduced to minority status in Hartford.

The response of Hartford's business community was manifold. Some leaders retreated, others fought the new governor, and a third sector adapted.

Cross's reign came to an end in 1938. Several financial scandals in his administration and an alliance between the Socialists and the Republicans led to his loss to Raymond Baldwin, a Republican attorney who believed that business should be friendlier to the federal government, who was less hostile to labor, and who was more in favor of government intervention in social policy. The GOP took back four congressional seats and one U.S. Senate seat. Yet Hartford remained Democratic.

This shift toward Republicanism coincided with an isolationist fever that spread throughout Connecticut during the early stages of Hitler's aggression. The sentiment did not last long, however. Once the United States entered the war, isolationist feelings diminished and, stimulated by war production, steady economic growth resumed.

The nation's legions of unemployed had been almost fully absorbed into the war economy by the fall of 1943, but large shortages of skilled labor were still a serious problem in New England.[6] Workers from all parts of the country flocked to Connecticut lured by the prospects of lucrative jobs. As the center of the aircraft industry, Hartford had become a highly sought destination. In 1941 alone, 18,620 newcomers moved to the city. In 1942, workers were recruited from all of New England, the Midwest, and Puerto Rico. This effort was led by the Electric Boat Company of New London, assisted by the U.S. Employment Service through a special office in Groton and another in San Juan. The War Manpower Commission also played a role, installing one of its branches on the island for a short while. Altogether, 130,000 workers moved into the state during the war period, more than two-thirds settling in Hartford, Bridgeport, and New London. The proportion of Puerto Rican workers was small, but they became the nucleus of a significant settlement.

POWER SUCCESSION AND THE REFORM MOVEMENT

In the 1943 municipal election, Republicans carried the city of Hartford for the first time since 1935. This change was more formal than substantial. Democratic boss and mayor Thomas J. Spellacy had opened the door to the mayoralty when he resigned in the midst of a financial crisis, created in part by his decision to stop borrowing to pay municipal expenses.[7] Spellacy was a conservative Democrat, and his power rested on a coalition with the Republicans. His resignation hardly weakened this coalition; nor was his power seriously undermined by the change from Democratic to Republican mayor. City voters continued to support the Democrats at other levels. In the presidential election of 1944, for example, Roosevelt did better in Hartford than he had in 1940. Although the Italian vote fell from 72 percent to 65 percent from 1940 to 1944, support from the Jews and the Yankees rose. Declining Irish support was arrested, and French-Canadian and black areas held steady, giving Roosevelt 80 and 75 percent of their votes respectively.[8]

Spellacy ran in the following election, and this time his coalition fell apart. He was defeated by his Republican opponent by more than ten thousand votes. In spite of its acknowledged "normal republican predilections," the *Hartford Courant* endorsed Spellacy, recognizing him for his concern for the city's welfare.[9] The voters, however, rejected his bossism and administrative record and punished him for deserting them in 1943.[10] This defeat set the stage for power succession within the Democratic party organization and for revision of the city's charter.

By the time of Spellacy's resignation, his former "errand boy," John M. Bailey, had already challenged his leadership.[11] The break with Spellacy and Bailey's takeover of the Democratic party organization in the city occurred in 1946. In a power struggle over the nomination of candidates for state senator that was truly Byzantine, Bailey's mettle was tested again and again, first over the nomination of candidates, then over the selection of delegates to the party's city convention, and, finally, during the proceedings of the convention. By winning the battle over the selection of the convention chair, Bailey was able to secure control of the nomination process. Further maneuvers gave him control of the delegates to the state convention. At this point Spellacy was done for; he and his supporters were excluded from the delegation. The vociferous round of insults and accusations that followed did nothing to alter the course of the session. Bailey's victory became official when the convention's chair adjourned the proceedings, declaring "We have a new Democratic party in the city of Hartford."

After their 1945 victory, Hartford's Republicans renewed their attacks on the city's government. Janick summarizes their arguments: "The main obstacle to progress in Hartford was an antiquated form of government based on ward representation, favoritism, and patronage."[12] By 1946, this was a very old charge and ineptitude, corruption, and mediocrity were seen as the order of the day. In response, the Citizens Charter Commission (CCC) campaigned for a change of structure.[13] CCC emphasized that the proposed council-manager form of government would make the city's government efficient and keep tax rates down. Some argued that the new charter would reform the civil service, give city employees new protections, establish a merit system, increase job security, and encourage the creation of a better pension plan. Claims that it would destroy collective bargaining and obliterate municipal unions were vigorously contested. Others argued that it would enfranchise the 25,732 independent voters who were barred from seeking office through the parties. Candidates for ward representation under the existing form of government were hand-picked by the party bosses—a nonpartisan system would bring openness to government by allowing a wider public to serve. A spokesman for a professional organization conceded that corruption was not prevalent among city employees. This, however, was no reason to keep an inefficient form of government that did not allow, among other things, for systematic planning; efficiency, he argued, not corruption, was the issue.

Opponents argued that the proposed charter undermined democratic principles, that reform was unnecessary, and that nonpartisanship would hinder progress by eliminating interparty competition. Some voiced a concern with communistic tendencies in the proposed charter. Others thought it an attempt to impose a dictatorship. Without the support of the parties, went another argument, working people would be shut out of the electoral process; it was estimated that a candidate would need $10,000 to run a nonpartisan campaign. One local judge blasted the intent of the reformers by arguing that the charter revision was the brainchild of "every discredited and disgruntled politician of the past." Finally, some suggested that bloc voting would produce domination by officials from one geographical section, one political party, labor radicals, racketeers, or an interest group, none of which would be restrained by the veto power of the mayor.[14]

The debate climaxed on 3 December 1946, when in fourteen of Hartford's fifteen wards, the voters supported CCC by adopting nonpartisan elections and establishing a nine-member city council elected at large. The council selected a deputy mayor and appointed a city manager and, along with the city treasurer and corporation counsel, they ran the city. The deputy mayor became the most powerful figure in this group. From then on, the mayor was a figurehead whose power was defined not by his office but by circumstances. The *Hartford Times* distilled the meaning of the election: "The citizens are at last on top."[15]

The citizens had indeed voted for reform, but the implications of their decision were not straightforward. A few years would pass before they would realize that they could not eliminate partisan considerations from electoral and policy processes and that the new form of government did not necessarily widen the pool of candidates. By the 1960s, members of the Chamber of Commerce also realized that, in the absence of partisanship and without a unifying executive, a coherent policy agenda was less likely.[16]

These events signaled closure for two processes. On the one hand, the sweep that made John Bailey the Democratic boss completed a process of power succession within the Democratic party. This changed the composition of the dominant party elite, a crust that had ruled the city's Democratic politics in alliance with the Republicans for a quarter of a century. Bailey's ascendancy within the party, however, was offset by Spellacy's appeal within the rank and file and among independent voters.

On the other hand, the consolidation of Republican control of the city, which culminated with the revision of the charter, not only altered the structure of government but buttressed the legitimacy of the business credo in local politics. To paraphrase Goodrich's assessment of nearly a hundred years earlier, the city took its hue from the entrepreneurial class and its allies, turning local government into a mirror image of the civil society. Politics was again conceived as a technical enterprise. Efficiency, not equity, became the bottom line.

POLITICS IN THE POSTWAR PERIOD

In 1948, the Hartford Democratic machine was controlled by an Irish-Italian combine that focused its activities on the state level. The party did not pay much attention to nonpartisan contests in Hartford until 1953, when Bailey decided to devote a great deal of resources to that year's municipal election. Not since 1946 had the Democrats run a serious campaign in the city.

The renewed interest occurred for two reasons: First, local Democrats needed support to compete with the powerful CCC and requested the assistance of the state organization. Second, Bailey saw an opportunity that he could not pass up, namely, to extend and consolidate the reach of his network. The Republicans cried foul, arguing that Bailey's entrance violated the spirit of the new charter, to which Bailey replied that they were the power behind the CCC throne. The contest became a partisan election within a nonpartisan system. The result was that nearly 50 percent of registered voters participated, the largest rate since the triumph of nonpartisanship in 1946. The Democrats staged a comeback. Eight of the nine elected council members were registered with the party.

The return of the Democrats in Hartford was followed by increasing political demands by blacks and by suburban flight. Blacks have a history in Hartford that stretches as far back as 1765. By 1900, 45 percent of the city's blacks lived in various neighborhoods in the north end of the city.[17]

In 1943, Governor Baldwin established the State Interracial Commission, and for two years this body helped expand the employment of blacks in industries throughout Connecticut. The commission sponsored workshops, forums, and radio programs on human relations, and it published pamphlets on issues such as discrimination in housing and union membership. In 1947, the legislature enacted the Fair Employment Practices Act to prohibit discrimination in hiring. In 1949, the state guard was desegregated.

These events notwithstanding, in the mid-1950s observers in Hartford predicted that blacks would explode in anger if their socioeconomic situation did not improve. And indeed blacks organized, demanded, and obtained a voice in municipal affairs in the 1950s. John Clark, Jr., the first African American to sit on the city council, was elected in 1955. The *Hartford Chronicle*, a newspaper established by Urban League member George Goodman, took off. And the NAACP attacked landlords, which were characterized by councilman Clark as "vicious rent gougers." [18]

During the 1960s, black militancy intensified. Janick argues that blacks in Connecticut were increasingly contentious, exclusive, and extreme during the last third of the decade. In civil rights organizations, whites were ousted from positions of leadership. Blacks also insisted that social service programs for their community should be run by blacks. Some leaders demanded inclusion in the decision-making process, while others advocated for its radical transformation. The Black Caucus, an organization that promoted violent action, was a prominent example of the extremist groups that peppered black politics at this time.[19]

Suburban flight also intensified during this period. The city's population peaked at 177,397 in 1950 and subsequently began to decline (see Table 2). A large segment of the middle class made prosperous by the war left the city. During the 1950s, 56,000 people moved into Hartford and

Table 2. Total, White, Puerto Rican, and African American Population in Hartford, 1950–1990

		Whites		Puerto Ricans		African Americans	
Year	Total	Number	% of Total	Number	% of Total	Number	% of Total
1950	177,397	164,743	93	*	*	12,774	7.2
1960	162,178	108,334	67	*	*	25,138	15.5
1970	158,017	105,383	67	8,543	5.4	44,091	27.9
1980	136,392	52,180	38	24,615	18.0	46,186	33.8
1990	139,739	55,869	40	38,176	27.3	54,338	38.8

SOURCES: U.S. Department of Commerce, Bureau of the Census, *County and City Data Book* 1956, 1962, 1977, 1983, 1994. Puerto Rican numbers for 1970 and 1980 from Hartford Capitol Region Council of Governments.
* Census data not available.

NOTE: The figures for whites and Puerto Ricans are not entirely reliable. The 1956 *County and City Data Book* distinguishes only "nonwhites" from the total. Puerto Ricans could be included in the "white" category. The 1962 edition disaggregates the total as "nonwhites" and "foreign-born." Puerto Ricans could be counted as either one. The 1970 figure is considerably lower than local estimates and so are subsequent numbers as well. This table, however, illustrates well the dominant demographic trend since 1950.

95,000 left, a loss of almost 10 percent. Former residents settled in adjacent towns, such as Bloomfield, East Hartford, Wethersfield, and Windsor. In 1950, these towns, plus West Hartford, Windsor Locks, Avon, and Simsbury, had a total of 133,145 persons. By the end of the decade, their combined population had increased by 68 percent. Much to Hartford's disadvantage, although the residents of these towns depended on the city for jobs, shopping, culture, and entertainment, they adamantly rejected any and all attempts at annexation.[20]

Suburban flight and the city's inability to extend its boundaries meant that blacks and the newly arrived Puerto Ricans were left behind, not only physically but socioeconomically as well. This was not necessarily a problem. Early migrants remember the city during the 1950s as a place where jobs were abundant and life was good.[21] But as industries also fled to avoid the burdens of urban taxes, traffic, and deterioration, the prospects for poor blacks and incoming Puerto Ricans began to look less bright.

Ironically, urban renewal did little to improve the situation. Rather, it destroyed ethnic and minority communities and replaced them with hotels, a shopping mall, and office space. This was the legacy of Constitution Plaza, a complex of buildings and open spaces designed to serve as a business and financial center. White ethnics moved to the suburbs or to new enclaves. Blacks also moved, mostly farther north within the city. There they confronted an influx of Puerto Ricans coming from the island, from the tobacco camps in Windsor, and from other states.

During the 1950s political changes occurred that would benefit both blacks and Puerto Ricans later on. Reform of the charter depressed political participation rates, of course, especially among low-income groups such as blacks. Yet the Puerto Ricans were encouraged to participate, especially when the level of intraparty competition was high.[22]

The introduction of primaries in 1955 changed the dynamics of politics in both the state and the city. Initially, the proposed primary legislation exempted localities of fewer than five thousand residents, effectively placing the burden of intraparty competition on the urban-based Democrats. Another provision introduced by the Republicans required would-be challengers to receive 20 percent of the vote at a party convention to run in a primary. The bill did not pass. Then, in a special session of the legislature on 22 June, an amended bill that eliminated the exemption on localities with fewer than five thousand residents passed both houses and was signed into law.

Near the end of the decade, legislation was passed banning discrimination in housing in residences with five or more contiguous units for reasons of race, religion, or nationality. Only a few states had such statutes, but initiatives such as this were in large part the result of pressures from urban blacks and liberals with urban constituencies within the Democratic party.

POLITICAL AND ECONOMIC CHANGE

Political reforms in 1964 redressed an imbalance in representation between Connecticut's big cities and small towns. Early in that year two lawsuits challenged Connecticut's apportionment of seats in the Assembly and Congress as unconstitutional. Hartford was the site of talks held between Democrats and Republicans seeking a state-based rather than a court-imposed solution. John Bailey consulted with the state delegation in Washington. As a result, a proposed solution reconciled the "one-man-one-vote" standard with the need to protect congressional incumbents. The state legislature approved the plan. State reapportionment, however, did not proceed until after the national election. By December, the parties reached agreement on a 36-member Senate and a 180-member House.

Drawing the lines was another matter. By mid-January 1965, a number of towns, including Hartford and Bridgeport, remained without new lines. A compromise was reached, and on 19 January the Assembly approved a Democratic-Republican plan calling for 36 Senate members and 177 House seats, of which 44 of the latter would come from Hartford, New Haven, Bridgeport, Waterbury, and Stamford.[23]

These reforms provided added opportunities for urban minorities to seek electoral representation. A new constitution, approved in 1965 by a two-to-one margin, buttressed these gains and added new ones: the party lever was made optional, segregation and discrimination were prohibited, free public elementary and secondary education was guaranteed, the University of Connecticut was created, and a home-rule guarantee was established, applicable to all communities throughout Connecticut.[24]

The combination of political reforms and inter- and intraparty competition should have suggested to members of minority communities that openings were available and inroads could be made through electoral strategies. This indeed happened, but by 1967 collective behavior exerted greater power. Context and action related chromatically rather than in harmony. Hartford, Bridgeport, Waterbury, Middletown, New Britain, Stamford, Norwalk, and New London all had riots that year. The worst occurred in Hartford. In July and September 1967, blacks took to the streets. In April 1968, following the murder of Martin Luther King, North End youth surged through sections of the city, throwing bricks and stones at police and firemen while chanting, "You Killed Martin Luther King." On Labor Day of 1969, they raged over the killing of a black youth. Janick states that arrests during the Labor Day riot included "for the first time" a large number of Puerto Ricans.[25] Actually, a large number had been arrested in August during an earlier disturbance.

The turmoil was underscored by important changes in the city's political economy, some of which had been in the making for some time. The Greater Hartford Chamber of Commerce spearheaded the return to partisanship in 1967, hoping to establish a strong mayoralty that, following Mayor Richard Lee's example in New Haven, would spur downtown development.[26]

After partisan elections were restored to Hartford, the Democrats achieved control of the mayoralty and the city council in 1971. Hartford was now a one-party city dominated by the Democrats. Interparty competition waned. Intraparty divisions and the politics of identity waxed. Electoral contests began to be fueled by racial, ethnic, and geographical factors. Business, however, continued to figure prominently in public affairs, although the composition of capital was not the same as it had been in the 1950s and 1960s.

Historically, both manufacturing and services have been significant in Hartford. This was true as late as 1965, when manufacturing and service jobs were close to 20 percent each of total nonagricultural employment in the city. In 1970, however, service jobs were 19 percent of the total, while manufacturing jobs were only 15 percent. By 1975, manufacturing jobs had been reduced to 9.2 percent of the total, while service jobs had climbed to 23.1 percent. Changes in the proportion of jobs in the financial, insurance, and real estate sector (FIRE) were also significant. These climbed from 24.4 percent of the total in 1965 to 26.1 percent in 1970, to almost one-third (30.3 percent) in 1975 (see Table 3). This trend continued during the 1980s, although both the proportion and the actual number of FIRE jobs declined slightly during the second half of the decade (see Table 4).

These changes were mirrored by shifts in land-use patterns. As the proportion of land devoted to industrial use declined, office and commercial

Table 3. Selected Nonagricultural Employment in Hartford, 1965–1980

Employment Sector	1965	%	1970	%	1975	%	1980	%
Total	117,780		134,450		125,450		143,180	
Manufacturing	23,100	19.6	20,030	14.9	11,600	9.2	12,210	8.5
FIRE[a]	28,450	24.4	35,040	26.1	38,020	30.3	45,200	31.6
Services	21,900	18.6	25,690	19.1	29,023	23.1	34,560	24.1
Government	12,980	11.0	20,530	15.3	20,870	16.6	22,720	15.9

SOURCE: Connecticut Department of Labor data assembled by Louise Simmons.
Financial, insurance, and real estate.

Table 4. Selected Nonagricultural Employment in Hartford, 1980–1990

Employment Sector	1980	%	1982	%	1984	%
Total	143,180		137,220		142,890	
Manufacturing	12,210	8.5	11,020	8.0	9,390	6.6
FIRE[a]	45,200	31.6	43,760	31.9	45,550	31.9
Services	34,560	24.1	35,870	26.1	39,630	27.7
Government	22,720	15.9	20,200	14.7	20,980	14.7

Employment Sector	1986	%	1988	%	1990	%
Total	152,650		158,600		151,380	
Manufacturing	9,720	6.4	8,260	5.2	6,620	4.4
FIRE[a]	46,690	30.6	46,050	29.0	43,020	28.4
Services	43,950	28.8	50,190	31.6	48,540	32.1
Government	23,010	15.1	24,340	15.3	24,890	16.4

SOURCE: Connecticut Department of Labor data assembled by Louise Simmons.
[a] Financial, insurance, and real estate.

areas expanded. Between 1967 and 1984, residential use declined from more than 30 percent to 29 percent of all land. The proportion of vacant land also decreased, from a little over 10 percent to 8 percent. In contrast, the proportion of land used for institutions, government, open space, parks, cemeteries, and transportation increased from about 45 to 49 percent. Office space expansion climbed from 2.3 million square feet in 1972 to 7.5 million in 1984. By 1995, however, land use was virtually the same as it had been a decade earlier.

It was against this backdrop of political and economic change that Nicholas Carbone, who was a neighborhood activist in the 1960s and a real estate developer in the 1980s, made his way onto the city council. First appointed in 1969, he subsequently became deputy mayor and the city's most powerful political figure.

CARBONE'S REGIME

To some extent the economic transformation of Hartford made no difference to Carbone's agenda. He believed that structure was important but not as much as leadership. Two years before his descent from formal power, he wrote: "It does not make any difference what the system is. . . . If committed people are in power, they can change the structure overnight."[27]

The focus of his strategy for tackling the city's social and economic ills was an alliance between public and private power, represented respectively by the city council and the Greater Hartford Chamber of Commerce. His role model was Arthur Lumsden, who, in his capacity as chief executive of the Chamber, brought together politicians, opinion leaders, and leaders of corporations. "Out of this kind of interaction," Pierre Clavel writes, "there developed an approach to public-private cooperation . . . whereby the business leadership would take initiatives to preserve those aspects of the city that it valued."[28] According to Lumsden, his role as economic mediator was to gather "the head of Travelers, the head of Aetna, the publishers of the two newspapers, and sometimes the head of the Chamber [to decide] who ought to be mayor."[29] In contrast, Carbone acted as political mediator, using his network to influence and exploit the process of economic development.

The changing composition of the economy and the agenda of the business community suggested a strategy whereby measures to redistribute resources would be linked to downtown development. Business wanted to make Hartford a better place for itself, and in Carbone it found the analogue to Mayor Lee in New Haven—a strong executive and a policy entrepreneur friendly to business despite his social agenda. To enact policies that increased employment and revenues, Carbone needed the corporate sector. This meant working together not with the manufacturing principals of yesterday but with the insurance giants of the moment. According to Carbone, to have redistributive impact, public policy had to go with the flow of current corporate preferences and interests. But the development strategies pursued by Hartford's corporations favored office construction, gentrification, and real estate speculation, as well as upscale retail centers, rather than neighborhood revitalization, housing construction, or neighborhood retail outlets.

The coalition between business and city hall was formed, and Carbone's strategy was put into effect, with several impressive results. Clavel argues that Hartford became a progressive city during this period because Carbone pushed for public co-ownership of private property, broad political representation, public planning, redistributive policies, and grassroots participation.[30] But this characterization is an example of mistaken identity, an instance in which abstract criteria are substituted for reality and a part is taken for the whole. Although it is true that Carbone negotiated jobs, quotas, and contracts, steering them toward Hartford residents, the distribution of these benefits proved to be skewed and their collective impact negligible. Between 1970 and 1982, for example, 7 percent of Hartford's housing stock was lost. By 1985, of thirteen chain grocery supermarkets, only two remained in business.[31]

The resignation of city manager Elisha Friedman in 1970 gave Carbone an opportunity to fill a policy vacuum, and he took it. In the process he subverted the council-manager form of government, becoming a de facto strong mayor. In this role he distinguished himself by a governing style that combined autocratic, technocratic, and neocorporatist tendencies, all of which he focused on the establishment of linkage policies and downtown development. Seen in context, his approach was radical and his strategy bold. But his regime was more dictatorial than progressive. Carbone had good intentions, but this was not enough. As one of his allies put it: "He didn't necessarily badmouth the neighborhood agenda. But he didn't feel accountable to the neighborhoods." [32]

Clavel argues that his reliance on market approaches and public-private partnerships "demonstrated Carbone's business side and the willingness of the city council to operate in an entrepreneurial way on behalf of public objectives." [33] But Carbone's accomplishments are testimony to the work of his technocratic assistants and his leadership abilities. The city council did little more than follow. He was a master at grasping the intricacies of complex development proposals. He absorbed the work of his experts quickly and made it intelligible to lay audiences. His boundless energy gave him citywide presence and visibility. The flow of federal resources to the city was expedited by his national connections. Thus, he was quickly recognized as the key figure on the city council, a status that corporate leaders supported and that he maintained for nearly a decade. Carbone was successful in part because, in a city whose political culture favored business approaches and interests, the odds were in his favor.

THE CONTEXT FOR PUERTO RICAN POLITICAL MOBILIZATION

What kind of place was Hartford during the 1970s and 1980s? What effects did political and historical context have on Puerto Rican political mobilization? In 1968, Henry Roberts, president of CIGNA, emphasized that the benefits of development ought to be enjoyed by the city as a whole, not just by the businesses downtown. [34] Two years later, Arthur Lumsden told his peers that "the [1969] riots have made the choice clear. We will remake our cities into fit places for the little family to live and work and grow or the city will be blown up; bombed out; burned down in our faces." [35] By 1975, however, corporations began to retreat from the Hartford scene, and some of its leaders pursued a national agenda.

Carbone's defeat in 1979 coincided with the emergence of a new breed of corporate managers whose ties to the city were nurtured by careerism rather than by civic commitment. Because most did not live in the city, their relationship to the urban environment was circumstantial and detached. In this, they conformed to a general pattern. Between 1960 and 1970, the number of jobs in the city had increased by 16 percent, while the number of jobs held by Hartford residents had decreased by 8 percent. By 1980, the number of jobs had increased by 24 percent, but the proportion held by city residents had declined by 21 percent [36] (see Table 5).

Table 5. Resident/Commuter Employment and Unemployment Rate, Hartford, 1960–1993

	1960	%	1970	%	1980	%	1990	%	1993	%
Total jobs	115,840		134,450		143,180		151,380		134,170	
Hartford jobs	55,628	48.0	42,281	31.4	33,556	23.4	32,565[a]	21.5	57,662[b]	42.9
Commuter jobs	60,212	52.0	92,169	68.6	109,624	76.6	118,815[a]	78.4	n/a	—
Unemployment rate	5.6		4.5		7.7		10.7		10.4	

SOURCES: Department of Planning, City of Hartford, *Hartford, State of the City, September 1983* and *State of the City 1995*.
[a] U.S. Bureau of the Census data provided by Benjamin Barnes, Planning Department, City of Hartford.
[b] Hartford labor force.

These changes did not allow any among Carbone's successors to nurture the public-private linkages he developed; those who tried found a stratum of corporate actors with diminished stakes in the city. As Lumsden put it in 1981: "These companies don't need Hartford. Aetna could lose the entire Hartford city budget in one year and it wouldn't affect its operations."[37]

During the 1980s the city was a study in contrasts. While downtown Hartford offered a gleaming skyline, residential areas were a locus of poverty and decay. The urban environment consisted of an array of classic juxtapositions: wealth and poverty, downtown corporate growth and neighborhood economic deprivation, political equality and economic inequality. The leading political actors were the city's corporate leaders, real estate investors, members of the city council, public administrators, and representatives of the leading newspapers. In the view of some, ordinary citizens had only a residual role in the political process, as ballast against "pervasive business domination in the city and the indifference of city government to neighborhood needs."[38]

Thus, Puerto Ricans asserted their claims in the context of two sets of variables. Business hegemony, a successful reform movement, and one-party domination shaped the historical context. The contemporary context included demographic change stimulated by the events of World War II, corporate-centered development, civic unrest, and urban decay.

The dominance of business suggested that Puerto Rican interests would be considered marginal. This was indeed one effect of Carbone's development strategy. Although nonpartisanship had been abolished, at-large elections remained in place. Given the size of the city, it was possible to campaign across neighborhoods without much difficulty, but as a demographically concentrated enclave, the Puerto Rican community had only minimal electoral impact. Furthermore, the lack of party competition diminished its bargaining capacity. This left Puerto Rican leaders at the mercy of party bosses and the community with no forum other than the streets. Demographic changes set the stage for alliances between Puerto Ricans and African Americans. Corporate-centered development, civic unrest, and urban decay were causally related, and Puerto Ricans experienced all three firsthand.

Context is a significant variable because it organizes the structure of opportunities available to political actors. In the case of Puerto Ricans, for example, differences between island and mainland participation have been largely attributed to factors that promoted participation in Puerto Rico and suppressed it in the United States.[39]

Yet context does not tell the whole story because it does not determine the *timing* or *content* of action, and whether a group decides to participate or not is ultimately an intersubjective calculus. In other words, nothing will happen, even in a favorable context, if political actors choose not to act. Favorable circumstances might not be matched by internal capability, resources might be inadequate, or leadership might be unprepared or weak. Furthermore, the group might be unable to distinguish favorable from unfavorable circumstances and therefore might hesitate to act; or it might simply miss an opportunity entirely. Conversely, a restrictive context might so infuriate a group that it simply springs to action in desperation or to create more favorable circumstances.

Puerto Ricans in Hartford faced constraints that limited their participation, yet they mobilized anyway. In part, their response was self-propelled. At times restrictions prompted them to act. During bouts of Democratic intraparty competition, they were courted by the warring factions, and sometimes Republicans vied for their support. Some Puerto Rican candidates took the initiative and used the Republican party as a wedge. Others concluded that responsiveness could be exacted only through extra-partisan organization and action. Carbone's neocorporatist experiment, the Citizens Lobby, excluded Puerto Ricans; his control over the party organization and autocratic style limited their access to positions and candidacies. This discouraged many, intimidated some, but steeled the resolve of others. The sense that neighborhood needs—and nested within these, Puerto Rican needs—were subordinated to corporate interests prodded even the timid to act against a lopsided development strategy and against Carbone himself. Puerto Ricans used their ethnicity to weave themselves into the political fabric of the city, sometimes reacting to developments, often turning long-standing needs and aspirations into programs of political action.

The Hartford context presented Puerto Ricans with the challenge of transforming the interactions between social, economic, and political interests into a match between political capability and systemic feasibility. To be meaningful, the match could not be a mere index of potentiality but had to be a record of actual instances of interest articulation producing political effects. In this process, no variable was isolated from others. Contextual variables interacted with political variables. Context was not everything, but overlooking its demands proved fatal.

The following chapters show how contextual constraints doubled as inducements to mobilization. Puerto Ricans matched capability with feasibility by turning ethnic identity into a rallying point for action. As the community developed from settlement to enclave, it used its inner resources—ethnic solidarity being the most prominent—to incorporate and confront elements of a tradition and a set of arrangements that were, simultaneously, models to emulate, a source of assets, and a wellspring of discontent. Ethnicity became an expression of political capability—identity claims articulated interests, and mobilization led to their satisfaction through elections, appointments, and policies. Identity politics represented the convergence between ethnic awareness and power awareness, between interests and political mobilization. Parity in representation and access to power were, among many outcomes, the most significant.

3 Puerto Ricans in Hartford: From Settlement to Collective Behavior

THE PUERTO Ricans coming into Hartford in the 1950s were from diverse backgrounds. Some were from the semi-isolated mountain regions of the island who came to work the tobacco farms. Others came from larger towns—such as Ponce in the south—with skills that were mismatched to the jobs they took upon arrival. "Recent migration statistics," reads one story of the early 1950s, "indicate that less than a third of the Puerto Rican newcomers are classified as unskilled workers. . . . Draftsmen take jobs as restaurant workers, school teachers become machine operators and carpenters work as maintenance men."[1]

According to another early account, "The Puerto Rican has come from New York City or direct from the island. He has come by invitation to fill critical labor-shortages in industry and agriculture. He has come to seek opportunities outside of the big isolation of Manhattan. He has come in answer to one of his strongest compulsions, the family"[2] (see Map 1).

Family lured Zoilo Caraballo and Julián Vargas to Hartford; others, such as Pablo Román, left Puerto Rico simply to transcend familiar boundaries. Many who came were transient farm workers looking for relief from seasonal unemployment. They came, beginning in 1951, to harvest the tobacco fields and wound up staying. As an occupational group they were defined less by what they had to offer the economy than by what the economy had to offer them—namely, jobs in restaurants, stores, and factories and on farms.

Pablo Román came to Hartford in 1950. "When I came here," he said to a *Hartford Times* reporter in 1957, "there were maybe three, maybe four, Puerto Rican families."[3] The son of a landowner from the coastal town of Mayagüez, Román had a high school diploma and knew English when he moved first to Michigan, where he and his brother worked in a mushroom factory for eighteen months, and then to Hartford, where he arrived invited by his sister and prompted by his desire to see more of the country. Hartford offered him a blue-collar job, which, in the economic climate of the 1950s, was still seen as a path to a better life.

From a meat refrigeration plant, Román moved on to a factory and then to G. Fox and Co., where he was in charge of filling orders in the

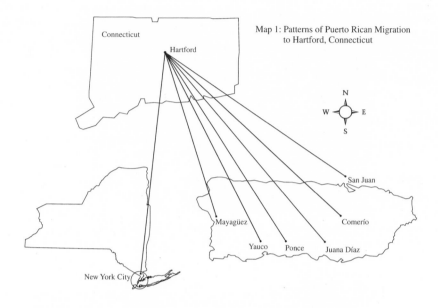

Map 1: Patterns of Puerto Rican Migration
to Hartford, Connecticut

Connecticut
Hartford

N
W — E
S

San Juan

Comerío

Mayagüez

Yauco   Ponce   Juana Díaz

New York City

The family of Venan Rodríguez, typical of the Puerto Rican settlers to Hartford in 1957. *From left to right:* Inocencia holding Wilfredo, Venan Rodríguez, Mrs.Rodríguez holding José Manuel, Olga Iris, and Mary Lou. Hartford Times *photo by Charles Vendetti. From the Hartford Collection, Hartford Public Library.*

Unidentified Puerto Rican farmworker. *From the Hartford Collection, Hartford Public Library.*

stockroom of a gift shop. From G. Fox, Román went to work at the Statler Hilton, where he hoped to become a waiter.

Unlike Román, Zoilo Caraballo went to school for only three years before he started working to help support his thirteen siblings.[4] In Yauco, a hilly Puerto Rican town famous for its flavorful coffee, Caraballo worked on a farm seven days a week. As an *arrimao*, he had a house provided by the landowner, but his pay amounted to a meager $8.75 a week.

Caraballo wanted his children to go to school, but they had to cross a river to get there, and during the rainy season, this was dangerous. A move to rent-free government housing meant he was farther from his job, and the cost of feeding his family went up as well. All the while a brother-in-

Mrs. Joaquín Vargas, an employee at Hartford Live Poultry, 15 May 1957. *From the Hartford Collection, Hartford Public Library.*

Antonio Gómez, a Puerto Rican worker at Royal Typewriter. *From the Hartford Collection, Hartford Public Library.*

law who was working on a farm in Pennsylvania had been writing to him about the opportunities there: plenty of work and $46 a week.

After his move to Pennsylvania, Caraballo worked shifts of sixty-six hours a week and missed his family terribly. He had a sister living in Hartford who suggested he move there. Once in the city, Caraballo landed a job at a tree nursery and later as a laborer and a machine operator at Royal Typewriter.

At Royal Typewriter, newcomers like Caraballo communicated with foremen by using Spanish phrase cards while taking advantage of on-the-job classes in English. These were given by the Bureau of Adult Education

Julián Vargas at La Popular, Bodega Hispana, 7 May 1957. Hartford Times *photo by Charles Vendetti. From the Hartford Collection, Hartford Public Library.*

of the Hartford Board of Education, and the company paid half the fee for the one-hour sessions.[5]

Soon Caraballo sent for his wife, who started work in a tobacco factory, and, in two months, with their combined $52 in savings, they sent for their two daughters. Of his life in Hartford, Caraballo liked the cold weather and the better pay best.

Julián Vargas heard about Hartford from friends there. He had been earning $8 a day as a "railroad engineer," which was a good wage by Puerto Rican standards. But it was not enough to feed a family of ten, and in 1953 he and his family moved to Hartford. Vargas arrived in the city with $500—a gift from his mother—and for two years he steadily saved the money he made from killing chickens at Hartford Live Poultry. A diagnosis of diabetes prompted him to quit his job and invest his savings of $350 in a jeep, a driver's license, and a load of vegetables from New York City.

Life as a peddler did not turn out to be what the doctor ordered, however, and after some setbacks Vargas established the first Puerto Rican *bodega* (grocery store) in Hartford. In 1956, La Popular, Bodega Hispana, opened on Main Street in the Clay Hill neighborhood (also known as Clay Arsenal), the first Puerto Rican enclave in the city.

A few other Puerto Ricans arrived earlier and under different circumstances. Olga Mele, who was married to an American serviceman, came
in 1941. Her husband's connection with the military and her education
gave her security, comfort, and a middle-class perspective. But Román,
Caraballo, and Vargas were more typical members of Hartford's burgeon-
ing Puerto Rican community.

ETHNIC AWARENESS: AN AMERICAN OTHERNESS

The notion of an American otherness was best expressed in 1965 by
Florencio Morales, a social worker formerly in the employ of the Community Renewal Team (CRT), Hartford's leading antipoverty agency for
more than two decades, during an interview with a reporter for the *Hartford Courant*: "The Hartford community must understand Puerto Ricans
as Puerto Ricans. . . . Yes, we are Americans, but we don't look like Americans. Americans must look for what the Puerto Rican has to offer." [6]

Morales's notion of an American otherness rang both alien and true to
many in and around Hartford. It was alien to those who connected Puerto
Ricans with the "heritage of the sugarcane cutter," which reportedly made
them "turn to guile and wile and the steel blade." [7] In the eyes of dubious
Connecticut citizens, Puerto Ricans presented too many "rough edges and
blank spots," [8] and that the newest of the new spent most of their free time
quartered in camps owned by the Shade Tobacco Growers Agricultural
Association (STGAA) did not forestall mean expressions. As a barber
from nearby Windsor put it: "You hear talk they're treacherous and carry
knives. We don't like to have them around too much." [9]

Yet this otherness was precisely what made Puerto Ricans not just a
group of people with foreign ways but a reminder of previous chapters in
the history of the American polity. Residents of the neighboring town of
Meriden watched in amazement as an entire family—mother, father, sib-
ling, and uncle—paraded from home to school to escort a single Puerto
Rican child to kindergarten. [10] "They are strangers," reads a 1957 account,
"facing pretty much the same things other immigrants confront: isolation
from the rest of the community because of their language, their strange
ways, their poverty and their tendency to stay together." [11]

In Hartford this feeling was often tempered by the idea that, like previous waves of new Americans, this one would ultimately adapt and assimilate. Thus, although it was difficult to get them to wear warm clothing
in the winter [12] and Puerto Rican men had to be told that it was "not considered good taste to comment . . . about the looks of the girls that pass
by in the street," [13] in the end they were thought of as "good people"
whose problems would disappear given time and instruction booklets in

Spanish priming them on the ways of the new polity. "If the citizen new-comers follow the pattern of the immigrants before them," wrote a jour-nalist for the *Hartford Courant* in 1954, "their first generation will gain only a foothold. Their language and 'foreign' culture will be a block to better jobs, the education and the homes most Americans are used to. But their children, and their children's children, will gradually break the barriers." [14] That Puerto Ricans were regarded as aliens is ironic since an argument that federal officials used to justify their recruitment as contract laborers during the 1940s was that "preference should be certainly given to citizens as against foreigners if laborers are to be brought to the main-land from off-shore localities." [15]

But language and culture were not the only obstacles these "foreign" citizens would have to surmount. Attitudes toward Puerto Ricans had hardened in reaction to events in Washington, D.C. Suddenly, Puerto Ri-cans were nationally visible, and the city was taking notice of them under adverse circumstances.

COMING INTO THE PUBLIC EYE

On 2 March 1954, four members of the Puerto Rican Nationalist Party took their claims for Puerto Rican independence directly to the U.S. Con-gress, not in the form of a signed petition or through a formal process of consultation, but with guns in their hands. They placed themselves on the visitors gallery, just above the floor of the House of Representatives, and from there opened fire.

For maximum publicity, the date of the shooting was selected to co-incide with the opening of the InterAmerican Conference in Caracas, Venezuela, where all a dumbfounded secretary of state John Foster Dulles could say upon hearing the news was "What?" [16]

The nationalists wanted to alert the world that Puerto Rico was not the showcase of democracy touted by the United States at the United Nations and throughout Latin America but a colony of an imperial power. The United States was not Puerto Rico's senior partner but its ruler. The United States had masterminded and controlled the repression of pro-independence advocates on the island, of which the most visible example was the jailing in a federal prison of nationalist leader Pedro Albizu Campos.

Reactions to the shooting, however, were highly unsympathetic. In Puerto Rico and Washington, the attack was characterized as "savage and unbelievable lunacy" [17] and, "contrary to our belief and our peaceful nature," an instance of "the misbehavior of a very few." [18] In New York, Felipe N. Torres, a Puerto Rican assemblyman from the Bronx, introduced a resolution condemning the shooting, which the state assembly approved.[19] And in Maywood, Illinois, a suburb of Chicago, a group of twenty-one Puerto Ricans presented themselves at Hines Veterans Hospital to donate blood as a gesture of sympathy for the wounded representatives. "We want to show the American people that the people of Puerto Rico do not hate them," said Luis Martínez, a bodega operator. "The nationalists are not representative of our native country. We are proud to be citizens."[20]

On the day of the shooting, a grand jury indicted Pedro Orozco Sánchez, a twenty-four-year-old Puerto Rican from Hartford, on charges of threatening to kill the president. Sánchez had been arrested on an unrelated matter and while being fingerprinted said, "What did I do, kill Eisenhower?" It was that statement that prompted the charge.[21]

The next day the *Hartford Times* ran a story titled "Local Puerto Ricans, Few in Number, Deplore Shootings."[22] Julio Falcón, a Puerto Rican liaison officer for tobacco workers, was quoted as expressing his dismay over the incident. Defined as transient tobacco and apple harvesters, Puerto Ricans were said to be unhappy about the shooting. The report included a message from the fire chief of Puerto Rico to "the fire chiefs of every town and city in the United States," reassuring them that "the vast majority of the people of Puerto Rico are indignant at the unbelievable and criminal aggression of which the members of the United States Congress have been victims." Hartford residents were reminded that no significant number of Puerto Ricans applied for relief or actually were on welfare. They were told that of those Puerto Ricans who settled in the state, more did so in towns and cities along the Connecticut shoreline than in Hartford.

This was an inauspicious moment for Puerto Ricans in the city, although they were far from the scene of the crime. No one, perhaps, understood this better than Pedro Orozco Sánchez. It was a counterproductive way of becoming visible, but then communities are seldom allowed to choose the way they come into the public eye.

SOCIALIZATION

For Hartford's new citizens, who still lacked a shared sense of place, politics was a rare but not absent endeavor. In Puerto Rico, political participation was common and intense. In Hartford, there was much to be learned, but from the island experience the migrants knew the value of electoral politics and were not strangers to its ways. At this early stage there were few signs of "mobilization on the basis of belief which redefines social action."[23] The community was small and therefore the most salient stirrings of organization were felt in nearby Bridgeport. There Antonia

The civic organization that Olga Mele helped create in 1955 was reactivated in 1960 and renamed Liga Cívica Puertorriqueña de Hartford. *From left:* Nilda R. Royo, secretary, and Osvaldo Torres, president (*seated*). Luis A. Marrero, vice president, and Virgilio Meléndez, treasurer (*standing*). Hartford Times *photo. From the Hartford Collection, Hartford Public Library.*

Pantoja, a social worker from the island led the effort. Although Hartford's Puerto Ricans had a comparable dynamo in the figure of Olga Mele, they had no seasoned leader who could give coherence to their social experiences and open up paths of opportunity.

The newcomers to Hartford did, however, have common-enough aspirations: education for their children, better employment, payment of debts, home ownership. Some saw politics as a path of opportunity. In addition to her church activities, Mele, perhaps the first Puerto Rican in the city, acted as a job developer and helped register Puerto Ricans to vote. In 1955, she and others formed the first Puerto Rican association in Hartford, a civic group that included voter registration among its proposed activities. Yet, at this point, society, not politics, was at the center of their action. Social life meant everyday survival, charitable activities, baseball tournaments, and cultural celebrations; in other words, the life of family, church, and friends.

Between 1951 and 1953, no Puerto Rican newcomer to Hartford was convicted, fined, or sent to prison by the state's superior court. In only two cases were Puerto Ricans charged with crimes severe enough to bring them before the high court, and both resulted in acquittals.[24] "Thefts by Connecticut's Puerto Ricans," reads a 1954 account, "are virtually unknown. Law enforcement officials from throughout the state can recall fewer than five in the past three years."[25] Common crimes were misdemeanors, such as drunkenness, breach of peace, and motor vehicle infractions, usually driving without a license.

But such particulars did not prevent city court officials from declaring in 1954 that the Puerto Rican was "a problem." Hartford was the only Connecticut city to do so that year. In the 9 May 1954 edition of the *Hartford Courant*, one state official was quoted as saying, "They're not moral or immoral—just unmoral," and another declared: "I don't think we have much to worry about. As soon as times get a little rougher they'll all be going back to New York or to Puerto Rico."[26]

Not knowing what to make of Hartford's "problem," these officials decided that Puerto Ricans were best left in the netherworld of the "unmoral" and, ultimately, back in the tropical zone where they originated. Certainly the experiences of the early migrants provided some grounds for this attitude.

During the summer, tobacco companies recruited between five and eight hundred Puerto Ricans, mostly men, who returned to the island at the end of the season. Some were hired to work in orchards. As if to emphasize their status as temporary workers, they were housed in barracks inside the farms, and rarely, if ever, did they venture into Hartford. Even those who came to the city on their own, with other plans, remained isolated. "I was very lucky," said Angel Colón, who left the town of Comerío in 1951. "I got a job on what you call the bull gang [a crew of laborers]. I worked there for seven years. I used to go to sleep early every night to save money. I never went anyplace."[27]

For Colón, and many others, his statement that he "never went anyplace" meant that he stayed put until the end of the harvest. But his statement could be interpreted in another way: work on the farms offered almost no chance for advancement. Puerto Ricans were stuck in the camps, and, to compound matters, returning to the island was not much better. Contrary to the hopes of their hosts, for many farmworkers, the tobacco fields were a halfway point between Puerto Rico and Hartford. Some could not afford to go back; others, like Juan "Johnny" Castillo, who came to Hartford in 1953, simply preferred to stay, which meant moving to the city: "I would say that [Hartford] was the perfect city. Coming in you found a good environment, there was housing; everything was good. Farmworkers came into the city to visit family or friends, and they liked it. They found jobs, because there were plenty of jobs then, and they preferred to make $8 or $10 in a factory than making $4 in the farms."[28]

In 1953, fewer than twenty Puerto Ricans were on welfare in Hartford.[29] The following year, welfare enrollment was still low and there were no indications that more Puerto Ricans applied than members of other groups, proportionate to their number.[30] According to Housing Authority reports for 1954, only five Puerto Rican families lived in public housing and four others had recently become eligible for low-rent apartments.

The extent to which Puerto Ricans rely on the mechanisms devised by the state to protect its less fortunate citizens has always been a sensitive point in communities throughout the mainland. And so it was that in 1959, Felisa Rincón de Gautier, the mayor of San Juan, proudly stated that of six thousand Puerto Ricans in Hartford only 120 received public assistance.[31] This evidence, according to Rincón de Gautier, proved that Puerto Ricans moved to the United States in search of gainful employment.

Rincón de Gautier was both right and wrong. Puerto Ricans did, indeed, move to Hartford seeking economic opportunities not available on the island. But by 1960 the welfare department was already concerned about the high proportion of the caseload that was Puerto Rican. According to department records, in July 1958, 12 percent of the caseload in the city was Puerto Rican; by July 1959, the figure had increased to 16 percent. In contrast, the department estimated that Puerto Ricans were 3 percent of Hartford's total population.[32]

Socialization proceeded in tandem with growth. By 1957, three thousand Puerto Ricans lived in Hartford. In only three years, that number increased by tenfold, in part because of the state's booming economy, in part because of intercity migration between Bridgeport and Hartford. "In Hartford and 100 other cities, Puerto Ricans are filling labor shortages in every type of industry," reads one account.[33]

According to a spokeswoman for the Greater Hartford Council of Churches, the newcomers were "definitely not an overflow from New York."[34] This caveat was considered necessary in view of the image held by many in Hartford of the "knife-flashing, drinking and fighting Puerto Rican"[35] from New York, an image reinforced by the comments of none other than the governor of Puerto Rico, Luis Muñoz Marín. In an interview with a reporter from the *Hartford Courant* early in 1959, Muñoz said that problems such as juvenile delinquency were unknown in Puerto Rico "until some of the families returned and their children brought bad habits . . . that they had learned in New York City."[36]

The Puerto Ricans' actual behavior was far more benign. A common complaint was that they disappeared from work for three or four months at a time, only to return, saying simply, "Wife sick" or "Go to Puerto Rico for Christmas." And because they were not required to take special classes to become citizens, they were considered to lack the incentive to become assimilated—an important factor in the incorporation of Germans, Poles, Italians, and other immigrant groups. Still, in 1956, about two hundred Puerto Ricans were registered to vote, a fact that came as a big surprise to many in the city.[37]

In 1958, the STGAA brought 984 Puerto Rican workers to Connecticut under an arrangement with the governments of Puerto Rico and the state.[38] This was quite a leap from the original three hundred brought in 1951, when the STGAA recruitment program began.[39] The increase coincided with the first signs of the formation of a Puerto Rican settlement on Hartford's South End.[40] Also for the first time, tobacco workers were paid $.90, either by the hour or on a piecework basis. Housing in the association's camps was free, and, for $2.10, which was deducted from the workers' pay, they were provided with three meals a day. There was also a deduction for medical insurance, which many resented.

From 1957 to 1959, the Puerto Rican population in the city increased by 100 percent, from three thousand to six thousand. No longer were they reported to be mismatched for their jobs. Further, few residents are likely to have believed about Puerto Ricans in Hartford what a 1948–49 Columbia University study found about Puerto Ricans in New York, namely, that "the migrants are more likely to have had industrial experience than members of the labor force in Puerto Rico; more likely to be skilled; and less than half as likely to be unskilled."[41] To Hartford residents, the growing settlement on the North End and the spotty enclaves developing near the South Green Park and Chapel Street area, as well as in Frog Hollow and Parkville, were populated by uneducated and unskilled workers fit for no work other than harvesting tobacco farms.

The front page of the 15 March 1959 edition of the *Hartford Courant* features a most interesting set of photos of two groups of Puerto Ricans. One photo was taken in Orocovis, Puerto Rico, and shows three men squatting on their heels, presumably talking. The second photo shows three men in Hartford, also squatting, apparently chatting away. The basic difference is that in the second image snow is falling.

"Whether in the sunny warmth of their native villages," reads the caption, "or the wintry streets of Hartford, when Puerto Rican friends meet they talk and when they talk they squat on their heels." The caption's lead—"It's their way"—suggests a resigned acceptance to a form of behavior that, while incongruent with the Hartford setting, was nonetheless understandable. According to the *Courant*, squatting was a pose Puerto Ricans fell "naturally into," even in the falling snow.

The two images must have provoked comments by readers regarding the weird ways of the newcomers: What were they doing on the street with no coats on? Why would they carry on a conversation in such an uncomfortable position? How long could they sustain their conversation with snow falling and no warm clothing? It is impossible to know what the men did after the photo was taken, but it is doubtful that they stayed outside for long. Did the photographer mean to suggest that not even a snowstorm could get them to change their behavior? Even if that wasn't what the photographer meant to convey, it is likely that the photo gave some readers reason to question the sanity of Puerto Ricans as a whole.

Many of the Puerto Ricans who came to Connecticut became, as the Reverend Andrew Cooney, pastor of the Sacred Heart Church of Hartford, put it years later, the Germans of their day, a reference to the fact that German immigrants had preceded them in some neighborhoods, had worked in lowly occupations, and had also been perceived as strange.[42] Standing—or squatting, for that matter—on street corners was not what was expected of Puerto Ricans, and some were either sent home or arrested for what were seen as their strange ways.

EASING THE TRANSITION

Help in easing the transition from life in a mostly rural to an urban environment, with new customs and a new language, came first, as early as 1952, from the Greater Hartford Council of Churches. Also in 1952, the government of Puerto Rico expanded the Migration Division of its Department of Labor to cover the Connecticut-Massachusetts region. In 1955, "La Oficina del Commonwealth," as it was commonly known, was opened in Hartford to act as liaison between the tobacco growers and contract workers recruited in Puerto Rico.[43]

A guide printed in Spanish by the Council of Churches gave newcomers their first lessons in acculturation: "In this country one uses only the name of the father and not that of the mother as in Puerto Rico. For example, Juan Antonio Garcia Lopez in this country is called Juan A. Garcia."[44]

The council's concern was molded by the immediacy of the migrants' problems—their lack of warm clothing and their ignorance of their new home. But some within the council were quick to realize that more formal, institutional responses were necessary. Thus, in 1956, the San Juan Catholic Center was established on Albany Avenue by Archbishop Henry J. O'Brien. Within three years, the center was offering family counseling and help in writing letters and translating documents and giving its clients referrals to other providers. The opening of the center did not preclude more modest initiatives, however, such as Mille Marchese's program for non-English-speaking children at the Barnard-Brown school, also begun in 1956, when only five Puerto Ricans were enrolled there.[45]

At the commonwealth's office, classes in conversational English and instruction booklets covering everyday life situations were available to anyone coming to Hartford from the island.[46] By 1967, staff were telling its clients, even transient workers, that a modicum of acculturation was the best way to stay out of trouble:

In the city you should not walk alone through alleys and should not gather in groups in front of Hispanic businesses or on street corners. Americans are not used to the joyful banter characteristic of our race, and to them a friendly but loud conversation between three or more people is sign of an argument or the beginning of a riot. If you go to the city with more than $15 or $20 and you get drunk or decide to visit unfamiliar apartments, you risk losing your money and ending up in a hospital.[47]

The Greater Hartford Council of Churches continued its charitable efforts, and in 1959, with the United Church Women of Greater Hartford, it cosponsored a project to train fourteen women to go to the homes of Puerto Ricans to teach them English. These women saw their pupils twice a week for an hour at each visit. They used the Laubach system of instruction, in which pictures were used to identify letters. The emphasis was on the sound of letters, not their form—in this way the pupil did not need to be literate to learn English, and the teacher could spare herself the trouble of learning Spanish.

Although more systematic than before, these initiatives were still affected by the quality of residuum that has characterized the charitable spirit throughout much of its history.[48] These independent charities were needed and welcome but in large part alleviated the distress of only those individuals whom they noticed.

To most Puerto Ricans in Hartford, these efforts did not begin to address their problems. Rather than disappear, the problems seemed to get worse. For example, the lack of housing was compounded by the unsanitary conditions in what was available, the discriminatory practices, and the long waits for public units. The problem of low pay and a high cost of living was exacerbated by high rents and the common practice among landlords of charging above the city council's welfare fair rent formula. Unable to complain in English, Puerto Ricans relied on interpreters to tell public officials their problems.[49]

Then, in October 1959, Gilberto Camacho, an organizer with the Commonwealth of Puerto Rico's Chicago office, was transferred to Hartford to coordinate the services of existing social agencies for Puerto Ricans and to establish worker education and orientation programs to incorporate Puerto Ricans into the American way of life. Camacho was to pursue these projects not just in Hartford but in cities in Massachusetts and Rhode Island as well. In Hartford, Camacho's first promise was to establish an organization of Puerto Ricans.[50]

POWER AWARENESS: A NEW SENSE OF SELF

In comments made to the local press in 1961, San Juan's mayor, Felisa Rincón de Gautier, indicated that the yearly celebration of St. John the Baptist Day marked the time when "all Puerto Ricans on the mainland wish they could come back."[51] Perhaps she was right. But by 1964 demographic and attitudinal indicators suggested a dissonance between wishes and reality.

In April 1964, two thousand Puerto Rican workers arrived to work in the tobacco fields. A similar group had come to the Hartford area the previous year, and, according to Gilberto Camacho, the similarity was not just in their numbers but that they were all coming "to take jobs which apparently [were] not acceptable to area residents."[52] Considering that many came for economic reasons and culturally were out of place, it was not surprising that Camacho expected the Puerto Ricans to leave soon. He predicted that "the group would dwindle as Puerto Rico's agricultural and industrial programs develop further."[53] This, however, did not come to pass. During the 1960s the number of Puerto Ricans in the city tripled instead. Camacho could not see it yet, but members of the Puerto Rican community were also beginning to take steps toward getting organized.

In the fall of 1964, about twenty thousand people lined up along Main Street to watch the celebration of the first Connecticut Puerto Rican Day

Parade, a festivity designed "to honor the state's Puerto Rican population and to encourage voter registration and participation in the coming election."[54] The parade began at the intersection of Main and Ely Streets, a short distance from where Main became Albany Avenue and downtown gave way to Puerto Rican and black neighborhoods. The marchers proceeded through the city to Dillon Stadium, a municipal facility near Colt Park, not far from the Colt firearms factory on Huyshope Avenue.

After the parade, approximately three thousand marchers filed into Dillon Stadium for a rally. John Davis Lodge, a Republican candidate for the Senate, and Thomas J. Dodd, Jr., son of the Democratic senator, spoke to the crowd. "The fault [for low voter turnout] lies not with the Puerto Ricans," said Lodge, "but with the state of Connecticut . . . which demands that every elector be able to read any portion of the state constitution in English."[55]

The celebration was not just a momentary escape from the grim facts of life in poverty and isolation. It was also a signal that, as a group, Puerto Ricans were developing a sense of political self. Their move out of the fringes into the realm of political alignment was simultaneously the means to and the expression of that change. However tentative, the rally was evidence of identification with the local political parties, and the parties in turn were struggling with the realization that Puerto Ricans needed to be given greater recognition.

Nicholas Carbone became involved with the Puerto Rican community in 1965 while working as a campaign coordinator for George Ritter, a local Democrat, who was running for city council. Carbone brought María Sánchez, a Puerto Rican pioneer in the city, into the effort, in an attempt to register and get Puerto Ricans to support his candidate.

Carbone's approach conveyed both a common-sense realization and the need for strategic planning. He and others within the Democratic party saw an emerging community—the Puerto Ricans were in Hartford to stay. The feeling was that if they were recognized and integrated, everyone else would be better off in the long run.

"We were looking to win an election, and every vote was important," said Carbone, recalling his more self-interested motives. "[We] wanted them to identify with the Democratic party in the city. There's very little patronage per se in the city . . . so the best thing we had [to offer to get the] involvement of the community was to be involved in the policy decisions that the city was going to be making."[56]

Formal Organizing: Adapt, Assimilate, Fight

In 1965, Puerto Ricans began to organize on their own. In February, the Puerto Rican American Association of Connecticut was formed to promote employment opportunities and voter registration. In April, the Spanish American Association of Hartford was organized to assimilate migrants into the social and cultural life of the city. Camacho assisted this group. In May, he reported to his supervisor: "The Association is formed by a group of young Puerto Ricans anxious and willing to push themselves and to help the Puerto Rican community in matters pertaining to education, housing, employment, registration and voting. They are specially interested in Puerto Rican youngsters and have started a drive to raise funds to build their own 'Casa de Puerto Rico.'"[57]

Also in 1965, the Latin American Action Project was established to provide services and information on employment and housing. And during the summer, the first specifically political organization of Puerto Ricans was founded. On 20 July 1965, fourteen Puerto Ricans met at the North End Democratic Club on Barbour Street to organize the Puerto Rican Democrats of Hartford. José Cruz, a public school teacher, was elected president. Julián Vargas, whose business ventures exemplified both integration and economic success, became vice president. Flavio Reverón, a community organizer with the commonwealth's office, was elected secretary, and María Sánchez, a key member of the Democratic party, became the group's treasurer.

Cruz described the role of the group in no uncertain terms: "We have to make this community our community, and make it help us fight our problems. We have to show people around us that we can live with them and successfully adopt their way of life."[58]

This was probably more than Carbone and his associates wanted from Puerto Ricans. Those two simple sentences suggested a program that went beyond the immediacy of an electoral contest. The message, in fact, spoke as much, and perhaps more, to Puerto Ricans themselves as to everyone else in the city, and it included an explicit call for action: adapt and assimilate, but also fight to solve the problems plaguing the community.

Other Puerto Ricans, however, were less willing to "fight," as illustrated in the comments of Irene Montalvo: "I'd never believe it if someone told me the Puerto Ricans were picketing. We'd never do that. To us picketing is like showing off. It offends people. We go the other way. You can never argue rights."[59]

In this view, it was preferable to go slowly, to educate the public through civic activities and cultural events, and to groom Puerto Ricans for individual success. Furthermore, there was skepticism that Puerto Ricans could form an organization for purposes other than to promote and enjoy their culture. The reasons for this were not given, and the very example of the group they had just organized was ignored. Instead, history became prophecy: since Puerto Ricans had not organized to combat social evils in the past, it was unlikely that they ever would.

A reporter for the *Hartford Courant* put it this way: "Leadership has always been lacking among Puerto Ricans here, and that which has advocated sudden change and urged a strong voice in behalf of better opportunities has usually fallen under the weight of political apathy, civic passiveness and the ever-present resignation to a second-rate standard of living."[60]

"[They] are the city's most exploited tenants and their housing is the city's worst," said Juanita Williams, the supervisor of the city housing department's North End field office, in November 1965.[61] With rent payments averaging about $8 to $10 per room per week, Puerto Ricans paid 20 percent more than any other city dwellers. Discrimination kept them from choosing better housing. "I go to the apartments," said Haydee Feliciano, from the San Juan Center, "They think I am Italian. Then they look at who I bring with me. They ask, 'Are they Italian too?' . . . I'm sorry, the apartment is rented."[62] The Puerto Rican Democrats of Hartford proposed to tackle these and similar problems. And, unlike the *Hartford Times* reporter, they did not doubt their ability. Instead, the most pressing question in their minds was how to make change happen.

Collective Behavior

Early in 1966, the Latin American Action Project delivered on its promise to provide information on housing conditions, and the news was bad. A survey of two hundred families in the North End's Tunnel area confirmed what many, albeit anecdotally, already knew: Puerto Ricans lived in inferior housing and paid inflated rents. "The general housing picture is nearly identical to that of the Negro in the North End," the survey report declared.[63] The Tunnel was the area of the Clay Hill neighborhood of Hartford's North End that was home to most Puerto Rican families in the city.

In 1967, only two years after the Puerto Rican Democrats of Hartford promised to combat the problems besieging Puerto Ricans, the prophecy of its detractors seemed fulfilled. "The English language continues to create the same problems for the Puerto Ricans that it did ten years ago," reads one account.[64] Language barriers and discrimination were the top two problems forestalling the fulfillment of the group's agenda.

Instead of action, the collective response was continued, sometimes self-imposed isolation.[65] Groping for an explanation, a frustrated José Cruz put the blame on the continuous flow of uneducated migrants from the agricultural regions of Puerto Rico, while Joseph Monserrat, director of the commonwealth's office in New York, and Santiago Polanco Abreu, then Puerto Rico's resident commissioner in Washington, pleaded for the public's sympathy by emphasizing that 80 percent of Puerto Ricans were white.[66]

Events took a different turn in 1969 when on the evening of Sunday, 10 August, rumors circulated through Hartford's South Green that the Comancheros, a white-ethnic, Hells Angels–type motorcycle gang, had assaulted an elderly Puerto Rican man at Friar's restaurant on Main Street.[67] The relationship between the Puerto Rican residents of the South Green neighborhood and the motorcycle gang was marked by long-standing ill feelings. But no previous incident had provoked the response that followed the alleged assault.

At the time "there was a lot of police brutality to begin with," recalled Antonio Soto, then a neighborhood resident and community organizer. "The Comancheros was just a group that we used to throw bricks at because they would be kicking Puerto Ricans in the ass all the time. So when we had the incident at the Main Street bar, all hell broke loose."[68]

On the night of the assault, Puerto Ricans were not to be confused by conflicting stories or troubled by doubts. "The rumor was enough to knock the top off the steam kettle that has been simmering for years," one account said.[69] In no time crowds gathered in various neighborhood spots, fights broke out, rocks and Molotov cocktails flew. The first arrests were of Puerto Ricans, which further incensed the rioters. Cars were set ablaze. A motorcycle shop was firebombed, and at about 1:00 A.M. someone broke into a mattress company and set between twenty and thirty mattresses on fire. The motorcycle gang was seen in the area throughout the night, but no members were arrested. This led to charges that the police were singling out Puerto Ricans while looking the other way where gang members were concerned.[70] Antonio Soto saw the riot precisely that way: "The cops turned their dogs on us," he recalled, "and the Comancheros had started the [incident], so we realized even further that the cops were more against us than the Comancheros were, and it just got totally out of hand."[71]

On Thursday, 14 August, after four days of bottle throwing and window smashing marked by tear gassing and arrests, María Sánchez, the only Puerto Rican member of the Democratic Town Committee at the time, requested a meeting with city officials to resolve the tensions underlying the rioting. Earlier, she had placated a crowd of about 150 young men who had gathered at the intersection of Park and Main Streets. City Manager Elisha Freedman was not convinced that a meeting was needed. "This seems to be a problem that can best be resolved through existing neighborhood organizations," he told a *Hartford Times* reporter.[72]

María Sánchez at a community meeting during the 1969 riots. *Photo by Juan Fuentes. Courtesy of Juan Fuentes.*

After some equivocating on the part of the concerned parties, a meeting was finally held that night at the South Green Multiservice Center on Main Street.[73] As the proceedings unfolded, Sánchez, Nicholas Carbone, and Freedman listened patiently. Residents complained that although they had been attacked, only Puerto Ricans had been arrested. Some mentioned unreasonable searches. In one case, a man was detained after a police officer found a chain, baseball shoes and gloves, and a baseball bat in the trunk of his car. Another explained that he had been arrested while telling people, in Spanish, not to throw rocks at police cars. This prompted Police Chief Thomas Vaughan to promise that interpreters would be hired to work full time at the front desk of the police station and that more Puerto Rican policemen and civilian aides for investigative work would be hired. Near the end of the meeting, Councilman George Athanson, a Democratic candidate for the nomination for mayor, urged the Puerto Rican community to run a candidate for city council. Many thought that was a good idea, but it would not happen for some time.

At the end of August, Bill Ryan, a reporter for the *Hartford Times*, wrote an assessment of the riots. Until 1969, he said, Puerto Ricans had caused no trouble in Hartford. Then suddenly the South Green was "a place of broken store windows and police throwing tear gas and people screaming defiance." A conflict with a motorcycle gang had turned into an event of social and political significance, and "after years of inaction, the Puerto Ricans were angry and making their presence known." [74]

Ryan's article revealed that Puerto Ricans were deeply resented. A fireman from the South Green was quoted as saying: "They are pigs, that's all pigs. A bunch of them will be sitting around drinking beer and when one is finished . . . he just throws the bottle anywhere. . . . They dump garbage out of their windows. They live like pigs." An unidentified South End resident said: "They insult women on the street. They ought to go back to hell where they came from." [75]

Ryan probably didn't even think about the impact of his harsh words when he wrote them. Even if the charges were true, insults led nowhere. To discourage littering, what was needed was regular trash collection and perhaps education. Hartford was clearly not Puerto Rico, where *piropos* were common practice, but even if complimenting women was uncalled for, the intention was not to offend but to flatter. In any case, Puerto Ricans did not stop to distinguish the civic minded from the pigs in their midst or to accept the charge that piropos were thinly disguised sexual innuendos. Ryan's comments rekindled their anger.

The day after Ryan's article appeared, the Puerto Rican community reacted, once again, with violence. This time the response was not entirely spontaneous. Two community leaders, Alejandro La Luz and Ramón Quiroz, began inciting friends and neighbors to reject the insults. While doing this, they allegedly accused María Sánchez of collaborating with the *Hartford Times* simply because the newspaper had announced that a profile on her would appear in a follow-up story. [76]

The violence was so intense that at the end of the first day and a half of rioting, hundreds of blacks and Puerto Ricans had ravaged a forty-block area of the North End, throwing fire bombs and bricks and sniping at police and firemen from rooftops and windows. Sixty-seven stores were looted, one policeman was shot, and 133 individuals were arrested. Forty-seven percent of those arrested were Puerto Rican, most of whom were charged with breach of peace or failure to disperse. [77] The reaction of the mayor was to declare a state of emergency, including a twelve-hour curfew.

The violence was random. This was particularly evident in the extensive damage suffered by a branch of the Hartford Public Library and the headquarters of the Hartford Board of Education. The day after the riot broke out, witnesses were already declaring that it was the worst Hartford had ever suffered. The mayor concurred. [78] But on the second night, the trouble spread farther, from the Clay Hill and Arsenal neighborhoods on the North End to the South Green and Charter Oak areas in the South (see Map 2). By 8:00 A.M. Wednesday, 266 arrests had been made on

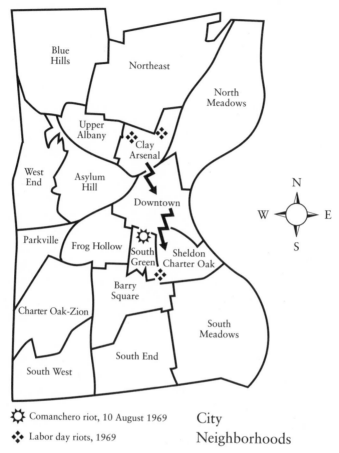

☼ Comanchero riot, 10 August 1969

❖❖ Labor day riots, 1969

City
Neighborhoods

Hartford, Connecticut, 1969 Riots

charges that included violation of curfew, breach of peace, attempted arson, breaking and entering, and loitering. Almost half of those arrested were Puerto Rican.[79]

On Thursday night, seventy more arrests were made. By Friday, 5 September, more than five hundred people had been detained.[80] Four people had been shot. The following Monday, Mayor Uccello lifted the state of emergency with a plea for help from the suburbs. "The suburbs must absorb some of the population of the inner city," she said. But her analysis of the disturbances did not help her cause any: "This activity was instigated by agitators and carried out by hoodlums . . . who would steal no matter what the social conditions."[81] Then she proceeded to echo the words of Wilber Smith, an NAACP officer and mayoral candidate, who had earlier cautioned the white community not to issue a "blanket indictment of all Negroes and Puerto Ricans." [82]

According to Uccello, the lawbreakers were aberrant members of the Puerto Rican and black community. She did not make it clear who the suburbs should welcome, the troublemakers or law-abiding blacks and Puerto Ricans. Republican Collin Bennett explained the events differently. The riot was evidence of a "poor relationship and lack of communication between the city government and members of the Spanish-speaking community. This segment of our society feels that there is no one to represent their interests in city hall, and this has been partly responsible for the increased tension . . . between the Spanish-speaking community and our city government." [83]

Father Segundo Las Heras, a Spanish priest with close ties to the Puerto Rican community, offered another judgment. In a newspaper interview, his explanation for the events combined elements of the mayor's and Councilman Bennett's interpretation. He recognized that agitators played a role and referred to the bitterness and disgust of ghetto dwellers over living conditions that turned anger into violence. Then he singled out the language barrier as the main cause of the Puerto Ricans' inadequate education and lack of integration.[84]

During the crisis, the Puerto Rican leadership and its allies scrambled to get outside help and attention. The Reverend Charles Pickett, a former head of the Spanish Action Coalition, a group that formed in late 1967, telephoned Jorge Luis Córdova Díaz, Polanco Abreu's successor as resident commissioner in Washington, and asked him to come to Hartford. His hope was that the commissioner would unite the leadership and bring peace to the community.[85] Córdova Díaz demurred. He was following the debate in Congress on electoral reform and did not want to miss it, he said. Also, he indicated, the governor of Puerto Rico had not asked him to go to Hartford. Finally, he was concerned that his visit might be construed by city officials as interference in local affairs.

Later that day, Pickett joined others at a meeting at the South Arsenal Neighborhood Development Corporation (SAND), a black agency, to discuss community unity. City officials were asked to attend, but none responded. There were about forty people in attendance, mostly Puerto Ricans. The central disagreement revolved around strategy. Some felt that more militant action was needed; others decried militancy.

The group agreed to call for a halt to federal funding to the city until an investigation of the disturbances was conducted. The next day, Alejandro La Luz, president of Puerto Rican Action for Progress, announced that telegrams had been sent to all funding agencies, including the Departments of Housing and Urban Development; Labor; Health, Education,

María Sánchez and Alejandro La Luz, 1 April 1970. Hartford Times *photo by Ronald Dundin. From the Hartford Collection, Hartford Public Library.*

and Welfare; and the Office of Equal Opportunity. Telegrams were also sent to Connecticut's governor, John Dempsey, and to Mayor Uccello.

"The needs of the Puerto Ricans in Hartford are not being fairly or adequately served," read the telegram. Signed by leaders of the Spanish Action Coalition, Puerto Rican Action for Progress, the Spanish American Association, the Comerieños Ausentes, and the Hijos de Santurce, the telegram claimed that, compared with other cities in the state, Hartford was not acting in good faith toward Puerto Ricans. The city's leadership as well as the federal government were warned that inaction would lead to more violence. "We demand that all funds be suspended pending an impartial investigation by your office," the signatories declared.[86]

Mayor Uccello offered no comment. But Reverend Las Heras, upset by the use of the word "demand" rather than "request," resigned as chair of the Spanish Action Coalition. "I certainly think we're getting a younger, very vocal group in SAC," said Reverend Pickett, remarking on the resignation, "and their attitude is that they are just not going to be pushed around anymore."[87]

A spokesman for the group of signatory agencies explained that Puerto Ricans were tired of playing games. "We are all trying to keep things cool but there's only so much we can do," he said. Keeping tempers under control was especially hard because the riots raised the issue of fairness.[88] For example, a call from the Greater Hartford Chamber of Commerce for tough measures against those who were arrested struck a sensitive chord. Puerto Ricans felt that looters and arsonists should be punished, but "at the same time we would like to hear the mayor be as strong for the punishment of others who violate the law, such as slumlords."[89]

The same day these complaints were heard, the Greater Hartford Community Council announced a membership meeting for 23 September for which the title of the program was to be "Our Puerto Rican Fellow Citizens." Gilberto Camacho was scheduled to speak about the "Puerto Rican Heritage and the Shock of Mainland Living" and Antonio Soto about "Organizing the Puerto Rican Community."[90] Ten days later, the president of the Puerto Rican Parade Committee, Feliciano Martorell, announced that Puerto Ricans from more than ten towns in the state would march on 28 September from West Avon to a rally at Bushnell Park.

The theme of the parade was "Register and Vote." So it had been since the first parade in 1964. But in the context of the recent disturbances and the claims of disfranchisement, the theme acquired a freshness and urgency not felt before. This was apparent in Martorell's pronouncement: "From now on we are going to show the administrators throughout the state that we want improvements in the areas of housing, employment, education, health and civil rights."[91] This was a comprehensive agenda, and it was strongly articulated.

The meeting on 23 September gave Puerto Rican leaders an opportunity to reiterate the main points in their social agenda. Once again, long-standing grievances were aired. Tales of rejection and misunderstanding were offered. Complaints about inadequate education, poor medical care, and expensive housing were also heard. In his talk, Camacho deplored mainlanders' ignorance of Puerto Rican culture. He also referred to the barriers Puerto Ricans faced. "We migrate to Hartford to better ourselves," he said. "We are told of a lack of skilled labor. A Puerto Rican comes here with $100 in his pocket. Where can he find an apartment?" Soto's presentation emphasized the relationship between the well-being of Puerto Ricans and the city's welfare. "If we have problems, you have problems," he told the leaders of the council. He then blamed the Labor Day week disturbances on lack of support of Puerto Ricans from city and state officials.[92]

These themes were further hammered into the city's consciousness the day of the parade. Feliciano Martorell said to a reporter that it was time to make the political establishment more responsive to Puerto Rican needs. Since 1964, the parade had reminded residents of the city that Puerto Ricans were living in Hartford. "From now on," he said, "we are

Connecticut palm trees. Scene from the 1969 Puerto Rican Day Parade in Hartford. *From the Hartford Collection, Hartford Public Library.*

going to show [everyone] that we are not only here, but that we want improvements. . . . We plan to follow through with our plans of bettering and upgrading the whole concept of the Puerto Rican around the state." [93]

ASSESSMENT

It is tempting to see the path from settlement to collective behavior as a succession of causally related events. Yet there is no way of proving that the establishment of, say, La Popular, Bodega Hispana, in 1956 or the celebration of the first Puerto Rican Parade in 1964 were causally connected to the 1969 riots. What is clear is that collective behavior was predicated on a set of preexisting conditions. But this is no proof that these conditions were necessary for such behavior to take place. Even what were considered proximate factors—such as electoral disfranchisement and linguistic barriers—cannot be construed as definitive causes, although they certainly were the sources of cumulative tensions that the Comanchero incident brought to a head. Furthermore, although their collective behavior represented a new era in the Puerto Ricans' experience in Hartford, traces of the past still remained. In fact, the riots made it clear that the present bore a rather disquieting likeness to the past; Puerto Ricans still faced many of the same difficulties they confronted upon arrival, and their political status was still marginal. Yet the conditions under which their current experiences were beginning to unfold were no longer the same as before.

After the dust of the riots settled, Córdova Díaz made an appearance. At the parade's closing rally, he said the riots represented a confrontation between two cultures but then corrected himself. "Actually, what I think we have seen is not a confrontation between Puerto Ricans and other Americans but an outbreak of the same conflict that is troubling this entire country." The rioting, protests, and unrest afflicting the nation, he said, were signals of conflict "between the young, the poor, the black—and the more experienced, perhaps the more affluent." In his own way, Córdova Díaz was intimating that the Puerto Ricans' problem was one of power not ethnicity. In his view, progress would come through politics. "It is the weight of our votes that will gain us respect," he concluded.[94]

In retrospect, it is easy to agree that the political process had much to offer. The role of ethnicity is also apparent, although Cordova Díaz's implicit assessment that it was secondary is questionable. The riots were a transitional moment. Martorell's statement best summarizes how Puerto Ricans connected ethnic awareness—a sense of who they were—with power awareness—a sense of their relative disadvantage. The connection suggested that change was needed, in how Puerto Ricans were perceived and in how they were served. It was clear that the "concept of the Puerto Rican" was firmly established. Now it was necessary to "better" and "upgrade" that concept through improvements in socioeconomic status. Thus, he was calling upon the community to "register and vote," and the mayor and the bureaucracy were urged to bring about equity.

This is not to say that Puerto Rican leaders in Hartford had never connected ethnic and power awareness before but that the collective action they took in 1969 made the link vivid. Puerto Rican leaders used the opportunity the riots provided to demand accountability from the political stratum and to encourage further political action. They made it clear that while most Puerto Ricans behaved responsibly, not all enjoyed the benefits they deserved or equal protection under the law.

Calls for political action presumed the existence of a community—not a mere settlement or a group of transients—and community meant the presence of ethnic-based needs. Housing, employment, and education were collective goods that although deserved by all were susceptible to unequal distribution. As Juanita Williams of the city's housing department put it and the Latin American Action Project confirmed, disparities of access existed, and these correlated with ethnicity.

Citizenship complicated matters because legality did not transcend culture. By law, Puerto Ricans were not aliens, yet many were excluded from voting de jure by literacy requirements, an issue that was related to their language, itself the product of their different culture. They were not completely marginal to politics, but the prevailing, and to some extent self-fulfilling, perception was that their interest in the political process was nil. Citizenship was supposed to make them instant participants, even if the city's political culture—with its one-party system, at-large elections, and corporate priorities—kept them in the shadows. But context was not the only disfranchising factor; ethnicity also contributed to the extent that language barriers restricted participation.

Speaking to a reporter at the end of the turbulent summer of 1969, Camacho, in a reversal of attitude, downplayed characterizations of Puerto Ricans as transient. The Puerto Rican community in Hartford was still young; yet, according to Camacho, their roots were already firmly planted.[95] Puerto Ricans were not leaving Hartford, and, as Martorell put it, their presence was no longer a question mark. The crucial issue now was how to command the attention of the political society, how to move from social visibility to political access.

The 1969 riots added to the political capital Puerto Ricans had accumulated since entering the political arena. The process of accumulation was not foreordained, and there was no guarantee that assets could be cashed in on at any particular time. In fact, the response of community leaders, taking advantage of the situation to make claims and press demands, .was as unpredictable as the opportunity provided by the riots. They put forth a plan—to seek improvements in education, housing, health, and so on—but it was one they had pursued for some time. They had no preconceived notion that disorder could be exploited; in fact, many avoided disruption like the plague. They took advantage of an unforeseen and unintended opportunity without really knowing that they were building upon a foundation of experience and resources that was there.

In 1969, with their numbers estimated at about twenty thousand, the Puerto Rican community in Hartford was demographically significant but unrepresented. No one could claim that its institutional maturity had peaked, but its level of institutional development was significant nonetheless. The office set up by the Commonwealth of Puerto Rico had been active for more than a decade, the San Juan Center was thirteen years old, and the Puerto Rican Parade had just celebrated its fifth anniversary. Moreover, many individuals had some political experience, after registering and mobilizing voters locally and having worked at the state level as organizers of political campaigns. Thus, Puerto Ricans appeared positioned to make inroads into the political structure. They were demanding power, and, within the political stratum, some recognized that if it was not given to them they would grab it themselves.

By the end of 1969, Puerto Ricans were politically energized, but representation did not seem close at hand. What was the net result of the riots? What internal assets could Puerto Ricans count on at the beginning of their third decade in the city? What factors helped them accumulate political capital, and what was the structure of the political choices available to them? What role did their relationship with blacks have in this process? These questions are answered in the next chapter.

4   From Collective Behavior
to Brokered Representation

POLITICAL CAPITAL is the balance of assets and liabilities that defines organizational capacity and the level of knowledgeability that enables political action. Ethnicity prompted and structured Puerto Rican political action, but this process did not take place in a vacuum. Instead, several variables—demographic growth, leadership development, and organizational efforts—shaped and influenced the expression of ethnicity. Similarly, rather than being a mere reflection of ascriptive traits, identity politics was a response to both endogenous and exogenous factors.[1] Black politics was of some assistance in this development, but it was also a source of tension and conflict. In seeking representation, Puerto Rican leaders negotiated the relationship between capability and feasibility, maximizing opportunities as best they could.

POLITICAL ASSETS

The 1969 riots gave Puerto Ricans in Hartford one asset: added visibility. The press was suddenly more accessible than before and eager to help rebuild their image. Although historically city newspapers had been largely sympathetic and willing to portray Puerto Ricans in the best possible light, now they acted out of a sense of guilt because of the role the article by Bill Ryan had in triggering the Labor Day riots. This attitude was exemplified by the coverage given to the activities of Sylvia Vargas née Carrasquillo, the state queen of the 1969 Puerto Rican Parade. "I could speak English, I was a nice girl and future social worker," she recalled. "I said all the politically correct things, and because they wanted to put forth a positive image of the Puerto Rican, I got a lot of press."[2] So did sixteen-year-old Rosa Delia Crespo, queen of the Hartford chapter of the parade, who was highlighted in a *Hartford Times* article on the dance where she was crowned.[3]

By journalistic standards, coverage was mixed, so that some issues were reported on prominently and others were simply buried in articles deep inside the papers. Still, the frequency of press coverage was good even if the stories didn't always report on issues of substance.

The year after the riots, the press coverage was also mixed. These articles emphasized the Puerto Ricans' wish to incorporate, as well as the difficulties they encountered. PUERTO RICANS PLAN TO ORGANIZE; JOBS, FRIENDS DRAW PUERTO RICANS TO "DESIRABLE" HARTFORD; AMERICAN DREAM SUFFOCATING; ETHNIC NEED: POLITICAL MUSCLE were some of the headlines from this time. Of the ten stories on Puerto Rican issues that year, six appeared on the front page.

Collective behavior also stimulated unity and formal organization. Responding to the question "What do you remember about the 1969 riots?" Gerardo "Jerry" Zayas, a resident of Hartford since 1959 who was elected to the city council in 1980, said: "That was one of the incidents that contributed to the unity of the Puerto Rican community. It generated a lot of interest in the goals of community improvement, building our own organizations, and developing our own political efforts—not that there weren't others, like María Sánchez, interested in these things and working in the community—but I think that's when the community began to unite." [4]

Olga Mele was one of the most socially active members of the community, and she had numerous connections throughout the city. She also was sanguine about the riots: "Not that many people condemned the riots, and criticism was only made behind closed doors." [5]

Johnny Castillo was not as politically involved as Mele but had a good grasp of local opinion from his neighborhood activities, which included the organization of baseball tournaments. He remembered how the treatment of Puerto Ricans by the authorities prompted feelings of bitterness and disgust. His assessment suggests that, despite the destruction and violence, the riots were an affirmation of ethnic needs that united the community:

> The riots were a movement for recognition. María Sánchez did a lot to stop the rioting, to maintain communication with the police, the firefighters, and the general public. There was no division whatsoever within the community. People were not ashamed [about the riots]. In reality, we were very angry because we were all portrayed as savages, but it wasn't like that; all we wanted was recognition, and it was not just one group [of Puerto Ricans] but all throughout the city. [6]

Juan Fuentes, a Hartford resident since 1963, had a similar assessment: "People were sick and tired of being used, just as today. There was no good housing, no services. Many thought the results were negative, but there were positive things, too. The Community Renewal Team was strengthened, a number of new programs were established, people got involved, and the politicians got very worried. You know, Americans move like old oxen; if you don't pinch [them], forget it, [they] get stuck." [7]

The riots had two other notable consequences. Three days into the dis-

From left: Roger W. Lindgren, in charge of social ministry at the Church of Christ the King; Gilberto Camacho; and Wallace A. Curtis, vice president of the Windsor Human Relations Committee, as they discussed the participation of Puerto Ricans in Connecticut's economy, 1 February 1970. Hartford Times *photo by Ronald Dundin. From the Hartford Collection, Hartford Public Library.*

turbances, the Hartford Foundation for Public Giving announced that it would donate $78,640 to the Greater Hartford Community Council to hire a full-time community organizer to work with Puerto Ricans. The three-year grant specified that the organizer would be a liaison between the council and community residents. Most important, it provided seed money to later establish La Casa de Puerto Rico, the first Puerto Rican antipoverty agency in the city.[8]

From the island, Governor Luis Ferré declared that his government would study the possibility of sending representatives to Hartford to assess Puerto Rican needs and to work with the state governor to assist the community. Nothing came of this promise, but it gave local leaders a cue to follow. For years Gilberto Camacho had pleaded with his superiors in New York for more resources for the commonwealth's office, but to no avail. A few days after the riots, Camacho wrote requesting an assistant, claiming to be under enormous pressure. In response, he was curtly told that no assistance was forthcoming and to put a stop to his requests.[9] Camacho, however, did not desist and used the riots to bolster his argument. When the Republicans captured the governorship in 1970, he shifted his focus. In a letter to Governor Thomas J. Meskill, he said: "The time has come for the Office of the Governor to be staffed with a Special Assistant knowledgeable in background, experience, an[d] academic education of the idiosyncracy of the Puerto Rican Americans."[10]

Meskill did nothing. But the idea was planted, and the position was created four years later by Ella Grasso, his Democratic successor.

Other political assets included an increase in and demographic concentration of the Puerto Rican population, leadership development, and a seemingly inexhaustible organizational drive. Because these were, in fact, crucial building blocs of political capacity, I discuss them separately below.

POLITICAL LIABILITIES

Olga Mele had been a catalytic agent in the community since the 1950s, on her own and as part of the pioneering efforts of the San Juan Center. According to Mele, "We began registering voters in 1950. . . . I helped the Americanos [non-Hispanic whites] get the Puerto Rican vote. I registered María [Sánchez] in 1955, I believe, and her husband and her whole family."[11] Yet, although they were socially visible, politically it was as if Puerto Ricans did not exist. Their political involvement had spanned more than a decade, but their impact was nil.

There was no single cause but rather many factors that kept Puerto Ricans at the margins. In 1970, the community was relatively young, not just in its age structure but in its acculturation, skills, political strength, and experience. Prejudice and discrimination were also contributing factors. This was substantiated in 1972 in a report commissioned by Nicholas Carbone. The authors found that residents of the South End had largely negative perceptions of Puerto Ricans, and a significant number favored limiting their population in the area.[12] But the most significant liabilities were endogenous: Puerto Ricans lacked resources and, despite sporadic moments of cohesion, were not united.

In fact, that Puerto Ricans were marginalized politically is not that surprising considering that in 1970, 43 percent of the community's adult population had lived in Hartford for no more than six years.[13] What is remarkable is that despite the recency of migration, by 1970 Puerto Ricans had developed a distinct institutional and communal life.

Human Capital

In 1970, nearly half the Puerto Ricans in Hartford were under eighteen years of age. Only 56.5 percent had lived in Hartford for more than six years. Almost half, 44 percent, had migrated to Hartford to improve their economic status. More than a third, 35.5 percent, came with or to join their families. A similar proportion had less than seven years of schooling. Only 23 percent had a high school diploma or its equivalent, and only 1.5 percent had a college degree. Among those employed, 52 percent were manual workers and 72.3 percent of these workers were men.[14] According to the Census Bureau, 27.6 percent of "Spanish-language" families, most of whom were surely Puerto Rican, and 45.1 percent of "Spanish-language" families below the poverty level received welfare in 1969. Median earnings among Hartford's Puerto Ricans were $4,556 that year.[15]

Only black males came close to Puerto Ricans in age structure; half were under 19.7 years of age. The median age for black females was 22; for white males, 30; and for white females, 34. Puerto Ricans were the youngest population cohort in Hartford. They were also the least educated and the poorest. Among blacks, 25.4 percent were high school graduates, and 3.2 percent, twice the percentage of Puerto Ricans, had four years of college. Although the proportion of black families below poverty level who were receiving welfare—45.2 percent—was just about the same as the rate for Puerto Ricans, only 21 percent of black families received public assistance; this was 7 percentage points lower than the Puerto Rican rate. The median earnings for blacks in 1969—$4,755— were slightly higher than for Puerto Ricans, but the median earnings of black males were more than $600 higher than the median earnings of Puerto Rican men and more than $2,000 higher than the median earnings of Puerto Rican women.[16]

Except for her age and welfare status, María Sánchez, who was literate but uneducated, employed but poor, was emblematic of the human capital profile of Puerto Ricans. In addition, she had to contend with perceived deficits that, in all likelihood, besieged others in the community. Said Carbone:

> I remember when we ran María for the school board and she spoke broken English. She wasn't an attractive woman, she was heavy, so where would you take her? How did you sell her? How did you get people to vote for her? And how [did] you get over the prejudice that she spoke with a thick accent? So we didn't take her into a lot of neighborhoods. . . . You had to be practical as you were trying [to get her] on the school board.[17]

Johnny Castillo's daughter, Yolanda, was elected to the city council in 1991. In 1992, she was the first Puerto Rican elected majority leader. Although a neophyte candidate, she was knowledgeable enough to manage the intricacies of Democratic party politics and the electoral process. This was an advantage that her father, and many Puerto Ricans like him, did not have. Castillo said: "When I came here [in 1953,] I knew nothing [about politics]. My political affiliation came through my family. I knew about the Populares, but here [I knew nothing]." [18]

Castillo's situation was not as difficult as that of other migrants. When he arrived in Hartford, he had a high school diploma, knew English, and quickly found work at Royal Typewriter. Yet his involvement in politics was always peripheral. The comparative advantages he had upon arrival suggest that politics must have been a great challenge for those who had even fewer cultural resources.

In the late 1950s and early 1960s, Olga Mele spent many hours helping her compatriots get jobs. According to Charles Quinn, the director of the Adult Counseling Service of the Hartford school system in the mid-1960s, "The natives [of Puerto Rico] were not interested in what we had to offer. Until we received the support of Olga and a few other field workers, we were unable to reach the people we desired to help. She became the link, our means for helping the community." [19]

Mele encountered countless individuals whose skills were just not up to par for the jobs that were available. She recalled:

> The men we worked with were destitute; they had nothing to offer, but we helped them. I went from factory to factory, [but] first they had to be interviewed by a representative from the Labor Department. And he saw that they only had a second grade education, or were illiterate farmworkers, or had never worked and so he said, "No, there's nothing." So I found them jobs where no English was needed—moving laundry bags or putting laundry into washing machines. [20]

Community Cleavages

In her 1970 analysis of the state of the Puerto Rican community, Janet Anderson of the *Hartford Courant* wrote about divisions among the Puerto Rican leadership, noting that at least thirty individuals considered themselves leaders, each one with a different viewpoint. "We don't have leaders, we have speculators," said Alejandro La Luz. True leaders, he added, must come from the community, "with intellectual honesty and in the spirit of sacrifice." Pedro Meléndez, from the Department of Community Affairs, declared, "We should organize for one common thing—to solve the poverty in our community." And Julio Quiñones, a businessman, said: "Our leaders are not united now, but this doesn't mean they cannot be. We're going to break out of this hole in the next two years." [21]

With all the issues that divided the community, it is not surprising that the future was not as Quiñones predicted it would be. As more Puerto Ricans moved to Hartford, a new enclave—and new divisions—developed. During the 1970s, newcomers added to the settlement around Park Street, colonizing portions of the Italian South End. But displacement caused by willful neglect of properties and redevelopment also contributed to movement from Clay Hill in the north to the South Green, Frog Hollow, and Parkville neighborhoods in the south.[22] Juan Fuentes witnessed this transformation: "Our people lived in the North End. They began to move to Park Street when housing displacement began in the North End. That began to happen around the 1970s when they started demolishing buildings. Some buildings burned and others were burned on purpose."[23]

Max Fernández, a director for more than fifteen years at TAINO Housing, a community and housing development agency, agreed that displacement was a force in shaping the formation of the enclaves, moving Puerto Ricans from the North End to the South, from Congress Street to Frog Hollow, out of Main and into Park Street. This occurred when developers promised to include low-income housing in their projects and then, citing changing economic conditions, gave up their plans. "Development, when it's done," concluded Fernández, "doesn't include our people."[24]

Residential fragmentation resulted in cleavages between North and South End residents. María Sánchez, for example, was unhappy when La Casa de Puerto Rico moved from Albany Avenue to Wadsworth Street. In her mind the move meant that South End Puerto Ricans would benefit, leaving those in the North End forlorn. Changes like this made residents of different neighborhoods eye each other with suspicion, making coalition building and political mobilization much harder.

Community organizations were polarized along an axis of militancy to moderation. On the moderate side, organizations such as Services for Puerto Ricans, created during the summer of 1970 with the blessing of Councilman Collin Bennett, proposed a strategy of government and foundation fund-raising to provide services.[25] Other groups, such as the San Juan Center, the Spanish Action Coalition, and La Casa de Puerto Rico, fell within this category. The militant tendency was illustrated by the People's Liberation Party (PLP), a group composed of Puerto Rican youth, organized in 1969. The group's slogan was "Power to the People!" Its strategy was summed up by the party's seventeen-year-old chairman, José Claudio, when he declared that "we tried to deal with city hall . . . with no results. The North End and South End ghettos are in terrible condition—and the city has not lived up to its promises. Hartford needs more demonstrations."[26]

With its younger, impatient activists, the PLP was a vivid reminder of the generational gap that divided the community. These Young Turks were eager to be "part of the action" while professing to being tired of "playing games." The Puerto Rican Socialist Party (PSP) and its fronts—the Brigada Venceremos, the Comité Villa Sin Miedo, the Comité de

Apoyo a Vieques, and so on—also illustrated the militant and generational split within the community.

Finally, cutting across divisions between militants and moderates, young and old, were differences in strategy—with some arguing for alliances with African Americans, others pressing for the creation of a pressure group—and a three-way disagreement over the solution to the status of Puerto Rico.

The status issue was a source of additional cleavages. In a survey conducted by Elwyn Nicholas Kernstock in 1970, Puerto Ricans were asked the following questions: "(1) Has Americanization destroyed your culture? (2) Do you support independence for the island? and (3) Do you identify yourself primarily as Puerto Rican?" The answers revealed a pattern of attitudes that he classified as nonnationalistic, passive nationalist, active nationalist, and aggressive nationalist. Those in the latter category answered "yes" to all three questions but comprised only 7 percent of the respondents. At the other end of the spectrum were the nonnationalists—those responding "no" to all three questions, and these were 33 percent of the respondents. Active nationalists were a notch below "aggressive" but represented only 23 percent of the respondents. Last, those responding "yes" to only one question fell in the passive category and constituted a plurality of respondents, or 39 percent. Among the passive nationalists, 10 percent supported independence. The majority—65 percent—declared that their primary identity was Puerto Rican regardless of whether they related to nationalism as an ideology or preferred Puerto Rican independence.[27] This led Kernstock to note a contradiction in "the strong indication of consciousness of national identity and the lack of a desire to create a Puerto Rican nation-state."[28]

ACCUMULATION OF POLITICAL CAPITAL

Demographic Growth

To bolster their social and political claims, Puerto Ricans could count on their growing numbers. According to local estimates (see Table 6), from 1960 to 1970, the Puerto Rican population almost tripled. Twenty years after settlement, the Census Bureau counted 8,543 of them, a figure well below the estimate of more than twenty thousand cited at the time in the *Hartford Courant.*[29] According to the census count, Puerto Ricans represented 5.4 percent of the city's population in 1970; according to local estimates, 12.6 percent. Even if the census count is accepted, their numbers clearly grew significantly during the 1960s.

According to census figures, from 1970 to 1980, the population almost tripled again—from 8,543 to 24,615 and from 5.4 to 18 percent of the

Table 6. Estimated Population Growth of Puerto Ricans
in Hartford, 1954–1970

Year	U.S. Census	Local Estimate	% Change
1954	—	500	
1956	—	2,000	300
1957	—	3,000	50
1958	—	4,500	50
1959	—	6,000	33
1961	—	7,000	17
1969–70	8,543	20,000	186

SOURCES: Culled by José E. Cruz from the *Hartford Courant* and the
Hartford Times (1958 only); U.S. Bureau of the Census.

NOTE: Census figures before 1970 not available.

total population. In contrast, the census count for blacks showed a small
increase—from 44,091 to 46,186 and from 27.9 to 33.8 percent of the
total population.

But sharp population increases did not occur only during the 1970s.
Population estimates indicate a 300 percent increase in the number of
Puerto Ricans from 1954 to 1956, 50 percent growth between 1956 and
1957 and between 1957 and 1958, and a 186 percent jump between 1961
and 1970. Based on census figures, the 1960–70 increase is 22 percent,
still a respectable change.

The increase during the 1970s coincided with a new migratory pattern
nationwide. Between 1965 and 1980, the so-called revolving-door migration to the United States resulted in fluctuating rates and high numbers of
return migrants. But in 1969, when the growth rate for Puerto Ricans to
Hartford appears to have been the highest since 1956, migration to the
mainland also registered its highest level overall since 1955.[30]

By 1970, there were forty to sixty Puerto Rican–owned businesses in
Hartford.[31] There were two Spanish theaters, on Main and Park Streets,
and one, the Lyric Club on Park Street, also held dances.[32] Connecticut had
no Spanish newspapers, but two national dailies—*El Diario-La Prensa*
and *El Tiempo*—circulated locally.[33] In 1973, Hartford welcomed the first
bilingual community newspaper in New England, *La Prensa Gráfica*,
which circulated locally for almost a decade.

Puerto Ricans in Hartford and throughout the rest of the state were
able to enjoy the Spanish broadcasts of Dinorah Maldonado and Yolanda
Carrera, hosts of the local TV programs *Adelante* and *Barrio* respectively.
Radio broadcasts were the source of much information, and these were
provided by Hartford-based WLVH, a Spanish-language station offering
news, community-interest programs, and Latin music.

In the North End, the Church of the Sacred Heart, once a German parish, was almost completely Puerto Rican by 1970. On the South End, Puerto Ricans attended St. Peter's, previously an Irish church. A pentecostal church, Templo Fe, was also established, gaining adherents at a rapid pace.

All of these developments were clear signs of enclave formation, signals of a strong and growing demographic presence.

ASSESSMENT

Demographic growth strengthened the community socially and provided a base for political mobilization. The social life in the Puerto Rican community indicated a new sense of self, distinct yet integrated. Spanish-language radio broadcasts celebrated Puerto Rican culture but also kept citizens informed about general issues, thus helping them integrate. Puerto Rican religious organizations and activities were the best known and the most frequented. These put dampers on political mobilization but did not discourage efforts by Hartford's Puerto Rican elite. In fact, the most recognized community leaders—María Sánchez, José Cruz, Esther Jiménez, Julián Vargas, Antonio Soto, and Florencio Morales—were those involved in political activities; they were also regarded as the most influential.[34]

Not all politicians grasped the implications of demographic trends. Those who understood what was happening knew that, to survive politically, they needed to integrate and co-opt the newcomers. By 1965, Nicholas Carbone was already arguing that Puerto Ricans had to be recognized or else the opportunity to forge a permanent alliance would be lost. He referred to the experience of blacks, in which he saw an important lesson, to further his argument.

> One of the lessons we learned at the board of education was that . . . when blacks were coming up during the 1950s and becoming a part of the Hartford community, the board didn't understand the demographics. . . . The result of that is when the NAACP made an effort [to talk] about affirmative action . . . we had basically a white middle-class teacher community with very few blacks. That was in the late 1960s, and there was a lot of tension.[35]

Once at city hall, Carbone supported the long-standing efforts of María Sánchez and Esther Jiménez, then a field worker with CRT, to address the educational needs of the increasing number of Puerto Rican children in the school system. School enrollments indicated a growing presence, and, according to Carbone, it was best to act swiftly rather than wait. Inaction meant that before long school officials would face a "gigantic problem." Therefore, Carbone said, "We then talked to the board [of education to start] recruiting teachers from Puerto Rico so we could match our growing population."[36]

Two generations of community leaders. *From left:* Mildred Torres, Sarah Romany, Olga Mele, and Diana Alverio. *Photo by Juan Fuentes. Courtesy of Juan Fuentes.*

In 1971, a teacher recruitment program, known as the Teachers Corps, funded by the federal government, began operations out of the University of Hartford. The program was conceived in the late 1960s by Perry Alan Zirkel, a professor at the university, and María Sánchez.

Leadership Development

Political capital also accrued through leadership development. The first institution to take an interest in Puerto Ricans was the Catholic Church, and it was through the church that the first cadre of leaders emerged. Some of these leaders became politically involved at this stage, but the main concerns of these early activists, most of whom were women, were social and cultural.

Baseball also played a strong role in the political socialization of Puerto Ricans and the development of political leaders. For many, the activities of the various teams provided cultural solace away from the home country. Baseball tournaments were structures of dissociation: from the rigors of work, from economic preoccupations, from melancholy brought on by feelings of nostalgia. One of the earliest sports associations, the Julián Vargas League, also served as a social network that brought party regulars, such as Vargas, and ordinary citizens, such as Johnny Castillo, to-

Julián Vargas (*second from left*), and members of the Juana Díaz baseball team. *Photo by Juan Fuentes. Courtesy of Juan Fuentes.*

gether to exchange views on issues, fostering their involvement in civic and partisan activities. It was a letter from Castillo, in which he sang the praises of Hartford's abundance of work and sought help in organizing a baseball league, that brought Eugenio Caro, who was elected to the city council in 1987, to Hartford in 1956.[37]

Community agencies also were a source of leaders.[38] In 1970, more than 60 percent of the recognized leaders in the Puerto Rican community had affiliations with CRT or other agencies.[39] Long before landing a position at Aetna Life Insurance, Mildred Torres, the first Puerto Rican to serve on the city council, was involved with the city's social service agencies. Before his election to the council, Jerry Zayas was the director of the Spanish American Center, an agency he helped establish in the mid-1970s to provide social services. Yasha Escalera, the first Puerto Rican executive director of the San Juan Center, developed his statewide political network through his work as president of the Connecticut Association of United Spanish Administrators (CAUSA), a group established in 1974 to represent and advocate for Hispanic agencies. According to Escalera, "In the early seventies [Puerto Ricans had] an emerging political presence not only in Hartford but in most of the small towns. What was more developed were the civic organizations and nonprofit organizations. So whatever political activity [there was] took place via that route."[40]

Yasha Escalera, the first Puerto Rican director of the San Juan Center, who helped organize Puerto Rican Democrats statewide. *Photo by Juan Fuentes. Courtesy of Juan Fuentes.*

The teacher program that Zirkel and María Sánchez established also became a source of leaders. Edwin Vargas, Jr., the first Puerto Rican to challenge the Democratic machine, was brought to Hartford by Sánchez under this program. Other participants, including Calixto Torres and Edna Negrón Smith, also went on to assume positions of prominence in the community. In 1977, Torres played a role in the organization of what later became PRPAC; and in 1990, Negrón took over Sánchez's assembly seat after her death in 1989.

In their attempt to co-opt promising individuals, machine politicians nurtured their eventual challengers. They could not foresee that co-optation would succeed only partially. Initially, Puerto Ricans played the protégé game; eventually, they challenged and displaced their mentors. Edwin Vargas, who constantly straddled the mainstream and the margins of politics, was one such challenger; María Sánchez, who clashed with

Edna Negrón Smith testifying in support of bilingual education in 1971. *Photo by Juan Fuentes. Courtesy of Juan Fuentes.*

Carbone in 1977 and replaced her mentor and associate Abe Giles at the state legislature in 1988, was another, as was Yolanda Castillo, who had a brief association with state representative Arthur Brouillet.

Similarly, dissatisfaction with the work of the commonwealth's office encouraged the emergence of new leaders. According to Gilberto Camacho, by 1970 the Puerto Rican leadership had multiplied since his arrival in the city in 1959. This was, to him, a sign of political maturity, a reflection of the increasing number of agencies serving the community. It was also a sign of what he called "resentment on the part of many of our initiatives."[41]

ASSESSMENT

An unintended consequence of leadership development was increased factionalism as the emerging cadre of activists competed for preeminence within a growing but still small community. During his tenure at the Spanish American Center, Jerry Zayas had a gentleman's agreement with Yasha Escalera, then director of the San Juan Center, not to encroach on each other's turf. They decided that Zayas's group would serve Puerto Ricans from downtown Hartford to the south and the San Juan Center would focus on Puerto Rican neighborhoods in the North End. But this arrangement was the exception, not the rule.

Factionalism within and among political groups was also common, in part because of the absence of a consensus on how best to advance the interests of the community. Puerto Ricans, like African Americans and others, were caught between wanting to provide advocacy and services, and this dilemma structured much of their actions and arguments over welfare policy and social change during the late 1960s and early 1970s. In addition to these conflicts, there were other ideological fish to fry, such as the question of colonialism in Puerto Rico and radicalism among Puerto Ricans in the United States.[42]

But the competition also had a positive side: recognized leaders had to prove their mettle, and in the process new activists emerged. Competition also fostered coalition-building efforts. For example, in 1973, La Casa de Puerto Rico created a group to bring together organizations and individuals throughout Hartford. Called the Forum for Participation, the group tried to provide a unified voice for Puerto Ricans, seek joint funding for projects, and define areas of responsibility for other organizations. The group also intended to advocate on behalf of Puerto Ricans, especially on redevelopment issues. Unfortunately, this particular effort dissolved, yielding nothing but a smart plan and an afterglow of good intentions. Later on, around 1974, the concept was rekindled and CAUSA was organized. CAUSA was used for both advocacy and political purposes. By 1989, it was exclusively concerned with advocacy and services. It provided its members mostly with technical assistance.

Organizational Efforts

When Kernstock asked survey respondents what they would do "If you believed that the Democratic or Republican party in Hartford cannot, or will not, give you any help in your problems," 5 percent said they would join a militant group and 43 percent declared that they would form a new party. To him, this confirmed the view that Puerto Ricans were more pragmatic than ideological and more inclined to seek solutions to their problems within the establishment.[43] But the findings also suggest that Puerto Ricans were one of the most enterprising groups in the city, assuming, of course, that behavior followed attitudes.

That was, indeed, the case. Puerto Ricans organized promiscuously, building upon and expanding existing resources, even if efforts were not always productive. Their presence was most prominent in community-based groups and agencies. In the 1950s, political action was not absent, but the Puerto Ricans organized mostly for religious and cultural purposes. While the San Juan Center provided a mix of social services, it did not become a Puerto Rican–controlled organization until 1974.

During the 1960s, cultural and political concerns merged. These came together in the Puerto Rican Parade Committee, and the mixture was sustained through other ventures. For a number of years Gilberto Camacho tried, unsuccessfully, to transform the parade organization into a federation of community groups—in much the same way the commonwealth's office tried to co-opt community agencies in New York in 1952 by creating the Concilio de Organizaciones Hispano Americanas.[44] In 1969, the Spanish Action Coalition, the first umbrella group incorporating Puerto Ricans, gradually gave way to La Casa de Puerto Rico. La Casa in turn generated a number of spin-offs, such as TAINO Housing Development and the Hispanic Health Council. The network formed by these groups, though not political, became a source of leaders and contacts that buttressed political action.

A detailed discussion of all the groups Puerto Ricans organized in Hartford is beyond the scope of this book. In the following sections I highlight significant examples to specify the dynamic at work and to assess the role played by these efforts in the community's political development.

COMMUNITY GROUPS

Community groups organized for cultural, social, recreational, and self-help purposes. Between 1952 and 1964, the commonwealth's office assisted in the formation of nearly twenty-five such groups, providing leadership seminars and direct organizing. Between 1952 and 1960, the office spent more than 50 percent of its time organizing the community. In part because of the number of self-generated initiatives and partly because of its lack of resources, by 1965, six years after Camacho promised to step up the office's efforts in that area, it dedicated no more than 30 percent of its time to organizing activities; by 1969, no resources were devoted to organizing except for assistance provided to existing groups after the 1969 riots. By 1970, the number of groups in the office's service area exceeded fifty, though it is impossible to tell how many were social or political or how many were based in Hartford.[45]

After the San Juan Center opened in 1956, the Puerto Rican Parade followed in 1964. Then came the Spanish Action Coalition (SAC), which was organized in late 1967 by a group of Protestant and Catholic clergymen and Puerto Rican leaders as an umbrella organization for Puerto Ricans and others in need. In January 1969, it was described by the *Hartford Courant* as "a little-known group which is emerging as the most unified voice among the city's Spanish-speaking population."[46] The group had members but no formal structure, no staff, and no offices. With support from the churches, it mobilized Hartford residents around political and social issues, such as electoral representation and service provision. What distinguished it from similar groups was that its membership was multiracial. According to Antonio Soto: "What made [SAC] strong was the fact that just about everybody who was involved in any community issues in all these different ethnic groups was part of it. We had an agenda that included more seats in the council, voter education; we needed Puerto Rican firefighters and policemen, an end to police brutality, a whole number of things."[47]

The group did not last long, however. After the 1969 riots, Puerto Ricans in SAC created La Casa de Puerto Rico with financial assistance from the Hartford Foundation for Public Giving, and SAC "little by little dissolved."[48] La Casa de Puerto Rico generated two important subsidiaries that eventually became independent organizations: TAINO Housing and the Hispanic Health Council.

Other groups included the Association of Puerto Rican Businessmen, the Clay Hill Mothers Club, Puerto Rican Action for Progress, the Puerto Rican Families Association, the Puerto Rican Federation for Self-Help, the Puerto Rican Historical Society, the Spanish American Civic League, various baseball leagues, and an assortment of hometown clubs. These groups held picnics, organized banquets to honor Puerto Rican celebrities— such as the Puerto Rican Miss Universe, Marisol Malaret—solved specific problems, provided services, and offered opportunities for socialization.[49]

POLITICAL GROUPS

The first political club of Puerto Ricans was the Puerto Rican Democrats of Hartford, organized in 1965. José Cruz, the group's first president, described its activities and accomplishments as follows: "We conducted awareness programs in the community, we registered voters, and on election day we got out the vote. . . . We got María Sánchez into the town committee. She gave us a voice there, and subsequently she became an important figure in Hartford politics. She then became a member of the board of education and that was an offshoot of the [group's work].[50]

The Puerto Rican Democrats was active for a number of years, maintaining a loose operation until 1979. During that time it was entangled with sufficient infighting and personality conflicts that it did not become coherent enough to change from a loosely knit network into a formal organization. Johnny Castillo, who knew some of the group members, said that it quickly divided over partisan rivalries and petty disagreements.[51] Furthermore, in the early 1970s, one of the group's leaders, Angel Ocasio, became so fed up with what he felt was the utter neglect of Puerto Ricans by the Democrats that he joined the Republican party, taking some of the club's members with him and thus debilitating the group further.[52] Rather than disbanding formally, it simply faded out.

During the 1960s, the GOP organized a small political club to incorporate Puerto Ricans, and this club remained in existence into the 1970s. But after a massive defeat suffered at the hands of the Democrats in 1966, Republicans made no significant efforts to involve Puerto Ricans. In 1967, Hartford reinstated partisan elections, and by 1971, with nearly two-thirds of the voters identifying themselves as Democratic party members, Democrats were clearly the dominating force in the city. In that year, Puerto Rican William J. Pérez ran for city treasurer on the Republican ticket, but this was more an act of desperation by a life-long Democrat grown tired of being taken for granted by the party than a sign of a strong courtship by Republicans of Puerto Ricans.[53]

On 21 May 1970, Gilberto Camacho wrote the following in a report to the national director of the commonwealth's office:

> During the years 1968–70 the age of contract workers has ranged from nineteen to twenty-eight years old. Only a few hundred are over thirty, and a significant minority is between sixteen and nineteen years old. Not many have experienced the hardships of farmwork. Also, this new generation has been influenced by the socioeconomic revolution and the protest movements that are shaking the nation. This new generation feels compelled to demand ideal working conditions that the farmers cannot provide.[54]

In his report Camacho mentioned the existence of a small sector within the leadership of the community that "influenced and supported by the antiestablishment movement participates and encourages Puerto Ricans to protest and rebel."[55]

One such group was the People's Liberation Party.[56] Started as a copycat version of the Black Panthers, the PLP began its activities as a local chapter of the Young Lords party in New York City, with the authorization of Pablo "Yoruba" Guzmán, the Young Lords' minister of information.[57]

The PLP was active from 1969 to 1975. It had a radical shell and a mainstream kernel. Members participated in the riots that rocked the city in 1969 but then, in 1973, worked to elect a Puerto Rican to Hartford's board of education. They organized marches and rallies to protest the housing and working conditions of migrant workers but also met with city officials to discuss issues. They refused to support politicians such as Nicholas Carbone and saw themselves as street-level enforcers of civil rights. In short, the members of the PLP wanted to penetrate the system, but instead of knocking at the system's door, they tried to kick it down.

Nineteen months after Camacho warned his superiors of radical elements in Hartford's Puerto Rican leadership, the Movimiento Pro Independencia (MPI) began its activities in the city, targeted at the "new generation" of farmworkers mentioned in his report. "The struggle has begun in Hartford," reads the first issue of the group's newsletter, *Mete Mano*, "and the exploiters of our people are trembling." A section titled "El

Foreground, from left: José Claudio and Eugenio Caro marching into Hartford City Hall circa 1970. *Photo by Juan Fuentes. Courtesy of Juan Fuentes.*

Trabajador Migrante en Los Campamentos Agrícolas" ["The Migrant Farmworker"] describes the housing provided to farmworkers as concentration camps and refers to Puerto Ricans as "slaves of the tyrants ruling our homeland." [58] "I wonder," wrote Camacho to his boss in New York, "whether the Division will provide the Hartford office with the resources necessary to fight, not only the radical groups that already exist, but also the Movimiento Pro Independencia, which has now begun to operate in our service area." [59]

In 1972, the MPI changed its name to the Puerto Rican Socialist Party. Its activities continued for more than a decade. The party had an official platform and a national presence. In Hartford, it challenged the legitimacy of the mainstream community leadership, and its issues became a rallying point for the white/ethnic left. Its presence was prominent in various local struggles. PSP initiatives often provided the impetus for ancillary action through ad hoc groups, including ventures in labor organizing. The party's priority, however, was "the fight for independence and socialism in Puerto Rico." [60]

Efforts to organize extra-partisan pressure groups were abundant and, for a long time, mostly unsuccessful. In 1991, Mildred Torres said: "A [political action committee] has been discussed and attempted, oh God,

Puerto Rican rally outside Hartford City Hall circa 1970. *From the Hartford Collection, Hartford Public Library.*

for over twenty years, . . . but every time it was discussed there was always a group or faction that [said], 'No, it's got to be Republican,' [or] 'No, it's got to be Democrat,' [or] 'No, if that person participates, I won't participate,' and so always something interceded to break down the discussion."[61]

In 1976, a decade after the Puerto Rican Democrats of Hartford organized, Andrés Vázquez, the special assistant to Governor Ella Grasso, launched another effort. The Puerto Rican Democratic Club was an attempt to create a power base and penetrate the city's town committee to secure support for the governor. Vázquez realized that local town committee chairs had much to say about key appointments and thus decided to organize Hartford to get a grip on that source of influence. He was also prompted by the lack of a self-sufficient Puerto Rican political network in the city.

One important challenge facing this initiative was how to neutralize Carbone's network, whose evolving feud with Ella Grasso did not bode well for initiatives sponsored by her minions. Vázquez was unable to tackle this obstacle, and in 1978 he abandoned the effort after declaring an interest in a city council seat. As a result, the group faded.[62]

ASSESSMENT

Although community and political groups were distinct, the line that separated politics from cultural, recreational, and self-help activities and especially from the provision of social services was at times somewhat thin. During the 1970s, community groups were more successful than political organizations. The former had more resources, clearly defined short-term objectives, and more stable leadership. This was true of the San Juan Center, La Casa de Puerto Rico, and other groups, such as the Hispanic Health Council and TAINO Housing.

Efforts to organize politically were marred by an uneven ratio of issues to resources. Political and social issues competed for the attention of a limited number of activists, who often spread themselves rather thin. Nicholas Carbone describes the situation well: "You'd go to one meeting at CRT and you'd go to the next meeting, same people—and it was to do something with the schools. You'd go to another meeting, same group of people; they were there to deal with a health issue. You'd go to another meeting, same group of people, an elderly center. I'd go to a political meeting, same group of people." [63]

In part, resources were limited because the number of political opportunities had increased beyond the community's capacity to take them. In March 1970, for example, José Cruz complained publicly about the lack of interpreters in city agencies. Even if the city had been willing to hire some interpreters, it probably would not have been a simple task, given the qualifications required. But when the mayor asked for names of individuals to sit on city commissions, a comparatively easier request, it took Cruz a month to submit one name. "It has been very hard," he wrote the mayor, "trying to get the best qualified people for your consideration." [64] This was ironic. On the one hand, Puerto Ricans had migrated as surplus labor, and now they were confronted with surplus opportunities—and in both cases they found themselves unable to cope. On the other hand, the most qualified to exercise leadership were not always willing to participate. Said Antonio Soto:

> The problem we faced at the time was, who the hell do we begin to move into those situations where political opportunities happen? At the time we were beginning to get Puerto Rican professionals; because there weren't any [before]—you basically had tobacco workers and factory workers, we had a couple of people who thought of themselves as super leaders, but in reality they lacked [leadership skills]. There were some [qualified individuals], but they were not interested; they were scared. It was still a young community; the average age was sixteen years old. [65]

Despite these difficulties, groups proliferated. But proliferation was indicative of a key feature of the process of group formation: frequent and troublesome starts and stops. Groups often lasted more than a year, but most were unable to become coherent or effective. This was partly related to their ad hoc quality. According to Yasha Escalera, "There have been [many] Democratic clubs, but they would flash at the election and go away. . . . Whenever there was an election, there would be no real follow through; the political effort was very disorganized; once the campaign was over, there was no documentation of what the vote was."[66] In many cases the would-be organizers were not even able to get beyond discussing what to do. But even those groups that had a more extended shelf life often struggled hard for the smallest accomplishments.

The Puerto Rican Democrats of Hartford, for example, came and went, leaving what some regarded as a small record of success. According to Sydney Schulman, a Hartford lawyer with a long history of involvement with Puerto Ricans in the city, the group never had a clear agenda or a program of action, a defect that compromised its ability, and it was therefore limited to the occasional endorsement of candidates.[67] Said José Cruz: "At the time, the leadership lacked education and know-how, and the question was, How can our community leaders prepare themselves? The answer was practical experience, which meant that we learned the hard way. So the criticism is valid. At the time we focused on the short term; we did not have enough foresight, nor the education, to look beyond that, but we laid the ground for later accomplishments."[68]

According to Cruz, factionalism was ideologically benign—mostly personality conflicts—but organizationally deadly. He did not agree that by testing the character of leaders, factionalism had a positive side. This is hardly surprising. The benefits of conflict are always best appreciated by those who are removed from its most immediate and visible effects, which tend to be centrifugal and disorienting. From his description it is clear that the group's membership was both small and overcommitted and that some divided their time between the Puerto Rican Democrats and several other community organizations. "There was a whole bunch of other groups at the time. We were in all of them trying to move forward toward integration within the city," said Cruz.[69]

As for radical groups, the PLP was formed with a bang and dissolved with a whimper. The PSP was notorious for alienating people with its ramrod approach. Yet radical action represented a form of interest articulation that, although largely unwelcome, had a significant impact on the accumulation of political capital. These efforts provided much-needed impetus for several grassroots campaigns. In particular, the PSP brought attention to bear on the plight of Puerto Rican farmworkers, the most disadvantaged sector of the Puerto Rican community in the city and the state.

Paradoxically, these multiple initiatives, false starts, flashes in the pan, and so on, while a symptom of the difficulties, incoherence, and precariousness of organizational efforts, also helped maintain the organizing momentum. The experience of the most repudiated of these groups, the

PSP, provided resources and strategic insights. In 1976–77, just as the PSP was blowing itself to pieces in Puerto Rico and New York, Puerto Ricans in Hartford began to cash in on the political capital accumulated over two decades. Ex-members of the group contributed by shifting the focus of their activities to the electoral process and the Democratic party.

STRUCTURE OF CHOICES: BROKERED REPRESENTATION

In the 1955 municipal election, James Kinsella sought a second term on the city council.[70] During the contest he was embroiled in a fight with two other Democrats—Mayor Dominick J. DeLucco and councilman Joseph V. Cronin. Kinsella wanted to be mayor, and to do so in Hartford's nonpartisan system he needed to be the top vote-getter of nine elected candidates. This did not happen as Joseph Cronin won the position with 24,608 votes against Kinsella's 22,793.[71]

In 1957, Kinsella tried to capture the mayoralty again, only this time he made sure to secure every vote available. This is when Puerto Ricans first became involved in the political process. At the time they were a negligible electoral force, but every single vote counted. Olga Mele recalls how Puerto Ricans entered the contest: "That happened when the San Juan Center got into politics. They were not supposed to do it because they were a social services agency, but Nilda Ortíz, who was the social worker, and Reverend Cooney were approached to help with the Puerto Rican voters, and we began by registering them and they were used as bullet votes for James Kinsella."[72]

Kinsella was elected by a margin of more than forty-five hundred votes.[73] Clearly, he did not need the Puerto Rican vote to win, but he courted the Puerto Rican leadership and they in turn got voters to support him.

In Olga Mele's view, Puerto Ricans were shortchanged by the Democrats. Political candidates sought Puerto Rican support but used their office to benefit their own group, themselves personally, or both. She did not level this charge against Kinsella. Instead, she referred to an associate of María Sánchez, state representative Abe Giles: "María helped Giles a lot. That man used the votes of Puerto Ricans for personal gain. I never liked that. But, you know, María was alone; there wasn't a group that could say, 'Fine, we'll vote for you but what are we going to get?' María never did that."[74]

Looking back to the 1960s, Antonio Soto had similar thoughts about the Democrats. In fact, it was his dissatisfaction with them that led him to join the Republican party. It all began with a knock on his door by a fellow Puerto Rican, Jesús "Wito" Martínez, who asked Soto to become involved in politics. Martínez was convinced that Puerto Ricans could benefit from political participation, although, according to Soto, he could not say precisely how. "Sure, why not," Soto said. The next thing he knew, the Republican Town Committee chair, Albert Miller, asked him to join the party.

> [Miller] said, "Well, if you become involved with the Republican party, I'll do something for you." And I said, "What would you do for me?" He said, "What, do you think the Democrats are doing something for you?" And I said, "No, they aren't doing shit. They know they got our votes; therefore, they don't do crap for us, so I'm disgusted with them." He said, "I can make you a town selectman if you become a Republican," and I said, "OK, but I don't want to sit around and talk to you guys and you guys not listen; I want to be part of the action." [75]

Soto quickly discovered that he gave something for nothing. Had he made his bargain in the nineteenth century, when selectmen controlled Hartford town, his position would have been meaningful. But this was the 1960s. Selectmen simply registered voters, one of the few town functions that the Act of Consolidation of 1896, which united Hartford town and city, did not transfer to city commissions.

When María Sánchez got wind of Soto's deed, she went after him, but she was unable to bring him into the Democratic fold. "That's how I met María Sánchez," Soto said. "She was a gung-ho Democrat, and she immediately heard of the Puerto Rican Republican and she wanted to see who the hell it was. So I got the first punch in the face by her. *'¿Qué carajo tú haces con esa gente?'* ['What the hell are you doing with those people?'], she said. She kept me in check; I knew she was watching my ass, so I had to be cool." [76] Two years after his appointment as a selectman, Soto was elected. He then resigned after passing his seat on to a compatriot.

The bargain that gave Soto his seat among Hartford's selectmen constitutes the earliest instance in the Puerto Rican experience in which choices were negotiated based on brokered representation. It did not mean much, but it was a start.

Despite their strong identification with the Democrats, Puerto Ricans were first put in the political spotlight by the Republicans. In 1966, Dolores Sánchez, a Puerto Rican businessman, ran for the state senate to represent the second district, encompassing the northern half of Hartford. According to fellow Republican José Garay, this nomination showed that the Republicans were more responsive to Puerto Ricans than the Democrats. [77] José Cruz had a different, more sensible, analysis: "Our community was overwhelmingly Democratic and the Republicans were trying to gain our favor. So they promised Dolores heaven and earth; he was not recognized by the community as a leader, and he fell for it." [78]

From left: William Pérez, press secretary, and Wallace Barnes, a candidate for the Republican gubernatorial nomination, holding a boot to "kick the rascals out." Pérez ran for city treasurer in 1971. Hartford Times *photo by Wayne Carter, February 1970. From the Hartford Collection, Hartford Public Library.*

Puerto Rican voters did not support Sánchez, and Puerto Rican leaders failed to use his candidacy as a bargaining chip to wrest concessions from the Democrats. In hindsight, it doesn't seem likely they could have succeeded in extracting any concessions, but at the time no one thought of finding out. For this reason, Sánchez's defeat by Boce W. Barlow, Jr., the first black to be elected to the upper house of the state legislature, was seen by some as a double loss.[79]

In 1971, a Puerto Rican ran for city treasurer on the Republican slate. William J. Pérez, an attorney, opposed city treasurer John J. Mahon, a nine-term incumbent first elected in 1953. The 1971 election was the second held under the partisan system restored in 1967. The Democrats had not won a partisan election since 1941, and this encouraged the Republicans. After going through a tough primary, the Democrats ran a unified ticket and won.[80] Pérez received 7,890 votes against Mahon's 20,887.[81]

The first Puerto Rican to run for city council, René Rodríguez, did so as a Republican. After joining the army in 1964, Rodríguez moved to Hartford in 1966 to work as an assembler in the firearms division of Colt Industries. He went on to become a successful businessman. He ran for city council in 1973, the same year María Sánchez sought a seat on the board of education. Rodríguez had no name recognition, and shortly before the election the *Hartford Courant* indicated that his was one of three Republican candidacies that had failed to excite major public interest.[82] While his bid failed, Rodríguez received only 928 votes less than María Sánchez, who came in third in the board race with 4,955 votes.[83]

Brokered Representation: Elected Office

The first instance of brokered representation involving an elective post of significance occurred in 1973. In November, the Democrats were seeking reelection to the city council on their record. They had a four-to-one voter registration lead. Nicholas Carbone was the council's majority leader, and this would be his third term in office.[84]

By 1973, María Sánchez had lived in Hartford for twenty years and was the owner of Henry's Newspaper Stand on Albany Avenue.[85] She became interested in a seat on the board of education, although her primary aspiration was to be a councilwoman. According to Soto: "María wanted to sit on the council, and Nick Carbone would not let her. [Carbone's argument was simply that] the time [was] not right. You are gonna get in there, and you are going to be all alone, and you are not going to have anybody on your side. . . . They made her feel that she just wasn't ready."[86]

Ready or not, in 1973 Sánchez ran for a seat on the board. Her liabilities had not dissipated, yet the Democratic machine supported her. This support did not come easy, however. Carbone's preferred candidate was Edna Negrón Smith, who bluntly told him to go to hell when he suggested that she was better than María Sánchez. "My English was good, but María had the experience and the guts to do the job," said Negrón, "Besides, she had accomplished a lot—the bilingual program, the teachers corps—in spite of her 'broken English' and lack of education. So the community stood solidly behind her and we forced Nick to accept her."[87] That point was clearly made in a meeting held at the Caminemos Adult Learning Center on Albany Avenue, where about fifty people told Carbone that they were for Sánchez and that was that.

During the campaign Sánchez was recognized as an experienced advocate of bilingual education. Her Democratic party endorsement was emphasized and juxtaposed with the greater political, administrative, and educational experience of other candidates. Her candidacy was considered a gauge of partisan influence and strength as well as a symbol for a community with no political representation.[88]

Aided by the resources of the Campaign Committee of the Bilingual Task Force, an advocacy group organized by La Casa de Puerto Rico, Sánchez became the first Puerto Rican elected to public office in Hartford. Shortly after the election, the *Hartford Courant* declared her campaign the cheapest ever financed by the committee; receipts had totaled $910.[89]

Brokered Representation: A Closer Look

Brokered representation brought a few Puerto Ricans into political positions between 1962 and 1979. But except for city commissions and the seat on the board of education, the posts they occupied—such as town selectman and justice of the peace—were of little political importance. The Republicans gave Puerto Ricans opportunity—to run for the state senate, for city treasurer, and for city council. The Democrats, despite their shortcomings, gave them access. The key power broker during this period was Democrat Nicholas Carbone. Carbone helped elect María Sánchez in 1973 and made possible the appointment in 1979 of Mildred Torres, Antonio Soto's sister and a political player in her own right, to fill a vacancy on the city council.

The charges Mele leveled against the Democrats were correct. Yet if Puerto Ricans were electoral fodder, the cunning of hoodwinking Democratic politicians was only a contributing factor. The model described by Elmer Cornwell applies: political submission rested on the assumption that political independence was surrendered in exchange for something more essential—political appointments, jobs, programs, services.[90] Puerto Rican leaders were not able to make the exchange yield the expected reward, but this was in part because they failed to specify their claims and to make the machine accountable. Further, even when they made demands, the choices were restricted. To many, this appeared to be the case even as late as 1979. Recalling the appointment of Mildred Torres, Jerry Zayas said: "There were meetings and negotiations. María had political savvy, but at the time Mildred was better equipped to work in the council. But it was Nick Carbone's decision; the group had no choice but to go along because it was Mildred or nothing. At that time we didn't have the political muscle we have today."[91]

Mary Ellen Flynn, a Democratic regular, offered an amendment to this assessment: "I would say [the Puerto Ricans] gave Nick the name. I wouldn't say Nick would do that [impose his choice]. Knowing Nick, no; if he told you a group went [to him with a recommendation,] he's telling you the truth. . . . Nick wouldn't lie. . . . If there was a group and that was the name he was told to go with, he would honor that.[92]

What this suggests is that the structure of choices available to Puerto Ricans in the 1970s was configured as much by their political muscle as by subjective perceptions of their bargaining power. In a sense, capability and feasibility were not polarities along an axis of subjectivity versus objectivity, agency versus structure. Subjectivity—that is, the perception of contending political actors of each other's relative power—was an objective element, contributing to assessments of what was feasible. The subtext in Zayas's statement is this: Carbone and the Puerto Ricans eyeballed each other and the Puerto Ricans blinked first. Torres was not the only choice, but the Puerto Ricans gave in to Carbone's desire, thinking that if they challenged him an opportunity would be lost. Flynn implicitly suggests that a little more staying power could have carried the Puerto Ricans farther. This is doubtful. Yet the ambivalence in Zayas's assessment of the situation—Mildred was the best candidate/It was Carbone's decision—also suggests that the decision to go along was the result of conviction as well as compromise.

Mildred Torres's account of the process lends some support to this judgment. From her testimony, the picture that emerges is one in which Carbone is firmly in control but Puerto Ricans decide, based both on self-determined preferences and a pragmatic awareness of the limits to their choices. She said:

> The Hispanic political leadership had been after Nick, who was the controlling factor in the Democratic political machine, to have a Puerto Rican seat, and so when that opportunity arose, they went to him and said, "You have no excuses now, there's a vacancy and we want it and you committed it and you are gonna give it to us." "So who is the candidate to be," he asked, . . . "Who do you want?" So there was a lot of discussion and a lot of talk. Edwin Vargas surfaced as a candidate. Edwin had a very bad reputation in this town; he still carries some of that baggage; [he] was very much identified with the socialists, and the community at that time, and I think still today [has] an ogre mentality about socialism and communism, so he wasn't a very attractive candidate. María Sánchez identified herself as a candidate and people felt that she had the seat on the board of education and she should stay there. I was approached by a group of my peers and asked if I would be interested. I said, "Sure, why not? I know the political system. I know how it works."[93]

The statements of Zayas, Flynn, and Torres indicate that the choice made on behalf of the community was determined by the tension between Carbone's actual and perceived willingness to acquiesce to Puerto Rican demands. In 1991, Carbone declared that "the argument I used back then

[1969] was, if people have to fight you for political power, they will never become your ally; if you give it to them before they take it away from you, then you can share with them and you have a permanent alliance."[94]

Puerto Ricans never really divined this. To them, the opposite was apparent: Carbone would share power according to his own timing and on his own terms only. This followed logically from his reputation and actual ability to influence and control people. Also, Puerto Ricans were affected by the impact of Carbone's political style. As Mary Ellen Flynn put it:

> If [Nick] had a thing in his head, he was going to do it and there was no talking to him; you could talk to him and he said yes, but he was going to do just as he pleased anyway. I don't think [he] ever did anything that he didn't think was right. The only thing is that if he thought it was right, he didn't want to hear anybody else telling him it was wrong. He just went forward. It got to a point that you just didn't talk [to him].[95]

To Puerto Rican leaders, Carbone's resistance to demands for increased representation was just as strong in 1979 as it was before. But the cumulative effect of that resistance was simply that Puerto Ricans eventually altered their structure of choices to be proactive rather than reactive.

Structure of Choices: Puerto Ricans and Blacks

Rufus Browning, Dale Marshall, and David Tabb suggest that the stimulus of black demand-protest substantially increases similar political activity by Hispanics but that the resistance of a dominant coalition does not appear to have that effect.[96] They define demand-protest as "mobilization efforts including violent and nonviolent protest . . . and more traditional demand-articulation tactics such as mass turnouts at city meetings, press conferences, neighborhood meetings, petitions, and formal and informal exchanges with city officials."[97]

Generally, the experience of Puerto Ricans in Hartford suggests a different relationship. Demand-protest was contingent, sometimes occurring in response to resistance from power elites, sometimes influenced by similar activities by blacks, but for the most part emerging in fits and starts, typically after a triggering situation or event made Puerto Ricans explode in anger. When this happened, Puerto Rican leaders made connections between the context of disadvantage in which the community lived and the factor or factors that caused them to respond, usually arguing that while the context created dissatisfaction, the catalytic event turned discontent into action. In the absence of mass action, leaders made similar connections in order to provoke it.

In relation to blacks, the Puerto Rican experience fit, to some extent, within the model of brokered representation that defined their relationship with whites. But the black–Puerto Rican relationship was more difficult because blacks were simultaneously powerful and oppressed. Politically, they were above Puerto Ricans but below whites. Therefore, what would have been a relationship based mostly on solidarity under conditions of equality became a relationship charged with ambivalence in the context of inequality, at times cordial and cooperative but often conflictive and racked by suspicion and hostility. In 1981, for example, the support of the Greater Hartford Labor Council contributed to the election of Thirman Milner, the first African American mayor of Hartford. Puerto Rican Edwin Vargas was president of the council at the time. He actively campaigned for Milner and brokered the support of Congressman Robert García, who, as the only member of the U.S. House of Representatives of Puerto Rican background, was influential in Puerto Rican communities outside his home base in the Bronx's sixteenth district. Conversely, when African American leaders challenged the Democratic party's Irish leadership in 1985, Puerto Ricans withdrew their support, afraid that a black victory might undermine their position within the city council.

The political experience of blacks in the city ran parallel to that of Puerto Ricans and thus did little to provide a stimulus to action along similar lines. By the time black representation was achieved, for example, Puerto Ricans had barely begun to settle in Hartford. This meant that the reservoir of shared experience that was necessary for Puerto Ricans to begin to emulate the actions of blacks was simply not there. The Spanish Action Coalition tried to provide some cross-pollination of efforts, but its presence was short-lived. Groups such as the NAACP were not attractive to Puerto Ricans. The NAACP's patronizing attitude became especially clear during the 1969 riots when at a meeting, James Frazier, treasurer of the Hartford branch, admonished Puerto Ricans as follows: "If you don't think you're colored like me, you've got something to learn." He exhorted them to join the NAACP and then walked out.[98] To a large extent, Puerto Ricans had no example to follow except their own.

As the community developed, Puerto Ricans found themselves living side by side with blacks. In time, a subordinate relationship did emerge. The relationship between María Sánchez and Abe Giles, which lasted well into the 1980s, is an example. Another is the quasi-monopolistic control of the distribution of program services that blacks exerted during the 1960s. About this, Mele said:

> Blacks care only about blacks, and they use us. All this time they have used us politically. They work for themselves, not for us. At CRT I worked with blacks for a long time and I noticed that. I had a program for the families of alcoholics, and the blacks looked for money for their programs but not for

mine. With all the antipoverty programs, blacks would always overlook us. Every time there was a new program, blacks would give us nothing.[99]

It was not that Puerto Ricans did not have bonds of solidarity with blacks or that they did not benefit from the programs that blacks controlled. Rather, the problem was that Puerto Ricans overestimated the degree to which black activism could incorporate their interests.

Mele is hard on African Americans, but her testimony overlooks the fact that Puerto Ricans often competed with them for elected positions, thus undermining the chances of forging mutually beneficial alliances. For example, it is likely that when Dolores Sánchez ran for the state senate in 1966, he was being used by the Republicans to undermine a black aspirant. Because Sánchez was virtually unknown and they were loyal Democrats, Puerto Ricans voted for the black candidate. Boce Barlow won by 14,914 to 5,501 votes. But given that Puerto Ricans had a reputation for ethnic bloc voting, Sánchez's challenge heightened suspicions among blacks about their Boricua neighbors.[100]

The attitudes and behavior of blacks toward Puerto Ricans were structured by the following premises: (1) blacks came to Hartford first and therefore should not be upstaged by more recent arrivals; (2) blacks had a longer and more tormented history of suffering, and the plight of Puerto Ricans paled by comparison; (3) blacks worked hard to achieve positions of leadership and influence, and no upstart group was going to benefit without paying its dues, especially since black suffering was not yet a thing of the past.

The resultant attitudes—self-righteousness, arrogance, ethnocentrism, paternalism—were evidenced in the behavior of blacks during the 1969 riots and subsequently as well. Blacks saw themselves as leaders and Puerto Ricans as followers. If Puerto Ricans did not accept their prescribed role, they were advised to "think again." They had to embrace black leadership, by joining the NAACP or working to elect black candidates, or they would be left behind. Such attitudes, according to Soto, "opened a lot of people's eyes because a lot of people thought that because we were all minorities we were in the same boat."[101]

Two years after the riots, at a meeting sponsored by the Hartford Foundation for Public Giving, a group of Puerto Rican community leaders that included José Cruz and Eugenio Caro told foundation officials that funding the black-controlled CRT would be a waste of their money. They protested that no Puerto Ricans were involved in CRT's decision-making process and that "even though CRT serves many Puerto Ricans," there was no Puerto Rican delegate agency.[102]

If the experience of Hartford's blacks stimulated the Puerto Ricans' action and choices, it did so in negative ways. The process involved emulation but also a great deal of conflict. Throughout the years, black–Puerto Rican coalitions developed. To some extent these were prompted by abstract notions of racial/ethnic solidarity that were shared mostly by Puerto Rican progressives and radicals. If Puerto Ricans (or blacks) could challenge the power structure on their own, they would gladly do so. But this approach was limited by a demographic reality: no single group had the numbers to impose its agenda on the others; in addition, identity politics did not allow Puerto Ricans (or blacks) to portray themselves successfully as a universal class. In that context, cooperation was rather forced and both groups remained vigilant, no doubt to learn from their mutual experiences but also to keep each other in check.

BROKERED REPRESENTATION AND BEYOND

Ethnicity is not an independent variable, but the Puerto Rican experience in Hartford shows that it was a constant factor. After analyzing the political attitudes and behavior of the Puerto Ricans in 1970, Kernstock concluded, "The Hartford Puerto Ricans seem to be a distinguishable group only by virtue of their ethnicity and prior experience; they appear to be neither distinguishably nor discretely a social force in and of themselves in this city."[103] They organized and mobilized to maintain religious traditions such as the Rosario Cantado (sung Rosary) and cultural practices such as St. John the Baptist Day. Some organized hometown clubs and baseball leagues named after their towns of origin. Political and economic action was driven by perceptions of disadvantage, and social and political status was correlated with ethnicity. Identity politics was, therefore, the lifeblood of the community and its principal means for integration. The basic mission of the Puerto Rican Parade, for example, was to affirm Puerto Rican culture and encourage political participation. SAC was an effort to transcend identity politics, but it paved the way for La Casa de Puerto Rico.

Between 1969 and 1979, identity politics yielded only brokered representation. After the election of María Sánchez in 1973, Carbone denied Puerto Ricans an open seat on the city council in 1975 and refused to include a Puerto Rican on the party's slate in 1977. In 1978, he was pressured to fulfill a promise that won Puerto Ricans representation on the city council for the first time. In the process, he bypassed the will of the community to impose his candidate. In 1979, Carbone was ousted and identity politics took a new turn. By 1991, Puerto Ricans achieved representation commensurate with their proportion of the city's population. How they accomplished that, the problems they faced, and the implications of identity politics are the subject of the following chapters.

5   From Brokered Representation
to Political Mobilization

To MAKE public officials accountable and expand political representation, the Puerto Ricans in Hartford organized and mobilized inside
and outside the Democratic party. They lobbied city hall, but they also
organized marches and rallies, often storming into the chambers of the city
council. Although they were reluctant to mount challenges within the
party, they were quick to protest perceived threats to the physical and
moral integrity of the Puerto Rican community. Their identity politics was
both expressive and instrumental, helping them to articulate demands for
respect and for political representation as well.

In 1975, Puerto Ricans pressed for representation in the city council
and were not successful. A seat on the council was a coveted prize among
the elite but not among all. The community supported calls for representation and policy responsiveness but only in the context of mass action in
response to specific triggers, such as a redevelopment proposal that recommended curtailing Puerto Rican migration to Hartford and a series of
ethnic jokes that ridiculed Puerto Ricans in the United States and on the
island.

An open challenge to Nicholas Carbone in 1977 was followed by the
appointment of a Puerto Rican to the city council in 1979. The battle for
the appointment generated the ingredients for a model of political action
that shook the system of brokered representation and set the stage for
extra-partisan political mobilization. In this process, ethnic claims were
prominent, orienting and anchoring political mobilization and political
demands.

The Mary Heslin Vacancy

Early in 1975, Deputy Mayor Mary Heslin left the city council to join
the administration of Governor Grasso. At the end of January, an editorial
in Hartford's Spanish-language newspaper *La Prensa Gráfica* entitled IT'S
ABOUT TIME! demanded that a Puerto Rican fill the vacancy. The editorial read: "The Hispanic population in Hartford now exceeds 42 thou-

sand. . . . In the recent state elections, many Hispanics contributed with their votes, and with their efforts as volunteers, campaign workers, to the Democratic landslide victory. The time has come for Nicholas Carbone and the Democratic Party to reciprocate. We are not asking for special favors. We are talking about political realities." [1]

Part of the political reality in 1975 was that Puerto Ricans had not succeeded in obtaining representation by working outside the Democratic machine. This the editor of *La Prensa Gráfica* was quick to emphasize. The opportunities provided by the Republican party had been fruitless in Hartford's one-party system. Radical demand-protest brought visibility and forced political responses, but by its very nature it could not accomplish representation.

The editorial argued that representation should reflect demography and identity. It suggested that Puerto Ricans had paid their political dues, most recently during the 1974 gubernatorial campaign, and thus should be given something in return. The editorial was directed at Nicholas Carbone, the recognized Democratic power broker in Hartford. While it argued that Puerto Ricans no longer needed to depend on Carbone's "good intentions," it recognized that if brokerage was the method, the last word was his. Some within the community wondered how and when they would be able to bypass Carbone, but there was no challenge to his power.

Instead, a group of community leaders met with Councilman Richard Suisman to suggest that Lionel DeJesus, a lawyer with Neighborhood Legal Services, be appointed to fill the Heslin vacancy. Suisman demurred. Allyn Martin, an African American councilman, proposed that another black be appointed, either George Goodman, a columnist with the *Hartford Times*, or Thomas Harris, of the chamber of commerce. Carbone declared that he would support the best qualified candidate regardless of race or ethnic origin. [2]

Meanwhile, in March 1975, a group of Puerto Rican women launched a new group called Voto Boricua (Puerto Rican Vote or I Vote Boricua if "Voto" is read as a verb) to register Hispanic voters throughout the state. "We congratulate the organizers of Voto Boricua," said Daniel E. Gold, senior vice president and general manager of WSFB-TV Channel 3 of Hartford, on a TV editorial. "They are encouraging the Spanish-speaking people to become Connecticut voters. They are increasing their political power and they are helping to restore a most laudable tradition of political activism." [3]

During the summer, notices were sent to community leaders, community groups, and organizations interested in voter registration, inviting them to come to a statewide meeting on 5 August 1975 at the Spanish

American Development Agency in Bridgeport. The purpose was to prepare for a meeting with the secretary of state at which obstacles to registration would be discussed.

In July, Doris Roldán, one of the founders of Voto Boricua, and sixteen other women representing seven towns throughout the state gathered at the YWCA in Hartford to form another group, Mujeres Unidas for Justice, Equality, and Reform, or MUJER, which means "woman" in Spanish. According to Roldán, the name was chosen because it reflected "the marriage and integration of two cultures, that of the Spanish and Anglo-American."[4] The goals of the group were nonpartisan, but it was willing to work in partisan coalitions. Roldán argued, however, that MUJER was a political organization because "it's about time we realized that politics affects all of us one way or another in our daily lives."[5] They made Connecticut's Permanent Commission on the Status of Women the focus of their attention, while trimming down an excessively ambitious set of goals to the single pursuit of Puerto Rican representation on this body.

Both Voto Boricua and MUJER emerged to fill gaps in voter registration and gender-oriented efforts. These groups could have joined the call for a Puerto Rican to be appointed to fill Mary Heslin's seat, but they didn't. According to Diana Alverio, a founding member of Voto Boricua, they did not see the need to do so because others in the community were already focusing on that objective. It is not clear, however, whether this was the main reason they did not even suggest the appointment of a Puerto Rican woman, a strategy that was compatible with their stated goals.[6]

In August, the council seat was still available. Early that month, in response to an invitation from Wilber Smith, a black legislator representing Hartford's second senatorial district, a group of Puerto Ricans met with black leaders to discuss what to do about the vacancy. The meeting did not go well. The Puerto Ricans alleged that the blacks were manipulating them. The attitude on both sides was one of suspicion, and the proceedings were tense. The chances of participants being able to forge a mutually beneficial alliance were not great. After all, the opening salvo of the battle had been *La Prensa Gráfica's* angry editorial, and Hartford's blacks seemed poised to fill the vacancy with one of their own. The meeting adjourned without an agreement between the parties. The Puerto Ricans publicly suggested that the blacks wanted to use them to serve their own agenda.[7] According to one of the Puerto Rican participants:

> The meeting broke apart because Wilber walked in and said, . . . "This is a political meeting not a social services meeting," and then he looked at me. He didn't want me in the meeting. Félix Irizarry [another participant] blew up at him. And Wilber, instead of letting it go, kept going, saying, "We don't

have to get with you, you have to get with us, we came here first, you are behind us; until you guys understand what you have to do, you're not going to get anyplace."[8]

Without a black/Puerto Rican alliance and with Puerto Rican efforts split between filling the vacancy, voter registration, women's issues, and a major fight against the so-called Hartford Process, the Democratic party saw no need to pay heed to Puerto Rican (or black) demands. As a result, the daughter of former Democratic boss John Bailey, Barbara Kennelly, was appointed to fill Mary Heslin's seat on the council.

GREATER HARTFORD PROCESS

Early in 1969, executives from United Aircraft, Connecticut General Life Insurance, Aetna Life and Casualty, and Travelers Insurance formed the Greater Hartford Corporation, ostensibly to deal with the problems associated with decaying urban structures and suburban sprawl. In 1970, a subsidiary, the Greater Hartford Process, Inc. (GHP), was created. In two years GHP developed an ambitious $800 million, fifteen-year plan to renovate Hartford. GHP's operational arm, the Greater Hartford Community Development Corporation, or Devco, was in charge of managing GHP's integrated plan for twenty-nine towns in the north-central area around Hartford. This initiative was referred to as Hartford Process.

The reasons for GHP's demise are complicated, but in the end it failed because the voters rejected it out of fear that in a regional scheme their power would be diluted by that of the towns in the suburbs and because citizens were angry at what they perceived was GHP's elitism and utter disregard for their concerns.[9] Pierre Clavel's explanation for GHP's failure is terse: "It fell victim to shifts in the political climate that made social engineering more difficult and it succumbed to increasing interest rates."[10] In his account Hartford's Puerto Ricans are invisible, although they played an important part.

In 1971, Eugenio Caro left the Hartford Police Department and shortly thereafter went to work for the American City Corporation, led by James Rouse, a mortgage banker turned urban developer. This group had been granted a $350,000 contract from GHP to develop the methodology for a "life-systems" and institutional study of Greater Hartford. Caro's job was to organize workshops and other activities in the Puerto Rican community.

After this stint, Caro went to work for GHP. His job at GHP did not last long, and shortly after leaving (some claim he was forced to quit), he circulated a copy of a confidential memo, dated 20 November 1974, outlining a proposed "geopolitical or demographic strategy for the city."

Feeling that the contents of the memo were explosive, Caro shared it with the board of directors of La Casa de Puerto Rico, of which he was a member. La Casa leaked the memo to the press and a public outcry soon followed.

The memo read: "Puerto Rican immigration must be reduced. Efforts should be made to consolidate the welfare dependent elements of this population in Clay Hill and in eastern Frog Hollow, using Section 8 housing rehab to provide quality relocation resources in these areas and in the suburbs." It also suggested a policy aimed at removing low-income residents and measures to arrest middle-class flight and to encourage the return of suburban residents to the city. This included providing better educational services to residents with the "financial ability to pull out" while overlooking the needs of poor residents.[11]

Puerto Ricans construed the contents of the memo as "machinations that strike at the very root of our community's survival."[12] La Casa de Puerto Rico quickly joined forces with others to mobilize the community, arguing that the Hartford Process "was not in the interests of the city's poor but a strategy to keep them in certain neighborhoods and to prevent others from coming into the city."[13]

On 21 January 1975, two days after the memo was published, between fifteen hundred and two thousand Puerto Ricans rallied to protest. They gathered at Sacred Heart Church on the city's North End and at St. Peter's Church on the South, and from there marched toward the recently inaugurated Civic Center, where they were joined by residents from neighboring communities. Spokespersons expressed their outrage at the memo's proposals, which, in their view, represented "an infringement of [their] rights under the Constitution." Although there was great anxiety and tension in the air, the rally ended with no confrontations. According to one account, "the participants showed how much they respect law and order."[14]

Peter Libassi, the chair of GHP, tried to muffle the controversy by declaring the memo's proposals illegal, unconstitutional, and largely irrelevant. Both the NAACP and the Black Political Leadership of North Hartford repudiated the memo as a racist attack against blacks, Puerto Ricans, and poor people in general; however, the NAACP refused to give in to the urging of some Puerto Ricans that the blacks resign from the board of Hartford Process. The NAACP claimed that such action would leave blacks and Puerto Ricans unrepresented. For its part the Black Political Leadership of North Hartford exonerated Libassi of any responsibility for the memo and strongly supported the continuation of GHP.[15] The national director of the commonwealth's office, Rafael Torregrosa, expressed dismay at the memo's recommendations but found comfort in Libassi's admission that they were unconstitutional. He called for a better understanding of the role of migrants in American society and for GHP to demonstrate charity of spirit.[16]

These reactions generated controversy and division between blacks and Puerto Ricans and among Puerto Ricans themselves. "The only way I can begin my analysis of the statement by the NAACP," wrote the editor of *La Prensa Gráfica*, Juan Fuentes, on 31 January 1975, "is by saying IT STINKS."

Once the GHP memo became public, Puerto Ricans Sarah Romany and Jerry Zayas quit the Hartford Process board in protest. It is not clear whether this action or the desire to disguise a self-interested motive prompted the claim that a black presence on the board was necessary to ensure Puerto Rican representation. The claim, however, was considered insulting to Puerto Ricans, a reiteration of black paternalism. For that, the NAACP was criticized. "Thanks, but no thanks," said Fuentes, "we are capable people, we have well-prepared people, who can help us with our problems." [17]

Other Puerto Rican leaders were aghast at the timidity of Torregrosa's protest. A spokesperson from the Puerto Rican Socialist Party charged that Torregrosa's concern with restrictions on Puerto Rican immigration was simply a sign of desperation, an expression of his fear that the government of Puerto Rico might not be able to ship one million Puerto Ricans to the United States by 1980. The PSP argued that both the message and the messenger were inadequate. Nothing short of a statement of protest from the governor of the island himself would suffice.[18] Speaking for La Casa de Puerto Rico, Edna Negrón Smith declared: "An explanation is owed to the Hartford community as a whole, and irresponsible statements such as those voiced by Mr. Peter Libassi dismissing the significance of this memorandum cannot be tolerated." [19]

From the onset of the initiative, Hartford Process officials emphasized that they were concerned with the quality of life in the city, not with the needs of any one specific group. To Puerto Rican leaders, this suggested a reluctance on GHP's part to be accountable to Hartford's citizens. If a private group eschewed responsibility for the needs of particular groups, it was up to city hall to pick up the slack. But city council members were seen as confederates rather than as overseers of GHP. The council was not dominated by GHP, but the two were, indeed, close. Although the council was of little operational help to GHP, in some instances their relationship resembled that of interlocking directorships.[20]

The memo contained a serious proposal, but the backlash against it was so strong that GHP's officers pretended it was not. A 1972 letter provided a precedent for this pattern. At that time officials had suggested a financing mechanism for the redevelopment of North Hartford that would shelter the city from a public referendum. When their scheme was made public, they also took pains to deny that the idea was being given serious consideration.[21]

GHP's spin doctors were assisted by city officials, who argued that Hartford Process had considered hundreds of ideas over the years, that the financing proposal of 1972 and the geopolitical strategy of 1974 were only two ideas among many, and that it made no sense to single them out in importance. But the way a number of community groups and leaders saw it, the two documents revealed a consistency of purpose and a bias against black and Puerto Rican neighborhoods. The 1972 letter in particular spoke to the issue of accountability, and GHP was perceived as determined to decide the fate of whole communities without the consent of their residents.

In light of these documents and GHP's secretive behavior, it didn't much matter whether Hartford Process was truly a racist, anti-Puerto Rican conspiracy or not. "For years we have suspected that illegal, exploitative, and racist plans were being put together behind closed doors," declared Edna Negrón Smith at a press conference in February 1975. "Now we know it for a fact."[22] An overweening reaction came from a member of the Hartford Board of Education, who suggested that the proposed policy of containment was comparable to Nazi policies against Jews during World War II.[23] Not to be outdone, the leadership of the PSP argued that the memo was evidence of a conspiracy against Puerto Ricans, orchestrated by the corporate sector in Hartford, its subsidiaries in Puerto Rico, and the island's government. To PSP's leaders, redevelopment was not a misguided strategy but a calculated attempt to destroy a bothersome national minority that refused to assimilate.[24]

Early in February, evidence of specific wrongdoing on the part of GHP was revealed. According to *La Prensa Gráfica*, a 1974 report prepared by the Office of Equal Opportunity (OEO) of the Department of Housing and Urban Development had found that the Capitol Region Council of Governments (CRCOG) had violated provisions of Title VI of the Civil Rights Act of 1964. CRCOG had allowed GHP to exert undue influence in the selection of a national consulting firm, in disregard of a recommendation from CRCOG's technical committee to hire a local 60 percent minority-owned firm. GHP's argument was that if CRCOG hired a local minority-owned firm known for its civil rights advocacy, white suburban communities would be less likely to accept plans for fair housing. The OEO report concluded that "program objectives with respect to minorities were defeated or substantially impaired" by CRCOG's "acquiescence to racial hostility in the structuring of the project and the consultant selection process."[25] Puerto Ricans accused CRCOG and GHP of suppressing the report's findings and vowed to sustain their effort to convince GHP's financial backers to withdraw their support.

By the end of the month, the anti-GHP campaign took a satirical turn when a coalition of labor, community, and leftist groups led by Puerto Ricans awarded Hartford Process a so-called Tory Award for its "service to the rich and powerful in Hartford, its racist and undemocratic practices concerning the future immigration of Puerto Ricans into Hartford, and its secret meetings and conspiracies to bypass citizen participation." Members of the coalition brought the award over to Peter Libassi's office at Constitution Plaza. He was not there to receive it, but they left him a mock one-way ticket to Nova Scotia and a rail.[26]

Pressure against GHP continued to mount, and in March blacks and Puerto Ricans mended fences. Members of the Blue Hills Civic Association, a group of black residents, unanimously voted to join Puerto Ricans in their repudiation of the GHP memo and in their request for a public meeting with GHP's board. In a letter sent to the chairman of the board, the association stated, "We believe that the Greater Hartford Process has the responsibility to prove by actions its intentions toward the minority groups in the city of Hartford."[27]

When GHP's memo became public, the Hartford Process was nearly paralyzed. Millions of dollars had been spent, but key projects were shelved. Puerto Ricans had set off a chain of events that made GHP profoundly unpopular. According to Kenneth Neubeck and Richard Ratcliff, "The controversy cost Hartford Process further legitimacy,"[28] and although it continued to meander through Hartford's political landscape for several years, it was effectively killed in 1975.

THE 1977 CONVERGENCE

In 1977, Puerto Rican leaders developed a strategy that synthesized several models of political mobilization and leadership. The process was not entirely coherent, and it is best appreciated in hindsight. The protagonists were leaders whose focus of action shifted from island issues, namely, the status question, to mainland concerns. While combining militant and moderate styles of action, they put the goal of independence for Puerto Rico aside to seek local representation. Ethnicity structured both demands and action.

"By 1977 the Democratic machine had failed to nominate a Puerto Rican candidate for city council," recalled Edwin Vargas. He added: "When Carter was elected, [Nicholas] Carbone had direct connections with the White House and [he] used those connections to promote Hartford as a model for urban development. But Carbone's progressive vision was marred by his alliance with the corporate sector to reinvest in Hartford to develop the downtown commercial center, and this did not benefit local minorities. The beneficiaries were the region—in terms of jobs for suburban residents—and the developers."[29]

Carbone disagreed:

> Any time I called the White House . . . I asked for ten million dollars for the city of Hartford. I asked for a UDAG, for the office of economic development to run a demonstration project in Hartford . . . . We sued the suburbs, the city of Hartford, and we won the lawsuit, that they were using community development block grant funds wrong. . . . These were all federal grants we were getting that were going into city agencies, the programs La Casa ran, the Hispanic Health council; where do you think all those monies came from? . . . We also won a lawsuit against the electricians, in which we got blacks and Hispanics into the building trade. We created minority contractors.[30]

While all of this was true, some Puerto Rican leaders were disenchanted with Carbone. As a consequence, they mounted a challenge that merged the following two strategies. One was to join the Democratic party and work from within to exact programs and services. María Sánchez was the most in favor of this alternative. As she put it, "One of the reasons why I'm with the Democratic party is to see what can be done for those of us who are here that are suffering the consequences of the decisions that are made without consulting the thirty thousand Hispanics that live in this city."[31]

The second strategy was to work outside the party, challenging the city council, mobilizing the community to demand rights and to promote systemic change. The 1969 riots were a spontaneous expression of this approach, the PLP was its initial articulation, and the PSP represented a sustained attempt to put it into practice. Other groups straddled the fence between the fringe and the establishment.

José La Luz and Edwin Vargas provide the clearest link between these alternatives. By focusing on them I do not deny the contribution of other people who were part of long-standing discussions on strategy and who also put their shoulders to the task of building an extra-partisan pressure group. In fact, long before any of these individuals made their contributions, the PLP, with its radical shell and mainstream kernel, was trying to combine insider and outsider strategies. Their work constitutes the earliest precedent for convergence. The emphasis of the PLP, however, was on outsider strategies, and for most of the party's short existence it avoided a relationship with elected officials and administrators. La Luz and Vargas not only provide a better example of leaders who espoused convergence, but it was under their leadership that the strategy succeeded.

José La Luz was originally from the mountain hamlet of Ciales, Puerto Rico. He moved to Bridgeport with his parents in 1964 at the age of fourteen. His family came to Hartford after María Sánchez enticed his father to work there as a community organizer. Continuous fistfights with his Italian schoolmates drove young La Luz back to the island. "I told my parents, 'Someone is going to die here and it's not going to be me.' They asked me what I wanted to do and I said, 'I'm going to Puerto Rico.'"[32]

In Puerto Rico, La Luz worked with groups seeking Puerto Rico's independence from the United States. Upon his return to the mainland, he went to Springfield College, where he joined the radical reform organization Students for a Democratic Society. In 1970, while Puerto Ricans in Hartford were putting forth their social and political agenda, La Luz helped coordinate a national strike protesting the U.S. invasion of Cambodia.[33] "I was in New York for a while and then I went to Connecticut," he recalled. He continued:

> There I helped organize several chapters of the Movimiento Pro Independencia before it became the Puerto Rican Socialist Party. In the PSP I was responsible for organizing the farmworkers, and we created the Asociación de Trabajadores Agrícolas [Farmworkers Association] and the Comité de Apoyo al Trabajador Agrícola [Farmworkers Support Committee]. Wilfredo Vélez and I and a whole bunch of reverends and ministers did this until about 1974–75. Then I was asked to be the organizing director of the PSP and went back to New York until 1977, when the party divided.[34]

Party responsibilities took La Luz all over the Northeast. But it was in Brooklyn that he met his first wife, Isabel Carrasquillo, the sister of Sylvia Carrasquillo, wife of Edwin Vargas. Marriage brought La Luz into contact with Vargas and a political partnership developed. Up until he left Hartford in 1989, La Luz was regarded as Vargas's main strategist and right-hand man.

Edwin Vargas was born in Sunset Park, Brooklyn, into a working-class family and moved to Puerto Rico in 1960 at the age of eleven. He came to Hartford in 1972, after graduating from the University of Puerto Rico. He earned a master's in public administration at the University of Hartford but worked as a public school teacher. A devoted chess player, he became Hartford Chess Club champion in 1972 and Hartford County knockout champ in 1973. In 1975, Vargas was president of the Hartford chapter of the PSP. His involvement in the teachers union led to his position as vice president in 1979.

The challenge La Luz and Vargas orchestrated in 1977 was the trial run of a strategy that combined bargaining and compromise with extra-partisan organization and pressure. The objective was simple: to mobilize the electorate to increase Puerto Rican political representation. Within the PSP, La Luz was part of a faction that advocated such a strategy. He, and many others, argued that the focus of radical action in the United States needed to be mainland rather than island issues. According to La Luz:

> We became heretics. The party line was that we had to wage [Puerto Rico's] national liberation struggle in the United States. . . . So there was a struggle within the party. Some people tell me now that we could have taken over the party. At the time I was just fed up with the whole thing. I said to myself, "Whether Menshevik or Bolshevik, I'm going forward," and that's how we came up with the idea of a nonpartisan political action committee and we organized an informal coalition to support Edwin [Vargas] as an independent candidate [in 1977]. Today I see that what we were saying made sense because people supported the effort whereas [the PSP] ended up nowhere. The battles we had in the PSP laid the ground for many initiatives later on.[35]

Vargas used the labor movement as a vehicle to blend militant and moderate leadership styles, while also focusing on mainland issues. Like La Luz, he argued that the PSP in the United States was a fan club for the independentista movement on the island, in his own words, a "committee in support of Puerto Rican independence." He proposed that any U.S.-based mass movement of Puerto Ricans worthy of the name had to concentrate on winning and securing democratic rights, using the electoral process as the arena and means to representation and power.

Socialist politics and the labor movement were the key formative influences in La Luz and Vargas's political development. From SDS La Luz moved to the PSP, a shift that took him from organizing students to organizing workers. In Hartford, Puerto Rican farmworkers gave La Luz a point of entry to the community. Under his leadership the party mobilized around a host of local issues, always connecting these to the goal of independence for Puerto Rico. As a teacher Vargas gravitated toward the union. Once there he pursued political goals—mostly to advance a Puerto Rican agenda.

La Luz and Vargas's outlook combined class and ethnic politics. The PSP and the union were vehicles for action, providing resources and standing. La Luz and Vargas believed that the working class was the historical subject of the socialist revolution, and even after they lowered their sights from revolutionary change to Democratic party politics, they kept their focus on workers—not just any workers but the Puerto Rican working class. Their goals were power and change, but the force that drove them was ethnic solidarity. As individuals they performed various roles as teacher, administrator (in 1988, La Luz was assistant city manager), prop-

From left: José La Luz, Yolanda Carrera, Edwin Vargas, Jr., and Esther Vargas. *Photo by Juan Fuentes. Courtesy of Juan Fuentes.*

erty owner, labor official, media personality (Vargas was host of the TV program *Mano a Mano con el Pueblo*, broadcast locally on Channel 13), and so on; but in politics they were, above all, Puerto Rican activists.

In July 1977, Carbone defeated Vargas in his attempt to get the endorsement of the Democrats for a position on the city council, but subsequently Vargas declared his intention to take Carbone on in a primary. On 2 August 1977, accompanied by community leaders Eugenio Caro, Mildred Torres, Cesar Carmona, Angel Ocasio, and José La Luz, Vargas announced the formation of a nonpartisan Puerto Rican political action committee to increase voter education and elect Puerto Ricans to office. La Luz, who at this point was an employment specialist at La Casa de Puerto Rico, declared, "We should pressure the political parties to become more responsive to the needs of this community." [36]

Of the six Democrats on the council, Carbone was the lowest vote getter. By now, his popularity and neighborhood support were low compared with his political power. "[Carbone] embodies the machine better than any other councilperson," Vargas said, "and it is the machine which has been insensitive to the needs of the Hispanic community." [37] Andrés Vázquez, a Vargas supporter, added: "The only way you can participate in this city is to challenge the machinery. We take the people out to vote election after election, and what do we get? Unemployment, discrimination, housing I don't have to describe to you. So what do we have to lose?"[38]

Vargas proceeded to collect signatures to force the primary. But at a meeting in a local hotel he was pressured to desist. Later, Carbone recalled the situation:

> What I explained to Edwin then was that if he ran, if he forced a primary, we were going to beat him. It would cost the party money, and once we did that there was no future [for him] with the Democratic party. If he wanted to see what his strength was, he should run as an Independent and that would allow him to do voter registration and build a political organization.[39]

Vargas agreed to run as an Independent if Carbone agreed that the next vacancy on the council would go to a Puerto Rican.[40] According to Vargas, Carbone agreed to appoint a Puerto Rican as soon as possible, but according to Carbone and other sources, this was a commitment he had originally made with María Sánchez.[41]

During the general campaign Puerto Ricans were not unified behind Vargas. For example, the Hispanic Democratic Reform Club, a loose organization of Puerto Rican community leaders and activists, endorsed, among others, Carbone, Vargas, and José Garay, who was running as a Republican candidate.

Vargas obtained support from the Hartford Federation of Teachers and from the Greater Hartford Labor Council, over which he presided. A group of volunteers interchangeably calling themselves People for Vargas and Comité Vargas Para Consejal organized press conferences, placed ads in community newspapers, and distributed campaign flyers listing an impressive array of supporters. Dorothy Billington, president of the teachers federation, declared, "Mr. Vargas has his hand on the heartbeat of the Spanish community, as well as the Hartford community."[42]

The Democrats ran on their record as the party that won increased state and federal aid, while Vargas ran as the advocate of a state income tax to increase aid to local schools.[43] As a result, Carbone was reelected with 11,845 votes, while Vargas, with 2,547 votes, ran a distant thirteenth in the sixteen-candidate race. Of the elected councilmen, the lowest vote getter—also an Independent—received twice as many votes as Vargas, and even Garay outdid him.[44] But no matter. For the first time Puerto Ricans had run independently against the machine. They used the tools that later helped them bypass the party: media visibility, pressure exerted through extra-partisan alliances, and grassroots mobilization. These tools enabled them to develop an autonomous power base and to force the hand of party leaders.

SWANK MAGAZINE INCIDENT

The incident involving *Swank* magazine is somewhat bizarre. It occurred in 1978 while Hartford's Puerto Ricans were already having to confront the triple whammy of redevelopment, unemployment, and relative political invisibility.

Although Puerto Ricans continued to reside in the North End, the area around Park Street was recognized as a strong Puerto Rican enclave. In September community newspapers were openly speculating about the impact of government neglect, increasing evictions, suspicious fires, and the subsequent demolition of buildings in various neighborhoods. These features illustrated the twisted course of redevelopment in Hartford. The Greater Hartford Process was on its last legs, and what redevelopment activities remained reflected a strategy that predicated the creation of something new on the senseless destruction of the old. In some cases, destruction served no creative purpose whatsoever. Puerto Ricans faced the twin assaults of bulldozers and arsonists.

A September editorial in the community newspaper *Qué Pasa* concluded, "The employment situation of Puerto Ricans has not improved." [45] Between 1963 and 1972, the city had lost ninety-four hundred manufacturing jobs, a reduction of 42 percent. [46] These jobs, which had employed Puerto Ricans throughout the 1950s and 1960s, had been replaced, in large part, by positions created under the Comprehensive Employment Training Act (CETA). But now even CETA jobs were being eliminated, and Puerto Ricans were feeling the impact disproportionately. [47]

As if redevelopment and unemployment were not bad enough, the Puerto Rican community was almost invisible politically. In 1967, partisan elections had been restored in the city. This was favorable to Puerto Ricans, who were likely to vote for slates rather than candidates. But now all electors had a bigger window of opportunity for participation since the state had made the party lever optional in 1965 (it was eliminated altogether through constitutional amendment in 1986), a change that was supported overwhelmingly in Hartford. Yet in 1968 only 53.3 percent of registered Puerto Ricans voted in the general election, versus 83.5 percent of all registered voters. Considering that the number of registered Puerto Ricans was about half the number of those qualified to vote, the participation rate was actually about 25 percent. [48]

The termination, in 1976, of literacy requirements to register should have encouraged higher registration and voting rates. But in 1978 a low level of electoral participation was still a problem. In any event, during the 1970s Puerto Rican registered voters were about 3 percent of all registered voters in the city, a proportion too small to make the group feel that its votes counted. This diminished their participatory drive. Some within the Puerto Rican community exonerated Puerto Ricans from responsibility for their political behavior, while others concluded that they were just apathetic.

Not all was gloom and doom, however. In June 1978, the mood of the community was festive. Hartford's mayor, George Athanson, made an appearance at the Park Street Festival to preside over an awards ceremony. Throngs of jubilant Puerto Ricans witnessed the ordaining of Father Peter Rosazza, known affectionately as "Padre Pedro," as bishop of Hartford. Padre Pedro was highly regarded, and Puerto Ricans saw him as one of their own. Then, in July, Ella Grasso made appearances before the San Juan Center's baseball league and at the San Juan Center headquarters, where she was given an effusive welcome by Yasha Escalera, the center's director, and community notables Jerry Zayas and Andrés Vázquez. In September, at the annual Puerto Rican Parade, held in Bridgeport, the Hartford delegation offered participants a taste of Puerto Rican music. By mid-October, community newspapers, labor and community activists, and local businesspeople celebrated the conclusion of a voter education and registration campaign.

Such was the context in which the *Swank* incident occurred. The community mobilized over the publication of ethnic jokes in this pornographic magazine with an intensity not provoked by far more serious concerns. Because the magazine was disreputable, Puerto Ricans became subject to charges of tawdriness: after all, why were they "reading" *Swank* in the first place?

In August 1978, the magazine, published in New York, printed the following jokes:

> Tell me the truth, said the man, would you allow your daughter to marry a Puerto Rican or a circus monkey? It depends, responded his friend, does the monkey work full time?

> Puerto Ricans really like to work. One opened up a jewelry store recently. The problem is he got caught by the police.

> What do they call a beautiful woman in Puerto Rico? A foreigner.

> When a Puerto Rican woman says "my man," she means "any man."

> Why is it that Puerto Ricans don't commit suicide? You cannot kill yourself jumping out of a basement window.

> How do you count the number of Puerto Ricans in New York? Count the number of basements and multiply them by fifteen.

> Why do Puerto Ricans wear pointy shoes? So they can kill roaches as they pile up in corners.

One hundred-fifteen Puerto Ricans died last night. . . . Their bed broke.

Puerto Rico wants to be the 51st state. What should its name be? The welfare state.[49]

The way Eugenio Caro tells the story, someone in the leadership of the PSP brought the jokes to his attention and asked him to organize a response. "You're the only one who can start something here," he was told by the president of the party's local chapter. In October Caro called a community meeting and 120 people attended. "If anybody is interested in following up on this issue," Caro told the gathering, "please sign." Twenty-four participants signed up to organize a protest against *Swank* and named themselves the Committee of 24.[50]

On 7 November, the day Governor Ella Grasso was reelected, the Committee organized a march and rally, dubbed the "Dignity March" by the community press, that attracted more than four hundred people who protested in front of city hall and at the headquarters of the Democratic party. Speakers condemned the jokes in *Swank* as racist, demanded better coverage of Puerto Rican issues from the local media, and clamored for better economic opportunities from the local government.

The marchers held signs that read: DOWN WITH PREJUDICE; CHANNEL 3 YOU'RE JUST LIKE SWANK; EQUALITY OF RIGHTS FOR RICH AND POOR; OUR WOMEN ARE DECENT; BORICUAS UNITED WILL NEVER BE DEFEATED. At the Democratic headquarters, they were met by a group of Governor Grasso's campaign workers, who at first thought the crowd was celebrating her victory. After all, Puerto Ricans had worked hard for her during the campaign. Caro explained the real issue and told the campaign workers that the crowd wanted Grasso to condemn *Swank* magazine. "We are not here to congratulate you or to tell you that we are on your side," said Caro, "We are here to tell you that we are tired of being used and tired of the status quo. We want Ella, and we want to tell her that we want dignity not demagoguery; we want employment and housing. We want to tell her that we are tired of being humiliated."[51] The campaign workers were dumbfounded. When the governor arrived, the crowd jeered, waving signs and Puerto Rican flags.

There was a second demonstration on 13 November, and, according to Caro, the Committee of 24 decided to take advantage of the momentum to mobilize on social issues and to keep an eye on city hall. "That's when we declared war on [Councilman] Robert Ludgin because he was against us. Every two weeks we would bring five hundred or six hundred [people] to city hall—even the gangs participated."[52] In February 1979, Caro offered to dissolve the Committee into a coalition, to work for increased political representation independently of the political parties. He proposed a strategy based on voter registration, identification and selection of candidates, and the celebration of public forums to educate voters.[53] This was an attempt to bring back to life the concept behind the short-lived organization that had backed Edwin Vargas in 1977.

By the end of 1979, however, the Committee of 24 was simply struggling to stay alive. The group needed to broaden its membership to counter attacks that it was an elite group that gave access only to carefully chosen people. A spokesperson invited anyone who cared to join to do so, while warning that only those who were willing to work long and hard would be welcome.[54] According to Caro, the group dissolved because of ideological infighting. In vanishing, it left a trail of sustained protest, sharp denunciations, and angry demands.

A PROMISE FULFILLED, A WILL BYPASSED

Just as Puerto Ricans were protesting "el insulto de *Swank*," Councilperson Barbara Kennelly was celebrating her election as secretary of state, which created an opening on the city council. At the council's meeting of 11 December, Councilman Ludgin introduced a resolution calling for public hearings so that candidates interested in filling the vacancy could be "interviewed publicly regarding their background, their attitudes and their inclinations and so that the public may have an opportunity to express their ideas concerning said appointment."[55]

Ludgin supported bringing in black civil rights activist Wilber Smith. Edwin Vargas understood that Carbone's commitment to filling the next vacancy was directly related to Vargas's 1977 candidacy and therefore felt entitled to the seat. According to José La Luz, no one ever said that the position would go to Vargas, but in his mind that was the implicit understanding.[56] Vargas argued later that the original commitment had been reinterpreted in three different ways. The first "revision" was that offered by La Luz. The second version was that the vacant seat would go to someone in the Puerto Rican community, selected by the community itself. The third version held that the seat would be occupied by one of Carbone's minions, someone selected by Carbone's Puerto Rican circle with his approval.[57]

Carbone claimed that his plan was that Puerto Rican allies would propose a candidate that he would then ratify, and, further, as noted earlier, that the original commitment was to María Sánchez, not Vargas. Whatever the truth, it is likely that Carbone simply deceived Vargas in 1977, leading him to believe that he had Carbone's commitment to appoint a Puerto Rican when there was a council vacancy in exchange for not running as a Democrat in a primary. As Carbone later explained:

I had a meeting with the community leaders, I don't know whether it was 1977 or 1976, and told them that the next vacancy on the city council I would try to fill it with someone from their community, who is going to be picked by the thirty-five leaders [the group associated with María Sánchez]. Even when I met with Vargas and María to talk about his running as an Independent, we talked about the community selecting a person to fill the vacancy [who] was acceptable to me.[58]

Vargas began discussing his interest in a council seat with community leaders and council members as early as June 1978, shortly after rumors began to spread that Kennelly's seat might become available. A newspaper account reads: "Edwin Vargas, who ran as an independent last November, is optimistic about filling one of the vacancies."[59]

On 4 December, Andrés Vázquez declared his candidacy, announcing that "my conviction that this vacancy should go to a Puerto Rican is above my own personal interest in the position."[60] On 30 December, Mildred Torres held a press conference to express her interest in the position. "I understand municipal government and I'm not wedded to any politician. My interest is to serve the city of Hartford and Hispanics," she said. At a Democratic town committee meeting held on 2 January 1979, María Sánchez expressed her desire to join the council. From outside the community, Jack Dollard, an architect, Mary Ellen Flynn, a public school paraprofessional at the time, and Loretta F. Fox, a real estate broker, were also candidates. The town committee interviewed two other Puerto Ricans, Félix Ortíz and María B. González, but they quickly withdrew in support of Sánchez.

Meanwhile, Carbone acknowledged his commitment to fill the vacancy with a Puerto Rican, bluntly stating that the applications of non-Puerto Rican candidates would be filed for future reference.[61] From interviews with Carbone, Vargas, and Torres, it is apparent that three sets of players approached Carbone vying for the seat. María Sánchez represented the Puerto Rican party regulars; Mildred Torres was the figurehead for Puerto Rican Democrats who were within Sánchez's sphere of influence but, on this issue, not completely within her camp; and, finally, a mixture of radicals, populists, and activists, some of them marginal to the party but longing to be on the inside, rallied around Edwin Vargas.

After Carbone told him that the right to determine who would fill the vacancy was not his but the Puerto Rican community's, Vargas, in consultation with José La Luz and Father Rosazza, decided to force Carbone's hand. As a result, a community forum was held on 7 January 1979, which attracted more than three hundred Puerto Ricans who gathered in the basement of Immaculate Conception Church to hear the Hispanic candidates. To organize the forum, La Luz enlisted the support of Oscar Nieves, from the commonwealth's office, who arranged a press conference and announced the following:

> We are not happy with the process being used by Deputy Mayor Nick Carbone in identifying a Hispanic candidate for the council vacancy that will occur when councilwoman Barbara B. Kennelly resigns to become Secretary of State. Mr. Carbone is indicating that Mildred Torres is the leading contender to fill that vacancy, when the Hispanic community and the citizens of Hartford were not even aware that she was interested in the position. The Hispanic candidates that have expressed interest in the position apparently are not even being considered by Mr. Carbone. At the same time, Mr. Carbone is saying that he will accept the recommendation of the Hispanic community in this decision.[62]

The press conference was covered only by the community press, and, according to one of the participants, Vargas, La Luz, and Nieves were there.[63]

Mildred Torres knew nothing about the press conference, which is not surprising since it was staged to question her legitimacy as a candidate. This is her version of how her candidacy and the forum came about:

> What we did was we went I guess to Nick and we said, "María is on the board of education, she should stay there, and Edwin is a loose gun. He doesn't know anybody, and we are not sure that we can trust him." The Democratic party, to get out from under, suggested that we might want to hold some kind of public thing. So we did. The three of us got together with our seconds if you will; mine was Alberto Ibargüen, and Edwin's was, of course, José La Luz, and I don't remember who María's was. We arranged to publicize it on the radio and to hold a forum at the basement of the church on Park Street and for the three of us to come and speak on why we were interested and what we felt we could accomplish, Oh, I'm sorry, there was a fourth candidate, Andy Vázquez.[64]

Torres's comments suggest that the idea of holding a forum came from within the Democratic party, but that was not the case. Further, her phrase "to get out from under" suggests that once the forum became a reality, Carbone did what he could to help win a victory for her. But although Torres, as well as Vargas, mobilized their supporters, Carbone denied helping out.[65] He accepted the forum for what it was—an attempt to force his hand—knowing that it would not change his mind. Carbone remembered the situation this way:

> I told Eddie Vargas, "You don't change the rules; so I sit down and negotiate with you, this twelve people, and it's twelve people who are going to make the decision. You couldn't get the twelve people to vote for you, so you went to a priest to call a forum; that wasn't the deal. I don't care if you get two

thousand people, I don't care if they all come to city hall, that wasn't the deal I made."[66]

At the forum, the first to speak was Eugenio Caro, on behalf of the Committee of 24. The committee, Caro said, had decided not to support any candidate. The candidates followed, all agreeing that the Puerto Ricans in the city were in bad shape. All saw the vacancy as an opportunity to make public policy more responsive to Puerto Rican needs.

Vázquez was an assistant to Governor Grasso but spoke in a confrontational and dramatic tone. "The whole educational system is worthless and has to be changed," he shouted at one point in response to a comment about education from the audience.[67]

María Sánchez was fiery yet guarded. "I know the problem," she said about housing, "because I suffer it myself. I also live in a building where the rent is too high and it gets cold in the winter. I make no promises, because in the council it will be one against eight, but if elected I will do my best."

Vargas lashed out against the "big corporations" and the municipal neglect of Puerto Rican neighborhoods. "As our people begin to move into a neighborhood, the city begins to move out," he said. "The city abandons those neighborhoods in terms of maintenance, police protection, and yet property taxes for small businesses on Park Street are $3.00 per square foot, while Travelers, Aetna, and G. Fox pay $1.50."

Torres, like Sánchez, offered no promises. She was thrown on the defensive when someone in the audience asked about her connection to Aetna. There was some booing and hissing, and the audience was asked to behave. That Torres works at Aetna has "nothing to do with her political position," snapped the moderator, Calixto Torres. "I've always had to work," Torres responded. "I've always worked with the community on nights and weekends. The council's business is not only conducted during the day. I work for an insurance company because I have to support my family." At this point the crowd erupted in a mixture of cheers and jeers. As the clapping, shouting, and whistling began to subside, the moderator once again begged for order: "One more time I'd like to request the public keep this forum at the highest possible level."

The audience saved its loudest reaction for responses to a question from the president of the Hartford chapter of the PSP. "Do you think," asked José Ramos, "that the educational development of our community requires discussion of the political situation of Puerto Rico, and how do you plan to deal with it?"

Vargas responded first:

> The political situation of Puerto Rico is of great interest to me, and when I came to Hartford I put a lot of my energies to that issue. But after being here

for a while, dreaming about going back, I realized that I had married and had two children, born here in Hartford. I realized that there was a growing Puerto Rican community that is here to stay. When I realized that, I said to myself, "*Caramba*, the political situation of Puerto Rico is important, but isn't also important the political situation of Puerto Ricans in Hartford, where we are born, live, and die?" So, even though I read the newspapers and try to keep up with events on the island, and I would oppose any actions against the will of Puerto Ricans there, and I want their rights to be respected, my main concern has to be the future of our children here in the United States.

Vázquez agreed with Vargas but then restated the PSP's position that in the resolution of the status issue, the role of the stateside community was crucial. "So we have to develop enough political muscle," he said, "to influence the U.S. Congress and decide what's best for Puerto Rico."

Torres offered a variation on this theme: "Whatever happens there affects us here. What I'm trying to do is to make the information on all positions available to all, so that we can be informed, to make sure that we have a say in what happens there even though we live here."

Only María Sánchez was in full agreement with Vargas. "What happens in Puerto Rico makes me sad," she said, "and I wish luck to those that are fighting for what they believe Puerto Rico should be, but as for me, my priority is to get involved here for the benefit of what is ours."

The forum ended with a straw poll in which Vargas received 157 votes; Torres received 100; Vázquez, 17, and Sánchez, 15.[68] The chair of the town committee's selection panel, Thomas Ritter, and the organizers of the meeting agreed to keep the results secret, but to the astonishment of many, the tally was trumpeted the next day in the *Hartford Courant*. The community press denounced the *Courant*, not knowing that José La Luz had leaked the results.[69]

After the forum, there were claims of manipulation, that the church had been packed with people from Bridgeport and other outsiders to tilt the vote in favor of Vargas.[70] "I can't say that's true," said the forum's moderator. He agreed that the perception was valid, however, since many people who previously were not active had turned out.[71] Ultimately, though, according to Carbone, the forum was insignificant:

[There were] incidences when we had civil disturbances in the city where the police union [collected] ten thousand petitions for me not to change the gun guidelines. So I wasn't gonna be impressed by who could drag out 150 people to a forum. That was not how you chose the members of the council. That's why I said the forum had no influence. We were looking at qualifications, their understanding of government, their ability to work as a team.[72]

From left: Andrés Vázquez, Mildred Torres, Eugenio Caro, and Edwin Vargas, Jr., at the 1979 press conference at which Vázquez and Vargas withdrew their candidacies for Barbara Kennelly's seat in the city council. *Photo by Juan Fuentes. Courtesy of Juan Fuentes.*

On the morning of 8 January, radio station WTIC announced that "Hartford's Spanish community would like to have a voice on the city council and is now eyeing the seat recently vacated by Barbara Kennelly. Chosen the most likely to succeed in the balloting is a Hartford schoolteacher, Edwin Vargas."[73]

Before the Democratic town committee's selection panel made its decision, Carbone told its members that Mildred Torres was his candidate. For two hours, he made his case, but to no avail.[74] On 10 January, the panel announced its endorsement of María Sánchez, who was recognized as community oriented, for having a good record as a board of education member, and enjoying the support of the three Puerto Rican town committee members.

That same day Vargas and Vázquez withdrew their candidacies in support of Mildred Torres. At a press conference, Eugenio Caro, flanked by the three contenders, announced that the Committee of 24 also was endorsing Torres. Caro explained that the committee had decided to interview Torres because her support seemed to be growing. The group endorsed her after knowing how she stood on such issues as housing, education, and employment.[75]

According to Vargas, "unity was necessary to avoid loss of the seat." [76] "I was approached by [Mayor] Athanson [who had a quarrel of his own with Carbone] but went along with Carbone," said Vargas. "I was afraid that a Democratic party with no Hispanics under its wing would lose federal funding for youth programs." [77] Thus, the same day that radio station WTIC was predicting Vargas's victory, he was with Vázquez, Torres, La Luz, and Torres at a meeting where he stepped aside, once he realized that his chance of being selected was nil.

On 22 January, seventeen Puerto Ricans signed a petition requesting the appointment of Mildred Torres. Her bid was also supported by Councilman Raymond Monteiro. Meanwhile, María Sánchez wanted the seat badly, and she had been endorsed by the mayor and several other council members. The Hispanic Democratic Reform Club, which had refused to support her in 1977, lobbied on her behalf.

But two days later, resolutions in favor of Wilber Smith and Sánchez were withdrawn. Carbone had the five council votes needed to ratify Torres's appointment. On 25 January 1979, with five votes in favor, two absences, and one abstention, Torres became the first Puerto Rican to occupy a seat on the city council. A promise to the community was fulfilled, but its will was bypassed.

ASSESSMENT

The Heslin episode coincided with extra-partisan organizing but did not provoke a rush of political mobilization. Instead, it reflected the persistence of a pattern Puerto Ricans had followed since their earliest efforts to gain representation. Up until the 1969 riots, they had worked diligently within the parties, mostly with Democrats, exchanging electoral support for limited gains. During the 1970s they organized outside the parties, while still relying on their relationship with Carbone to negotiate access and concessions. As the community grew, new groups emerged, adding layers of action to layers of experience. The result was a pattern of political action that combined brokerage with mobilization. In the Heslin case, however, mobilization and brokerage ran along parallel lines as groups such as Voto Boricua and MUJER had no bearing on the selection of Heslin's replacement. Furthermore, brokerage was weak. The meeting between the blacks and the Puerto Ricans failed because they did not trust each other. Yet neither group was able to influence the selection process on its own. The militant tone of *La Prensa Gráfica*'s editorial did not translate into decisive pressure on the Democrats. In the absence of such pressure, the Puerto Ricans were ignored.

The 1978 protests over the ethnic jokes in *Swank* might appear heavy-handed and even silly in retrospect, but the demands that rode the coat-tails were substantial. A member of the Committee of 24 explained events this way: "[*Swank*] was the straw that broke the camel's back. Combined with the lack of housing, employment, and education, the insults became intolerable. We just could not let [the jokes] pass without doing something about it." [78] By turning ethnic slurs into a political issue, the Puerto Rican leadership broadened the scope of conflict. But pursuing the matter was risky since a protest against a pornographic magazine also exposed the tawdry side of some within the community.

Recalling what surely was an exciting time, Caro inflated the number of people attending the protests organized by the Committee of 24. Mo-bilization was massive, although not all rallies were successful. Some sug-gested that Robert Ludgin encouraged the rash of protests that followed the *Swank* incident as part of his ongoing feud with Carbone; anything that made Carbone look bad, such as frequent picketing at city hall, strengthened Ludgin's cause. But this was just coincidental. It is not clear the extent to which Puerto Rican unrest hurt Carbone, since his popu-larity was already on a steep decline. What is certain is that the causes of the Puerto Ricans' discontent—displacement caused by redevelopment, unemployment, lack of representation on the council, and a general sense that they were not respected—were neither artificial nor manipulated by the council.

The *Swank* incident brought some measure of unity to the community, although the tensions and conflicts that had prevented unified action in the past had not gone away. Puerto Ricans remained divided along parti-san, organizational, and ideological lines. The legitimacy of community leaders whom critics accused of being inconsistent was still questioned.

Finally, while the response to the jokes in *Swank*, like the response to the GHP's memo, was swift, the same was not true of the responses to other, sometimes more deserving issues. In December 1978, the group Vecinos Unidos, which was active around housing and redevelopment is-sues affecting Puerto Ricans on Park Street, organized a community meet-ing with the director of Hartford's housing authority. The meeting was advertised for more than a week on the Latino radio station WLVH. At the meeting, however, organizer Roberto Laboy wondered why the hun-dreds of Puerto Ricans living in substandard housing were not there. "An outsider," he later wrote, "would have concluded that the Puerto Rican community has no need for better housing." [79] Meetings with government bureaucrats, of course, are not crowd pleasing, whereas demonstrations and marches can be dangerous and do not guarantee results. One can only speculate as to why the *Swank* incident generated an upswing in mobili-zation while other issues did not. It appeared that ethnic insults were more deeply felt than discrimination in housing; perhaps Puerto Ricans were already inured to the uncooperative and indifferent attitude of most city officials and therefore had no reason to expect that yet another meeting would make them change.[80] In any event, the wave of mobilization the *Swank* incident triggered produced few specific gains. The Committee of 24 was an important by-product, but, like many organizations in the past, it drove itself to exhaustion without leaving much to show for its efforts.

After 1977, the system of brokered representation changed. Demands were still for the most part negotiated, but independent mobilization began to take root. In 1979, Puerto Ricans were still timid about challenging Nicholas Carbone. Yet, in a small but important number of cases, they asserted their power. In 1973, Carbone was forced to accept the candidacy of María Sánchez. In 1977, Edwin Vargas flaunted an unsuccessful but unprecedented challenge that planted the seed for what later became PRPAC. In 1979, Vargas and La Luz tried again and made it impossible for Carbone not to honor a commitment to appoint a Puerto Rican to the city council. There is some ambiguity here, however, because it is not known whether Carbone would have kept his promise if Puerto Ricans had not mobilized.

In their pursuit of the council seat, Puerto Ricans were faced with strategic differences and factionalism. Paradoxically, these divisions worked in their favor as they translated into a multiple set of pressures bearing on Carbone. Again, it is difficult to know for sure what difference this made, since Carbone was publicly committed to filling the vacancy with a Puerto Rican. The factions involved represented the elements of what eventually became a new model for political action, combining back-room negotiation, extra-partisan organization, coalition building, and community pressure. "Eventually" is the key word here because, as the 1978–79 appointment battle unfolded, what was apparent to Puerto Ricans, especially Edwin Vargas, was that they could not avoid the reach of Carbone's long arm.

6   Identity Politics: The Puerto Rican
Political Action Committee of Connecticut

ALTHOUGH THE Puerto Rican experience in Hartford cannot be
reduced to a single dynamic, ethnicity had a singular role in the set of
interrelated transitions that marked the community's political development. The first arrivals were quickly defined as "the Other." Initially this
was not detrimental because their presence was placed in the context of a
tradition of immigrant incorporation. Language, culture, and citizenship
made their experience distinctive, but the reception they were given was
similar to that offered their Irish, German, and Italian predecessors. Even
during the early years of settlement, there were indications that ethnicity
was a central category, not a temporary marker in a process of assimilation, as even those whose ties to the city were unambiguously permanent
sought to organize the community around the themes of cultural affirmation and socioeconomic progress.

Identity claims structured the Puerto Rican experience in Hartford
since settlement. The Puerto Rican Parade was the first organized, large-
scale attempt to connect the cultural life of the community with its political reality. But it was not until the 1970s that this connection was made
systematically, in efforts to address ethnic needs by achieving political access. The Puerto Rican Political Action Committee of Connecticut—the
most effective organizational expression of this process—became visible
in 1985, but the concept animating the group had earlier incarnations.

In 1976, Andrés Vázquez tried to organize a statewide Democratic club
with a strong base in Hartford as a vehicle for the 1978 campaign of Governor Ella Grasso. This project did not go very far. Local leaders organized rallies on behalf of non-Hispanic candidates seeking the support of
Hispanics, but a self-sufficient network, focused on electing Puerto Ricans
in Hartford, never gelled.

The embryo for what would become PRPAC emerged in 1977 to support the independent candidacy of Edwin Vargas. The next year, the stalwarts of this campaign outlined a set of criteria to ensure the selection
of a Puerto Rican to fill the city council position made available by the
resignation of Barbara Kennelly. The group faded, however, and did not
come back together because three leading members—Mildred Torres,

124

Edwin Vargas, and Andrés Vázquez—went their separate ways in pursuit of the vacant seat.

In 1979, Eugenio Caro, using the Committee of 24 as a model, advanced the idea of a political action committee in a call for the formation of an independent, progressive coalition to promote voter education and seek political representation. Also in 1979, in her *Qué Pasa* column, "Apuntes Políticos," Cecilia La Luz, a community activist and sister of José La Luz, referred to the Caucus Político Hispano, whose purpose was to ensure the involvement of citizens in the government process. La Luz argued that although it was fine for different groups with various strategies and ideologies to coexist, efforts should focus on penetrating the Democratic party.[1]

In 1981, the Spanish Democratic Club was formed, to promote unity among community leaders and party regulars. Its main purpose was to gain recognition from the Democratic party. Some of its members proceeded to form, also in 1981, the Puerto Rican Democratic Club of Greater Hartford, which was presided over by Olga Torres, a community activist, and came together to support the candidacy of Jerry Zayas for city council. Competing with this group was the Puerto Ricans and Hispanics for Political Progress, essentially an instrument for furthering the political aspirations of Mike Borrero, a professor at the University of Connecticut. When Borrero became director of a national organization, the National Puerto Rican Forum, the group vanished.

Many individuals were involved in all these efforts, and all the groups that made it from concept to reality—as Mildred Torres put it in 1991, not a few failed to go beyond the discussion stage—had overlapping memberships. The closest of these to PRPAC, in membership, goals, and structure, was the Puerto Rican Democratic Club of Greater Hartford. "We are called the Puerto Rican Democratic Club," read the minutes of its 14 December 1981 meeting, "yet we are not affiliated with any political party." The minutes of its next meeting, held three days later, refer to the group as the Puerto Rican Political Action Club.

The organization that came into the limelight in 1985 represented all of these initiatives and something else. Like a newborn infant, it incorporated various "family" traits, while having characteristics of its own. It was a brand-new entity grounded in the experience and resources of a variety of preceding efforts. Most who were involved were not aware of the genesis of their initiative or of the continuity between past and present. They could not, like the individual who delves into his past, look at photographs in a family album to establish the resemblance.

The likeness between PRPAC and its predecessors suggested not only continuity but a strong organizational impetus among Puerto Ricans. This impulse was propelled by the links they made between ethnicity and political status.

According to Eugenio Caro, the first two meetings of PRPAC took place in Nancy Meléndez's house sometime during her first term on the council. It was José La Luz's idea that it was time that the Puerto Rican community had its own PAC. "We discussed it and decided to do it," Caro said.[2]

Peter Ayala attended his first PRPAC meeting in 1984, while it was still struggling to establish itself:

> [Mildred Torres] invited me to a meeting at her home; I really can't tell whether the PAC had been around for a long time, but the meeting I went to seemed to be an organizational meeting where they still were laying out the foundations of the PAC. At this meeting, in the middle of 1984, there were Mildred, Eugenio Caro, Nancy Meléndez, who was councilperson at that time, Carmen Rodríguez [an education administrator], Becky Delgado Brito [a public school teacher]; Ed Vargas wasn't there. There were a number of other people there. It seemed to me that these were people that had been in the community for a long time. The house was pretty full. María Sánchez was not there. It couldn't have been their first meeting because it seemed that the foundations had been laid and they were agreeing on them at that meeting. I remember specifically that they charged Eugenio to incorporate the PAC.[3]

The PRPAC members who attended the meeting Ayala described were angry at the lack of responsiveness of the Democratic party. They were determined to influence the future selection of candidates. The idea was to have a say in the decision-making process *and* to have a Puerto Rican name on the next ballot.

VICTORY, BIGAMY, AND BETRAYAL

Nicholas Carbone's regime was a hard-driven effort to bypass the institutional weaknesses of city government: at-large representation, low pay for councilpersons, minority party representation by statute, and a ceremonial mayor. Though some have argued that these features buttressed the power of Hartford's corporations to dictate policy,[4] to Deputy Mayor Carbone they provided openings for the establishment of broad-based redistributive policies. Yet business-government linkages and tax initiatives promoted downtown development, while failing to arrest neighborhood decay. This prompted the formation of a challenge slate in the 1979 city council race, led by Mayor George Athanson and Councilman Robert Ludgin. Ironically, Athanson and Ludgin were supported by the forces Carbone was most keen on helping—blacks, Puerto Ricans, members of white ethnic neighborhoods—not merely because they felt left out but because, in contrast with its early history, Hartford had a strong distaste for autocratic, long-term incumbents. After having him at city hall for ten years, people tired of Carbone and felt he had too much power.

To balance their so-called neighborhood slate, Athanson and Ludgin needed a Puerto Rican. With help from María Sánchez and José Garay, they found their candidate in Antonio González, a Democrat from Sánchez's circle who owned a grocery store and was well known in the community.[5] González was not an outstanding candidate, and many could not understand why he was chosen. Two interrelated reasons account for his selection. Ethnicity was perhaps the most important: Puerto Ricans were the second-largest ethnic group in the city, and they felt entitled to representation on the council. Athanson was sympathetic to this; during the 1969 riots, his was the only voice publicly suggesting that Puerto Ricans needed political representation. In addition, he was an outspoken believer in the validity of ethnicity as a criterion for the selection of candidates. The second reason, although not substantive, was equally compelling. Like blondes in the land of Kong, good Puerto Rican prospects were scarce. Garay recalled:

> They wanted me, and we had many meetings. I had until February 28 to switch parties so that I could be on the Democratic slate during the primary. I was not convinced I should do it. I told them, "I want to do something, but this is not my party. But I'll get you a candidate." I talked to Jerry Zayas, and he declined. I talked to Olga Torres, and she said no. I talked to other people to help me find someone willing to go against Carbone. In the end we had no choice but Tony González.[6]

The November election brought Carbone's ten-year reign to an end. In a sense, Puerto Ricans were released from his yoke twice over since they also acquired new representation on the council. Although he was not the most qualified candidate, González defeated Carbone's protégé, Mildred Torres, in a September primary by a little over a thousand votes. In the election he received 10,458 votes, the lowest among the Democrats, but this gave him quite a comfortable margin of 5,342 votes over the lowest vote getter elected.

In 1980, González marched into city hall as the first Puerto Rican *elected* to the city council. This was a milestone for the community, all the more significant from a comparative perspective. The first African American elected to the council occupied his seat 190 years after blacks began to settle in Hartford, 107 years after slavery was abolished in Connecticut, and 79 years after blacks were granted the vote in the state. It took Puerto Ricans about forty years to achieve the same.

Mildred Torres campaigning in 1979 to retain her city council seat as Nicholas Carbone (*left*) watches. *Photo by Juan Fuentes. Courtesy of Juan Fuentes.*

The sense of accomplishment faded almost instantly, however, when it became known that González had remarried without divorcing his first wife. This made him liable to criminal charges, which was a political disaster for Athanson's coalition and for a community whose reputation as consumers of pornography was now further tarnished by having a bigamist as its highest elected official.

As stories expounded on the situation, rumors spread that González also was a wife batterer. In November 1979, opponents of his candidacy had organized a demonstration in front of his store on Park Street to denounce him. As a result of efforts by two prominent local feminists—

Antonio González, the first Puerto Rican elected to the city council, 1979. *Photo by Juan Fuentes. Courtesy of Juan Fuentes.*

Dr. María Bithorn and Edwin Vargas's mother, Esther Vargas—the picket line had included Gloria Steinem, who happened to be in town at the time. The revelations vindicated the organizers of the protest, but key people I interviewed stated that although González gave Puerto Ricans a bad name, the scandal was muffled rather quickly. Some argued that, had he sought a second term, the community would have supported him.[7]

One of the people willing to overlook these faults was Councilman Ludgin. "These things happen," he declared. "I don't think González acted in bad faith."[8] Ludgin's generosity was politically motivated, however. At the council, it quickly became apparent that González was in way over his head.[9] He had a gut feeling about certain issues but was unable to articulate policy positions. To find his way in the council's maze of resolutions, ordinances, and budget and policy matters, he depended on others.[10] He was not prepared to lead but was ready and eager to follow. This was good for Ludgin, who, after replacing Carbone in the powerful deputy mayor position, became autocratic in his leadership style and paranoid about Carbone's residual influence and therefore demanded blind loyalty from his allies. Having González's vote in his pocket gave him a good reason to be forgiving.

Whether González acted in bad faith or not was a moot issue. The revelation of bigamy and the accusation of wife battering sealed his political future. Come 1981 he "chose" not to run, and in April several individuals were suggested as potential replacements. The leading contenders were Mike Borrero, Yasha Escalera, then special assistant to Governor William O'Neill, and Alberto Ibargüen, a vice president at Hartford National Bank. A fringe candidate, Antonio Santiago, also surfaced. Because of the importance of the coming election, two separate voter registration campaigns were conducted, one led by Alfredo Rodríguez, who during the 1974 gubernatorial race had worked for Ella Grasso, and another spearheaded by the Concilio Latinoamericano Para el Avance Laboral (Labor Council for Latin American Advancement), an AFL-CIO organization headed locally by Edwin Vargas and José La Luz.

On 28 July, the Hartford Democratic Town Committee met at Hartford High School. Three hundred Democrats—including voting members and guests—attended the convention. The party's leadership had promised Edwin Vargas that Borrero would be chosen for the spot occupied by González. How they did it is not known precisely, but María Sánchez and Mildred Torres persuaded town committee leaders to forsake Vargas and support their candidate, who until that point had not surfaced officially as a contender. As a result, Jerry Zayas won the endorsement over Borrero, thirty-eight votes to nine.

Vargas criticized the nomination, giving as his reason not the fact that he had been deceived but that Zayas was employed by Northeast Utilities. Although Zayas said that he was not worried about the attack, he felt compelled to clarify that he had been a community activist before working for the company. "For ten years the community has known me and my work through the Puerto Rican Parade and as director of the Spanish American Center," he said.[11] Borrero and Santiago were also critical and pledged to force a primary. Santiago criticized the town committee for choosing Zayas "behind the community's back." There was no primary, however, and Zayas was easily elected with 11,356 votes.

Paralleling this drama, another power play was taking place at the Democratic convention. Blacks wanted Thirman Milner, a former state representative, endorsed for mayor. The party refused and chose to support the incumbent, George Athanson. Milner proceeded to challenge Athanson in a primary and was defeated. Not one to be denied, Milner questioned the primary results and obtained a favorable ruling in court. In the November election he rode to victory by a three-to-one margin over his Republican opponent, becoming the first black mayor of Hartford. His support came overwhelmingly from blacks and Puerto Ricans. This was a

From left: Edwin Vargas, Jr., and Thirman Milner, the first African American mayor of Hartford, elected in 1980. *Photo by Juan Fuentes. Courtesy of Juan Fuentes.*

milestone in Hartford's history and, given the city's council-manager form of government, a largely symbolic but important victory for blacks.

In the Puerto Rican community, Milner was backed by Borrero and his allies. Since the Democrats had double-crossed Borrero, Edwin Vargas and others encouraged Puerto Ricans, as a way of paying the Democrats back, to support Milner, who although a Democrat was not the party's chosen candidate. Milner's bid was assisted by local appearances from Puerto Rican congressman Robert García, whom Borrero's ad hoc group, Puerto Ricans and Hispanics for Political Progress, invited to Hartford. During his appearances García emphasized the need for mutual support among blacks and Puerto Ricans. This note was echoed by others. Thus, although Milner did not have a close relationship with the community, his candidacy appealed to Puerto Ricans because he was a black "outsider" whose challenge gave them vicarious satisfaction.

After the election, an editorial in the community newspaper *Qué Pasa* declared that Milner's election demonstrated the importance of a black-Hispanic alliance. "The black community has recognized that Hispanic support was crucial to Milner's election," reads the editorial. "Gone are the days when artificial barriers separated these two communities. Gone are the days when Puerto Ricans and Hispanics used racial epithets to refer to blacks. The time has come for these groups to join hands and face the challenges of the future." [12]

Both *Qué Pasa* and Milner commended Puerto Ricans for not pursuing a quid pro quo. Borrero was praised for giving his support without asking for anything specific in return. Incredibly, *Qué Pasa* saw this as a sign of political maturity. According to the editorial writer, what was important was the long-term vision of progress for all, not the short-term spoils of victory.

This was, perhaps, rhetoric intended to blunt the accusation that Milner was a biased candidate and to reassure those who predicted that his mayoralty would favor only his supporters. In response to these attacks, Milner was quick to declare that he would be "the mayor of Hartford, not of one specific group." [13] It is also likely that even at this stage there were some within the Puerto Rican community who could not follow the most simple rule of the political process: nobody gets something for nothing, unless the giver is a fool.

Meanwhile, a defeated and vengeful Ludgin became a thorn in the back of Puerto Rican leaders, as he used the little time he had left in office to unleash a probe of the San Juan Center. Ludgin was concerned that Community Development Block Grant monies were being used to organize tenants and lobby for more housing. More specifically, he was intent on punishing the center for its role in the overnight occupation of city hall by a group of homeless Puerto Ricans during the Thanksgiving holiday. [14]

In addition to Ludgin's persecution, Puerto Ricans were concerned about two other key issues. In 1980, they were 18 percent of the city's population and, with approximately six thousand electors, represented 12 percent of registered voters. Although close to parity, this was considered a low proportion. According to Mike Borrero, voting-age Puerto Ricans totaled a potential 38 percent of electors. Thus, it was crucial to increase registration and turnout if they hoped to turn the community into a powerful voting bloc. According to Borrero, "We can be the swing vote in Hartford if we use our votes intelligently and work in unity." [15]

The second issue was the never-ending factionalism among elites, a problem amply demonstrated by the competition between Vargas and Sánchez over González's successor. The new director of the commonwealth's office, Carlos Piñero, wrote: "We must take a hard look at our situation. We've had enough personality conflicts. . . . It's about time the so-called leaders begin to work together in a broad-based coalition. . . . Let's drop our pet peeves and hidden agendas." [16]

These were significant problems, and a third was soon added: the inability of Puerto Ricans to hold on to their council seat. Mildred Torres did not last a year as councilwoman; Antonio González lasted one term, but his tenure was tainted. Then, in the summer of 1982, after barely six months in office, Jerry Zayas left the council. Zayas's political involvement dated from the early 1970s. He had been the first Puerto Rican to sit on the city's Redevelopment Commission, as a Carbone appointee. He had also been a member of the board of the Greater Hartford Process. Yet, in retrospect, he admitted to being ill prepared for the council job, a post that demanded much and gave little back. Compensation, for example, was a meager $4,000, which meant that unless council members were independently wealthy, they were forced to hold other full-time jobs.[17] Zayas noted: "With all my contacts and experience, I was still not fully aware of how demanding the job of a councilperson can be, that is, if you want to be effective. The needs of our community were simply overwhelming. The potential for voter frustration, and actual dissatisfaction, was very high. I also wanted to change my personal life. I had been so involved that I had neglected my family, so I wanted to rectify that."[18]

Zayas recommended Olga Torres as his successor. Several others within the community began to eye the seat, and subsequently a meeting was held to manage the emerging factions and to strategize. Yasha Escalera was a key player in this process.

> When Jerry resigns, . . . we all agreed that we were going to go through a process to deal with the vacancy, . . . and that's when [Councilmen Frank] Borges and Rudy Arnold cut a deal and put in Olga Torres. [They cut a deal] with Olga because they had the votes. We wanted to go through a community process. They said [to her], "You don't have to go through a community process, it's the council that decides." So . . . we, [meaning] the people that [were] active politically—myself and Carmen Amore, Nancy [Meléndez], it was probably ten or twelve of us—we met at Aquí Me Quedo [a Puerto Rican restaurant]. . . . There were three or four of us whose names were in the hopper for the seat. . . . We all put together a meeting [with Borges and Arnold], . . . [but then at the meeting] at 5:00 P.M., Borges basically called Olga and said I've got the votes for you. If you want to wait two weeks, do what you want, but we got the votes and we are going to [choose a successor] tonight.[19]

Olga Torres succeeded Zayas. In 1983, at the end of her term, she decided to seek reelection and was endorsed by the Democratic party. But, to the surprise of many, she rejected the nomination. She felt that the Democratic slate needed more Puerto Rican representation and did not want to be used as a token by the party. Thus, she chose to run with a challenge slate of labor leaders and community activists who shared her concerns.

For Puerto Rican party regulars, such as María Sánchez and Yasha

Escalera, this was too much to take from someone who had dissed them in 1982 by bypassing the "community selection process." As a result, they withdrew their support for her.

Originally, the challenge slate included Nancy Meléndez, who at the time was director of the New England Farm Workers Council, as candidate for the board of education. Meléndez, however, was doubtful about her participation. Prodded by María Sánchez, she considered deserting the challengers to run with the endorsed Democrats. According to Sánchez, if Meléndez didn't go with the party, the sole Puerto Rican seat on the council would be lost. Escalera recalled:

> We [he and Sánchez] talked with Nancy about running. Nancy called me and all I told her was, "Nancy, if you are going to do this, you have no private life. Don't do it just for the glory." She said she understood, and then I went away. She said, "I don't know if I'm going to do it," and that's when I left, and then the next day, boom!, they pushed it, she went through; María convinced her [to run with the Democrats for city council].[20]

The challenge slate was unable to win the primary. Nancy Meléndez ran with the Democrats and was elected, saving the so-called Puerto Rican seat on the council. The community's leadership ended badly divided. María Sánchez and her minions were disappointed and angry at Torres for turning her back on the party. The challengers, who included Edwin Vargas and (behind the scenes) José La Luz, felt cheated by Meléndez, who neither shared her doubts nor warned them when she changed her mind. Both Torres and Meléndez were accused of betrayal, a charge that was perhaps too strong for what they had done. Before long, however, Meléndez became the rallying point for a coalition of forces that brought back to life the idea, first articulated in 1977, of forming a pressure group. Initially, the coalition was called the Hispanic Leadership Caucus. Later it was dubbed the Puerto Rican Political Action Committee of Connecticut.

THE TROUBLE WITH NANCY

In 1984, Edwin Vargas told a reporter from *Qué Pasa* that Puerto Ricans who worked for big corporations could not possibly represent the interests of the community. In his view, political virtue had a single source, the people, and its best measure was grassroots support. Nancy Meléndez had recently come into the employ of a large corporation and therefore failed to meet the standard, said Vargas.[21] Others disagreed. Many felt that Meléndez deserved only kudos for her council resolutions addressing housing, education, and employment issues. Early in 1984, she nominated Mildred Torres and Ramón Pacheco, a Puerto Rican lawyer, for the Personnel and Redevelopment Commissions, respectively. Some considered this "a taste of the good things yet to come from the new Puerto Rican representative."[22]

To move beyond resolutions and appointments, Meléndez needed to work closely with the rest of the council. Instead, she clashed almost immediately with black rookie councilman Charles Mathews over the appointment of a new city manager. The unofficial story is that Meléndez favored a Puerto Rican candidate who was rumored to be gay. According to Yasha Escalera, "Charlie Mathews came and told a group of us that there was no way he was going to support a Puerto Rican that was gay, because that wasn't good for us. . . . I don't know [whether] that was the issue, but basically that's when Nancy decides that she [is not going to support Mathews]."[23] To appoint his candidate, Mathews needed a yes vote from Meléndez. But she withheld her support, and in a five-to-four decision, in which Meléndez cast the deciding vote, the council selected Italian Alfred Gatta.

Like González before her, Meléndez was ill prepared to meet the demands of the council. Soon, she was, as she had been earlier, unemployed and worried about self and family. Personal problems compounded a highly stressful situation at the council. According to Escalera, "She was constantly putting herself in very controversial roles and taking stands that put her in a central position, but when the pressure came, she had difficulty dealing with what she had done."[24]

In 1985, Councilmen Mathews and Frank Borges rebelled against Democratic town chair James Crowley in protest over what they saw as the marginal inclusion of blacks within the power structure. Hartford had a black mayor and two black councilmen but no African Americans held what Mathews and Borges considered to be the truly important positions in city government. These were the offices of city manager, treasurer, corporation counsel, and deputy mayor. By leading the council and the city manager's office, the latter carried more weight than the mayoralty itself. The holders of these positions were, respectively, Alfred Gatta, Pete Kinsella, Richard Goldstein, and Alphonse Marotta, all of whom were white ethnics.

Mathews's argument was that since one-third of the city's population was black, African Americans deserved a corresponding share in the power structure. In his view, at least one of the "pillars of power" should have been in African American hands and more blacks should have been on the council. The party's leadership did not budge, however, and, by deciding to run a primary, the critics became insurgents. Their strategy was to run a slate composed of three blacks from the North End and three white ethnics from the South End, in effect cutting off the Puerto Ricans as payback for what Meléndez had done in 1984. Said Edwin Vargas: "Charlie Mathews and Frank Borges were riding high on the North End. They made the fatal mistake of trying to replace Meléndez with Abe Giles's son, [Radames,] who . . . was born of a Puerto Rican mother but culturally was black. We were sympathetic with Mathews, but we didn't like the idea of black power at Puerto Rican expense."[25]

As a result of a conversation between Eugenio Caro and José La Luz, a meeting was organized and a press conference held on 27 March to announce the commitment of a broad group of leaders to Meléndez. Dubbed the Hispanic Leadership Caucus, the organizing group laid the ground for the reincarnation of the Puerto Rican Political Action Club of Greater Hartford that Olga Torres and Juan Colón had organized in 1981 to support Jerry Zayas.

In a moment of rare unity, factions came together in support of Meléndez. Mathews and Borges were present but did not intervene. They didn't need to, since their position was known. According to Mathews, the movement to remove Meléndez was not a rejection of the Puerto Rican community. It was, instead, "personal, against Nancy Meléndez. This is about her and her actions."[26] They did not understand the self-evident truth that without a Puerto Rican occupying it, there could not be a Puerto Rican seat on the council. In that sense, the assembled leaders were clearly saying, an attack against Meléndez, deserved or not, was an attack against the community.

The outcome of the meeting was remarkable given the mixed reviews of Meléndez's performance and the profound aversion the likes of Vargas and La Luz felt toward her. Vargas claimed that his support did not reflect a change of heart. Instead, it was based on the fact that Mathews and Borges were opposed to linkage policies and low-income housing and were considered mouthpieces for developers and the big corporations. He also appreciated the symbolic power of ethnic representation, even if, in his mind, the representative left a lot to be desired. A bad representative was better than no representative at all. Further, Meléndez could always be replaced with a more qualified Puerto Rican, when Puerto Ricans, not blacks, decided that it was necessary. At the time, it was important to keep the seat for as long as possible, until it was accepted by others as a kind of Puerto Rican entitlement. If the pattern was broken, the long-run setback would be greater than having a lousy representative for one or two terms.

With few exceptions, those present at the meeting shared these sentiments. Radicals and conservatives, party regulars and outsiders, old guard and Young Turks, all jumped onto the Meléndez bandwagon, demanding not just the preservation of the Puerto Rican seat but a second seat on the

Nancy Meléndez. The battle to save her seat on the city council unified Puerto Ricans and launched PRPAC. *Photo by Juan Fuentes. Courtesy of Juan Fuentes.*

council. José La Luz declared, "We have witnessed the growth of our community, and at this time, rather than reducing our participation, it might be more appropriate to think that we deserve at least two seats on the council."[27] Subsequently, in an article they wrote jointly, Vargas and La Luz called for black and Puerto Rican unity. They pointed out that Puerto Ricans had made possible the election of Hartford's first black mayor and warned against divisions fostered by intergroup competition for resources, such as those that had doomed black-Hispanic coalitions in New York and Chicago.[28]

Within the Democratic party, support for Meléndez was spearheaded by Democrats Working Together, a group whose name projected an image of unity in contrast to the divisiveness created by Mathews's challenge. In May, group leaders met with Mayor Milner in an attempt to ease the tensions between blacks and Puerto Ricans. They emphasized that the attack against Charlie Mathews should not be interpreted as an attack against the black community. This argument, which Puerto Ricans did not buy from Mathews vis-à-vis Meléndez, blacks did not buy from them. Each party was convinced of its own sincerity, and neither believed the other.

On 7 May, the press reported that the activities of the Puerto Rican group were a sign that the Hispanic community had begun to "flex its political muscle." The story reads: "A group known as the Hispanic Leadership Caucus increasingly has been presenting a united political front, representing Puerto Ricans in a series of talks with the city's political powers. . . . It will soon take the next step toward political growth by creating the Puerto Rican Political Action Committee, an organization intended to raise money to finance political organizing in the city's Hispanic neighborhoods." [29] Meetings with "prominent black leaders," with the city manager, and with town committee chair James Crowley were reported, noting that Crowley had committed the support of the party machine on Meléndez's behalf.

The caucus established a campaign committee whose division of labor reflected a broad-based unity. Carmen Amore, a business leader, supervised the registration of new voters; José La Luz handled the press; Mildred Torres acted as treasurer; and Edwin Vargas headed the campaign. Vargas enlisted support from the Hartford Federation of Teachers, from the schools' superintendent, and from other individuals. One of his talking points for a meeting held on 15 May reads: "Discussion of need to keep unity of group led by Nancy Meléndez. Don't allow others to divide us, let's keep our differences of opinions among each other. Try to anticipate controversial issues ahead of time if possible and discuss them in the group honestly." [30]

At the party convention in July, as expected, Meléndez obtained the endorsement of the delegates. In the September primary the endorsed Democrats easily defeated the challengers. Although the primary victory almost guaranteed success in November, the caucus took nothing for granted and went all out in its efforts to get voters to the polls. Child care and transportation were provided to anyone who needed them. Volunteer workers literally got people out of bed to make sure they went to the polls, in some cases waiting for them while they dressed. [31] Meléndez's reelection marked the first time since 1979 that a Puerto Rican incumbent had the opportunity to serve a second term. She received 12,564 votes, the most a Puerto Rican candidate ever received between 1971 and 1991.

LEGITIMACY AND SUCCESS

By October 1985, Puerto Ricans had taken the "next step" announced by the *Hartford Courant* in May. The Hispanic Leadership Caucus was now known as PRPAC. Mildred Torres was selected president, a move that Vargas and La Luz supported as a conciliatory gesture to what they called the "old guard," a term used to refer to Sánchez, her associates, and leaders of La Casa de Puerto Rico.

Shortly before the election, PRPAC organized a relief effort in response to a mudslide in a small town in Puerto Rico. Nancy Meléndez and treasurer Peter Ayala, who led the statewide effort, formed an ad hoc subcommittee, the Comité de Auxilio a Puerto Rico, which collected nearly $250,000 to help the families of the 180 people who had died in the disaster.[32] For this work PRPAC was recognized beyond the Puerto Rican community as an important and legitimate organization, pursuing mostly political purposes but serving humanitarian causes as well. Between 1985 and 1990, PRPAC activities were prominent and systematic. By 1991, the group had become the most significant force of its kind on the city's political scene.

In 1985, in a bit of symbolic, island-based politics, PRPAC lobbied the school board to adopt a resolution naming the Kinsella School after the leader of the 1868 revolt against Spanish colonialism on the island, Ramón Emeterio Betances. That same year, Edna Negrón Smith became principal of the renamed school. When the election of Thomas B. McBride to the city council in November created a vacancy at the board of education, PRPAC lobbied for a Puerto Rican appointment, making its case both privately and in public. On the board, María Sánchez waged her own campaign; and, after much wrangling over the candidate, Puerto Rican María González-Borrero, a PRPAC member, was appointed by unanimous vote in January.[33]

PRPAC also highlighted the lack of Hispanic administrators in the public schools. After a series of meetings with key policy makers, the group succeeded in obtaining the appointment of several Puerto Ricans to administrative positions in the school system and in the city, including principals, a city personnel director, and an assistant city manager.

Mildred Torres did not hold the presidency of PRPAC for long. It is not clear exactly when she resigned—she was not sure of the date herself when I asked her—but it was probably sometime in 1986. When she stepped down, Vargas and La Luz were pleased but did not pursue the position. "She dropped it [the presidency] on my lap," said Caro, "because I was vice president. Peter Ayala was treasurer, and Frances Sánchez was secretary." According to Ayala:

Eugenio and I took the PAC under our wing and we structured it. We did a lot of organizing; we had regular meetings; things were done democratically. Around that time Edwin [Vargas] came in as a member; I don't know if Edwin was in before. We used to have meetings either . . . at the community center or at the National Puerto Rican Forum, and every time we had a meeting we would get more and more people. I really don't remember how Edwin got into it. But also José La Luz, I forgot to mention him. There was a lot of personalities now that they saw the PAC as a viable solution to the problems of the Hispanic community, the lack of representation.[34]

During the 1987 legislative session PRPAC worked with state representatives to ensure passage of the Direct Mail Voter Registration Bill. This legislation did not have much to do with the goal of increasing Puerto Rican registration, but it was favored by PRPAC for increasing voter registration in general. PRPAC lobbied Puerto Rican representative José Lugo, from Bridgeport, to support the measure, and Lugo in turn secured the affirmative vote of other legislators. During that same session, the group helped defeat an English-only proposal sponsored by right-wing senator Tom Scott. Key figures in this battle were Peter Ayala and future state representative Juan Figueroa, who worked with La Casa de Puerto Rico.

Also in 1987, PRPAC stalwarts bolted out of the party's convention, frustrated and angry, when the Democrats refused to endorse Eugenio Caro for city council—he was considered erratic, too radical, and a loose cannon[35]—and nominated María B. González, a Puerto Rican teacher, instead. This coincided with the formation of a white, liberal-progressive coalition known as People for Change (PFC), which set out to wrest the three minority seats on the city council from the Republicans. When Caro was rejected, the leaders of PFC jumped at the opportunity to form an alliance with PRPAC by offering to make Caro one of their candidates. The members of PFC thought, with good reason, that a PFC-PRPAC ticket would bring together the electoral expertise of a cadre of progressive activists and the grassroots mobilization and support of the Puerto Rican community.[36] The assumption underlying this strategy was that PRPAC was not only an effective organization but a legitimate one as well.

On their way out of the Democratic party convention, PRPAC members chanted, "Brouillet, Come November We'll Remember" and "Brouillet, We'll See You in the Streets."[37] Arthur Brouillet, a public school teacher of French-Canadian background, was singled out because he was a key voice against Caro and had brokered the candidacy of María B. González. He also represented the third assembly district, which demographically was now a Puerto Rican stronghold. Dissatisfied with this situation and with Brouillet's patronizing style, Edwin Vargas and others in PRPAC had been mulling over the idea of electing a Puerto Rican to represent the district. Thus, there was an anti-Brouillet sentiment in the air that was galvanized at the convention.

Said Juan Figueroa: "Edwin Vargas was the person who asked me to run. And it was after the Democratic convention of 1987, when Art Brouillet made his deal with Crowley to reject Caro and nominate María González. That same night or maybe the next day, Edwin openly proposed to have me run as a candidate for the third district." [38]

Once Caro accepted the PFC's nomination, José La Luz convinced him that he had to step down as president of PRPAC. This was a calculated move by La Luz and Vargas to regain control of what they considered their political child. When Peter Ayala told the story, he said that he did not suspect that the move was choreographed, and when the decision was made to make Edwin Vargas president, there were no accusations that the outcome had been planned. According to Ayala:

> I didn't want to be president, and now Danny Pérez [a labor organizer and close friend of Vargas] is with us and Edwin Vargas—they had become key players—so we all went to the Washington Diner—we are still without a president—so Danny Pérez says: "Why are you looking so much, here's the man for you." And we said, "Edwin? Hey, why not?" It went before a vote in our next meeting, but that's how he became president. [39]

Victory at the polls proved PFC's assumption and strategy right— African American Marie Kirkley-Bey and Caro were elected, nearly ousting the Republicans from the council. For the first time in the city's history, Republican representation was reduced to one councilman. But the results made some within the community uneasy, since Caro's competitor, María González, was also elected. This brought Puerto Rican representation on the council to the level demanded by the Hispanic Leadership Caucus in 1985. Although most PRPAC members had nothing but contempt for González, not everyone shared this attitude. The community press, for example, was quite pleased with this unanticipated development. [40] Unfortunately, on policy matters and as a political leader, González proved to be a disaster, a great embarrassment to her supporters and to the community at large. [41]

Following up on its threat to Brouillet, in March 1988 PRPAC achieved control of the Democratic town committee for the third assembly district. After this victory, the group boasted its "new clout" within the party by helping to elect Mary Phil Guinan, a progressive Democrat from Hartford's West End, as the party's citywide chair. In exchange, Edwin Vargas was elected assistant treasurer, and as part of the bargain, Raúl Rodríguez, a Puerto Rican lawyer, was elected secretary. "This is the first time," wrote Vargas, "that the Puerto Rican community elects one of its own to the five-member executive committee of the Democratic party." [42]

On 14 April, Juan Figueroa announced his candidacy for Brouillet's seat. Since this was a state seat, PRPAC broadened its pro-Figueroa effort by including not only PFC but the Legislative Electoral Action Program, a group formed in 1980 to elect progressive candidates to the state legislature. PRPAC did not know what Brouillet would do, but it was ready for and counting on running a primary against him. In preparation for that contest, the group organized a voter registration campaign in the third and sixth assembly districts.

In a September primary, Figueroa and Brouillet battled for the Democratic nomination. Once again, the marriage of electoral know-how, provided by PFC and LEAP, and grassroots mobilization and support, provided by PRPAC, proved crucial to success. Two other factors were equally important: Figueroa's appeal as a candidate and demographic changes in the district. This combination of elements gave him a margin of victory of 2.5 to 1.

Parallelling the Figueroa-Brouillet power play, a confrontation was taking place between María Sánchez and her associate Abe Giles. After more than twenty years of service, Sánchez was ousted from the town committee in the sixth district, where she lived and worked. According to Giles, Sánchez simply failed to come to meetings and did not sign the consent slip that would qualify her as a candidate. He saw her exclusion as "her mistake." In his view, this "mistake" could have been easily corrected, but "nobody seemed to want to."[43]

Sánchez saw it differently. She felt Giles, whom she had supported for well over a decade, had betrayed her. Also, her being ousted suggested an effort among blacks to squash Puerto Ricans. In a fit of ethnic indignation and personal anger, on 29 June, Sánchez announced she would run against Giles in a primary for candidacy as state representative. Because she had not supported PFC in 1987, PFC did not work for her in 1988, although the group endorsed her candidacy. PRPAC backed Sánchez, and its members participated in her campaign, also registering voters in her district. The combination of extremely hard work by her network of supporters, her appeal as a candidate, and, ironically, the poor state of relations between blacks and Puerto Ricans in the North End gave her a victory in the September primary, although by a narrow thirty-three-vote margin.

According to an analysis of the primaries, "What is clear . . . is the emergence of the Puerto Rican community in Hartford politics. The contrast in the political status of Puerto Ricans a year ago and today could not be more stark."[44]

In November, Figueroa and Sánchez joined Américo Santiago, a Democrat from Bridgeport's 130th assembly district, as the Puerto Rican delegation to the state legislature. Figueroa and Sánchez marched in to repre-

From left: State Representative Américo Santiago, from Bridgeport's 130th assembly district; Hartford's mayor, Carrie Saxon Perry; and State Representative Juan Figueroa. In March 1991, the 3rd assembly district's Democrats for Change gave Santiago and Figueroa political leadership awards for their "dedication and integrity to the state of Connecticut." *Photo by Juan Fuentes. Courtesy of Juan Fuentes.*

sent two heavily Puerto Rican assembly districts, but symbolically they were there to represent all the Puerto Ricans of Hartford.

In 1989, PRPAC scored another round of victories. It engineered the election of Frances Sánchez, a public school teacher, to the city council and, in collaboration with an ad hoc coalition, of Carmen Rodríguez and Pedro Ramos, a social worker, to the city's board of education. Caro considered going back to the Democratic party, but Edwin Vargas convinced him to run again as a PFC candidate.[45] Caro was reelected, although his support was 15 percent lower than in 1987 because María González, who ran as a petitioning candidate, diverted some of his votes.

The objectives of the 1989 campaign were ambitious. PRPAC and its allies intended to reelect Caro, place Frances Sánchez on the city council, and achieve control of the board of education by electing a majority slate that included a liberal white, an African American, two Puerto Ricans, and a representative of the gay community. The Puerto Rican candidates were not able to dominate the board of education, but they were elected. This was a net gain.

The elation came to an abrupt end, however, on 25 November 1989, when María Sánchez was found dead in her apartment, probably of a

From left, seated: Edwin Vargas, Jr., and Frances Sánchez. *Photo by Juan Fuentes. Courtesy of Juan Fuentes.*

heart attack. The search for her replacement in 1990 led to a clash between PRPAC's leadership, some of its members, and the leadership of the so-called Puerto Rican old guard.[46]

PRPAC had supported María Sánchez in 1988 but did not have a strong group of members in Sánchez's turf, the North End. The campaign to fill her seat gave PRPAC an opening to extend its theater of operations and truly become a citywide force. Within PRPAC, Eugenio Caro and Jack Cullin, who was its treasurer at the time, held the view that Sánchez's supporters on the North End—that is, those who worked directly for her and had traditionally been in her camp—should select her replacement. Outside PRPAC, Yasha Escalera, who was María Sánchez's campaign manager, was adamantly opposed to the group making any inroads on the North End. Escalera was willing to let PRPAC participate in the process but not as a major player; ultimately his network would designate a successor. The conflict over process overlapped with turf issues and old personal rivalries, threatening the loss of an assembly seat that Sánchez had won narrowly.

After interviewing four candidates, PRPAC decided that Edna Negrón Smith (now known as Edna Negrón) was the best. Negrón was a school principal but also had a long record of community involvement—most notably in the promotion of bilingual education and in the fight against the Greater Hartford Process—and thus satisfied both elitist and populist requirements. Escalera's "María Sánchez Committee"—a network of campaign workers and community activists in the North End—also ruled in favor of Negrón. Edwin Vargas initially encouraged a fifth candidate, policeman Edwin García, and after PRPAC endorsed Negrón, he refused to accept the result and decided to enter the primary contest on his own. Giles wanted his seat back and was endorsed by the Democratic party. With the situation out of control and fearing that a split Puerto Rican vote would lead to defeat, PRPAC decided not to campaign for Negrón or García. But Negrón won the primary and went on to replace Sánchez after easily winning the required special election. Her victory was celebrated, but it also left behind a divided community and a badly bruised PRPAC.

PRPAC acted rationally when it decided not to wage a battle it was not sure it could win; but some were not impressed by the group's pragmatism and saw its neutrality as political cowardice. Yet the following year, the group's leadership risked its very existence in an all-out challenge against an old nemesis, Charles Mathews—who was now Hartford's deputy mayor—and the six Democratic members of the city council. Frustrated by Mathews's insistence that blacks would not allow more than two Puerto Ricans on the council and by Frances Sánchez's alignment with Mathews, PRPAC decided to throw its weight behind black mayor Carrie Saxon Perry in her campaign to replace Mathews and the remaining Democratic councilpersons with a slate of candidates more responsive to her.

Before breaking off with Mathews, PRPAC negotiated the appointment of a Puerto Rican, Jorge Simón, as corporation counsel.[47] PRPAC had delivered the Puerto Rican votes that Mathews needed to elect an African American as city treasurer and himself as deputy mayor. After this, Mathews pursued the office of city manager. Vargas told him: "We already gave you the treasurer [Denise Napier], the deputy mayor, and now you also want the city manager's position? What are *we* going to get? I have to tell you now what you told Crowley in 1985: if you want our support, Puerto Ricans must occupy a position of power." With this gun to his head, Mathews agreed to appoint a Hispanic as corporation counsel.

Soon after Simón's appointment, Mathews began to backtrack and voiced regret over his decision. Vargas reminded him that the only time he had suffered a political defeat was when he crossed the Puerto Ricans in 1985 and that he seemed to be headed in that direction again. Then Vargas asked: "How about having a second Puerto Rican on the council?" To which Mathews responded that North Hartford and the black community were not ready to see a second Puerto Rican on the Democratic council and neither was he. "Well, maybe you are not ready, and the black community is not ready, but the Puerto Rican community is ready," Vargas replied.[48]

In the Mathews-Perry power play, the interests of five factional groups clashed. One group included Mathews and his supporters on the council. They had a stake in installing a mayor who would respect the institutional roles prescribed by the council-manager form of government to advance a corporate-oriented set of policies for Hartford. In this setup, the deputy mayor, namely Mathews, would call the shots.

The second faction included Mayor Perry and her supporters. Here the stakes were power and representation. Perry wanted two things: (1) a council that would allow her to become a de facto strong mayor and (2) charter revision to bring back de jure a strong mayoralty to Hartford. In her view, this would give all citizens a voice in the development of policies that would promote the economic well-being of the city and its residents.

The third faction included the members of People for Change and PRPAC. Both groups wanted effective representation of progressive and Puerto Rican interests on the council. PRPAC wanted a council that reflected Hartford's demographic reality. On the city's nine-member council, this meant one-third of the seats had to be held by blacks, one-third by whites (or white ethnics), and one-third by Puerto Ricans. There were two Puerto Rican councilpersons already, so the Puerto Ricans were asking for only one more. PFC wanted an additional minority seat and a policy process that welcomed minority input. In exchange for supporting Perry, PFC exacted a commitment to open the Democratic caucus to PFC representatives. Perry also agreed to support the PFC's candidates in the general election.

The fourth faction encompassed the Italians and other white ethnics of Hartford's South End. The issues here also were representation and power. The Italians felt cut off by a black-dominated city council, but they also wanted to arrest the increasing influence and gains of the Puerto Ricans. That these white ethnics joined the alliance was a sign of weakness, since this forced them to collaborate with rising Puerto Ricans. Yet allying with the Puerto Ricans was also a clever tactical move because insisting on disagreement would have kept the Italians on the sidelines.

Black leaders constituted the fifth faction. They were split between Mathews and Perry in a division that reflected conflicting corporate-oriented, middle-class, and populist agendas. Containment of the Puerto Ricans was also part of the blacks' motives. Within Mathews's camp, this meant securing a pliant Puerto Rican—namely, Frances Sánchez—within the council's Democratic majority and keeping Puerto Rican representa-

Celebrating their 1991 victory, Carrie Saxon Perry (*at the microphone*), Henrietta Milward (*to the right of the podium*), Wilber Smith (*directly behind Milward*), Edwin Vargas, Jr. (*holding the Puerto Rican flag*), Shawn Wooden (*in front of Vargas*), and Danny Pérez (*directly behind the flag*). *Photo by Juan Fuentes. Courtesy of Juan Fuentes.*

tion at the current level. Mayor Perry's version of containment was different. It allowed for three Puerto Rican representatives, split between the Democrats and PFC, but only on an obedient council.

What began as a PFC-Perry-South End coalition against Mathews became a PRPAC-Perry coalition during the primary campaign and election. PFC did not disappear; it provided volunteers and resources, and so did the network of South End leaders. But PFC's cadre deferred to Vargas and PRPAC. Vargas's charismatic leadership, extensive network, strategic insights, and limitless energy made him the most influential player during the campaign.[49] In exchange for his efforts, Vargas obtained a commitment from Perry that if the coalition was successful, the presidency of the city's Democratic town committee would go to him.

By the end of 1991, under Vargas's command, PRPAC helped oust Deputy Mayor Mathews and the six Democratic incumbents who supported him. This was an amazing accomplishment, especially given that the incumbents spent more money, by a ten-to-one margin, than the challenging coalition. The city council was now one-third Puerto Rican. Eugenio Caro was reelected as a PFC candidate, and newcomers Fernando

From left: council member Fernando Comulada, board of education member Carmen Rodríguez, Edwin Vargas, Jr., Councilwoman Yolanda Castillo, and State Representative Juan Figueroa. *Photo by Juan Fuentes, 1991. Courtesy of Juan Fuentes.*

Comulada, a businessman, and Yolanda Castillo, a city employee and the daughter of Johnny Castillo, were elected on Perry's slate. Two other PFC candidates were elected, leaving the Republicans off the city council for the first time in decades.

After Perry's victory, the council began to rotate the position of deputy mayor among its members. The Democratic caucus was opened to PFC. These arrangements proved ineffectual and short-lived. Perry's coalition soon divided and broke apart when key members became disillusioned with her leadership. Perry was also dogged by charges of corruption and failure to deliver on campaign promises. The council reverted to the old structure, and a new coalition of five members emerged. In this alliance, contemptuously named the "Gang of Five" by its opponents, Puerto Ricans held a majority of three votes.[50]

Thus, within the span of twelve short years, Puerto Ricans found themselves going from zero representation to having a formal lock on the policy-making process. Their grip was fragile, however, and the relationship between Puerto Rican power holders and PRPAC was problematic. Identity politics facilitated the transition from interests to interest group, from social and political needs to organized action. Puerto Rican activists rode the wave of demographic strength, leadership development, and organizational efforts. Coalition building was also a key instrument for access to power. But, alas, it was not easy to turn coalition dominance into coalition power. In other words, having a margin of power sufficient to influence the policy process did not guarantee that the Puerto Rican majority would be able to enact redistributive measures to benefit its immediate constituency.

ASSESSMENT

In 1985, history, effective leadership, and a sense of crisis combined to transform the Hispanic Leadership Caucus into PRPAC, catapulting the latter into the political limelight. Table 7 illustrates the electoral impact of PRPAC. Using the number of votes for Puerto Rican candidates in voting districts where they concentrated as a proxy for turnout, the table shows that the entry of PRPAC in the electoral process in 1985 correlates with the second highest turnout rate since 1971. In 1979, Antonio González was elected to the city council with 55 percent of the vote in Puerto Rican districts. In 1981, Jerry Zayas captured 50 percent of the vote, but in 1985 the candidate supported by PRPAC and the Democratic party won with 69.4 percent of the vote. Despite being opposed by PRPAC, María González also gathered 50 percent of the vote in 1987, but in 1989, when PRPAC candidate Frances Sánchez was endorsed by the party, she was elected with 68 percent of the vote in Puerto Rican districts.

These data also show that although identity politics was crucial to electoral success, it was not sufficient in and of itself. Even at its highest, the proportion of the city vote captured by Puerto Rican candidates in Puerto Rican districts was less than 40 percent. The highest proportion accrued by a *winning* candidate was 29 percent and the lowest was 21 percent. Thus, as important as ethnicity was, to get elected, Puerto Rican candidates had to receive between 22 and 30 percent of their votes from African Americans and whites.

Despite the constant turnover among the elite, by the mid-1980s Puerto Ricans could count on a cadre of leaders marked by varying degrees of political savvy, relative financial stability, and a demonstrable commitment to political action. These leaders provided continuity, stamina, and direction to the emerging pool of teachers, lawyers, and white-collar workers who occupied newly available positions of influence and power. They managed conflict by deftly making and breaking alliances—as the on-and-off relationship with Charles Mathews illustrates—and by ruling out no methods, from back-room wheeling and dealing to community pressure.

Table 7. Estimated Voter Turnout in Districts with High Concentrations of Puerto Ricans, 1971–1991

Year	Candidate	Total Vote for Mayor	Total Vote for P.R. Candidate	%	Citywide Vote for P.R. Candidate	% Cast in P.R. Districts
1971	William Pérez (R)	5,509	1,193	21.6	7,890	15.1
1973	René Rodríguez (R)	5,661	848	14.9	4,027	21.0
	María Sánchez (D)[a]		1,130	19.9	4,955	22.8
1975	José Garay (R)	4,914	584	11.8	2,769	21.0
1977	José Garay (R)	4,189	590	14.0	2,809	21.0
	Edwin Vargas (I)		579	13.8	2,547	22.7
	María Sánchez (D)[a]		681	16.2	3,133	21.7
1979	Antonio González (D)[a]	4,173	2,590	54.9	10,458	24.7
	José Garay (R)		726	15.4	3,255	22.3
1981	Gerardo Zayas (D)[a]	5,447	2,740	50.3	11,356	24.1
	María Sánchez (D)[a]		674	12.3	3,244	20.7
1983	Nancy Meléndez (D)[a]	4,596	3,275	71.2	11,344	28.8
	Angel Ocasio (R)		748	16.2	3,243	23.0
1985	Nancy Meléndez (D)[a]	4,459	3,097	69.4	12,564	24.6
	María Sánchez (D)[a]		1,095	24.5	4,307	25.4
	Antonio Santiago (I)		343	7.6	1,080	31.7
1987	María B. González (D)[a]	3,889	1,934	49.7	6,981	27.7
	Eugenio Caro (PFC)[a]		1,326	34.0	5,147	25.7
1989	Frances Sánchez (D)[a]	3,258	2,218	68.0	8,009	27.6
	Eugenio Caro (PFC)[a]		1,223	37.5	4,379	27.9
	María B. González (P)		556	17.0	1,410	39.4
1991	Yolanda Castillo (D)[a]	1,970	1,486	75.4	6,077	25.9
	Fernando Comulada (D)[a]		1,411	71.6	5,570	25.6
	Eugenio Caro (PFC)[a]		1,138	57.7	4,374	26.7

SOURCE: Data assembled by José E. Cruz from reports by the *Hartford Courant* and Hartford's town and city clerk's office. Puerto Rican turnout is estimated by comparing the vote for Puerto Rican candidates and the vote for mayor in voting districts where Puerto Ricans concentrated. In 1969–1971 Puerto Rican voting districts were 29–34, 36–38, 40–42. From 1973 to 1981 the districts with Puerto Rican concentrations were 8–9, 14–17, 23, 25, 32. From 1983 to 1991 the corresponding districts were 7–9 and 18–20. In 1971 Hartford was divided into 45 voting districts. In 1973 there were 32; in 1982 they were reduced to 23 and in 1992 increased to 27.

[a] Elected.

Because of their positions within the community, Puerto Rican leaders had access to a network of grassroots supporters who were used to mobilize Puerto Ricans in general and Puerto Rican voters in particular. For example, Vargas developed his network as vice president of the Hartford Federation of Teachers. Caro did likewise through baseball and other activities, including frequent ward heeling and hanging out at highly visible locations. La Luz was well known as a community activist because of his association with the PSP. Mildred Torres had a long-standing relationship with community agencies, particularly La Casa de Puerto Rico. María Sánchez was a stalwart of the Democratic party but, most important, a veritable community resource herself, pushing for programs at the board of education and dispensing all sorts of favors from her newspaper stand.[51] The twin forces that, in seesaw fashion, drove them apart and brought them together were in-group competition and out-group rivalry.

The 1985 process was reactive. Puerto Ricans responded to a black power play that threatened to shut them out. What was crucially important was the willingness of virtually all the factions in the Puerto Rican community to come together to tackle the challenge. This was predicated on the need to preserve ethnic-based political representation. The intervention was broad based and efficient. In other words, it incorporated the key factions, it was well organized, and it benefited from an alliance with the controlling faction within the machine—represented by party chair James Crowley—against the faction represented by Charlie Mathews.

The goal in 1985 was negative—stop Mathews—and prospective—increase representation. Success consolidated and legitimized PRPAC. In politics, as in gambling, it is hard to quit when one is ahead, and that is precisely how many felt. Vargas and La Luz, for example, decided that if Meléndez won, they would declare victory and get out of her camp, because they were still chafing from her disloyalty in 1983 and thought she was a terrible council member anyway. But PRPAC was successful beyond their expectations, and the victory was such a high that they could not extricate themselves from what followed.[52]

A key factor in securing continuity was smooth leadership succession, which assured stability and renewed energy. When Mildred Torres resigned from the presidency of PRPAC, Eugenio Caro easily moved into the position; when Caro in turn stepped down, Edwin Vargas quickly took command. But effective leadership always raises the difficult question of whether mobilization (as opposed to collective behavior) can occur in its absence. Vargas was as much a product of his ability and circumstances as the circumstances of PRPAC's political development and its success were a product of his intervention. Had Vargas not been there, PRPAC would have had to invent him. His leadership (with much assistance from

José La Luz) invigorated the group and made it more effective. Torres was
a single parent suddenly confronted with the responsibility of raising her
grandchildren; Caro was the head of a large family and had a history of
unstable employment. When the presidency of PRPAC was "dropped on
his lap," he concluded that he "wasn't ready for that."[53] In contrast, as an
official of the Hartford Federation of Teachers and a partner in a stable
marriage, Vargas was in a financial and personal position that was well
grounded; he also had more and better connections, a clear and realistic
mobilization strategy, and endless energy and drive. According to key political actors, some of whom did not consider themselves Vargas's allies,
he was the community's undisputed leader and PRPAC's rallying force.

> Juan Figueroa: [Vargas is] the central figure in Puerto Rican politics in the
> city right now. . . . What he's done is a lot of hard work. He's taken risks by
> taking stands.
> Antonio Soto: Edwin is the wagon train boss. . . . He's politically astute and
> ahead of his time.
> Edna Negrón: He likes to exercise power. But he's dedicated his life to this
> struggle. . . . I think the new unity of the PAC is a great thing.

In an article for the *Hartford News*, reporter Steve Walsh summarized these
sentiments thus: "Under Vargas's direction a new unity has been formed.
The Puerto Rican Political Action Committee is the vehicle Vargas and his
allies have used to forge this unity."[54]

This rosy picture, however, while accurate, was not without wrinkles.
In 1991, I talked to Jorge Simón and Juan Figueroa about the relationship
between ethnicity, organization, and power. According to Simón, developments in the Puerto Rican community were met with fear from a power
structure dominated by whites and blacks. The coalitions that were built
based on the Puerto Rican swing vote, he argued, were viewed with
weariness.

Elites in Hartford didn't quite know what to make of the whole situation. Blacks saw Puerto Rican progress as a challenge to their conquests
and were more fearful than anybody else about someone coming along
and taking away the power they had struggled so hard to attain. Simón
saw the emerging community only beginning to develop the expertise necessary to translate demographic numbers into real power.

> Until we do that, I think we [will be] somewhat fragmented. We've never
> been a one-voice type of group that can direct power where [it needs] to be.
> What I see as a problem is that, because we are such a younger voice, and
> by younger I mean newer, we are looked upon by those who have been here
> so much longer as a yelping type of people, biting at the legs of these people

and being more of a nuisance than anything else. So long as we have to fight to maintain our people in the small numbers that we have in the legislature, on the council, without the strength to really impact on those that are there above us, we are not a threat to anyone. We should be looking to expand the base so that, yes, we want Eugenio Caro, we want Frances Sánchez, we want Edna Negrón, we want Juan Figueroa, but we can really effect what goes on in the South End, too; we may not want just a Hispanic there but maybe one who is sensitive to the needs of the Hispanic and get commitments from that person so we control that seat, too.[55]

"This is one of the issues of debate I have with PRPAC," said Juan Figueroa. While arguing that progressives should be concerned with issues, that the emphasis should be on securing collective goods, he recognized that identity politics was necessary:

There is a constant tension. I don't believe that our political efforts should be focused on ethnicity regardless of qualifications, beliefs, or principles. And there's a lot of people who don't care who they have in a position as long as it is a Puerto Rican. Up to a point, that is a legitimate position because it is a way to advance. Some people get into the qualifications polemic and you get swallowed up and you don't get anybody [elected]; but, on the other hand, some people insist on Puerto Ricans and they don't deliver, or they are not progressive, their qualifications are not the best, and you end up doing greater harm if you look at it from a progressive point of view. We haven't confronted [this situation] that much because the relative power that we have is nothing when you compare it to the whites and to the blacks.[56]

Having said that, it was with no small sense of irony that Figueroa related how his election to the chairmanship of the state assembly's Housing Committee came about. First, he had to fight to prevent its elimination. Then, in lobbying for the position, he had to put aside, for a moment, substantive arguments about the importance of housing. "The committee had as a chair a black representative from New Haven who was retiring. Because a black had held the seat—you know how these things get molded—the most likely possibility was another minority to step in, so I made that pitch and talked to the speaker, [Richard J. Balducci, D-New Britain], and he gave it to me."[57]

No one could argue, however, that Juan Figueroa was your stereotypical ethnic politician, the kind who was "always ready to smoke a cigar, take a drink, play a game of cards, or tell a story."[58] He defined himself as a progressive, a reformer, someone who was unlikely to follow the advice given to legislators by Martin Lomasney, the political czar of Boston's Ward Eight for almost fifty years: "Never write anything down when you can say it, never say anything when you can nod your head."[59]

Figueroa wrote things down, spoke his mind forcefully, and, when necessary, played the ethnic card.

The tension between ethnicity and expertise was real, and it was one
challenge facing PRPAC in 1991. Rebecca Brito, who was PRPAC 's president for a short while, put it this way: "We first think about securing the
position and then we consider the candidate's qualifications. There is
room for improvement in this area." [60]

The backdrop for PRPAC's success was colored by paradox: economic
prosperity was joined by urban deterioration. Although the Central Business District experienced a boom during the 1980s in the construction of
office space and the real estate market was active both in residential and
commercial areas, the homeless population increased, public schools became overcrowded, and the income gap between the poor, the middle, and
the upper class widened. In the early 1990s, boom became bust, and layoffs exacerbated the economic picture.

In 1992, of twelve homeless shelters in the twenty-nine-town Greater
Hartford region, nine were in Hartford. While total enrollment in the public schools increased by 3.2 percent from 1980 to 1991, elementary school
enrollment grew by 10 percent. Between 1980 and 1990, the number of
families below the poverty level increased by 18.4 percent, and the highest
concentrations of poor families were in the Puerto Rican and African
American neighborhoods of Clay Arsenal (54 percent), Sheldon-Charter
Oak (47 percent), Frog Hollow (46 percent), the Northeast (41 percent),
and the South Green (35 percent). Office vacancy rates in the early 1990s
were higher than 20 percent, which, according to city planners, were "the
highest they have been in recent memory." Unemployment increased from
7.7 to 10.4 percent, and by 1993 nearly ten thousand people had left the
city, lured by prospects for employment elsewhere, by reduced prices for
suburban homes, or both. [61]

Was the prize of identity politics hollow? Let us now complete this
analysis by looking at the relationship between context and action and
addressing the question of identity politics and urban power.

7   Identity and Power

WHEN, AT the end of 1995, Hartford made it to the front page of the *New York Times* with the headline "'Insurance Capital' Hartford Finds Itself without Its Net," the wording suggested that another president had told a U.S. city in trouble to "drop dead," as President Gerald Ford had twenty years earlier when he had said that New York City's fiscal crisis was none of the national government's business. The Hartford story, however, was not about the abdication of federal responsibility. It was not about the loss of entitlements. Instead, it was about the decision by Aetna Life and Casualty Company to sell its casualty and property divisions to the Travelers Group, Inc., a move that represented the loss of thirty-three hundred jobs, fifteen hundred in and around Hartford.

The loss of jobs was not a new problem. In 1982, one thousand workers had been sent packing following the dissolution of a Connecticut General subsidiary. In 1990, Aetna had reduced its workforce by eliminating twenty-six hundred positions. Two years later, Travelers announced that it would lay off five thousand workers by 1994. In this context, it was not hard to understand why one of every ten buildings in Hartford was abandoned in 1995 or why in the short span between 1990 and 1994 the city lost 11.1 percent of its population.

"We are a ghost town," Nicholas Carbone told the *Times*. Yet political officials and business leaders asserted that the wave of mergers, acquisitions, consolidations, and layoffs affecting Hartford did not signal the death of the city but an opportunity for new growth. A merger between Travelers and Aetna, for example, was seen as leading to an increase in cash reserves that would enable the company to expand its Hartford operations. As an industry spokesperson put it: "As we grow, employment opportunities should be strengthened. We've been here 150 years, and we're not leaving." At the same time, a study of the insurance industry reported that although higher-end jobs were not leaving the city, less-skilled jobs were being farmed out to states and countries with larger supplies of cheap labor. "If I were Mayor of Hartford," said Carbone, "I would hire the best lawyers out there and make it clear that there'd be no mergers unless the companies make an explicit commitment to Hartford. These people have an obligation to employees, and they have to be forced to meet it."[1]

The theme of this story has played itself out in Hartford time and again. The cast of characters has changed, but the tension between corporate interests and citizen needs has remained. During the eighteenth century, political entrepreneurs promoted political and economic initiatives that transformed Hartford. Throughout the nineteenth century, city and state were inextricably bound in the transformation of national politics that resulted from the creation of the Republican party. During the twentieth century, the city's manufacturing base, its powerful insurance industry, its flow of immigrants and migrants, and the ascendancy of business made Hartford a commonwealth in which corporations often dictated the terms of policies and government had to be forced to provide equal protection for its citizens. Puerto Ricans joined this process as immigrant-citizens in the wake of World War II, just as the city changed its political structure and brought the Republicans back to power. Thus, the political context in which the Puerto Ricans mobilized contained elements of both change and continuity.

This context both constrained and facilitated political action. Business hegemony, political reform, demographic and economic change, civic unrest, and a one-party system formed the structure of opportunities within which Puerto Ricans organized and mobilized. Changes in the racial makeup of the city also were important, forcing Puerto Ricans to factor the competing interests of African Americans (and vice versa) into their mobilization calculus. The challenge the Puerto Ricans faced was how to match capability with feasibility, in other words, how to strike a balance between what they could do and what the systemic setting allowed.

In meeting this challenge, ethnicity was a key resource, especially in the context of demographic growth, leadership development, and a sustained organizational drive. This combination of factors facilitated incorporation, although in absolute terms the process was protracted and arduous. In 1954, when Puerto Ricans came into the public's eye, and in 1969, when collective behavior put them in the limelight, integration was considered important but difficult to achieve, because of their troubled and troublesome quality of otherness. Yet even when their numbers were small, they sought full membership in the political society using the electoral process, focusing on mainland issues, and carrying on both insider and outsider models of leadership and mobilization. In 1977, as a result of the independent candidacy of Edwin Vargas, a convergence of insider and outsider strategies set the stage for the emergence of PRPAC, a group that became the most successful example of identity politics.

Identity politics was, however, equally welcome and problematic. Ethnicity was both expressive and rational, and Puerto Ricans used the electoral process mostly to address the issues that affected their daily lives. Island issues concerned them, but these never fully engaged the community. Radicals attempted to make the status of Puerto Rico a central issue but were not successful. Some shed this outlook and helped empower the community by combining insider and outsider mobilization strategies. Ethnic-based action broadened representation, but the latter did not fully translate into responsiveness. This failure was not related to a dissonance between ethnic *values* and the requirements of the situation. Neither was it the result of the inability of the Puerto Rican elites to recognize differences within the community in nativity, gender, or class.[2] The dissonance was instead between campaigning and governing. These were discrete processes that required *different uses* of ethnicity. Yet this problem was not addressed because it was not recognized in the first place.

Thus, ethnicity represented an asset and a challenge. Nonethnic factors affected the exercise of power as well. PRPAC's mobilization strategy was effective, but its relations with institutions and individuals were undermined by its relative lack of standing. The policy process was daunting, and PRPAC's strategy did not allow the group to develop policy expertise, forcing a reliance on allies whose commitment to a Puerto Rican agenda was marginal. Several obstacles prevented PRPAC from maintaining the loyalty of candidates it helped elect: preexisting preferences stood in the way of new commitments, elected officials wanted to be effective rather than merely right, and the process of governing revealed differences with PRPAC theretofore unknown to these officials.

THE CITY AS POLITICAL CONTEXT

Despite obvious and not surprising differences between what was known as Suckiaug to its Native Americans, Newtown and Harteford to its English settlers, and contemporary Hartford, there is a pattern to the city's political history: periodic waves of outmigration mixed with a regular flow of immigrants and migrants; an instrumentalist view of politics, seen as a means to personal salvation, as a tool in the acquisition and accumulation of wealth, and as a method for achieving equality and justice; a commitment to constitutionalism and popular government; and power arrangements based on a concentration-diffusion pattern, that is, narrow at the top and broad-based at the bottom. The changes in the "agenda of urban resource allocation" that Robert Salisbury correlates with good government political reforms in the 1940s were fought out in the city beginning at the turn of the century. What he calls "politics for profit"— votes give power, power provides favors, favors provide votes—did not break down in Hartford.[3]

To highlight these continuities is not to say that the more things change the more they stay the same but to suggest that an awareness of links to the past amplifies the scope of urban possibilities and provides a deeper perspective on more recent events.[4] Puerto Ricans are not the first group in the city's history to take advantage of the instrumental qualities of ascribed traits, and the legitimacy of this approach is partially sanctioned by its precedents. That instrumentalist approaches have been used in the pursuit of equality belies the notion that means and ends must always be in moral synchrony. Finally, to know that power can be simultaneously concentrated and broad-based and that this pattern has a long history is sobering. In light of this knowledge, the judgment that Puerto Ricans achieved limited political accomplishments might be more tempered and less harsh. In terms of socioeconomic progress, the Puerto Ricans' access to power was insufficient. In the context of historical developments, however, it was rapid and dramatic.

According to Coleman, Hartford is in the middle range between business-controlled and citizen-controlled urban settings. In Neubeck's and Ratcliff's view, the city's politics are too rich and complex to encase them in a single theoretical shell. They conclude that Carbone's regime raised expectations to a point that made it difficult for citizens to accept the inherent limits to city politics.[5] Both commentators are right. In the twentieth century, Hartford's tradition of theocratic rule based on popular consent found expression in a business commonwealth in which the corporate bias of public policy was prominent, although at times offset by class, racial, ethnic, and neighborhood challenges. The Puerto Ricans provide an example of a group that mobilized successfully, effecting change from below. In their case, economic changes and political reforms shaped political mobilization based on identity claims. Hartford's demographic reality during the postwar period, its one-party system, and its at-large elections made coalition politics indispensable in accessing power. This did not preclude coalition dominance by a single group, as Puerto Ricans demonstrated in 1992, although economic contraction and fiscal stress imposed severe constraints on the exercise of coalition power.

The dynamism of Hartford's political system is partially grounded in the persistence of inequality. Religious conflict, cleavages between city and town, liberals and conservatives, Yankees and immigrants, Republicans and Democrats, business and labor, white ethnics and blacks, blacks and Puerto Ricans—all signal forms of political inequality. This feature simultaneously limited and enabled political action, an ambivalent view but one that is rooted in history. And although there is a respectable strand in the urban politics literature that sees political inequality as nearly insurmountable, even the most pessimistic scholars urge us, in the end, to "keep hope alive."[6]

The question is whether hope can be kept alive on grounds other than simple faith. For example, is there anything else that context can tell us about the prospects for political equality? The Puerto Rican political experience in the United States is increasingly framed by the parameters of politics in cities such as Hartford. What are these parameters? An important one is size. A medium-sized city offers advantages for political action that a metropolis like New York does not. It permits easy access to city hall, proximity to elected officials, an accessible media, and small electoral districts that allow direct contact with large numbers of voters even when financial resources are scarce. In a city like Chicago, it is difficult for insurgents to mount credible challenges, as three independent Puerto Rican candidates from Westtown/Humboldt Park and Lakeside discovered in 1975 when they ran against incumbents backed by Richard Daley.[7]

The story of the Puerto Ricans in Hartford shows that in smaller contexts the potential for disruption is much higher. There Puerto Ricans enjoyed the advantages of demographic concentration without necessarily suffering the disadvantages associated with social distance. The existence of a distinct ethnic enclave facilitated political mobilization but did not prevent the development of social and political connections with other similarly concentrated groups.

Most important, in medium-sized cities campaign finance is not as daunting a challenge as it is in larger settings. In the 1973 Hartford Board of Education race, for example, María Sánchez spent about $0.18 per vote. By 1991, costs were considerably higher, yet in that year's election, candidates on the victorious ticket spent an average of $3,200 per candidate. This was twice as little as opponents of charter revision argued it would cost candidates to run if Hartford switched to a nonpartisan, council-manager form of government, and this argument was made in 1946!

Life in a medium-sized city does not necessarily have a differential effect on aggregate socioeconomic status. Data from the 1990 census show that Puerto Ricans are economically worse off in midsized cities than in big cities. For example, in 1989, at $12,032, the mean per capita household income of Puerto Ricans in the Los Angeles Metropolitan Statistical Area (MSA) was almost three times that of Puerto Ricans in the Lawrence-Haverill, Massachusetts, MSA. In the Hartford MSA, which corresponds roughly with the city's boundaries, the mean per capita household income of Puerto Ricans that year was only $6,095, or 32.6 percent that of the population as a whole.[8]

Because scale is not an independent variable, it does not necessarily account for economic disparities one way or the other. Yet this analysis shows that for Puerto Ricans, there is a positive association between life in a midsized city and *political participation and representation*, the two most important ingredients of political equality. There is evidence that this is also true for other Latino groups.[9] Furthermore, to the extent that political participation and representation lead to socioeconomic progress, the context provided by life in midsized cities might be an important factor in the process leading toward material advancement. The story that opens this chapter is illustrative of this point in two ways: it shows that corporate decision making plays a crucial role in the economic health of a city, but it also suggests that these decisions can be tempered by what the political stratum does and how it reacts to the moves of other actors.

IDENTITY POLITICS: EXPRESSIVENESS AND RATIONALITY

In the case of the Puerto Ricans in Hartford, identity politics was simultaneously an expressive process and one in which prior organization and instrumental rationality played a role.[10] Mobilization was driven by cost-benefit calculations, but rationality was mediated by psychosocial factors. The Puerto Rican Parade and the *Swank* magazine incident are clear examples of the latter. Moreover, ethnic awareness did not collapse into solipsism; instead, it led to power awareness, thus prompting the pursuit of concrete political objectives. When Puerto Ricans organized and mobilized around ethnicity—that is, when a pressure group articulated ethnic interests—they were able to access power. This was not a matter of pure will but the result of an interplay between objective and subjective factors.

Although the desire for economic betterment was important, the earliest Puerto Rican associations were religious and cultural. Examples include the Legión de María and the Rosario Cantado, which Olga Mele joined and founded, respectively, in the 1950s, local baseball leagues, the Puerto Rican Parade, and other cultural celebrations, such as the San Juan Bautista and Park Street Festivals. In 1996, religious activities and organizations were no longer prominent, but cultural events continued to draw significant resources and energy. Examples were the Orquesta de Cuatros de Connecticut, Inc., a musical ensemble and community organization founded in 1988, and the Concurso de Trovadores de la Nueva Inglaterra, a day-long feast of creole food and folk music established in 1990. These expressions of identity intertwined with status, although a key question that observers asked during the 1960s was whether Puerto Ricans would ever tackle issues other than those related to their culture.

This question revealed an underlying ignorance, because when Julián Vargas opened La Popular, Bodega Hispana, in 1956, it quickly became the meeting place for Puerto Ricans interested in politics. Regulars met to plot strategies to penetrate the Democratic party and, if necessary, to fight city hall. María Sánchez was a key member of this group, and her true cause was educational policy. When Wito Martínez decided to recruit Antonio Soto for the Republican party, he felt that politics was important for the community, although he did not know exactly why. Others saw clearly that politics was a means to advance a Puerto Rican agenda that included bilingual education, the hiring of Spanish-speaking police and firefighters, the official celebration of Puerto Rican holidays, and better employment and housing opportunities. These topics were discussed in private homes and on the baseball field. Furthermore, cultural events served as political platform. Politicians have always been a regular feature of the Puerto Rican Parade and of other festivals. I attended the Concurso de Trovadores in June 1994 and saw Hartford's mayor Mike Peters doing his bit to further identity politics by praising Puerto Rican culture and emphasizing diversity as a collective asset that benefited all Hartford residents.

Edwin Vargas, whose rhetoric and strategy had a class hue, recognized that ethnicity was a crucial factor in mobilizing Puerto Ricans. In 1985, he tossed aside his socialist ideology to support Nancy Meléndez, the ethnic candidate. Subsequently, whenever he ran a campaign he took advantage of his candidate's position on row B of the ballot by using the slogan "Vota por la B de Boricua" ("Vote for row B, for Boricua), which, instead of reminding voters of issues, appealed to their sense of identity.

José La Luz began his mobilizing activities by organizing farmworkers, and although he did not relinquish his labor outlook, his focus always was on Puerto Ricans. In Hartford he quickly jumped onto the ethnic bandwagon. Initially, his attitude was separatist, but by 1977 he realized that Puerto Ricans in Hartford were cultural, not radical, nationalists and that identity politics was effective only as an integrationist strategy.

Was the advancement of identity politics in Hartford an opportunistic utilization of ethnicity designed to promote economic interests? Many have made this claim. David Ward summarizes this view: "Ethnicity is a label to describe reactive responses of interest groups that have perceived detrimental alterations in the allocation principles of public policies. Their political loyalties do not, therefore, reflect their interests in ancestral foreign causes but rather their concern over threats to their well-being from competing interest groups."[11]

Identity politics in Hartford was often reactive, employed to demand changes in the allocation of economic, social, and political benefits granted by the state. These demands were frequently framed by intergroup competition. But if ethnicity was a smokescreen for interest group activity, why would people answer its call? Either they were deceived or ethnicity appealed to them in ways that class did not. Or perhaps there is a third alternative: that ethnicity was both expressive of ancestral background and politically instrumental. This was, in fact, the case in Hartford. When Puerto Ricans organized, ethnicity was a central category, expressing cultural concerns and rallying people around sociopolitical demands; when they mobilized, ethnicity was often the triggering factor.

The argument that ethnic interests mask underlying economic concerns, effecting a kind of cultural placebo, makes ancestry the litmus test of authenticity. On the one hand, because identities are shaped by the politics of place, ethnicity does not need to be exclusively or predominantly related to a concern with an ancestral homeland to be authentic. On the other hand, to argue that ethnicity is a smokescreen for economic interests or a superficial index of social stratification suggests behavioralist and false consciousness explanations often used to account for political action.[12]

There is no point in denying the socioeconomic referents of ethnicity, but this does not justify reducing ethnicity to class. Douglas Gurak and Mary Kritz, for example, compared Puerto Ricans with Hispanic immigrants to the Northeast in the 1970s and found that in the Puerto Rican case ethnic identity in the second generation correlated with low socioeconomic status. Lloyd Rogler and his collaborators, however, found that ethnic identity was strong even when there were higher levels of acculturation among second-generation Puerto Rican families.[13] What these findings suggest is that ethnic identity is not driven by a single logic and that its expressions range from ancestral callings to leisure-time pursuits.[14] These brackets include a variety of expressive and instrumental examples, from ethnic pageants to the commercialization of ethnic symbols, from demands for better housing to struggles for political representation; and sometimes, as the case of Puerto Ricans in Hartford illustrates, the search for dignity and respect is expanded to include demands for jobs and better educational opportunities. For them, identity coincided with ancestry and it cut across class and generation; its symbolism was public and politically powerful.

Identity Politics: Interest Articulation

How did Puerto Ricans in Hartford articulate their identity claims? Initially, society was the principal venue; after 1969, the state became the target of action. Their agenda was centered on mainland issues and concerns. It is, in fact, interesting and remarkable that the intensity of nationalistic feeling among Puerto Ricans was not matched by an equally intense preoccupation with Puerto Rico's colonial status. The relationship between their identification as a culturally distinct group and their support of sovereignty for the island was inversely proportional. They defined themselves as Puerto Rican Americans and were intent on showing their fellow citizens that they could adopt the American way of life without losing their culture. To do this, they celebrated ethnicity while penetrating partisan structures, marching, rioting, organizing, and mobilizing independently to obtain cultural and political concessions.

Strategy: Electoral Politics

The assertion that before 1970 Puerto Rican electoral efforts in the United States were all but nonexistent is wrong.[15] In Hartford, electoral politics was a staple of Puerto Rican activities since the 1950s, when only a handful lived in the city.[16] As the community grew in numbers, so did its involvement and the number of Puerto Rican candidates running for office. Electoral participation was not sporadic or inconsistent; it was simply not prominent relative to the society at large.

The work of old guard leaders, such as Olga Mele, Julián Vargas, María Sánchez, and José Cruz, shows that electoral politics was very important to the community's early leadership. Their politics quickly became the politics of the local Democratic party. In 1964, they organized the Puerto Rican Parade under the slogan "Register and Vote"; the following year, they formed their first political club, the Puerto Rican Democrats of Hartford, although others had been working in local campaigns since 1955, first by registering voters and then, in 1957, by working for the election of James Kinsella. Of the cadre of community leaders that emerged during the 1970s, those who responded to the old guard were prodded to enter electoral politics through the Democratic party.[17] There were other venues, but, from the outset, electoral politics was a key component of a strategy aimed at social and economic betterment.

Determining electoral participation, however, is difficult because the data are either not available or unreliable. For example, based on 1970 census data for population, the registration rate for Puerto Ricans is 44.8 percent. But on the basis of local population estimates, the rate decreases to 13.5 percent. Using electoral support for Puerto Rican candidates as a proxy for turnout, it is clear that although participation was generally low, it had peaks and valleys.

Citywide support for Puerto Rican candidates is another proxy for participation and for the role of ethnicity in the process. The lowest level of citywide support for an elected candidate was 12.6 percent of the vote and the highest was 73 percent. Support surged when a Puerto Rican Demo-

Table 8. Electoral Support for Puerto Rican Candidates, 1971–1991

Year	Candidate	Total Votes	% of City Total
1971	William Pérez (R)	7,890	37.7
1973	René Rodríguez (R)	4,027	16.3
	María Sánchez (D)ᵃ	4,955	20.1
1975	José Garay (R)	2,769	13.0
1977	José Garay (R)	2,809	14.9
	Edwin Vargas (I)	2,547	13.5
	María Sánchez (D)ᵃ	3,133	16.6
1979	Antonio González (D)ᵃ	10,458	48.5
	José Garay (R)	3,255	15.0
1981	Gerardo Zayas (D)ᵃ	11,356	44.2
	María Sánchez (D)ᵃ	3,244	12.6
1983	Nancy Meléndez (D)ᵃ	11,344	57.4
	Angel Ocasio (R)	3,243	16.4
1985	Nancy Meléndez (D)ᵃ	12,564	60.6
	María Sánchez (D)ᵃ	4,307	20.7
	Antonio Santiago (I)	1,080	5.2
1987	María B. González (D)ᵃ	6,981	38.7
	Eugenio Caro (PFC)ᵃ	5,147	28.5
1989	Frances Sánchez (D)ᵃ	8,009	50.2
	Eugenio Caro (PFC)ᵃ	4,379	27.4
	María B. González (P)ᵇ	1,410	8.8
1991	Yolanda Castillo (D)ᵃ	6,077	73.0
	Fernando Comulada (D)ᵃ	5,570	67.0
	Eugenio Caro (PFC)ᵃ	4,374	52.6

SOURCE: Data assembled by José E. Cruz from reports by the *Hartford Courant* and Hartford's town and clerk's office.
ᵃ Elected.
ᵇ Petitioning candidate.

crat ran for the council for the first time. When PRPAC entered the scene in 1985, backing by Puerto Rican voters hit the highest point since 1971, and when a PRPAC candidate was endorsed by the Democratic party in 1989, her score was 12 percentage points higher than for the candidate endorsed by the party but opposed by PRPAC in 1987. In 1991, when candidates ran supported by a coalition of Puerto Ricans, African Americans, and white ethnics, they captured the highest proportion ever of the citywide vote (see Table 8).

Focus: Mainland versus Island

The push and pull of mainland issues and homeland concerns is central to the Puerto Rican experience in the United States. Although the presence of Puerto Ricans on the continent preceded the acquisition of the island by the United States, the process of community formation is an epiphenomenon of the colonial relationship established in 1898. For this reason, Puerto Rican politics in the United States has often been interstitial, although not all leaders and organizations have articulated this quality of in-betweenness in quite the same way.

During the postwar period, Puerto Ricans did not eschew island concerns, but the work of most community agencies focused on mainland issues. A radical ferment during the late 1960s and early 1970s proposed a complete subordination of local struggles to the national liberation movement, but by 1980 this movement was all but dead. The 1989–90 debate around the proposed plebiscite on the status of Puerto Rico led to a surge of interest and mobilization, but when Congress decided to do nothing, the issue went back into remission.[18]

In Hartford, the homeland-mainland dynamic was even more tilted toward mainland issues than elsewhere. Politically, Puerto Ricans moved more in the interstices of integration and marginality than between island and continental issues. The archives of the now-defunct Department of Puerto Rican Community Affairs in the United States contain a reference to forty tobacco workers from the Hartford area who flew to Puerto Rico allegedly to vote in the 1960 general election.[19] In August 1972, Gilberto Camacho requested absentee ballots from the national office because "there are contract workers that go back to Puerto Rico to vote a few days or a few weeks before the end of their contract thus losing at least $180 which they would get if they finished their term."[20] Camacho may not have been aware of it, but in February of that year, the Speaker of the Puerto Rican legislature's House of Representatives, Angel Viera Martínez, told the commonwealth's Secretary of Labor, Julia Rivera de Vincenti, that "the only persons that are allowed to cast absentee ballots are the members of the armed forces."[21] In any event, participation in Puerto Rican elections was not encouraged by the commonwealth's office.

Was the behavior of farmworkers representative of those in the urban community? Perhaps in the 1950s, but not in 1960 or thereafter. The first batch of Puerto Rican farmworkers to come to Connecticut in 1951 consisted of three hundred men. I found no records documenting the number of workers who failed to return to Puerto Rico, but it is likely that the initial group of three hundred provided Hartford with its first spate of new residents.[22] At that point, homeland concerns must have been prominent, given the recency of migration. Subsequently, between five and eight hundred farmworkers were recruited during the summer; the highest number was 984 in 1958. In that year Puerto Ricans in the city were estimated at close to five thousand. Thus, tobacco workers were a significant proportion—about 20 percent—but as time went by, that percentage decreased, and by 1970, even if we assume that recruitment continued at the peak figure, the proportion was probably around 5 percent. Consequently, after

1960, their behavior would not have been representative of the community's. Moreover, since they were on the outskirts of the city, confined to the tobacco fields and camps, they were hardly part of the community anyway, and those who moved to the city—probably an even smaller proportion of Hartford's Puerto Rican population since many farmworkers did go back to the island—eventually no longer had farmworker status and left that outlook behind.

From the evidence, it is hard to tell whether city residents voted in island elections in person or by casting absentee ballots. Until the mid-1970s, absentee ballots were not available to mainland Puerto Ricans, except military personnel. But even after more categories of people were allowed to use absentee ballots, it is unlikely that many did since to do so they needed the assistance of the commonwealth's office. In addition, they had to prove temporary residency status. Gilberto Camacho only encouraged contract workers to participate in island elections. He wanted Puerto Rican residents to register to vote in Hartford.[23]

In 1976, at a meeting organized by Camacho's office to plan a voter registration drive, the assembled community leaders were told that the governor of Puerto Rico wanted mainland Puerto Ricans to be "encouraged to enter the mainstream of political life in places where they live and work in order to obtain the full power needed to improve the quality of their lives."[24] Thus, although Puerto Rican residents were interested in island politics—they were kept informed of island events through family, friends, travel, and the community press—they participated in Hartford politics.[25] The curve of participation in local elections was like a sine wave, although the cycle was irregular. De facto disfranchisement, however, was determined more by structural conditions than by individual characteristics or community preferences. Groups such as Voto Boricua therefore focused their efforts on the elimination of obstacles to registration, even though they also emphasized the importance of civic participation.

Puerto Rican nationalists and radicals did try to steer the attention of the community from day-to-day issues to island issues. In 1971, for example, at a forum held at the University of Connecticut, Alejandro La Luz exhorted students to follow in the footsteps of Pedro Albizu Campos, the leader of Puerto Rico's nationalist movement, and not get distracted by joining radical groups in the United States. The PSP registered voters to cast absentee ballots and recruited poll watchers to volunteer their services on the island. At the 1982 Statewide Puerto Rican Convention, a Hartford-based initiative sponsored by the commonwealth's office under the leadership of Carlos Piñero, PSP members pushed hard for the adoption of their program, which gave the goal of independence for Puerto

Rico the highest priority. In 1983, Víctor Gerena, a Puerto Rican born in the Bronx and raised in Hartford, stole more than $7 million from a Wells Fargo branch in West Hartford, and in 1984 it became known that he was a member of Los Macheteros, an island-based independentista group that claimed responsibility for the robbery.[26]

Not only did Puerto Rican students not follow in the footsteps of Albizu Campos, but they failed to join U.S.-based radical movements to any significant extent. No one I spoke to in Hartford had any recollection of people other than party members paying heed to the PSP's call for absentee voting and poll watching on the island. The hard line adopted by party members at the 1982 convention alienated many participants and was an ingredient in the failure of the effort. In his chronicle of the Machetero episode, Ronald Fernández shows how the class symbolism of the robbery completely overshadowed its political intent. Puerto Ricans (and others) cheered Gerena, identifying him as a Robin Hood. So long as he represented a working-class David who inflicted damage on an exploitative Goliath, his deed was applauded. Once people realized that Gerena had acted in support of Puerto Rico's independence, however, they rejected him, sneered at his motive, and suggested that he had been taken for a ride by Los Macheteros.

In 1986, PRPAC issued a resolution condemning as a civil rights violation the arrest of a group of independentistas in Puerto Rico in connection with the Wells Fargo heist. But one looks in vain for indications that this case moved Hartford's Puerto Rican community beyond a sporadic expression of solidarity. The campaign of the PSP and its allies to free those arrested and to publicize the island's colonial status was marginal. As far as I can tell from interviews and documents, two rallies in support of the defendants took place, one each in 1986 and 1988.[27] But what little was done was not very effective, in part because of differences within the Hartford left.[28]

When the 1989–90 debate on the proposed plebiscite on the status of Puerto Rico raised the question of whether mainland Puerto Ricans should be allowed to vote, the overwhelming consensus among Hartford's Puerto Rican elite was that they should. In a policy forum held in New York, Edwin Vargas presented a spirited argument for participation, but on that occasion he was representing the National Congress for Puerto Rican Rights—a group with a programmatic interest in the status issue—not PRPAC. Still, Vargas began his presentation by regretting that the issue had surfaced to, once again, "threaten unity in our community," while simultaneously suggesting that it might be an ephemeral concern.[29] The issue, in fact, was forced on Congress by island leaders; once Congress killed the initiative, mainland interest faded. Hartford's Puerto Ricans went on with their lives, largely untouched by the brief controversy. PRPAC in particular kept itself busy figuring out how to make further inroads into local power.

Structure: Insiders, Outsiders, and Convergence

María Sánchez was the epitome of the ward-heeling politician, even if she conducted most of her business from behind the counter of her newsstand in Albany Avenue. While Sánchez was clear about the reasons for being a regular partisan, her version of the political exchange was limited. She was patient and loyal but knew when to be adamant about demands.

Mildred Torres was also a moderate insider, not so much as a party regular but as a loyal Democrat. Although bargaining and compromise were the forte of the initial group of leaders who coalesced around her 1979 candidacy, she was also associated with PRPAC. Moderates tend to use partisan reform as a vantage point for access,[30] but in Hartford they carved out their entry in part through independent groups such as Voto Boricua and MUJER. Their strategy was colored by a quasi-technocratic attitude that emphasized political acumen, knowledge of the rules of the game, and autonomy from the Democratic party.

The role of outsider never suffered from a scarcity of players. Some remained obscure figures, while others were prominent in the affairs of the community. Examples of the latter are Alejandro La Luz, who began his work during the 1960s, José Claudio and Eugenio Caro, who were highly visible in the early 1970s, and Edwin Vargas and José La Luz, who during the mid-1970s represented the far left among the Young Turks.

In Hartford, as elsewhere, demand-protest combined with mobilization that took advantage of the resources provided by community agencies. These agencies emerged as offshoots of the charitable spirit and were subsequently buttressed and expanded through state and federal programs. The San Juan Center was created by the Catholic Church. The Institute for the Hispanic Family also had church support through Catholic Charities. Groups such as La Casa de Puerto Rico, TAINO Housing, and the Hispanic Health Council were mostly funded by the government and foundations. These groups were not marginal, but they mediated between the community and the state, providing services and advocacy. In some cases, they employed militants and activists from the PLP and the Socialist party, but they also employed unaffiliated nationalists. Indeed, the use of community agencies as a base for militant activities was a constant source of irritation for people such as Gilberto Camacho.[31]

The emergence of the PLP in 1969 was a rudimentary expression of convergence. The party had a radical shell, a mainstream kernel, and

never went far beyond protests and rallies. For years, many tried to organize an effective pressure group, but success eluded them. In 1977, the
independent candidacy of Edwin Vargas was a second trial run for convergence. When Vargas and La Luz made the transition from pure radicalism to electoral pragmatism, they became the link between insider and
outsider strategies that crystallized in 1985 as PRPAC. Convergence resulted in an interlocking model of political mobilization. The connecting
parts were quid pro quo politics and up-front challenges. Its tools were
bargaining and compromise, community pressure, intrapartisan alliances,
and coalition building.

URBAN POWER: ACCESS

A discussion of the relationship between identity and power in Hartford
must begin by emphasizing that political mobilization had a limited impact on longstanding social and economic inequalities afflicting Puerto
Ricans. The power structure was not foreclosed. Instead, it was permeable—that is, sometimes insulated and sometimes penetrable. Pluralist
power succession was possible but problematic. Puerto Ricans accumulated political capital, marshalled resources, and achieved coalition dominance. But while identity politics facilitated representation, it was not
equally useful in promoting responsiveness through the exercise of coalition power.

In comparative terms, Puerto Rican political development occurred at
breakneck speed. For example, Italians organized their first political club,
the Italian American Democrats of Hartford, in 1959, seventy-nine years
after arrival. Puerto Ricans created their first civic association barely fourteen years after settlement, to register voters. The first political club, the
Puerto Rican Democrats of Hartford, was organized twenty-four years
after arrival. The first Italian representative took office twenty-nine years
after the great migration from southern Italy, and Puerto Ricans did the
same thirty-two years after coming to Hartford. These intervals were
close, but the Italian official, Salvator D'Esopo, went to the state legislature, while the Puerto Rican, María Sánchez, took a seat on the board of
education.[32] Yet eighty-three years passed before an Italian, Dominick J.
DeLucco, was elected mayor of Hartford, an event of purely symbolic significance since charter revision in 1946 made the mayoralty subordinate
to the city council. In contrast, in 1992, a Puerto Rican, Yolanda Castillo,
was selected the council's majority leader, and in 1994 Eugenio Caro occupied the position of deputy mayor, posts with far more power than the
mayor's. Puerto Rican accomplishments occurred in about half a century,
which was a short interval, especially compared with that for African

Americans, who had to wait seventy-nine years to elect their first council-man and more than a century to elect the city's first black mayor. What explains the relatively rapid acquisition of power by Puerto Ricans in Hartford? Puerto Rican politics during the 1970s was the politics of the social service agencies. Daniel Bell and Virginia Held write that "the community action provisions of the Poverty Act of 1964 established the basis for neighborhood organization by community groups."At the national level, Jeffrey Berry sees the rise of interest group activity in connection with the civil rights and antiwar movements of the 1960s.[33]

Puerto Ricans in Hartford, however, began to organize as early as 1955, almost a decade before the War on Poverty and the civil rights movement were in full swing.[34] They organized continuously, nurturing their impetus on cultural needs and a desire for economic betterment. Between 1956 and 1975, economic betterment was largely pursued through community agencies. In 1975, there were at least twelve organizations providing various services. Based on census figures, this meant one group/agency for every seven hundred Puerto Ricans in the city; based on local estimates, the ratio was sixteen hundred to one. But these groups provided indirect support to political activities. They were otherwise politically impaired since their primary task was to satisfy their clients. Also, agency administrators were busy developing programs, chasing grants, and managing resources.

Third-sector politics drew wedges among political players. The conflict between Wilber Smith and Yasha Escalera at the Comerieño meeting is one example. The protestations of Olga Mele, Eugenio Caro, and José Cruz are another instance of third sector rivalry that stood in the way of political solidarity. The link between politics and social services generated political capital but also presented constraints for independent political action.

A small group of Puerto Ricans that included Julián Vargas, María Sánchez, Esther Jiménez, and Antonio González were recognized within the Democratic party. Yet with only the voice of Sánchez on the town committee and that as party regulars these pioneers ranked low in the partisan pecking order, their claims for increased representation were either ignored or kept at bay. Within this group, only Sánchez had sufficient recognition and standing to be politically credible and influential in Hartford.[35]

It is worth noting how an observer characterized Puerto Rican political participation during the 1970s. Coleman writes: "The organization of a politically apathetic Puerto Rican community occurred due to its opposition to the Process memo."[36] This statement both understates the role Puerto Ricans played in that fight and reveals nothing about how their involvement crystallized. Puerto Ricans were a barely visible minority with low levels of voter registration and participation. But as a community they were clearly struggling to make themselves be seen and heard. This view of the community as apathetic prior to the mobilizations of 1975 and beyond was nonetheless widespread.

Based on her interviews of "influential Puerto Rican men in Hartford" in the early 1970s, Madelyn Colon drew a portrait of Puerto Rican politics whose most prominent feature was a largely ineffectual and unqualified cadre of leaders lacking substantive issues and whose practice was tinged with shades of corruption. She wrote: "There is a definite apathy on the part of Puerto Ricans in the city. . . . Frequently, Puerto Ricans have no time to become completely involved." [37]

In his study of Puerto Rican political behavior in Hartford in 1970, Kernstock came to conclusions similar to but far more extensive than Colon's. Based on a community survey, Kernstock found them unable to conceptualize or understand anything beyond the simplest political ideas and unwilling to communicate with community or political leaders.[38] Seeing only incoherence in their political development, he doubted that political socialization could proceed any further. Kernstock alleged that ethnic correlates did not appear to have much impact on the political behavior of Puerto Ricans.[39] He concluded that "there seems to be little opportunity for [Puerto Ricans] to play a significant role as an ethnic bloc in Hartford's political arena" and offered a dismal prognosis: "It does not seem likely that traditional indigenous leadership can be developed." [40] The hurdles were far too great: out-groups blocked opportunities for power, Puerto Rican organizations were controlled by cliques, and Puerto Ricans didn't seem willing to participate.

From these assessments, the statement that the offensive portions of the Greater Hartford Process memo thrust Puerto Ricans into action begs the question how such mobilization was possible at that point in time. Given the previous assertions of political insignificance, incoherence, and political apathy, it would seem that mobilization materialized out of thin air. The emergence of PRPAC and its victories become equally incomprehensible. Why were they able to mobilize as they did?

How the society perceived and treated the Puerto Ricans was an important factor in their emergence as an ethnic group. Harry Bailey and Ellis Katz argue that "the discriminatory practices of the majority of the society have been important in making ethnicity politically salient and in causing the formation of secondary groups based on ethnicity." Similarly, in her analysis of the politicization of Puerto Rican ethnicity, Judith Herbstein argues that an ethnic group is "a segment within an ethnic population which collectively organizes, at least at the local level, in response to the power structure of the national society." Herbstein agrees that ethnicity emerges in the intersection between ascriptive traits and structural conditions, but she confuses the emergence of ethnicity with its professionalization and gives little credit to Puerto Ricans themselves by emphasizing that ethnicity was merely a "label" given to them from the outside by labor unions, political parties, and the commonwealth's office in New York.[41]

Puerto Ricans in Hartford became an ethnic group as the result of the interplay between endogenous and exogenous factors. Ethnic awareness manifested as a sense of self in the context of place, but place was not the sole determinant of how and when identity surfaced and developed. Moreover, although national policies and events played a role, identity politics was fundamentally shaped by local interactions. Even though ethnicity was prompted by "labeling," this was not arbitrary; after all, these immigrants *were* Puerto Ricans and stood out as the newest "Other."

Political Responses to Exogenous Factors

The political-economic context provided both opportunities and constraints. In Hartford's one-party system, private power exerted a considerable influence on public policy. Although insurance companies were prominent in the city, manufacturing was important. Hartford's products ranged from horse nails and plumbing and heating supplies to atomic reactors and space hardware. Historically, the tobacco industry was also significant. As manufacturing jobs disappeared, the service sector grew but jobs for city dwellers declined. Thus, in 1980, the labor force participation rate of Hartford residents was lower than in 1960, even though the number of jobs in the city increased by 22 percent between 1965 and 1980, from 117,780 to 143,180. As the commercial-real estate boom of the 1980s ended, the service sector took a turn for the worse, leaving many stranded on the unemployment lines.[42] In 1990, 11 percent of the city's labor force was jobless, but for Puerto Ricans the rate was 18 percent, and 48 percent of Puerto Rican households had incomes below the poverty line.

Table 9 illustrates the reductions Hartford suffered during this period in the financial, insurance, and real estate sectors, in addition to losses in manufacturing jobs. These losses were partially offset by gains in the agricultural, forestry, fishing and mining, transportation, and business and repair sectors. Thus, although Hartford's labor force participation rate remained stable at about 61 percent, its rate was not as high as the rate for the state or six other cities (see Table 10). In contrast, the labor force participation rate among Puerto Ricans was 56 percent in 1990.

Since its transformation into a business commonwealth, an ideology

Table 9. Changes in Manufacturing and Financial, Insurance, and Real Estate (FIRE)
Jobs in Hartford in Comparative Perspective, 1980–1990

	1980	1990	% Change
Connecticut			
Manufacturing	458,816	346,552	−24.5
FIRE	118,702	176,421	+48.6
Bridgeport			
Manufacturing	23,847	15,846	−33.6
FIRE	2,916	4,427	+51.8
Hartford			
Manufacturing	13,742	8,656	−37.0
FIRE	9,096	8,770	−3.6
New Britain			
Manufacturing	14,570	8,416	−42.2
FIRE	2,785	3,849	+37.9
New Haven			
Manufacturing	11,619	9,545	−17.9
FIRE	2,403	3,418	+42.2
New London			
Manufacturing	3,376	2,225	−34.1
FIRE	322	570	+77.0
Waterbury			
Manufacturing	18,410	13,904	−24.5
FIRE	1,927	3,156	+63.8
Windham			
Manufacturing	2,730	1,737	−36.4
FIRE	337	561	+66.5

SOURCE: 1990 Census sample data assembled by Office of Policy and Management, State of
Connecticut.

that favors private power has prevailed in Hartford. During the 1950s and
1960s, the power of the insurance companies to dictate redevelopment
policy, for example, was nearly complete; Constitution Plaza, a complex
of office buildings and public space located downtown, is a testament to
that power. Throughout the 1970s, corporate influence was significant
but not monolithic: this is the period in which Carbone used his links
to the corporations and the White House to effect redistributive policies;
the arrangements that gave city hall a slice of the profits from the operation of the Civic Center is a good example.[43] As noted earlier, their analysis of this period led Clavel and others to declare Hartford a progressive
city, but these efforts had a strong autocratic and corporatist flavor and
ended up pitting the city against the suburbs, the governor against the city
council, and blacks and Puerto Ricans against business and political elites.
Racial/ethnic conflict was endemic. Restrictive voter registration procedures and literacy requirements to vote discouraged universal political
participation.

Table 10. Hartford Labor Force Participation Rates in
Comparative Perspective, 1980–1990

	Percentage of Persons 16 and Over in Labor Force	
	1980	1990
Connecticut	65.3	69.0
Bridgeport	59.8	64.6
Hartford	60.4	60.5
New Britain	64.4	65.3
New Haven	56.4	62.5
New London	63.9	68.1
Waterbury	60.8	65.0
Windham	63.1	64.9

SOURCE: 1990 Census data assembled by Policy Development and
Planning Division, Office of Policy and Management, State of
Connecticut.

For Puerto Ricans, the immediate consequences of these characteristics and changes were unemployment, poverty, welfare dependency, and political marginality. But low socioeconomic status did not deter political action. In this deteriorating environment, they found plenty of causes to rally around and mobilize: redevelopment initiatives, poor housing, and a sense that political representation favored downtown interests rather than the city's neighborhoods. Ethnicity was the prime mover. They said to themselves: We are Puerto Ricans. Although we don't look like Americans, we are that too, and we need to show everyone that we will not be denied. We are poor and disfranchised *because* we are Puerto Ricans, and it is as Puerto Ricans that we must organize and mobilize to make progress.

The organizational life of the community was intense and varied, with groups forming continuously from 1955 on to serve the gamut of perceived needs, from cultural affirmation to research, advocacy, revolutionary change, and electoral representation. Even when the leadership was less well prepared, organization and mobilization were relatively constant. As more financially stable and better-educated leaders emerged, political action became more effective.

To the extent that the configuration of the economy promoted population flight to the suburbs, Puerto Ricans benefited. The increase in the number of Puerto Ricans in the context of a shrinking overall population resulted in added demographic muscle. And as whites left for the suburbs, the better-prepared Puerto Rican leaders moved into the positions of power left behind. Economic changes favored social and political action, but these were dependent on such factors as when and how Puerto Ricans organized, the kind of leadership they had, and the kinds of coalitions they developed. In the absence of these subjective interventions, white flight, for example, would have been irrelevant. And what is distinctive about these emerging patterns is that their common denominator was the ethnic factor.

Political obstacles provoked selective involvement rather than alienation. Redevelopment policy, for example, which some informants correctly identified as dominated by private power, fueled political action — as a mobilizing issue and as a catalytic agent for neighborhood-based as opposed to downtown-oriented development. The secretiveness of the GHP incensed Puerto Ricans from the outset; dogged attempts to envelop GHP's proposals in the mantle of technical rationality did not insulate Carbone and the city council from heated attacks.

The mixed and paradoxical character of the Puerto Ricans' political action is clear in their perceptions, which guided it, of the responsiveness of Hartford's political system. For example, in the assertions by the PLP that they had "tried to deal with City Hall with no results," and in PSP allegations of collusion between GHP and government officials, Puerto Ricans perceived the political system as unresponsive. In the various attempts at penetrating the Democratic party, the perception was that it was up for grabs, that inclusion was possible although not automatic. At other times city hall was seen as a countervailing power, as in efforts to have city or state officials help the community redress grievances against corporations and other third parties.

Political Responses to Endogenous Factors

Puerto Ricans were able to mobilize because they had a history of organizational efforts behind them and a good measure of organizational resources before them. Demographic growth, leadership development, and organizational momentum were the internal factors that made their emergence possible. The latter included voter registration, initially carried out in the heat of electoral battles and later through the focused efforts of groups such as Voto Boricua. In fact, during the mid-1980s such efforts became well funded and systematic through the Atrévete campaign, a national program sponsored by the Office of the Commonwealth of Puerto Rico to promote voter education and registration among Puerto Ricans in the United States.

In 1975 and thereafter, Puerto Ricans mobilized when their capacity for local action intersected with events that were perceived as insults to their dignity or as attempts to take something away from them.[44] The GHP memo and later the ethnic jokes in *Swank* magazine triggered mobilization, either through existing outlets, such as La Casa de Puerto Rico and the PSP, or through new ones, such as the Committee of 24 and the coalition that gave Peter Libassi the Tory award. The rate of group formation both sustained organizational impetus and put a strain on limited human resources. The Puerto Ricans were not always effective, but they were certainly not inactive; the combination of cumulative resources and crisis facilitated their capacity for action.

Most important, political mobilization was driven by culture and language. In Hartford's changing political and economic landscape, these were constant concerns, determining responses as dissimilar as Olga Mele's religious initiatives during the 1950s—the celebration of the Rosario Cantado, her work with the Legion of Mary—and the mobilization against *Swank* magazine. The quest for economic progress was always important, but the desire for dignity and respect and even spirituality were key catalytic agents, forceful enough to override the constraints that discouraged political action. Comments from Olga Mele illustrate this dynamic: "We complained, María Sánchez and I, that we couldn't confess because there were no Spanish priests. We used to pay priests to come from New York so we could confess, so the church saw that there was a need and in 1955 Father Cooney was appointed to St. Peter's on Main Street and he was put in charge of the Hispanics and that's when he decided to create the San Juan Center."[45]

This cultural element was an important link between ethnic awareness and power awareness. In other words, ethnic issues and needs correlated with a sense of how the relative advantages of out-groups compared with those enjoyed by Puerto Ricans. Such comparisons shaped and promoted mobilization. PRPAC was not the only example of such a group, but it was by far the most successful.

URBAN POWER: EXERCISE

Contingency Factors

What factors account for the inability of Puerto Ricans to close the gap between representation and responsiveness? In 1981, Paul Peterson argued that structural conditions at the local level made it difficult, if not virtually impossible, for groups and citizens to have a prominent role in policy formation. Free-rider problems, closed decision-making processes, irrelevant partisan organizations, and issues of secondary importance, among others, were key factors in why he characterized the impact of organized groups as marginal.[46] More important and more limiting, however, was the place of localities, specifically their subordination, in the federal system.[47] But the paramount determinant of group marginality was the inherent and ineluctable interest of localities to promote development policies.[48]

While formidable, the critical response to Peterson produced only amendments to his argument. Browning, Marshall, and Tabb, for example, challenged the thesis that the economic determinants of urban policy were more important than political factors but concluded that political choices were constrained by the level of intergovernment support. Although they found that local political mobilization had a significant impact on policy responsiveness, other variables, such as the demographic makeup of the city and public opinion, also played important roles.[49] Similarly, Logan and Swanstrom rejected "the notion that there is a market logic of capitalism to which urban policy at all levels must submit," while recognizing that the limits to the scope and character of city policies are set by the national political economy and political structure.[50] In his *A Phoenix in the Ashes*, Mollenkopf provided the most detailed refutation of Peterson's economic model by showing how in New York City the Koch administration "pursued policies directly contrary to economic interests, while its efforts to promote private investment were motivated by political rather than economic concerns."[51] Lurking in the background of his account, however, was the federal government, providing resources and shaping local policies, playing a role that *A Phoenix in the Ashes* understates but that his previous book, *The Contested City*, highlights.[52]

Logan and Swanstrom's book is baffling because of the mutually exclusive answers it offers to the question of what determines local policy. For example, according to Parkinson, urban policy under Margaret Thatcher responded to ideology rather than to rational economic calculus.[53] But in the convergence of public policy in London and New York, Fainstein saw evidence of a single substance driving decisions, namely, global economic imperatives.[54] Sassen, by contrast, argued that "the fact that there is great variety in the local expression of economic restructuring and in local political responses and initiatives does not necessarily refute the proposition that economic restructuring is the dominant force in shaping local development. That variety describes a range of possibilities, not necessarily a systemic property."[55] Perhaps these opposite assessments should be regarded as proof that a single logic can produce different outcomes. Another possibility is that the question of policy determination ought to be answered through a historical rather than a theoretical analysis. Thus, in regard to the impact of economic restructuring on local policy, Walton argues that outcomes are determined not by ideology, as suggested by Parkinson, and not by economic restructuring itself, as noted by Fainstein and Sassen, but by the "interaction of the scope and timing of market reorganization and the history and organizational resources of local communities."[56]

Of course, the distinction between history and theory is deceptive, and to suggest that models that are deduced from a theoretical logic rather than from the ground up are inherently arbitrary is no less crude a form of positivism than the assertion that facts speak for themselves. But Walton's point is well taken because it avoids teleological errors by placing the causality and character of outcomes within the intersection between capability and feasibility—in the reconciliation of what political actors can do and what the systemic setting allows.

Such is the focus of what I call a contingency theory of power, which in the case of Puerto Ricans in Hartford means that the relationship between representation and responsiveness—that is, the exercise of power—was mediated by features of the economic, political, and fiscal setting, the context of political agency, and the resources available to political actors. In the context of demographic growth, leadership development, and a history of organizational efforts, Puerto Ricans used ethnicity as a key resource to mobilize. Economic change prompted them to seek redistributive justice, often making cultural demands the starting point of their actions. One-party politics and institutional bias prompted them to build extra-partisan organizations, while the demographic shape of the city and at-large elections promoted coalition building. Once representation was achieved, contingency became a matter of negotiating a new set of circumstances.

The Rules of Politics

Simmons refers to the situation created by access as one in which the critical dilemma is between meeting popular expectations while facing up to harsh economic realities. She refers to the resolution of this dilemma as a matter of "playing Solomon in an age of austerity," an approach that, as Claus Offe and James O'Connor have suggested, makes the state a battleground in which legitimacy and accumulation fight each other out.[57]

The dilemma described by Simmons is pertinent to this analysis. She was elected to Hartford's city council in 1991 after PRPAC's coalition with Carrie Saxon Perry, PFC, and disaffected Italian party regulars from the South End (hence referred to as the PRPAC-Perry coalition) trounced the Democratic incumbents and wiped out the Republicans from the council. For progressives, she argues, access is especially challenging because of their commitment to equity and innovation. More so than conventional politicians, they struggle with the tension between the ethical demands of conviction versus the pragmatic demands of responsibility;

they want to run the trains on time but not at the cost of acting like fascists. For Peterson, this dilemma is hardly worth agonizing over because if cities lose sight of their unitary interest, secondary interests become moot. For Simmons, the choice is between sustaining a political base and conforming to policy imperatives.

What are, in Simmons's analysis, the reasons that explain the failure of the PRPAC-Perry coalition? She writes: "The following factors combined to produce the loss: business and media opposition; internal dissension among office holders and fragmentation of the political base of the coalition; inability to address underlying needs of the population; our own blunders and miscalculations; and the fragmented and inhibiting structure of Hartford's municipal government."[58] This list raises several questions, such as, What were the grounds for media and business opposition? Was opposition selective or across the board? What was the internal dissension about? Why could it not be managed? How did government structure impair policy development? Simmons does not answer these questions, but it is clear that the council was overwhelmed by the enormity of its task. She tells us that "due to the severe fiscal constraints under which we operated we had to make horrendous choices . . . we had to balance developmental, allocational, and redistributive imperatives. . . . Choosing among them was a nightmare."[59]

Not only were Simmons and her colleagues daunted by their responsibility, but they also tried to please everyone, thus pleasing no one. She recognizes that voter anger could not be placated despite the council's best efforts but fails to see that the emphasis on principle, above all, was itself a problem. This emphasis created a tension between conviction and responsibility; and by favoring principles over outcomes, the council was penalized. "Without progressive approaches to economic development," Simmons declares, "the inequality of the present is perpetuated." In the same breath she realizes that "good intentions, good explanations, and even good analysis of issues simply are not enough; immediate needs challenge officeholders to construct immediate answers."[60] The belief that a government can live by good intentions and good analysis of issues not only qualifies as part of the council's "blunders and miscalculations," it also reveals a naive concept of politics, as if process were the only thing that mattered.

Although Simmons grants politics a role in her analysis, the overarching difficulty is said to have been structural: "The key constraint we faced, which permeated almost every policy decision, was that of the fiscal stress of the city."[61] What is clear from her account is that the dilemmas the council had to solve were Solomonic but the decision-making process was not; Solomon solved the adjudication problem he confronted. In contrast, although the council was not totally paralyzed, it was torn and indecisive. Council members could not bring themselves to answer the key question of politics: who gets what, how, and when? And when they did, they violated three basic political rules.

In *The Federalist Papers*, Madison writes: "In framing a government which is to be administered by men over men, the great difficulty lies in this: you must first enable the government to control the governed; and in the next place oblige it to control itself." The primary control on government is "a dependence on the people" but "opposite and rival interests" also are necessary to check and balance potential abuses of power.[62] To be sure, politics requires consensus and stability. Therefore, beyond a certain threshold, ambition not only counteracts ambition, it also prevents effective government. A climate of exacerbated differences in which opposite and rival interests could not find common ground was one of the reasons leading to the dissolution of the PRPAC-Perry governing coalition. Thus, by losing its bearings—by not being able to control itself—the council lost its base of support; it was unable to control the people.

There is plenty in Machiavelli's *The Prince* that would have been of value to the 1991–93 council. But two rules, which the governing coalition violated, stand out. The accuracy of Simmons's characterization of the council is dubious because the dissolution of the governing coalition itself suggests that not everyone was driven by the same set of motives and goals. But when she speaks of choosing between equity and inequality, she describes a situation that the council faced collectively and an approach that guided some of their decisions. This approach, in which right choices are given preference over pragmatic decisions, is best illustrated by the council's way of treating friends and enemies equally. Simmons commented on this: "Even the more conservative unions, such as the construction trades, who never contributed or participated in campaigns (and even supported opponents), were able to have issues heard. We could not represent ourselves as advocates of labor and then deal only with those unions in which we had friends."[63]

Machiavelli would reject this approach as nothing short of reckless, an outlook that by emphasizing principles over interests makes political survival impossible. "He who abandons what is done for what ought to be done, will rather learn to bring about his own ruin than his preservation. . . . Therefore it is necessary for a prince, who wishes to maintain itself, to learn how not to be good, and to use this knowledge *and not use it*, according to the necessity of the case."[64] The emphasis is added to make clear that focusing on interests as opposed to principles is not to say that anything goes, a caveat that introduces the kind of ambiguity into decision making that "the advocates of labor" in the council were unable to handle.

Finally, in his chapter entitled "Of the Civic Principality," Machiavelli argues that to a government constituted by the people, no resource is more valuable than the people's support. But should a prince find himself unable to count on that support, he must make sure that the nobility is dependent on him. If the powerful favor his rule, his chances of political survival are greater; if not, they "will help to ruin him when in adversity." [65] When the people are hostile, the worst thing they will do is abandon the prince, "but from hostile nobles he has to fear not only desertion but their active opposition, and as they are more far-seeing and more cunning, they are always in time to save themselves and take sides with the one who they expect will conquer." [66] This is very close to what happened in Hartford: the governing coalition faced the one-two punch of voter anger and business antagonism.

These are, in broad outline, the reasons why the exercise of coalition power by the alliance between PRPAC, Perry, PFC, and South End leaders was limited and why its representatives failed to win a second term. But the situation was even more complicated because each member confronted specific difficulties. In PRPAC's case, ethnicity became problematic as a source of conflict with blacks over the apportionment of positions and the distribution of benefits and as a proxy for interests. But nonethnic factors also impaired the exercise of power. Most important, the relationship between identity and power was not linear and could not be taken for granted. In campaigning, ethnicity was effective, but the circumstances of governing added wrinkles to its use that PRPAC did not anticipate. I proceed to discuss these issues in turn.

Puerto Ricans and Blacks

The night of 11 September 1991, after it was clear that the PRPAC-Perry coalition had won the Democratic primary, Edwin Vargas declared: "Before tonight there were three Hartfords—black, white, and Puerto Rican. After this election, there is now one Hartford." Mayor Perry echoed the sentiment during her victory speech by saying: "This is a beautiful coalition and it's going to continue—that is our commitment to you." [67] Barely two months later, PRPAC and Perry divided over the selection of a new city manager. Simultaneously, a previous conflict concerning the residency of the corporation counsel was resurrected and Perry insisted that "if [Jorge Simón's] contract is renewed, moving his family here will have to be part of it." [68]

A third conflict centered around the chairmanship of the city's Democratic party. Perry had agreed to help install Edwin Vargas in the position in exchange for PRPAC's support. After the election, a second condition was added: the dumping of the Puerto Rican corporation counsel. Vargas had no trouble with this, because by now he had become disillusioned with Simón. Ostensibly, Perry was firmly committed to Vargas, but in private she hesitated. Vargas argued that by forcing him to seek control of his district's town committee, a battle he knew he could not win, she set him up so as to relinquish her pledge. In fact, after the slate headed by Vargas failed to take over, many pressured Perry to desert him, claiming that his loss was a personal repudiation and a release of the mayor's obligation.

Some African Americans felt that the position should not go to a Puerto Rican, regardless of the vote. This sentiment was expressed to me by a local activist, who argued that Vargas had no right to be the Democratic party's chair because blacks were entitled to occupy the post first. Italian Democrats preyed on this feeling, taunting blacks with the notion that it was time for a black chairman. Others, like board of education member Thelma Dickinson, opposed Vargas out of simple fear. "I hope to God that Edwin Vargas is not the next town chair," she declared. "I think he's too possessive of people he works with. He thinks the city council is at his beck and call." [69]

In August, patronage emerged as another source of conflict. PRPAC accused Perry of regaling contracts and favors to her supporters in the black community while ignoring her Puerto Rican and Italian allies. Capitalizing on the sense of alienation of the South End councilman and the ambition of a black councilwoman, PRPAC engineered an alliance between them and the three Puerto Rican representatives to wrest control of patronage from the mayor and reinstate order in the council. The move distressed Perry so much that she shut herself in her office and refused to talk to anyone. But later on she was candid about her actions: "If they felt they were out of the loop I guess it was the patronage loop. . . . I'm trying to keep my eye on the prize and the prize is we have to start delivering in terms of services." [70]

The new coalition did something simple but substantive: its members reinstated legality to the council by eliminating the informal system Perry had instituted whereby the position of deputy mayor was rotated every month. This action was seen as the most significant and perhaps the definitive event that led to the break between PRPAC and Perry. Initially called "The Five in Control," in September, the community press referred to the group as "The Gang of Five." [71] The emergence of this coalition simultaneously pitted Puerto Ricans and blacks against each other and brought them together. PRPAC made enemies with Perry but compensated by making Henrietta Milward the new deputy mayor.

The PRPAC-Perry coalition was the product of back-room negotiations and deals among the various players. Yet shortly after the election Perry declared that she was no longer willing to entertain that style. "I don't like all that back-room stuff. That's what we got away from by running this campaign, and I won't tolerate it," she said.[72] When pressed to comment on the possibility that if a Puerto Rican was appointed city manager PRPAC would have to agree to the appointment of a black corporation counsel, she responded: "There's definitely not going to be any package deals. I can't deal with any more of that. The driving force behind this appointment [for city manager] is going to be who moves the people's agenda forward."[73] These were the first signs that something was amiss within the elected coalition, but no one noticed Perry's sudden memory lapse and retraction, and no accusations were made against her. No one told Perry that "back-room stuff" and "package deals" were instrumental to coalition maintenance and therefore necessary to fulfill her populist agenda. It took PRPAC nearly a year to understand that the terms of the alliance had changed and a realignment was required.

The sentiments around the candidacy of Edwin Vargas were symptomatic of a deeper problem, involving a history of troubled relations among African Americans and Puerto Ricans and a collective memory that, by being short and selective, airbrushed the record of cooperation and solidarity between the two groups. For example, after the 1991 election, a group of black leaders organized the North Hartford Alliance—also known as the African American Alliance—to develop a unified agenda for the predominantly black section of the city. The group used Mayor Perry as a rallying figure, arguing that her landslide victory in North Hartford districts mandated her to promote, first and foremost, the interests of African Americans and the North End. For this reason, alliance members opposed Vargas's bid for party chair, although many also perceived him as narrowly concerned with Puerto Rican interests.[74] No one seemed to remember that Puerto Ricans had helped elect Hartford's first black mayor, had facilitated the appointment of a black city treasurer, and had made possible Perry's 1991 victory. Only a few understood that although black and Puerto Rican interests were different, a mutually beneficial coalition was possible.

Nonethnic Factors

The leadership of PRPAC saw the process of "entry into the policy-making sphere" as more in keeping with Salisbury's model in which the political process is a succession of exchanges and Banfield's concept of political influence, in which the emphasis is on the ability to match intention with activity, than as a process in which groups consider various options, negotiate, bargain, and reach a consensus.[75] To influence policy making, PRPAC winnowed out candidates and elected them to office. The objective was to have representatives that would make policy on the basis of "loyalty to the organization." As partisan control over the nomination and policy process waned, PRPAC's control had to wax for the strategy to work. The idea was to turn the group into a nonpartisan political machine.[76] Yet once elected officials were in place, PRPAC lost track of their policy-related activities until the next election. There were exceptions to this pattern, such as Jorge Simón, who was closely watched, but there was no systematic follow-up of legislation in specific areas, no introduction of proposals, and no provision of expertise through hearings or direct lobbying. PRPAC members and public officials interacted in discrete electoral and policy power plays, but the group played a secondary role in defining the policy agenda and supplied no systematic input comparable to that provided by lobbyists or think tanks.

The most salient policy power play in Hartford was the adoption of the city's budget. If, for example, the school system was slated to suffer budget reductions, PRPAC took a position against such cuts. But this occurred not because the group followed the budget process or because any one member was charged with the task or was an expert but because of the overlapping enrollment of several of its members with the Hartford Federation of Teachers, a group with an obvious interest in school matters. This made input contingent rather than systematic.

In 1992, when the board of education proposed a privatization plan to deal with a budget deficit, PRPAC mobilized along with others to denounce the plan. It also demanded that the two Puerto Ricans it had helped elect to the board fight privatization, which they were reluctant to do. Some PRPAC members contributed to the debate on the proposal, but theirs was knowledge acquired as practitioners, not as experts. Their arguments were persuasive, but doubts remained among many whether they were defending a policy or their own jobs.[77]

PRPAC's lack of systematic involvement in the policy process was mostly due to its mobilization strategy, to how it related to other community groups and the candidates it elected, and to the circumstances of the process itself. A fourth factor was the strategy PRPAC chose to exert its influence. The imperatives of campaigning and governing introduced a subset of factors that also played a role. These elements are discussed in turn below.

MOBILIZATION STRATEGY

PRPAC's métier was electoral politics. The group knew that demographic concentration, voter registration, and voter turnout were the key elements of success. Its leadership mastered the art of coalition building and relied on all kinds of alliances to advance the group's objectives. Edwin Vargas was notorious for his willingness to confederate with just about anyone whom he felt could help advance PRPAC's objectives—blacks and white ethnics, progressives and reactionaries, labor groups, gay and lesbian groups, friends and former enemies. This was a mixed blessing, for it helped PRPAC achieve victories but it also gave Vargas, and by extension the group, a reputation for being too much of a fox and not enough of a lion.

PRPAC knew how to elect candidates, but its Machiavellian deftness in the electoral process was not matched by mastery over policy. This deficiency was readily accepted by PRPAC members, who rationalized it by noting that even the chamber of commerce was often lacking in this regard. According to Edna Negrón: "They [PRPAC] should get involved. They are not involved in that process, hardly at all. That would be perfect, first to identify the kind of legislation that would impact our community and that ought to be put through." When asked if PRPAC used or prompted Puerto Rican community-based organizations to use their expertise to bridge the gap—for example, having the Hispanic Health Council help monitor public health policies—Jack Cullin responded: "That doesn't happen. I don't think that we've [PRPAC] thought of it, but that's a good idea." [78]

Some Puerto Rican organizations did enter the policy process. Anyone reviewing the Journal of the Common Council can easily see the many instances in which groups such as La Casa de Puerto Rico and TAINO Housing were dispensed special treatment, through council resolutions or specific exemptions. Although these groups greatly favored having Puerto Ricans on the council, their presence was not necessarily seen as the one factor that made things happen vis-à-vis policy. According to one of TAINO's directors: "If we only had [representation] without any credibility, we wouldn't get things done." [79] This meant that community groups put more emphasis on developing and maintaining their credibility than on using PRPAC as a policy rod or vice versa. The relationship with Puerto Rican representatives was positive and welcome but tenuous. The relationship with PRPAC was one of sympathy and support, but for policy purposes these groups relied on their own expertise, resources, and connections.

INSTITUTIONAL AND INDIVIDUAL RELATIONS

To be effective in aggregating or distilling different policy positions, PRPAC needed standing. The concept of PRPAC emerged in the 1970s, taking practical form in 1977. The group's leadership in 1990 had been involved in Hartford politics from even earlier. Yet at their peak in the late 1980s, PRPAC's leaders were considered *arrivistes* by many. According to Juan Figueroa:

> The truce between the leading agencies and the leadership of the PAC has stood for only the past year and a half [1990 to mid-1991]. There were a lot of frictions before that, particularly between La Casa de Puerto Rico and some of the agencies close to La Casa and the PAC. It was an old guard versus new guard issue, with the PAC presenting itself as the avant-garde . . . and agencies such as La Casa being portrayed as the conservatives. . . . The idea of [PRPAC] bringing the agencies into the [policy] process is excellent, but the level of trust must be greater than what it is now.[80]

The problem of standing also applied to PRPAC's relations with elected officials, and in some cases even with those it helped elect. Elected officials either dismissed the group or feared its power. Some used PRPAC but resisted its authority. Eugenio Caro, for example, was elected with PRPAC support but was not willing to do the group's bidding on the council. He aspired to be Hartford's first Hispanic mayor and felt that he needed a personal political base to prevent being bypassed by a younger, better educated Puerto Rican candidate. Although Caro was a founding member of PRPAC, he was not representative of the new recruits who put him in office. This made him insecure about PRPAC's allegiance and, even though his logical course of action was to be cooperative and loyal, he resisted any pressure the group would exert. Caro thus went along with PRPAC only during campaigns or policy power plays, such as the installation of the Gang of Five; during the normal policy-making process, he was stubbornly independent, prompting some to consider him self-centered and unreliable. These qualities discouraged PRPAC from working closely with Caro on policy matters. And by not putting enough pressure on him, the group compounded its lack of standing.

By contrast, PRPAC had a great deal of influence over Yolanda Castillo, who in the 1992 council coalition of five was selected majority leader. Still, Castillo was no puppet. For example, she tried to steer PRPAC away from the issue of privatization of the school system and stuck to her guns when the majority sentiment was that the group should take a position against it. Furthermore, even though she was majority leader, she could not control the votes of her colleagues. Eugenio Caro joined the Gang of Five because he had been against Perry from the start. The emergence of the new coalition did not make him any more reliable. Fernando Comulada had his own agenda and so did Milward. The fifth member, Anthony DiPentima, responded to the Italian party regulars of the South End. Thus, for all practical purposes, even though PRPAC had elected three candidates, it could only count on one, often conditional vote.

PRPAC also was the victim of its own success. Its accomplishments showed that loyalty was not the sine qua non of electoral success, that changing sides when necessary was a better strategy. This lesson was not lost on its allies. Some of these, after getting elected by PRPAC, turned their back on the group to do the bidding of other coalitions both in and outside the Democratic party.

In short, PRPAC did not have a lock on the loyalty of the candidates it helped elect. Caro could justify his attitude by arguing that he had been elected by PRPAC and PFC and therefore had two constituencies to serve. Frances Sánchez, however, could not make this argument because, even though she was endorsed by the Democratic party, her candidacy was brokered by PRPAC and her campaign was run—to the last detail—by PRPAC members and volunteers. PFC contributed, but Sánchez was fundamentally a creature of PRPAC. Yet once elected, she turned around and refused to support positions favored by both groups. She also sided with Deputy Mayor Charles Mathews against PRPAC in the conflict that brought together Perry and PRPAC in 1991. During that year's electoral campaign, Sánchez waged bitter attacks against the group and especially against Edwin Vargas. She was not reelected but, instead of fading from the political scene, she became PRPAC's Frankenstein.

THE POLICY PROCESS

The circumstances of the policy process, combined with the problems in translating representation into responsiveness, and PRPAC's mobilization strategy further reduced the chances that PRPAC would have a systematic impact on policy. For example, the legislative package that the Hartford delegation to the state legislature presents every session is susceptible to external input, but effective intervention requires critical knowledge, access to policy networks, or both. PRPAC did not have either. A month before the session begins, the staff of the mayor's office and the legislative delegation meet to assemble the package. The process is open to all legislators regardless of rank, and they are free to seek input from lobbies or individuals. Each legislator focuses on bills that are relevant to him or her, but each has the option of endorsing each bill. When the legislative session starts, everything has been discussed and decided and all the bills are introduced simultaneously.

During his first legislative session, Juan Figueroa endorsed seventy-four bills and three resolutions. "In 1988, being new," he recalled, "I endorsed a great part of the package. I went to two meetings and had no problems with the package but didn't have a critical eye for it either like I have now after three years of service."

Figueroa's input was uncritical, but PRPAC's was nonexistent. Said Figueroa: "The PRPAC has essentially been a vehicle for campaign mobilization, a political instrument. In terms of legislative issues, I've had an informal relationship with individual members. One of the things I wanted to do and haven't been able [to] was [to organize] an issues forum where the members of the PAC could discuss issues. I even prepared a questionnaire that was sent to the members asking them to identify the three most important issues for the Puerto Rican community, but there are so many things to do that this one fell by the wayside." On the one hand, Figueroa wanted to make PRPAC more than a "vehicle for campaign mobilization" but dropped the ball; on the other hand, no one from PRPAC pressured him to follow up on his initiative.

At the state legislature, there are more committees requiring the attention of legislators than they can possibly attend, especially rookie legislators whose share of staff is apportioned by rank.[81] Edna Negrón, for example, sat on three committees—Commerce and Transportation, Education, and Public Health—while holding a full-time job as principal of a local school. To do her legislative work, she could rely on the assistance of a quarter of a legislative aide, who "basically answer[ed] phones and might be able to write a letter."

Committees meet twice a week, draft legislation, and hold public hearings. A member must be thoroughly familiar with the workings of these committees before he or she can accomplish anything in the area of policy. According to Negrón, the Hartford delegation endorses a significant number of bills without its members being consulted (that is, bills other than the Hartford package noted above). "We meet weekly, but there's always something that falls through the cracks," she said. Although rookie legislators receive a crash course, they are really on their own in learning the ropes. "They give us [a] two-day [orientation] of what the departments are. It's sink or swim." Keeping up with the volume of legislative proposals and tracking down specific bills can be daunting, at least initially. Representatives with a legal background have an easier time understanding simple matters such as the notation system of bills, but others must learn even that. Negrón said: "How do I read a bill? I mean it's in English, but the references are in Greek!"[82]

Within the city council, the policy process is fragmented. Power is shared by a weak mayor, the council, and the city manager. Since Carbone's defeat in 1979, the council had lacked a stable majority controlled by the deputy mayor. In Hartford's one-party system, fragmentation made policy dependent on a coherent Democratic caucus or a strong deputy mayor or city manager. Typically, coherence was impossible when the level of racial, ethnic, and/or geographic conflict was such that a clear majority could not be fashioned on the council. Referring to the 1991–93 term, City Manager Howard Stanback declared: "Ninety-five percent of the initiatives we are trying are supported by the city council. The only reason that it is not 100 percent is because we have a major split on the council, and 5 percent is caught up in politics." [83] This might have been true of the projects his office was sponsoring, but the fact was that the policy process itself was 100 percent caught up in politics, subject to the level and fluctuations between agreement and dissent. Louise Simmons, one of the councilpersons who voted to hire Stanback, confirms this in her analysis of policy making during her term. She identifies three basic cleavages that council members had to negotiate to make policy: (1) downtown and business interests competing with neighborhood interests; (2) planners thinking in professional terms and politicians looking at proposals through the lens of the next election; and (3) deciding among competing interests within the governing coalition itself. Rather than being technical, these conflicts were political to the core. [84]

In Hartford, the policy process all but obliterates the separation between the civil and the political society. Extra-institutional pressures are widespread and systematic; some actors wield more influence than others, but the regime—that is, the symbiosis between elected officials, groups, and citizens—is wide open and constantly being reconfigured. In the case of groups such as PRPAC, power assertions depend on their relative strength, which is measured by the extent and kind of rewards they control, their persuasiveness, which hinges on their ability to show that a policy option will yield a reasonable cost-benefit ratio, and their cleverness—in other words, the degree to which they know how to exploit competitive advantages. Cleverness includes the ability to manipulate issues through distortion and deception, but this is a double-edged sword. These qualities are crucial if basic rifts are to be negotiated successfully.

Thus, strength, persuasiveness, and cleverness were key resources in trying to secure a majority on the council who would favor the agenda of any one particular group. Although the leadership of PRPAC was unquestionably clever, it was not consistently persuasive or strong enough to transform coalition dominance into coalition power. Its greatest handicap, however, was its relative absence from the policy process itself.

POLICY STRATEGY

PRPAC's absence was relative, however, not absolute. Contrary to what Figueroa, Negrón, and Cullin suggest, PRPAC did have some input into the policy-making process. At the state level, the group channeled its contribution as a member of the Legislative Electoral Action Project and, consequently, its impact was indirect. Since 1986, PRPAC articulated policy objectives through LEAP's policy platform, over which it had veto power. But once the legislative session opened, LEAP pursued these objectives, not PRPAC. LEAP typically used PRPAC resources in three ways: (1) to influence legislators who might be more responsive to Puerto Rican input, (2) to mobilize the Puerto Rican community, and (3) to bring into the influence process the social and professional resource networks of PRPAC members and allies.

Both the policy strategy and its objectives were conceived and articulated in autocratic fashion. When LEAP discussed a legislative package, they heard from Edwin Vargas, not from PRPAC. Vargas consulted with PRPAC's membership, but often these meetings were pro forma, a measure of the extent to which the group's membership deferred to him. Of course, sometimes pro forma deliberations are worthy exercises, but there is a threshold beyond which they lose all democratic value. In the case of PRPAC, they gave Vargas legitimacy but did not enhance the group's resource capacity. When Vargas stepped down from PRPAC's presidency in 1989, he continued to be the liaison with LEAP. The new president, Ramón Arroyo, a social services administrator, accepted the arrangement and did not show any interest in having such access. But it is likely that Vargas did not want to give him access to LEAP's network. Arroyo's work in the third assembly district, obsessively monitoring the lists of voters, was efficient to the point of near perfection. He kept the city registrars of voters on their toes, constantly questioning purging decisions and making sure that no Puerto Rican voter was illegally disqualified. In other regards, he was mediocre.[85]

A similar dynamic developed at the city level. On the council, the ostensible policy articulator was PFC, but PRPAC often took the initiative and provided leadership in discrete policy power plays. For example, in 1986 PRPAC joined an effort to have the council adopt linkage as a policy concept. According to the group, linkage initiatives needed to include agencies providing employment and training services. PRPAC leaders also felt that linkage policies needed a mechanism to insure that the trickle-down effect of development projects was felt in Puerto Rican neighborhoods.[86] Another example was the school privatization issue. Here PRPAC took the initiative because the group felt that privatization would negatively affect

Puerto Rican children disproportionately. PRPAC's strategy was to draw the city council and the public into the fray to broaden the scope of the issue, which Hartford's board of education had the right to settle administratively.

PRPAC sponsored meetings with local officials to express Puerto Ricans' concerns, but these were sporadic and included no specific policy goals. For example, in 1986 Edwin Vargas requested a meeting with City Manager Alfred Gatta. He wanted to discuss "the role of our community in your administration." Gatta's response was as vague as Vargas's objective. Rather than focusing on Puerto Ricans, he declared he was interested in a discussion of the "issues that impact the city." [87]

A similar meeting was held in 1988 with Congresswoman Barbara Kennelly. I attended this one as a member of the staff of the National Puerto Rican Coalition (NPRC), a Washington, D.C.-based organization of which PRPAC was a member. PRPAC dubbed the meeting a "congressional update on Puerto Rican and Hispanic issues," but it was more a ritual encounter. Near the end, after all the pleasantries had been exchanged and the rhetoric had evaporated, PRPAC members were taken aback by the no-nonsense approach of NPRC's lobbyist, Segundo Mercado, when he asked Kennelly to endorse NPRC's public policy agenda. My perception was that Mercado's request, simple as it was, struck like a bolt of lightning. Perhaps because this was the first such meeting, PRPAC did not expect it to be more than a formality. But the feeling was that the members of PRPAC came unprepared to discuss actual issues or to make specific demands.

CAMPAIGNING AND GOVERNING

PRPAC emerged to combat perceived inequalities—of status and political access. Much of the initial impetus for the group's formation was provided by the desire to overcome unemployment, low voter turnout, cumbersome registration procedures, and inadequate political representation. Although PRPAC's leadership recognized that, to benefit the community, policies need not be effected by Puerto Rican representatives, it also acknowledged that in a situation of relative powerlessness, ethnicity was more likely to translate representation into responsiveness. Responsiveness, however, proved difficult to accomplish. As noted above, several mechanisms account for the discrepancy. In addition, the distinction between campaigning and governing structured another set of factors.

PRPAC developed a reputation in Hartford for running campaigns with machine-like precision and efficiency. Contest after contest, it had the candidates, the signatures, the state certifications, the headquarters, the fund-raisers, and a wide circle of volunteers registering voters, canvassing door to door, getting the vote out, and watching the polls for irregularities. None of this was done democratically. A great deal of centralization was required. PRPAC's leadership made most decisions unilaterally. Typically, during an electoral campaign, PRPAC members met infrequently, if at all. Whenever dissension reared its ugly head, the number of membership meetings was cut down to the barest minimum. Campaigns were hierarchically organized and conservatively managed. But once they ran their course, momentum subsided. After taking their places on the council, representatives altered their relationships with PRPAC. Three mechanisms account for the change.

The first mechanism was the existence of antecedent loyalties. The cases of Caro and Simón suggest that public officials defect from the groups or coalitions that help elect them not just because they realize that there are other alternatives but also because these commitments come into conflict with their electoral allegiances. These preexistent loyalties can be concrete—Simón's overriding commitment was to the Democratic party—or abstract—Caro's ostensible concern was with the democratic process and the welfare of the community.

The second mechanism was the effectiveness imperative. When Marie Kirkley-Bey abandóned the PFC/PRPAC coalition, many were disappointed and surprised. She explained her decision simply: the power in the council was in the hands of the Democratic caucus, so that it became apparent that "to promote the everyday person's agenda, [she] needed to have a voice in that caucus." In her view, the coalition's main objective did not match the requirements of the situation:

> They wanted to become a permanent third party and I said 'I won't do that.' As a minority party you can't chair a committee, so therefore you can't set the agenda. In contacts with business and others, it is best to be in the majority party because they know you have a greater capacity to deliver. Therefore it would have been easier for me to work on housing issues and those issues that I thought were important.[88]

The third mechanism was the "veil of ignorance" over the eyes of coalition members that slipped off shortly after a candidate took office.[89] This veil obscured goals, beliefs, ideological commitments, special concerns and interests, leaving in plain view only that which was relevant to winning the election. Frances Sánchez had no idea of what was in store for her when she accepted the invitation to be PRPAC's candidate. As a public official, she became aware of cleavages she never knew existed. Her own views on issues and her perception of which council alignments were more expedient created a gulf between herself and her supporters.[90] Some of her collaborators were so incensed by this situation and their criticism of Sánchez was so stern that it is hard to picture them supporting her enthusiastically as a candidate.[91]

IDENTITY AND POWER

Groups such as PRPAC claim to broaden political representation. The assumption is that interests within the civil society can be satisfied within the political society only if members or advocates of these interests are included in the policy-making process. This assumption is fraught with problems. It is not a given that all interest groups can have their day in the policy process. When the range of participant interests widens, conflict is more widespread and the possibility of stalemate increases. Satisfying all interests also raises the issue of limited resources. The claim is often made that identity politics inevitably leads to an endless war among innumerable factions for a small or shrinking amount of benefits.

One could argue that every possible group or interest need not be included. In this case, taking account of the "leading interests" suffices. The pertinent question then is how to identify those interests. Typically, representation is operationalized demographically. In Hartford, Puerto Ricans are a significant group because they are at least 27 percent of the city's population. There are Cuban, Colombian, and Peruvian residents, but their numbers are so small that they have been superseded by Puerto Ricans. This is illustrated by the fact that hardly anyone refers to the various groups by the umbrella terms "Latino" or "Hispanic." Yet in the past, when the community was small, Puerto Rican leaders were not deterred from demanding representation or special attention. This suggests that, although demographic criteria are important, they don't necessarily make exclusion of the less significant groups or interests acceptable.

An alternative is to satisfy all interests piecemeal and in turn. Here the problem is how to set a policy queue and its ordering. Who goes first? How much do they get compared to others, and on what basis are benefits allocated? What mechanisms are set to order the formulation and satisfaction of claims? Some of the literature on interest groups suggests that in fulfilling this function, the pressure system is an effective and desirable supplement to political parties.[92] But in the context of party decomposition, it is not clear that the pressure system alone suffices. Even when parties and pressure groups do supplement each other, policy proceeds either incoherently or through increments and thus always fails to appease someone or tests the patience of those who are temporarily excluded. This can be extremely problematic unless social, economic, and political relations are fundamentally trustworthy and the legitimacy of the state is rock solid, which is a clearly utopian situation if ever there was one. Finally, underlying all these objections is the problem that an identity between groups and interest representation cannot be automatically assumed, and, further, even interest representation does not necessarily lead to the advancement of the represented interests.

Remarkably, these difficulties do not diminish the appeal of identity politics because its claims, more often than not, are sculpted from beliefs that are impervious to argument. This is so not because identity politics is intrinsically irrational and based purely on sentiment and belief but because experience constantly tells us that someone, somewhere, has benefited from identity politics and therefore it must work. The dynamic here is similar to that whereby myths are fashioned: by the power of belief combined with anecdotal evidence.

The Puerto Rican story in Hartford, however, provides compelling evidence of the power of identity and its usefulness in the process of empowerment. To a large extent, the transition from ethnic awareness to power awareness made identity politics necessary. Thus, bilingual education in Hartford required Puerto Rican advocates; no one else really cared as much as those who were directly affected. Even Carbone, who was sympathetic, had to be prompted and pushed to act.

The social science evidence in favor of identity politics is inconclusive but strong. Browning, Marshall, and Tabb find important correlations between group representation and policy responsiveness. Estades has shown how identity served as the basis for political organization and participation of Puerto Ricans in New York City. MacManus and Bullock have identified correlations between gender, political roles, and policy preferences at the municipal level. And even Erie, who challenged the conventional wisdom on the urban political machine, recognized that it was an instrument of upward mobility, although the prizes were limited and were enjoyed more by Irish, southern, and Eastern European immigrants than by blacks. What Erie proved, in fact, was not that identity politics did not work but that it worked differently for different groups and that outcomes were shaped by such factors as the relationship between city and state governments and the fiscal strategy pursued by local machines.[93]

In terms of the exercise of power, does action based on identity shut the rest of the public out? There is no easy answer to this question. But, as Carmichael and Hamilton suggest, in-group coherence can help bridge the gap between a sense of belonging to and belonging with. On the one hand, the assertion of difference is not a precondition of incorporation but precisely the way in which it takes place. On the other hand, particularity can be representative if it fulfills for a specific group a general need or aspiration. Identity politics transcends its particularity when it produces a collective good or collective lessons. For example, Puerto Ricans demanded equal treatment and sought representation—a collective good—and their success showed that coalition dominance did not necessarily mean coalition power—a lesson for all.

To be acceptable in the exercise of power, identity must not undermine responsibility. In other words, policy needs to be responsive to identity claims without incorporating a *permanent* bias on policy, or the kind of monopoly that is associated with the notion of shutting the public out. For the reasons stated above, PRPAC's impact on policy was tenuous. This in itself prevented the corruption of the policy process but in a way that was detrimental to Puerto Rican interests. Three other factors prevented the entrenchment of a particularistic bias in policy making that, in contrast, were welcome. First, even though Puerto Ricans had common interests, they were not a monistic unit. The most vivid example of an absence of unitary interests is provided by the varieties of conflict within the community and the multiplicity of organizational vehicles these cleavages promoted. More often than not, groups and individuals pursuing similar objectives competed on the basis of their different versions of community interests.

Second, political judgment was not always colored by identity. Within PRPAC's camp not everyone took ethnicity for granted. Juan Figueroa, for example, saw a tension between identity politics and public policy. Like him, other leaders sought to reconcile identity with substance, and the voting behavior of the community also revealed concerns that went beyond simple correlations between identity and interests. The clearest example of this was the rejection of Dolores Sánchez at the polls in 1966.

Third, Puerto Rican interests were not per force distinct or in contradiction with the interests of others or with the public at large. Actions that were intended to benefit Puerto Ricans often had spillover effects. PRPAC brokered the appointment of Jorge Simón as corporation counsel expecting that he would channel patronage to Puerto Ricans and Latinos. Simón turned out to be intensely independent in his judgments, but on the question of patronage he and PRPAC were of the same mind. "My job is one of those jobs which is of political patronage," he said. "It was given [to me] because of certain things that the Hispanic community has done. . . . My policy has been that the city has been lackadaisical in providing opportunities for minorities. . . . That's what I have pushed."[94]

Beyond that, Simón stabilized an office that was dysfunctional, directed the attack on developers whose buildings were being foreclosed for tax delinquency, negotiated $4 million in back taxes from developers, and prevented the city council from hiring a private firm to conduct negotiations with the municipal unions, thus saving the city half a million dollars in legal fees. When the Connecticut Civil Liberties Union Foundation (CCLUF), in collaboration with PRPAC members, filed a complaint against Hartford's Republican and Democratic registrars of voters protesting existing purging practices, Simón was a firm ally. Its victory—although won on behalf of Latino voters—was a victory for all voters. This decision clearly addressed both specific and general concerns, and it enhanced accountability by making local government responsible for an equitable system of voter registration.[95]

In sorting out the mechanisms that mediated the relationship between identity and power, it is apparent that conceptual difficulties did not forestall practical success and that identity claims were not always narrow. But a climate of exacerbated differences, a focus on principles as opposed to interests, and business antagonism and the inability of players either to neutralize or to win the favor of the powerful did not allow Hartford's 1991–93 governing coalition to hit its stride. Furthermore, the mobilization and policy strategies chosen by PRPAC, as well as specific relations between groups and individuals, truncated the group's influence within that coalition. Finally, features of the policy process, preexisting loyalties, the desire to make a difference, and selective ignorance resulted in an environment of uncertainty, unpredictability, and flux that hampered the transformation of coalition dominance into coalition power.

ISSUES FOR FUTURE RESEARCH

This study opens up several areas for future research. The politicization of ethnicity raises questions about social and political boundaries that must be tackled in a realistic rather than a platonic fashion. Ethnicity is often associated with a hardening of distinctions that impairs dialogue and prevents the construction of an "inclusive commonality." When these particularisms are recognized by the state, the spillover into politics allegedly balkanizes the political society. Although state intervention is important to prevent the transformation of ethnic cleavages from social fault lines into full-fledged political earthquakes, some consider a policy of intervention ultimately self-defeating because it institutionalizes the conflicts that it is supposed to eradicate, thus laying the ground for political disintegration.[96]

The question is whether in the absence of state intervention other mechanisms can prevent ethnic explosions without encouraging and legitimizing ethnicity. Exogamy is said to be one such mechanism. According to David Hollinger, "The extraordinary increase in marriage and reproduction across the lines of the ethno-racial pentagon represents a fundamental challenge to the authority of descent-defined categories. A critical mass of acknowledged mixed-race people heightens the credibility of an ideal according to which individuals decide how tightly or loosely they wish to affiliate with one or more communities of descent. These Americans help move the society in a postethnic direction."[97]

Hollinger's vision of postethnicity attempts to reconcile the tension between prescribed and chosen affiliations and is indeed predicated on the notion that as intermarriage blurs the biological boundaries of ethnicity, choice will triumph over prescription and the tension between ethnos and species—that is, between particularity and universality—will be mitigated. At that stage, the politicization of ethnicity will not be necessary because ascriptive affiliations will have evolved into a matter of individual choice.

There are two problems with this approach: First, it is not clear what measures will pick up the slack between an ethnic present and a postethnic future. A postethnic vision is appealing, especially if it reconciles unity with diversity, but the question Hollinger does not answer is how to transform his suggested perspective into a program of action. Second, and most important, to solve social and political problems primarily through individual actions is unrealistic. In fact, it would be foolish to predicate the fulfillment of a social vision solely on individual choice. Furthermore, although exogamy has certainly been on the rise during the past twenty-five years, the number of people who have cut themselves loose from ascriptive unions is still quite small. From 1970 to 1994, the number of interracial couples tripled from 310,000 to 1.2 million, but the higher figure represents 2.5 percent of all same-race couples and only 2.3 percent of all married couples in the United States.[98] Not only are these small numbers but their impact is complex. Although intermarriage can certainly erode the ascriptive basis of ethnicity, it does not necessarily undermine its hold since individuals often change rather than shed their ethnic affiliations as a result of such unions.[99]

By 2030, Latinos are projected to be 19 percent of the U.S. population, and the estimate for 2050 is 25 percent. In that year, whites are anticipated to be about 53 percent of the total. Asians are expected to surge from the current 3.3 to 8.2 percent, while African-Americans will probably remain close to their 1995 figure, which is 13.6 percent of the total.[100] If immigration and fertility swell in a context of economic stagnation and nativism, will these increases be matched by comparable rates of intermarriage? What about the impact of a division of labor that reconfigures the ethnic cast but maintains and reinforces ethnic boundaries? To what extent does intermarriage actually obliterate prescribed boundaries, and to what extent does it merely restructure existing patterns?

In Hollinger's scheme, the protagonists of the conflict between ethnos and species are a business elite whose patriotic calling has been tempered by global economic realities, a set of transnational communities with little incentive to identify with the American nation state, and the assortment of religious fundamentalists and right-wing fanatics who have claimed America for Americans only. And while it seems that for the species to prevail over the ethnos, the choice must be over an Americanism that encourages diversity but does not promote in-group isolation, it is in the failure to "provide sufficient opportunities for poor people of all ethno-racial classifications," that, according to Hollinger, America's postethnic future lies in doubt.[101]

Although the constituencies Hollinger describes are real, his descriptions do not capture the complexity of their values, attitudes, and behavior. It is questionable, for example, that the intensity of ethnic identification among the various diasporas that populate the United States is inversely proportional to their commitment to the national community. This book shows that ethnic identity does not necessarily lead to separatism, and other research on Latinos clearly suggests that a "diasporic consciousness" is not incompatible with a commitment to the United States.[102] In rather contradictory fashion, Hollinger himself admits that "today's demography of immigration has its novelties, but uncertain attachment to the United States is not one of them."[103] Yet this is a complex issue that raises enduring and important questions both for society and politics.

The Puerto Rican experience shows that gender is an important category in the process of empowerment. Why did women take such a prominent leadership role in the early stages of the political development of Hartford's Puerto Ricans? What factors account for the shift that took place in the 1970s, from a political leadership that was predominantly female to one that was predominantly male?

Women have been politically active for more than a century. Although their activities have typically related to issues of home and family, their participation in local voluntary associations has focused on the responsibility of the state for the provision of social services. Two forces circumscribed the scope of women's participation: their role within the domestic sphere and the absence of opportunities for participation in public life.[104] Often, women took the initiative for political mobilization and even played leadership roles. But for the most part, political participation was parochial and led by men. When this was not the case, the struggles they initiated were eventually taken over by males.[105]

New ways of looking at women's political participation have revealed a richness previously missed. Their parochial concerns have been shown to have been intertwined with holistic effects, often broaching the separation of public and private spheres.[106] Furthermore, local action frequently drew on national connections.[107] A continuing problem, however, has been how organization and mobilization can overcome racial and ethnic barriers, both within and outside the groups in which women participate. It appears that women-led communal action reproduces existing patterns of racial and ethnic segregation and thus contributes to persistent inequality. Ideologies of domesticity also appear to play dual roles as public activities are rationalized as extensions of private roles. In New York, for example, Puerto Rican women who were reluctant to work convinced themselves that employment was acceptable as the only way to fulfill their domestic responsibilities.[108] In Hartford, a similar dynamic propelled women into the political process, but the precise circumstances in which this took place are not clear.

There is some evidence that although the mobilization of white women tends to focus on making the power structure responsive to community needs, the mobilization of Latinas focuses on the question of access.[109] In this regard, however, the record is ambivalent because in some cases responsiveness has been the main focus of political mobilization among Latinas.[110]

Puerto Rican political mobilization included a radical stream that was particularly active in Hartford during the 1970s. How did ethnicity figure in the origins, goals, and strategy of radical groups? Would a detailed analysis of the Puerto Rican left reveal a distinct set of lessons for future political action, or were these groups so out of touch with the community that they simply vanished without leaving a legacy or a trace? The radical experience is interesting because gender assumes a peculiar dimension, especially when compared with mainstream political participation. In Chicago, gender conflict within the fledgling Young Lords Organization (later the Young Lords party) led to the creation of a subdivision called the Lordettes.[111] In the New York branch, women held top leadership positions.[112] This was also true of the Puerto Rican Socialist party in New York. In Hartford, however, female leadership was more prominent and substantial among mainstream partisans than among radicals. Given the egalitarian emphasis of radical ideologies, this is paradoxical and deserves an explanation.

Although radicals in the United States have a rather sorry history, they have made residual and supplementary contributions.[113] Important figures, such as Eugene Debs, stand as exemplars of democratic leadership, prompting some to claim that although the careers of these radicals were a failure, their lives were a success.[114] In a number of cases, radical groups have played a role somewhat similar to that of electoral third parties.[115] In Hartford, it appears that radicals performed similar functions, providing effective leadership models and acting as catalytic agents of wider community mobilization. The causal link between radical militancy and mainstream success deserves further analysis, however. Convergence in Hartford was essentially effected by radical individuals. Although Vargas and La Luz appeared to become mainstream politicians, they were in fact hybrids, combining radical approaches and mainstream methods, carrying their radicalism in their heads while fashioning practical alliances that centered around electoral representation and policy responsiveness. The interesting question in this case is whether Puerto Rican gains occurred despite the input of radicals or whether representation was in part promoted by the establishment as a way of preventing the proliferation of an extremist version of identity politics.

In conclusion, Puerto Rican political mobilization was determined by endogenous and exogenous factors. When opportunities were favorable, political actors took them, and when they were not, participants figured out ways of overcoming the hurdles in their path. Political action demonstrated that power was permeable, even when the odds were against access. The inability of Puerto Rican elites to improve the socioeconomic status of the community is disappointing and troublesome. Yet one lesson of this story is that socioeconomic status is not everything. The rewards of politics can be material or symbolic, and their value is not intrinsic. Instead, this value must be measured against the objectives of action and the judgments of the political actors themselves of their accomplishments. Coalition power is real when the effects of political mobilization—of whatever nature—have an impact on those represented by a governing coalition. What this means is that, ultimately, the relationship between identity and power must be assessed discretely in terms of objectives and accomplishments rather than in reference to abstract standards. Unfinished agendas set the parameters for future action, but as criteria for the evaluation of outcomes, they have a limited value. How do we know that their goals could have been accomplished? If we judge what is done by what must be done, do we not risk overlooking the differences between the various logics of political action? Fortunately, the end of this narrative is not the end of the real story. The challenge is still on for those who insist that history is nothing but a record of dominance and subordination and who see the political behavior of ordinary peoples as not much more than a palimpsest inscribed from above.

8 Puerto Rican Politics and the Challenge of Ethnicity

THE ENTRY and meteoric rise of PRPAC in Hartford's political scene forced public officials to be mindful of its actions and heightened the vigilance of out-groups. Not knowing what to make of this phenomenon, white and black members of the power elite simply redoubled their efforts to keep public policy safe from the deleterious influence of special-interest groups. In the civil service and third sector, blacks saw the emergence of Puerto Ricans as a challenge to their conquests. They were fearful that Puerto Rican gains would take away the power they had struggled hard and long to get. One effect of this attitude was that the accountability of public officials became more important to them. And on the few occasions that Puerto Ricans and blacks healed their mutually inflicted wounds, the cost was new cleavages with whites.[1]

To some, identity politics means that blood is thicker than water; but they go no further than saying that identity triggers political action.[2] This account shows a positive relationship between identity and power that nonetheless is not linear and cannot be taken for granted. Identity claims were necessary and fruitful, but there were limitations as well, notably in the transition from the access of power to its exercise. The problem is not that identity politics is a sideshow; ethnic issues in Hartford were seriously regarded, and most were substantive. Although PRPAC's influence was limited, power assertions by the corporate sector did not appear to be a factor in the erosion of PRPAC's ability to control the candidates it helped elect. Corporate power was influential in other ways. The context was inhospitable, but this shaped the structure of opportunities, not necessarily the timing or content of interventions by political actors.

The evaluations of key protagonists of how identity affected power echoes the analysis above. Edwin Vargas remained convinced that Puerto Rican power was blocked by an Irish-Italian-Jewish network of political and economic entrepreneurs who constituted a permanent structure of influence in city politics;[3] in Juan Figueroa's mind, Puerto Rican power was insignificant compared with the power of whites and blacks. Jorge Simón recognized the advances made by the community while claiming that these had barely made a dent in the real structure of power. Similarly, when

201

declaring his intention to seek reelection in 1989, Eugenio Caro emphasized that much more needed to be done.⁴

The Puerto Rican elite was right in feeling dissatisfied with its achieve-
ments. But the disjunction between "what is" and "what ought to be"
should not be reified. Political change always leaves a residue of continuity
that appears to nullify its intent. But change does happen, and shifts in
the dominant political coalition—that is, changes in the interests represented within formal institutions—do affect the context and ways in
which coalition power is exerted and the role of organized constituencies.
In Hartford, Puerto Ricans effected a change of this kind by politicizing
ethnicity. Their strategy was to penetrate the power structure to change
existing correlations between ethnicity and status. Their success was limited. Does this confirm the notion that upward mobility strategies based
on access to power are *dépassé*?

A New Mode of Seeking Reddress

In his article "Ethnicity and Social Change," Daniel Bell characterizes ethnic groups as "pre-industrial units" and argues that receding class politics
have opened the way for a reawakening of primordial feelings leading to
a politics based on ethnicity. These feelings are, he claims, a "strategic
site" that gives disadvantaged individuals "a new mode of seeking political redress," especially when the state is receptive.⁵ These statements raise
several questions.

First, Bell's choice to set the boundaries of ethnicity in the preindustrial
world is not convincing, precisely because ethnicity surged in a post-
industrial context. Why would ethnicity emerge in circumstances in which
its "natural" referents were lacking? In the Puerto Rican case, the ethnic
surge cut across migratory and generational experiences. In other words,
identity politics was strong among the cohorts that migrated from the
rural Puerto Rican countryside, among those who had a more urban-
industrial background, and among those Puerto Ricans born and raised
on the mainland. In fact, PRPAC became the leading force of its kind in
Hartford precisely as a new generation of middle-class professionals took
control of the organization. Thus, the notion that ethnicity is naturally related to a certain economic order—with corresponding political actors—
is suspect.

Second, while it is plausible that in a context of attenuated class politics ethnicity will surge and fill the gap, the former condition is not a re-
quirement of the latter. Between 1965 and 1975, manufacturing jobs in
Hartford dropped from 20 to 9 percent of the total nonagricultural employment in the city, while service jobs climbed from 19 to 23 percent.

The proportion of jobs in the financial, insurance, and real estate sector also climbed during this period—from 24 percent of the total in 1965 to 31 percent in 1975.[6] Between 1960 and 1970, city jobs increased by 16 percent, while the number held by Hartford residents decreased by a whopping 24 percent.[7] In 1970, the citywide unemployment rate was 4.5 percent, but by 1980 it had climbed to 7.7 percent; in 1990, it was 10.7 percent. By 1991, service, financial, insurance, real estate, other service, and government jobs were 94 percent of nonagricultural employment in the city, while manufacturing jobs were a minuscule 4 percent.[8] In such a context ethnicity should have thoroughly superseded class as the engine of social and political conflict. But throughout this period and especially during the 1980s, both class and ethnicity played significant roles in city politics, sometimes separately, at times in tandem.[9]

Third, the emergence of ethnicity does not necessarily involve a reawakening of suppressed primordial feelings.[10] Puerto Ricans began to organize around ethnic issues almost instantly after arriving in Hartford. As the community grew in numbers, ethnic awareness grew, and it continued to exert a socializing influence. This was a systematic process that fueled organization and action, which in turn sustained a sense of ethnic identity. Ethnicity became salient politically once Puerto Ricans connected ethnic awareness with power awareness but not because it had once been suppressed and now was able to reassert itself.

Fourth, strictly speaking, ethnicity was no "strategic site," because ethnic solidarity was dynamic. In fact, there was no single strategic site for the articulation of claims; instead, there were multiple organizational efforts and many organizations that vented issues and structured action. Of these, the most effective was PRPAC.

Finally, Bell's most persuasive statement is that ethnicity provides a good basis for political organization and action when the state is receptive to ethnic-based demands. Thus, a fundamental boost to ethnicity comes from the willingness of the state to accept it as a criterion for allocational and distributive decisions. Yet when Puerto Ricans demanded bilingual education and the recognition of Three Kings Day as an official holiday, the government was not receptive at all. To make the fire department diversify its workforce, Puerto Ricans had to sue. The issue became more dramatic when the lack of Spanish-speaking firefighters contributed to the death of a Puerto Rican boy. Similarly, to satisfy some of their housing needs, they had to occupy city hall.

Some see nothing but false consciousness in politicized ethnicity and only conflict management in state responsiveness. In this view, ethnicity is a cover for class-based demands and the state responds willingly to secure social peace on the cheap. By focusing on ethnicity, the state diverts attention away from more fundamental issues such as poverty and income in-equality.[11] In the Puerto Rican case, ethnic-based claims were not diver-sions from real issues but the kind of issues that made a difference in the well-being of the community. Rather than a smokescreen, ethnicity was a resource, used by leaders and taken up by followers to articulate needs and to structure action.

The Role of the State

In "The Politics of a Multiethnic Society," Nathan Glazer argues that since 1970 a new pattern of ethnic politics has emerged in the United States, as a function of five characteristics defining recent ethnic groups: (1) these groups are not from Europe but from Africa, Asia, and Latin America; (2) the legality of immigration presents a different set of difficulties and concerns; (3) the groups's arrival has occurred in a context in which re-sponsibility for political enfranchisement and upward mobility is public rather than private; (4) new groups are more diverse than previous immi-grants culturally, linguistically, in their religious backgrounds, and in their skill levels; and finally, (5) some newcomers are loaded with old resent-ments against the United States. He concludes that these factors "create a heady brew, and turbulent as was the assimilation of the new European immigrant groups, the tensions of these five factors suggest a more turbu-lent period for the new groups."[12]

Glazer's analysis is accurate and relevant. His representation of the challenge posed by the new pattern is not. While nationally ethnic con-flict was not absent during the 1980s, contemporary disturbances were not any more threatening than in the past. As of this writing, Hartford, in particular, had not experienced any kind of political violence since 1970—instead it coasted through a quarter-century with relative political stability. During this period racial-ethnic tensions were successfully man-aged. Blacks elected a mayor and increased their political power. Puerto Ricans organized, mobilized, and achieved representation working to-gether with African Americans, progressives, and white ethnics.

Yet the debate concerning the impact of ethnicity on the political pro-cess continues to emphasize instability as an inherent feature of ethnic politics and conflict as an inevitable outcome. Even the metaphors chosen by analysts project images of violent agitation: from melting pot to bub-bling cauldron. Glazer suggests that the fundamental problem is twofold: on the one hand, there is the question of how to deal with ethnicity, whether to encourage assimilation or diversity. To this he answers that full assimilation to "a common national type" is the best alternative. On the other hand, there is the issue of the role that the state should play in the adjudication of ethnic claims, to which Glazer responds that it should play none. Both approaches are, in his view, indispensable requirements of stability, harmony, and political integration.[13]

On the one hand, assimilation has been held up as a normative ideal because it allegedly promotes stability and ameliorates conflict. But in fact cultural homogeneity is no guarantee of stability, and in the absence of cultural diversity other variables become a source of conflict. Instability and conflict cannot be prevented, they can only be transformed or managed. To manage instability and conflict, it is imperative to work within a framework of commonality, but this is not the same as striving for assimilation. Political incorporation is not the same as Anglo conformity, and neither is a condition for the other.

The state, on the other hand, always intervenes. It is naive to pretend that the state can adhere to a position of "benign neutrality," as Glazer recommends. The important question is not whether the state should intervene but how and to what ends. In this regard, John Higham has proposed a model that he calls "pluralistic integration." In this model the state supports only common interests and establishes only universalistic policies, while ethnicity and other types of particularistic categories are left to flourish, with varying degrees of intensity, within the society.[14]

This is an appealing model, but it has several problems. First, this division of labor is unrealistic, not because there are no boundaries between the political and the social, but rather because politics is as much about commonality as it is about difference—otherwise it would not be politics. Second, even if this neat division of labor were possible, it would be undesirable because, at best, it would produce a minimal state, and at worst there would be no state. Third, the model has important ideological implications. The general community, through the state, has always and will always support and strengthen particularity both for good and bad reasons. If particular interests are supported by the state for bad reasons but citizens become deluded into thinking that the state only addresses general concerns, they become ideologically disarmed against the hegemony of those interests. Yet, even if the idea of separation between the general and the particular is upheld as a normative aspiration, it is problematic because it does not provide for the support of specific interests by the state when this is good and necessary. One becomes, in short, unable to distinguish between what is good for the country and what is good for General Motors or, conversely, one reacts in knee-jerk fashion against the bailout of the Chrysler Corporation or affirmative action.[15]

In *Ethnic Politics*, Milton Esman, in referring to the role of the state in the management of ethnic conflict, places the burden of responsibility for this task on the shoulders of government officials. Rather than focusing on the impact of ethnicity per se or the ways in which its politicization may yield the best results for a particular ethnic community, Esman explores the ways in which the state can effectively juggle the opposite roles of creator and manager of ethnic conflict. "The normal inclination of political authorities," he writes, "is to defend existing structures of ethnic relations at minimum cost to the regime and to the dominant ethnic community," a pattern that fails to hold only when there is no dominant ethnic community or when conflict emerges from within the state itself. Because ethnicity poses a challenge that seldom yields definitive solutions, Esman focuses his analysis on the balance of power that results from the clash between ethnic groups and the state and the goals and methods the state brings to bear on the process.[16]

Esman's analysis of ethnic politics is one of the most fairminded and levelheaded among the many that crowd the academic literature; yet his emphasis is on the potentially destructive effects of ethnicity in the political process and the ways in which such potential can be minimized. In a statement reminiscent of Glazer and Moynihan's cool approach, Esman declares to "neither deplore nor celebrate the phenomenon of ethnic solidarity."[17] But his emphasis on conflict makes this statement rather disingenuous. There is not much room for anything other than a grudging acceptance of ethnicity if its salient feature is its potential destructiveness. In this view, the taming rather than the encouragement of ethnicity is the only adequate goal.

THE DISUNITING OF AMERICA?

In *The Disuniting of America*, Arthur M. Schlesinger, Jr., argues that the politicization of ethnicity in America in the post-civil rights period signals an emphasis on elitism rather than popular mobilization. In his view, ethnicity has become a cult, a rallying cry for "minority spokesmen—less interested in joining with the majority in common endeavor than in declaring their alienation from oppressive, white, patriarchal, racist, sexist, classist society. The ethnic ideology inculcates the illusion that membership in one or another ethnic group is the basic American experience."[18] Thus, ethnicity represents a threat to the American tradition of popular government, to the basic stability of the polity, and to the emphasis on individual as opposed to group rights.

Donald Rothchild and Alexander Groth analyze ethnic politics on the international arena and consider ethnic identity as "one of the well-established political fault lines of the modern world."[19] They identify internal and external variables—such as economic decline and the international environment—that magnify the "intrinsic" pathological tendencies of ethnicity. But they argue that the breakdown of the political order is the most significant magnifier of these pathologies. Drawing from the experience of the former Soviet Union and other Eastern European and African countries, they paint a portrait of exacerbated tensions and violent conflict in which ethnicity run amok plays a crucial role.

The Puerto Rican experience in Hartford is noteworthy because it does not illustrate any of these scenarios; nor does it suggest that identity politics is intrinsically destructive or a threat to the polity.[20] Instead, identity politics represented an alternative set of moorings securing a voice for a marginal group, structuring their agenda, and facilitating their incorporation. Contrary to what Schlesinger claims, political mobilization emerged out of the interaction between elites and masses. The notion of followerless ethnic entrepreneurs who manage to thrive despite the absence of grassroots support does not jibe with the Puerto Rican case. Ethnicity was an important trigger to mobilization, but the emphasis was on integration. In other words, although prejudice, disadvantage, and inequity were correlated with membership in a specific group, the correlations were used to promote political representation rather than to emphasize alienation. Thus, membership in an ethnic group was not only the Puerto Ricans' American experience but the context in which they sought objectives fully sanctioned by the civic culture.

Did ethnic politics represent a challenge to the government of the insurance city? To the extent that representation was an objective of mobilization, it did. But this challenge was not intrinsically destructive and, in fact, it was an antidote to the corrosive effects of exclusion and underrepresentation. If ethnicity is intrinsically pathological, as Rothchild and Groth claim, how often should it explode into violence and of what kind? In Hartford violence was not absent, but the tensions underlying violent conflict were managed and quickly ameliorated. Riots occurred only twice in more than forty years of community history, and in one of these instances Puerto Rican claims merged with the grievances of blacks.

Esman argues that ethnic politics is likely to degenerate into civic or violent conflict because the values that divide ethnic communities are unmistakably real. But this is an odd reason, in part because it suggests that peace and civility are the by-products of a politics devoid of substance. The Puerto Rican case shows that episodic violence was mostly defensive. Disfranchisement was compounded by ethnicity, but the combination did not make Puerto Ricans more prone to violence; instead, ethnicity made political exclusion vivid, thus energizing the quest for representation. This was not an entirely harmonious process, but neither was it pathological. On the contrary, ethnicity fostered solidarity and organization and it was a corrective to political inertia.

Even if ethnicity is not intrinsically negative, however, there is no denying that it is a fault line and a potential source of conflict. This should be taken for granted just as it is true for other categories, such as race or class. The really important question is not whether ethnicity is potentially a source of conflict but whether we can identify the conditions that prevent ethnic conflict from developing into full-scale violence. What prevents identity politics from exerting a destabilizing and destructive influence? As Esman suggests, this is where the state comes in, as a regulator and manager of conflict. Sociology also offers an answer, different in nature but complementary: to the extent that groups experience division from within and have affinities with other groups, tensions and conflict can be kept within bounds and in some cases even minimized or resolved.[21] Identity politics did not exempt Puerto Ricans from internal bickering. Similarly, in-group solidarity was punctuated by many instances of reaching out.

WHITHER IDENTITY POLITICS?

Steven Erie notes that there were differences in the extent to which first- and second-generation urban political machines were able to promote upward mobility among immigrants. Moreover, he recognizes that a strategy based on access to power produced both political and economic rewards that, although modest, were appreciated and used as a springboard to further gains by its beneficiaries. His assessment of machine politics is an important adjustment of previous analyses of the role of ethnic politics in the process of incorporation of new urban constituencies. But if the problem with pluralist interpretations is that they exaggerate the promise of ethnic politics, the problem with his evaluation is that it underestimates its deeds. Against an excessively high pluralist standard, actual gains appear substantially limited—although, as is clear from Erie's analysis, this was not true for everyone. By Erie's gauge, the strategy of "capturing the levers of urban power" to promote socioeconomic uplift appears misguided. His evaluation judges gains that fall short of "a pot of gold" as not even worth the effort.[22]

Although Erie criticizes Paul Peterson for "[freezing] his subject matter in time,"[23] his own negative assessment is in part determined by his projection into the future of the worst features of past and present: conservative national politics, uneven regional economic development, political challenges to accrued power, selective and unequal rewards, fiscal retrenchment, and fiscal crisis.[24] Yet isn't it possible that by applying the lessons of experience, political actors might use identity politics to change unfavorable circumstances? The irony of contingent political action is that, even when it conforms to the requirements of the situation, it creates opportunities for further action.

The Puerto Rican case suggests at least three important salutary effects of identity politics. First, it can be a venue for the resolution of claims, the righting of wrongs, and the integration of previously excluded actors; it fits well within the process of empowerment as a corrective to *entrenched* power. Second, by enlarging the scope of conflict, it can amplify and deepen the sense of political community. By widening the pool of participants in the political society, such mobilization increases the level of political equality. Third, by helping to change the face of power it enhances the level of political responsibility. As outsiders, Puerto Ricans could focus on their interests. Elected office forced them to consider a broader spectrum of demands even if their attempts to reach-out were not always selfless or effective.

In Hartford, integration, political community, and responsibility were served in concrete and symbolic ways. After Carmen Rodríguez was elected to the board of education in 1989, the number of Puerto Rican principals and vice principals in the schools increased from 6 to 31 percent. After 1991, the city began to do more business with Latino contractors and vendors. After Carrie Saxon Perry's reelection in that year, Puerto Rican department heads were kept and new ones were appointed. Puerto Ricans also increased their membership on a number of boards and commissions, including the Personnel Board, an important source of patronage.[25]

During the 1992 presidential campaign, the Clinton forces completely ignored the leading Puerto Rican organizations at the national level; in Connecticut, candidate Clinton visited El Mercado, a shopping center on Park Street, in the heart of Hartford's Puerto Rican community, and appeared on local Spanish-speaking TV. This had no significant effects on policies and resources. In fact, such token attention is derided by some analysts as "taco politics" and generally takes the form of photo ops and bland affirmations of cultural richness, resulting, at its worst, in a circus but no bread.[26] But to Puerto Ricans in Hartford, the equivalent tactic, or *cuchifrito* politics, was a signal of their newly acquired importance and developing power.[27]

In 1985, Hartford saw a motley crew of party regulars, radicals, and community activists come together to support Nancy Meléndez under the umbrella of the Hispanic Leadership Caucus before it permutated into PRPAC. Thereafter, Puerto Rican unity underscored a string of political victories that impressed both friends and foes. The comments of a conservative, and sometimes unfriendly, columnist are an example: "The most important voting bloc in Hartford today is Latino—mostly, but not entirely, residents of Puerto Rican background. . . . They are the best

Edwin García greeting Bill Clinton during his 1992 campaign visit to Hartford. García was elected state representative for Hartford's 6th assembly district in 1992. *Photo by Juan Fuentes. Courtesy of Juan Fuentes.*

organized, with the best voter-registration campaigns. Their Election Day get-out-the-vote effort rivals the now-fractured Democratic party and easily outstrips moribund Republicans'. . . . The city's most influential politician today may be Edwin Vargas, Jr. . . . Vargas heads the Puerto Rican Political Action Committee."[28] For a period of seven years there seemed to be hope in political representation, as the recognition that Puerto Ricans sought since the beginning of settlement began to be felt.

But identity politics was not just an instrument of in-group coherence, for Puerto Rican politics had a citywide impact. What this means was best described by Edwin Vargas: "PRPAC changed the cultural climate of the city. Puerto Ricans now have more respect, attitudes toward gays have changed. Within the community homophobic attitudes have softened."[29] The reform of purging procedures, spearheaded by the Connecticut Civil Liberties Union Foundation, PRPAC members, and others, provided for registration services in government agencies. Furthermore, the rule was changed so that special assistant registrars, who had been authorized to operate only on an ad hoc basis, could register voters all year round. These changes righted specific wrongs and were good for all.

These changes notwithstanding, the direct impact of PRPAC was most strongly felt in the electoral arena and in discrete policy power plays. Its record was mixed, so that persistent poverty robbed the gains secured by PRPAC leaders of some of their luster, inroads made in the governing structure of public schools were hampered by a relative disjunction from the policy process, and lasting divisions and conflict within and outside the community coexisted with the increased respect for otherness that PRPAC helped obtain for Puerto Ricans and non-Latinos.

Perhaps the best example of PRPAC's ambiguous policy role is the enactment of Public Act 91–392 in October 1991. Crafted and sponsored by Juan Figueroa, this legislation forced all jurisdictions in the state to take specific steps to encourage affordable housing. The bill was part of a package that included legislation to hold discretionary state funds from towns failing to develop affordable housing. Although legislators balked at the coerciveness of that approach, it forced them to pass compromise measures that were significant in breaking down exclusionary housing barriers.[30] Figueroa was very close to PRPAC; PRPAC helped elect him, but the group had little to do with this legislation. To be sure, this initiative did not spring, Athena-like, from Figueroa's head; but in the process of consultation and deliberation that preceded the legislation, PRPAC was one voice among many.

Identity politics was not an exercise in Pareto optimality although, in the end, some outcomes left all citizens better off. Puerto Ricans were able to achieve, albeit briefly, coalition dominance but were not flush in the exercise of coalition power. In 1993, Mayor Perry was defeated, PFC was ousted and replaced by a Republican minority, and Eugenio Caro, the only Puerto Rican from the Gang of Five to survive the electoral on-slaught, did so by running as a Republican candidate.

Meanwhile, in 1989, the mean household income per capita of Puerto Ricans in the United States was $8,379 but in the insurance city it was $6,095; relative to non-Hispanic whites, their income was 35 percent. In 1990, poverty among Puerto Ricans was 30 percent nationally but 47.5 percent in Hartford.[31] According to the city's Department of Planning and Economic Development, the number of persons twenty-five years and older who had completed four years of school or more had been increasing each decade since 1960, yet in 1990 less than 40 percent of Puerto Ricans in that cohort had done so. Not surprisingly, Puerto Ricans were almost one-third of the unemployed, a figure that belied the true scale of the problem since it did not include those who had ceased looking for a job.[32]

True, in the new arena of urban ethnic politics, welfare state bureaucracies perform a role that tends to ameliorate the impact of political disfranchisement.[33] Even when the winds of political change fail to blow in the direction of impoverished and/or unrepresented groups, bureaucratic inertia results, ironically, in a flow of benefits and services that helps them get by. Yet, the position of Puerto Ricans in Hartford was precarious given that, at 14.2 percent, the proportion of Puerto Ricans receiving public assistance in 1989 was small relative to their poverty rate: over two-thirds of those below the poverty level were left to fend for themselves.[34]

The case of Puerto Ricans in Hartford shows that the gap between coalition dominance and coalition power was not caused by an overestimation of the promise of identity politics but by discrepancies between capability and feasibility. The political context both constrained and promoted action. Conflict between Puerto Ricans and blacks, PRPAC's mobilization and policy strategy, and the dissonant requirements of campaigning and governing were some of the key factors that mediated the relationship between representation and responsiveness, coalition dominance and coalition power. Erie concludes: "The practitioners of the new ethnic politics are trying to consolidate power with limited local resources and diminished welfare-state largesse."[35] But it is not clear what "real" lessons can be extracted from this statement. If it means that class should substitute for ethnicity, how is this supposed to enhance local resources and increase benefits provided by the state?

It is unlikely that the factors and mechanisms that kept PRPAC from achieving one of its key strategic goals—that is, to control policy by becoming a non-partisan political machine—would have played a different role if the emphasis of mobilization had been class. Because out-groups perceived Puerto Rican gains as their losses, Puerto Rican ascent was seen not as a corrective but as a reinforcer of political inequality. The challenge for identity politics was to ride the wave of Puerto Rican interests and pride without exacerbating conflict and suspicions of partiality. As in other urban settings, in Hartford this proved to be achievable in campaigning but much more difficult in governing.

The Puerto Rican case illustrates how identity structures the process of empowerment by prompting and organizing mobilization around cultural, linguistic, and political issues. Puerto Ricans maximized the effects of mobilization from the vantage point of community characteristics that developed over time: significant demographic concentration, capable leadership, and effective organization. For a while this mobilization took place in the context of a political system in which the demands of a fractured public were managed in autocratic and exclusionary fashion. Subsequently, authoritarian control gave way to fractionalized administration. In this changing context, the challenge of ethnicity was to enhance the process of empowerment by transforming incorporation into responsiveness.

Identity politics gave Puerto Ricans representation but complicated the exercise of power. This was in part the result of the role ethnicity played in the process, in part the result of features of the political process itself.

THE CHALLENGE OF ETHNICITY

In politics, the challenge of ethnicity is one of ideological clarification concerning questions about the character of social integration, the nature and management of conflict, and the role of identity in representation and policy. Part of the challenge is related to the ability of political actors to disentangle obscure and complicated relations of causality. In other words, political actors need to sort out what is the result of ethnicity and what is the result of other factors, with special attention to changing circumstances. It would be foolish to claim that a clear understanding of these relations inevitably leads to favorable results, because knowledge is not an independent variable and action often has unintended consequences. Moreover, part of the political process always unfolds "behind our backs," as it were; sometimes political actors succeed in spite of themselves. Nonetheless, this level of understanding is important because it underscores the contingent character of political outcomes.

The larger problem, of course, is how to meet increasing social and economic needs in the context of decreasing resources; decreasing not because of a shrinking pie, even though productivity *is* a serious problem, but because of the relative size of distributive shares. In Hartford, the pov-

Table 11. Characteristics of Hartford's Puerto Rican Neighborhoods, 1990 (in percent)

	Citywide	Clay Arsenal	Frog Hollow	Parkville	Sheldon-Charter Oak	South Green
Families below poverty level	26	54	46	21	47	35
Persons 25+ years						
High School Graduate	59	41	47	52	46	52
Bachelor's Degree	14	3	15	11	15	14
Linguistically isolated households	14	13	32	22	21	25
Persons 16+ Years						
In Labor Force	61	45	51	61	49	58
Unemployed	11	24	18	8	16	12
Renter-occupied units	76	92	92	80	93	91
Occupied units without						
Telephone	14	25	27	7	28	29
Automobile	39	70	55	31	63	53
Occupied units with more than						
one person per room	8	14	18	7	14	17

SOURCE: City of Hartford, Department of Planning and Economic Development, *State of the City*, 1995.

erty rate in 1990 was 26 percent for all families but the proportion of poor families in Puerto Rican neighborhoods ranged from 35 to 54 percent. The proportion of people citywide that did not own a car was 39 percent but for Puerto Ricans the proportion ranged from a low of 31 to a high of 70 percent. Those residential units without access to a telephone in the city were 14 percent of the total. In contrast, in neighborhoods where Puerto Ricans concentrated the average was 22 percent, with a high of 29 percent in the South Green. Overcrowding was also a serious problem, with only 8 percent of residential units in the city housing more than one person per room compared to 14 percent of units in the Puerto Rican enclaves of Clay Arsenal and Sheldon-Charter Oak and 18 percent in Frog Hollow. Furthermore, of the eleven neighborhoods where renter-occupied housing units exceeded the citywide rate of 76 percent, five were Puerto Rican. Thus, at a time when only 40 percent of the population was white, the problem of distributive shares was not only critical but defined by ethnicity[36] (see Table 11).

In meeting social, political, and economic needs in such circumstances, the politicization of ethnicity is more part of the solution than part of the problem. The balkanizing effect of ethnicity is not absolute. However visible and threatening ethnicity might appear to be, it rarely stands unaffected by other factors. Ethnic polarization is often offset by forces that lean toward pluralistic inclusion. Usually both tendencies go together—polarization prompting pluralistic responses—causing a diffusion effect, as when inclusion desocializes ethnicity and makes it more symbolic than factual. When the latter is the case, ethnicity does not necessarily become less real or substantive, but it certainly loses its disruptive edge.[37]

Ironically, fragmentation and instability are more likely precisely when political actors refuse to acknowledge difference and either insist on non-ethnic approaches, as if ideals such as postethnicity or color blindness could substitute for reality, or prefer to ground their strategy in other categories. Some, for example, would just as soon replace ethnicity with class as the basis of a "better" kind of politics—one more realistic and inclusive, less diffuse.[38] In this view, class simplifies conflict by reducing it to capitalists versus workers, rich versus poor, or in contemporary parlance, people of color versus the white establishment. Such simplification makes everything else "clear," including the outlines of strategic action and the potential outcomes. The proponents of this scheme take their cue from "the real lessons at rainbow's end" and seek to move beyond a politics of identity that is, in their view, limited, murky, and balkanizing.

The response to this argument cannot be just a simple denial because an either/or outlook only substitutes one set of simplistic assumptions and propositions for another. The challenge of ethnicity is, in effect, perennial because accomplishments are never one hundred percent and political action is always tempered by unintended consequences. No category is exempt from this reality. Thus, while reductionist approaches satisfy the human craving for simplicity and coherence, they are nonetheless inadequate.

It should be clear by now that the argument made here for identity politics is conditional. It is sensitive to history, it does not presume to determine causality a priori, and it focuses on how individuals and groups reconcile capability and feasibility. In this approach, normative standards are *constructed* by political actors as they adapt will to circumstances. Moreover, in this process, protagonists recognize that capability is measured by how interest articulation produces political effects, not necessarily by how close or how far these effects fall from the chosen standard. The distance between outcomes and norms helps set the terms of prospective action. But in setting those terms, participants must keep in mind that politics is not reducible to a single logic. Further, they need to understand that the gap between ideals and practice is a reminder that in politics, as Machiavelli once said, "One change always leaves the way prepared for the introduction of another."[39]

Notes

Chapter One

1. Edward Ericson, "Meet the New Boss," *Hartford Advocate*, 12 November 1992, pp. 8–10, 15.

2. Edwin Vargas, Jr., interview, 4 May 1993. All interviews were with the author.

3. Classic works include Lawrence Chenault, *The Puerto Rican Migrant in New York City* (1938; reprint, New York: Russell & Russell, 1970); C. Wright Mills, Clarence Senior, and Rose Kohn Goldsen, *The Puerto Rican Journey,: New York's Newest Migrants* (1950; reprint, New York: Russell & Russell, 1967); Oscar Handlin, *The Newcomers: Negroes and Puerto Ricans in a Changing Metropolis* (Cambridge: Harvard University Press, 1959) and Joseph P. Fitzpatrick, *Puerto Rican Americans: The Meaning of Migration to the Mainland* (Englewood Cliffs, N.J.: Prentice Hall, 1971). For good contemporary theoretical and empirical treatments of the issues of Puerto Rican migration, see Centro de Estudios Puertorriqueños, ed., *Labor Migration under Capitalism: The Puerto Rican Experience* (New York: Monthly Review Press, 1979), and Francisco L. Rivera-Batiz and Carlos Santiago, *Puerto Ricans in the United States: A Changing Reality* (Washington, D.C.: National Puerto Rican Coalition, 1994).

4. Puerto Ricans have lived in the United States since the mid-nineteenth century. In 1844, the family of José de Rivera moved from New York to Bridgeport, Connecticut. According to the 1860 census for New Haven, there were ten Puerto Ricans in the city, one of whom appears to have fought in the Civil War. See Helen Harrison, "Edward Johnson House," *Bridgeport Daily Standard*, 31 October 1914; Neil Hogan, "The Actual Enumeration: New Haven and the U.S. Census," *Journal* (New Haven Colony Historical Society) 38 (Fall 1991): 9, 17.

5. The heavy machinery used in Puerto Rican *haciendas* during the last quarter of the nineteenth century came from the United States, France, and England. See Carlos Buitrago Ortiz, *Los Orígenes Históricos de la Sociedad Pre-capitalista en Puerto Rico* (San Juan: Ediciones Huracán, 1976), pp. 35–36. In 1892, the Puerto Rican newspaper *El Imparcial* noted that if U.S. imports were restricted to implements, machinery, and codfish, Puerto Rico would not be a prisoner of the American market. During the 1894–95 session of the Spanish courts, a petitioner suggested that Puerto Rico would be better off importing codfish from Nova Scotia than from the United States. See Lidio Cruz Monclova, *Historia de Puerto Rico,* vol. 3, *Siglo XIX* (Rio Piedras, P.R.: Editorial Universitaria, 1979), pp. 272, 278.

6. National Puerto Rican Coalition, *A Demographic Profile of Puerto Ricans in the United States* (Washington, D.C., 1992), p. 15.

7. Edwin Maldonado, "Contract Labor and the Origins of Puerto Rican Communities in the United States," *International Migration Review* 13 (Spring 1979): 107.

8. Mills, Senior, and Goldsen, *Puerto Rican Journey*, p. 53.

9. Clarence Senior and Donald O. Watkins, "Toward a Balance Sheet of Puerto Rican Migration," in *Status of Puerto Rico: Selected Background Studies Prepared for the United States-Puerto Rico Commission on the Status of Puerto Rico* (Washington, D.C.: United States-Puerto Rico Commission on the Status of Puerto Rico, 1966), p. 706; in her study of Puerto Ricans in Milwaukee, Anne Akulicz de Santiago documents the importance of family in the decision to migrate. In 1952, 66 percent of migrants were persuaded to move by their spouses, other relatives, and friends. In 1978, 53 percent of migrants moved to Milwaukee for similar reasons. See *The Puerto Rican Community of Milwaukee: A Study of Geographic Mobility* (Milwaukee: Spanish Speaking Outreach Institute, University of Wisconsin-Milwaukee, 1980), pp. 44, 46.

10. Dispersion has been noted since the 1950s, but it was not significant until 1980. See Clarence Senior, "Puerto Rican Dispersion in the United States," *Social Problems* 2 (October 1954): 93–99; Kal Wagenheim, *A Survey of Puerto Ricans on the U.S. Mainland in the 1970s* (New York: Praeger, 1975), pp. 11, 74.

11. The pattern of demographic dispersion that characterized Puerto Rican migration and settlement during the 1980s is not well understood. Partial evidence suggests that economic and quality of life factors were crucial components in an array of incentives fostering mobility and the choice of location. See Rivera-Batiz and Santiago, *Puerto Ricans in the United States*, p. 114.

12. Philip Gleason points out that "the most important single factor in the ethnic revival [of the late 1960s] was the new spirit of group-centered militance shown by American blacks." *Speaking of Diversity, Language and Ethnicity in Twentieth-Century America* (Baltimore: Johns Hopkins University Press, 1992), p. 75.

13. Miren Uriarte, "Organizing for Survival: The Emergence of a Puerto Rican Community," Ph.D. diss., Boston University, 1988; Gloria Bonilla-Santiago, *Organizing Puerto Rican Migrant Farmworkers: The Experience of Puerto Ricans in New Jersey* (New York: Peter Lang, 1988).

14. Articles and studies about Puerto Ricans outside New York City from the 1950s and early 1960s include J. E. Koch, "Puerto Ricans Come to Youngstown," *Commonweal*, 8 October 1953, pp. 9–11; Isham B. Jones, "The Puerto Rican in New Jersey: His Present Status," New Jersey State Department of Education, Division against Discrimination, July 1955; Fred Golob, "The Puerto Rican Worker in Perth Amboy, New Jersey," Occasional Studies no. 2, Institute of Management and Labor Relations, Rutgers University, March 1956; Daniel Donchian, "A Survey of New Haven's Newcomers: The Puerto Ricans," Human Relations Council of Greater New Haven, May 1959; Thomas P. Imse, "Puerto Ricans in Buffalo," City of Buffalo, Board of Community Relations, 1961; Alvin String, "Puerto Ricans in New Jersey," *Public Health News*, August 1962; City of Philadelphia, Commission on Human Relations, "Philadelphia's Puerto Rican Population with

1960 Census Data," March 1964. None dealt with politics or with the relationship between ethnicity and political incorporation, although Golob's article noted that Puerto Ricans did well in the labor market and Imse declared that Puerto Rican children were Americanizing rapidly.

In 1984, James Jennings and Monte Rivera edited a volume that addressed the geographical imbalance of research about Puerto Rican politics only in its title. In *Puerto Rican Politics in Urban America* (Westport, Conn.: Greenwood Press, 1984), five out of seven chapters are about New York City.

15. Joan Dee Koss understands community organization as a cultural expression in "Puerto Ricans in Philadelphia: Migration and Accommodation," Ph.D. diss., University of Pennsylvania, 1965; in *The Puerto Rican Community of Milwaukee*, Akulicz de Santiago devotes two sentences to their political status and aspirations.

16. In "Organizing for Survival," Uriarte conceptualized the process of community formation as one aspect of the political process. But her objective was to explore the role of community organizations in the development of ethnic identity.

17. The epiphenomenal approach and the internal colonialism thesis can be found in Felix M. Padilla, *Puerto Rican Chicago* (Notre Dame, Ind.: University of Notre Dame Press, 1987), pp. 6, 13.

18. The English founders of Hartford called the settlement Newtown—after the Massachusetts town they came from—and in 1637 renamed it *Harteford*, after an English town. The Native Americans who originally occupied the land called it *Suckiaug*, meaning "black earth."

19. William DeLoss Love, *The Colonial History of Hartford* (Chester, Conn.: Centinel Hill Press, 1974), p. 349.

20. Republicans regularly called for "businesslike government, without concern for the feelings of the would-be bosses and spoils-mongers." *Hartford Courant*, 9 April 1895, p. 6.

21. A recent analysis characterizes Hartford during this period as a bifurcated economy and a paternalistic society. Stephen Valocchi, "Hartford Voices: Race, Ethnicity, and Neighborhood during the Great Depression," September 1993, unpublished manuscript. On the one hand, inequality was a feature of the city's economy even before incorporation in 1784. On the other hand, it is unclear how one can consider Hartford paternalistic, as riven with conflict as it was during the first three decades of the twentieth century.

22. Herbert F. Janick, Jr., *A Diverse People: Connecticut 1914 to the Present* (Chester, Conn.: Pequot Press, 1975), p. 102.

23. The separation of church and state was officially effected in 1818. In 1852, Harriet Beecher Stowe, a Hartford resident, published her antislavery novel *Uncle Tom's Cabin*. In 1854, a member of the Know-Nothing party purchased Hartford's daily newspaper, the *Courant*, transforming it into a partisan vehicle. With the help of the *Courant*, the Know-Nothings captured the governorship in 1855. Anti-immigrant feelings in the city were so strong that in 1894, to prove their loyalty to American ideals, the Irish decided to terminate the Saint Patrick's Day Parade. In the state, women were granted the right to vote in 1893 but were limited

to school matters. In 1895, three women were for the first time nominated to partisan positions in the city. In that same year the state legislature refused to extend the franchise so as to shield women from the "satanic" influence of politics.

24. Kwame Ture and Charles V. Hamilton, *Black Power: The Politics of Liberation in America* (New York: Vintage Books, 1992), p. 44; emphasis in original.

25. Browning, Marshall, and Tabb offer a narrower definition: incorporation occurs when a group achieves a presence in governing coalitions. Rufus Browning, Dale Rogers Marshall, and David H. Tabb, *Protest Is Not Enough: The Struggle of Blacks and Hispanics for Equality in Urban Politics* (Berkeley: University of California Press, 1986), pp. 24–25.

26. As suggested by Robert A. Dahl in *Who Governs?* (New Haven: Yale University Press, 1961) and by Kathleen Neils Conzen in *Immigrant Milwaukee: 1836–1860* (Cambridge: Harvard University Press, 1976).

27. Identity is constant in that the self is constant; what changes is the content of identity, while there is a shell that is less susceptible to outside influence. For example, I will always be Puerto Rican, but I am no longer a monolingual Puerto Rican nationalist.

28. In electronics, the cycle of a sine wave is the portion of the wave that establishes the pattern from point 0 to the peak, from the peak to the lowest point, and from there back to 0. Cycles are regular in duration; thus, the first cycle tells the story of the whole wave. This is therefore a good but imperfect analogy since sine waves are repetitive and politics is not.

29. Kathleen Neils Conzen et al., "The Invention of Ethnicity: A Perspective from the U.S.A.," *Journal of American Ethnic History* 12 (Fall 1992): 3–41, and the response by Lawrence H. Fuchs, "Comment: 'The Invention of Ethnicity': The Amen Corner," *Journal of American Ethnic History* 12 (Fall 1992): 53–58; Herbert J. Gans, "Symbolic Ethnicity: The Future of Ethnic Groups and Cultures in America," *Ethnic and Racial Studies* 2 (January 1979): 1–20; Irving Howe, "The Limits of Ethnicity," *New Republic*, June 25, 1977, pp. 17–19.

30. Wallerstein and Horowitz use similar terms to define ethnic identity. Wallerstein's context, however, is West Africa and the role of ethnicity in the achievement of national integration in decolonized settings. Horowitz focuses on how action changes group identity, whereas I emphasize the effect of identity on action. Immanuel Wallerstein, "Ethnicity and National Integration in West Africa," *Cahiers d'Etudes Africaines* 1 (July 1960): 131, 133–34; Donald L. Horowitz, "Ethnic Identity," in Nathan Glazer and Daniel P. Moynihan, eds., *Ethnicity: Theory and Experience* (Cambridge: Harvard University Press, 1975), pp. 111–40.

31. Padilla, *Puerto Rican Chicago*, p. 4.

32. Glazer and Moynihan, eds., *Ethnicity: Theory and Experience*, p. 15.

33. The notion of power awareness was suggested to me by Lloyd Rogler, *Migrant in the City: The Life of a Puerto Rican Action Group* (New York: Basic Books, 1972), p. 5.

34. A 1974 analysis of criminal justice statistics indicated that the person most likely to be arrested in Hartford was young, unemployed, male, and Puerto Rican. Moreover, although the evidence was not conclusive, an analysis of the disposition of cases strongly suggested a law enforcement system "biased in favor

of light-skinned defendants, especially those for whom English is a native language." Walter Gray Markham, "Chromatic Justice: Color as an Element of the Offense," paper presented at the annual meetings of the American Political Science Association, Chicago, August 29–September 2, 1974, pp. 5, 15.

35. A correlation between ethnicity, race, and status is sometimes used to suggest the existence of discrimination regardless of whether the affected parties see it that way. See, e.g., Robert D. Bullard, *Dumping in Dixie: Race, Class, and Environmental Quality* (Boulder, Colo.: Westview Press, 1990), and D. R. Wernette and L. A. Nieves, "Breathing Polluted Air," *EPA Journal*, March/April, 1992, pp. 16–17. Bullard is not shy in charging that the siting of environmentally noxious facilities in and around black neighborhoods is not random. Wernette and Nieves do not explicitly make a case for discrimination, but they note that the disproportionate exposure of African Americans and Latinos to air pollutants cannot be explained either by their geographic distribution or their economic status.

36. Wrinkle et al. find that "both Mexican Americans and Puerto Ricans who report being victimized by discrimination are more likely to report engaging in non-electoral participation, and for both groups, this is the strongest cultural predictor [of participation]." Robert D. Wrinkle et al., "Ethnicity and Nonelectoral Political Participation," *Hispanic Journal of Behavioral Sciences* 18 (May 1996): 146.

37. Rodney Hero, *Latinos and the U.S. Political System: Two-Tiered Pluralism* (Philadelphia: Temple University Press, 1992), p. 133; Andrés Torres, *Between Melting Pot and Mosaic* (Philadelphia: Temple University Press, 1995), pp. 19–20, 166.

38. Coalition power is exercised when the legal, administrative, and policy capacities of the state are used to produce benefits to specific constituencies and/or to the public at large. The flow of benefits can be steady or episodic, and the rewards can be material or symbolic.

39. Herbert Gans, "Foreword," in Neil C. Sandberg, *Ethnic Identity and Assimilation: The Polish American Community* (New York: Praeger, 1974, p. vii.

40. *Quinceañera* are coming-of-age parties, much like debutante balls, at which fifteen-year-old girls celebrate their passage into womanhood. See Daisann McLane, "The Cuban-American Princess," *New York Times Magazine*, 26 February 1995, p. 42.

41. See, respectively, Jonathan Rabinovitz, "An Editorial Provokes a Debate on Intermarriage; Jewish Weekly Touches a Nerve in Connecticut," *New York Times*, 13 July 1995, p. B1; Matthew Purdy, "Symbols of Exile Bloom in Jews' Yards," *New York Times*, 14 October 1995, p. 21; Neil Strauss, "Seder for Rock Musicians," *New York Times*, 4 April 1996, p. C14. Sukkahs are open-air huts used during Sukkoth, a seven-day holiday celebrating the harvest and commemorating forty years of wandering in biblical times.

42. See, respectively, Mireya Navarro, "New Policy on Cubans Met by Protest Drive," *New York Times*, 17 May 1995, p. A12; David Gonzalez, "Puerto Ricans Get Freedom, Culturally," *New York Times*, 26 March 1996, p. B1;

43. See, respectively, Pam Belluck, "Sinn Fein's Leader Raises Funds at Queens Reception," *New York Times*, 13 March 1995, p. A2; Selwyn Raab, "64 Indicted as Gangsters in Chinatown," *New York Times*, 24 February 1996, p. A23.

44. Daniel Bell's benign assessment of identity politics as a "new mode of seeking political redress" (see "Ethnicity and Social Change" in Glazer and Moynihan, eds., *Ethnicity*, p. 169) contrasts with more recent and harsher evaluations.

Vered Amit-Talai, for example, documents how in Greater Montreal ethnic activism has resulted in instances of neo-corporatist inclusion that blunt criticism and that, in rather circular fashion, incorporate minorities as advisers on how minorities can be incorporated. See "The Minority Circuit: Identity Politics and the Professionalization of Ethnic Activism" in Vered Amit-Talai and Caroline Knowles, eds., *Resituating Identities: The Politics of Race, Ethnicity, and Culture* (Peterborough, Canada: broadview press, 1996), pp. 98–100.

Other critics include Paul Berman, "In Defense of Reason," *New Yorker*, 4 September 1996, p. 94; Eleanor Heartney, "Identity Politics at the Whitney," *Art in America* (May 1993): 42–47; Arthur M. Schlesinger, Jr., *The Disuniting of America* (New York: Norton, 1992); and Manning Marable, "Building Coalitions among Communities of Color: Beyond Racial Identity Politics," in James Jennings, ed., *Blacks, Latinos, and Asians in Urban America* (Westport, Conn.: Praeger, 1994), pp. 29–43.

The voice of Todd Gitlin is one of the most ardent. He argues that identity politics only leads to "a grim and hermetic bravado which takes the ideological form of paranoid, jargon-clotted, post-modernist groupthink, cult celebrations of victimization and stylized marginality." See "From Universality to Difference: Notes on the Fragmentation of the Idea of the Left," *Contention* 2 (Winter 1993): 21.

According to Betty Friedan, identity politics leads, at best, to "a rights-based focus on narrowly defined grievances and goals" and, at worst, to "a future of separate and warring races, genders, and generations." See "Children's Crusade," *New Yorker*, 3 June 1996, p. 6.

Frances Fox Piven joins these critics while recognizing that identity politics is here to stay. See "Globalizing Capitalism and the Rise of Identity Politics," *Socialist Register 1995*, pp. 102–16.

Although Roger Waldinger and Mehdi Bozorgmher's *Ethnic Los Angeles* (New York: Russell Sage, 1996) is not about identity politics per se, it identifies the conditions that ensure that ethnicity will continue to be salient and relevant in society and the economy. Theirs is a voice of sobriety amid the prevailing hyperbole.

45. Edward C. Banfield and James Q. Wilson, *City Politics* (Cambridge: Harvard University Press, 1967), pp. 46, 95, 131, 170, 171, 230.

46. Michael Peter Smith and Joe R. Feagin, "Putting 'Race' in Its Place," in Michael Peter Smith and Joe R. Feagin, eds., *The Bubbling Cauldron: Race, Ethnicity, and the Urban Crisis* (Minneapolis: University of Minnesota Press, 1995), p. 4.

47. Rita Jalali and Seymour Martin Lipset, "Racial and Ethnic Conflicts: A Global Perspective," in Demetrios Caraley and Cerentha Harris, eds., *New World Politics: Power, Ethnicity, and Democracy* (New York: Academy of Political Science, 1993), pp. 55–76; Donald Rothchild and Alexander J. Groth, "Pathological Dimensions of Domestic and International Ethnicity," *Political Science Quarterly* 110 (Spring 1995), pp. 69–82.

48. Glazer and Moynihan, *Ethnicity: Theory, and Experience*, pp. 8, 15; see also Daniel P. Moynihan, "Patterns of Ethnic Succession: Blacks and Hispanics in New York City," *Political Science Quarterly* 94 (Spring 1979): 3.

49. Alejandro Portes and Robert L. Bach, *Latin Journey: Cuban and Mexican Immigrants in the United States* (Berkeley: University of California Press, 1985).

50. Harry A. Bailey and Ellis Katz, "Ethnic Groups and Political Behavior," in Harry A. Bailey and Ellis Katz, eds., *Ethnic Group Politics* (Columbus, Ohio: Merrill Political Science Series, 1969), p. 60; Scott Cummings, *Immigrant Minorities and the Urban Working Class* (Port Washington, N.Y.: National University Publications, 1983), pp. 8, 9, 126; Rodolfo O. de la Garza, Robert D. Wrinkle, and Jerry L. Polinard, "Ethnicity and Policy: The Mexican American Perspective," in F. Chris Garcia, ed., *Latinos and the Political System* (Notre Dame, Ind: University of Notre Dame Press, 1988), p. 438; John D. Buenker, *Urban Liberalism and Progressive Reform* (New York: Scribner's, 1973).

51. As suggested, respectively, by Rivka Shpak Lissak, *Pluralism and Progressives: Hull House and the New Immigrants, 1890–1919* (Chicago: University of Chicago Press, 1989), and Mary C. Waters, *Ethnic Options: Choosing Identities in America* (Berkeley: University of California Press, 1990).

52. As indicated by Lawrence H. Fuchs, *The American Kaleidoscope: Race, Ethnicity, and the Civic Culture* (Hanover, N.H.: University Press of New England, 1990), and Nathan Glazer, *Ethnic Dilemmas* (Cambridge: Harvard University Press, 1983).

53. Juan Flores makes this recommendation in *Divided Borders: Essays on Puerto Rican Identity* (Houston: Arte Público Press, 1993).

54. The literature that documents and analyzes this role spans two decades and cuts across disciplines. See, e.g., Raymond E. Wolfinger, "The Development and Persistence of Ethnic Voting," *American Political Science Review* 59 (December 1965): 896–908. Wolfinger's article was incorporated in his book *The Politics of Progress* (Englewood Cliffs, N.J.: Prentice Hall, 1974); Michael Parenti, "Ethnic Politics and the Persistence of Ethnic Identification," *American Political Science Review* 61 (September 1967): 717–26; Elmer E. Cornwell, Jr., "Bosses, Machines, and Ethnic Groups," in Lawrence H. Fuchs, ed., *American Ethnic Politics* (New York: Harper Torchbooks, 1968), pp. 194–216; Nathan Glazer and Daniel P. Moynihan, *Beyond the Melting Pot: The Negroes, Puerto Ricans, Jews, Italians, and Irish of New York City* (Cambridge: MIT Press, 1970); Michael Novak, *The Rise of the Unmeltable Ethnics* (New York: Macmillan, 1971); Glazer, *Ethnic Dilemmas*; Fuchs, *American Kaleidoscope*; Milton J. Esman, *Ethnic Politics* (Ithaca: Cornell University Press, 1994).

55. The accounts of Nicholas Lemann, "Black Nationalism on Campus," *The Atlantic*, January 1993, pp. 31–47, and James Traub, "The Hearts and Minds of City College," *New Yorker*, 7 June 1993, pp. 42–53, illustrate the paradoxical and ambiguous character of identity politics. Identity politics can be the source of both reasonable and unreasonable attitudes and behavior.

56. The nature of urban discourse itself is contested. A recent illustration is the exchange between Robert A. Beauregard, Sam Bass Warner, Jr., and Robert Warren in the *Journal of Urban Affairs* 18 (1996): 217–43.

57. E. E. Schattschneider, *The Semi-Sovereign People* (Hinsdale, Ill.: Dryden Press, 1960), p. 59.

58. Rudolf Hilferding, "The Materialist Conception of History," in Tom Bottomore, ed., *Modern Interpretations of Marx* (Oxford: Basil Blackwell, 1981), p. 128.

59. See, e.g., C. Wright Mills, *The Power Elite* (New York: Oxford University Press, 1956); Arnold M. Rose, *The Power Structure* (New York: Oxford University Press, 1967); Floyd Hunter, *Community Power Structure* (Chapel Hill: University of North Carolina Press, 1953); G. William Domhoff, *Who Really Rules* (Santa Monica, Calif.: Goodyear, 1978).

60. See, e.g., Dahl, *Who Governs?*; Edward Banfield, *Political Influence* (Glencoe, Ill.: Free Press, 1961); Nelson Polsby, *Community Power and Political Theory* (New Haven: Yale University Press, 1963); Robert J. Waste, *Power and Pluralism in American Cities* (Westport, Conn.: Greenwood Press, 1987).

61. See, e.g., Phillipe Schmitter, "Modes of Interest Intermediation and Models of Social Change in Western Europe," *Comparative Political Studies* 10 (April 1977): 7–38, and "Still the Century of Corporatism?" *Review of Politics* 36 (January 1974): 85–131; Leo Panitch, "Recent Theorizations of Corporatism: Reflections on a Growth Industry," *British Journal of Sociology* 31 (June 1980): 159–87.

62. See, e.g., John Manley, "Neo-Pluralism: A Class Analysis of Pluralism I and Pluralism II," *American Political Science Review* 77 (June 1983): 368–83; David Harvey, *Social Justice and the City* (Baltimore: Johns Hopkins University Press, 1973); Charles Tiebout, "A Pure Theory of Local Expenditures," *Journal of Political Economy* 64 (1956): 416–24.

63. See, e.g., John H. Mollenkopf, *A Phoenix in the Ashes* (Princeton: Princeton University Press), especially chapter 2. This chapter is a comprehensive survey and assessment of theories of urban power and includes an extensive bibliography on the subject except as it relates to neocorporatism; see also Clarence N. Stone, *Economic Growth and Neighborhood Discontent* (Chapel Hill: University of North Carolina Press, 1976) and *Regime Politics: Governing Atlanta: 1964–1988* (Lawrence: University Press of Kansas, 1989). In *Theories of Urban Politics* (London: Sage, 1995), David Judge, Gerry Stoker, and Harold Wolman review and update the theoretical spectrum summarized here, including discussions of urban social movements, gender in urban politics, and so-called regulation theory.

64. Paul E. Peterson, *City Limits* (Chicago: University of Chicago Press, 1981), p. 5.

65. Stone, *Economic Growth*, pp. 8, n.16; 228; Stone, *Regime Politics*, p. xi.

66. Peterson, *City Limits*, p. 5.

67. Doing this is not easy, in part because the prescriptive capacity of historical knowledge is sometimes erroneously construed as axiomatic. In other words, by establishing and examining precedents to situations, political actors might be able to identify a range of probable outcomes following action, which might put them in a better position to act, but it will not necessarily indicate an appropriate strategy. Furthermore, even if the strategy is right, action might be miscarried by unforeseen events and circumstances. To say that the examination of the past helps

us understand the present and tells us where to go in the future does not mean that our understanding is necessarily correct or that we will get to our destination.

68. V. O. Key, *Politics, Parties, and Pressure Groups*, 4th ed. (New York: Crowell, 1958), pp. 166–68.

69. Gitlin, "From Universality to Difference," p. 35.

70. Philip Gourevitch, "Misfortune Tellers," *New Yorker*, 8 April 1996, p. 98.

CHAPTER TWO

1. Quoted in James E. Smith, *One Hundred Years of Hartford's "Courant"* (New Haven: Yale University Press, 1949), p. 116.

2. James C. Welling, *Connecticut Federalism or Aristocratic Politics in a Social Democracy* (New York: New York Historical Society, 1890), p. 7.

3. Joseph Lieberman, *The Power Broker* (Boston: Houghton Mifflin, 1966), p. 57.

4. Quoted in Lieberman, *Power Broker*, p. 33.

5. Stephen Valocchi, "Hartford Voices: Race, Ethnicity, and Neighborhood during the Great Depression," unpublished manuscript, September 1993, pp. 5, 7.

6. Henri Michel, *The Second World War* (New York: Praeger, 1975), p. 435.

7. Jack Zaiman, "Moylan Elected Mayor in Landslide Vote; Republicans Increase Council Majority," *Hartford Courant*, 7 November 1945, p. 1. Spellacy resigned over a dispute concerning residency requirements of municipal employees. See "Thomas Spellacy, Connecticut Aide," *New York Times*, 6 December 1957, p. 29.

8. John W. Jeffries, *Testing the Roosevelt Coalition* (Knoxville: University of Tennessee Press, 1979), pp. 200–202.

9. *Hartford Courant*, 1 November 1945, p. 8.

10. *Hartford Courant*, 1 November 1945, p. 8; 2 November 1945, p. 16.

11. The account in this paragraph is drawn from Lieberman, *Power Broker*, pp. 40–82.

12. Herbert F. Janick, Jr., *A Diverse People: Connecticut 1914 to the Present* (Chester, Conn.: Pequot Press, 1975), pp. 84–85.

13. In 1946, the group changed its name to the Citizens Charter Committee.

14. *Hartford Courant*, 6 November–15 December 1946.

15. Quoted in Janick, *A Diverse People*, p. 85; see also Keith Schonrock, "Republican State Ticket Sweeps to Victory, City's Democrats Give Snow 11,745 Plurality, GOP Making Gains in Congress Contests," *Hartford Courant*, 6 November 1946, p. 1.

16. What Hartford's business leaders and residents understood in the late 1960s, political scientists discovered in the 1950s. See Charles R. Adrian, "Some General Characteristics of Nonpartisan Elections," *American Political Science Review* 47 (September 1952): 766–76; Oliver P. Williams and Charles R. Adrian, "The Insulation of Local Politics under the Nonpartisan Ballot," *American Political Science Review* 53 (December 1959): 1052–63.

17. Sondra Astor Stave and Bruce Stave, "Making Hartford Home: An Oral History of Twentieth-Century Ethnic Development in Connecticut's Capitol City,"

in Sondra Astor Stave, ed., *Hartford: The City and the Region* (West Hartford: University of Hartford, 1979), pp. 31–49.

18. Janick, *A Diverse People*, p. 83.

19. Janick, *A Diverse People*, p. 94.

20. See Glenn Weaver, *Hartford: An Illustrated History of Connecticut's Capital* (Woodland Hills, Calif.: Windsor Publications/Connecticut Historical Society, 1982), pp. 127–28. It is the inability to extend city boundaries that, according to some, accounts for Hartford's urban decay. See David Rusk, *Cities without Suburbs* (Washington, D.C.: Woodrow Wilson Center Press, 1993).

21. Eugenio Caro and Juan "Johnny" Castillo, interviews, 14 August 1992. José Garay, interview, 25 January 1993.

22. Olga Mele, interview, 6 August 1992, and James Kinsella, interview, 19 July 1994.

23. In 1996, the House consisted of 151 members. Hartford had two senators and nine representatives.

24. *Hartford Courant*, 15 December 1965, p. 16.

25. Janick, *A Diverse People*, p. 95.

26. Dahl analyzes the mayoralty of Richard Lee as part of his classic study of New Haven politics. See Robert A. Dahl, *Who Governs?* (New Haven: Yale University Press, 1961). Stone and Sanders reassess the New Haven case in "Re-examining a Classic Case of Development Politics: New Haven, Connecticut," in Clarence N. Stone and Heywood T. Sanders, eds., *The Politics of Urban Development* (Lawrence: University Press of Kansas, 1987), pp. 159–81.

27. Nicholas Carbone, "The General Assembly's Failure to Help Its Capitol City," in Clyde D. McKee, Jr., ed., *Perspectives of a State Legislature*, 2d ed. (Hartford: n.p., 1980), p. 220.

28. Pierre Clavel, *The Progressive City* (New Brunswick, N.J.: Rutgers University Press, 1986), p. 21.

29. Morton Coleman, "Interest Intermediation and Local Urban Development" (Ph.D. diss., University of Pittsburgh, 1983), p. 162.

30. Clavel, *Progressive City*. See also Harry C. Boyte, *The Backyard Revolution: Understanding the New Citizen Movement* (Philadelphia: Temple University Press, 1980), pp. 159–63, and Eve Bach, Nicholas Carbone, and Pierre Clavel, "Running the City for the People," *Social Policy* 12 (Winter 1982): 15–23.

31. Kenneth J. Neubeck and Richard E. Ratcliff, "Urban Democracy and the Power of Corporate Capital: Struggles over Downtown Growth and Neighborhood Stagnation in Hartford, Connecticut," in Scott Cummings, ed., *Business Elites and Urban Development: Case Studies and Critical Perspectives* (Albany: State University of New York Press, 1988), p. 311.

32. Quoted in Clavel, *Progressive City*, p. 51.

33. Clavel, *Progressive City*, p. 36.

34. Quoted in Coleman, "Interest Intermediation," p. 170.

35. Coleman, "Interest Intermediation," p. 170.

36. The trend continued unabated, and by 1990 residents held only 21.5 percent of the total jobs in Hartford, versus 78.4 percent for commuters. The disparity was compounded by an 11 percent loss of jobs between 1990 and 1993.

37. Coleman, "Interest Intermediation," p. 241.
38. Neubeck and Ratcliff, "Urban Democracy," p. 311. Coleman is less categorical. He finds that politics in Hartford ranges between the extremes of corporate elitism and neighborhood-based pluralism and that business groups, politicians, and community-based organizations engage in on-and-off relationships punctuated by conflict and cooperation.
39. See Dale Nelson, "The Political Behavior of New York Puerto Ricans: Assimilation or Survival?" in Clara Rodríguez, Virginia Sanchez Korrol, and José Oscar Alers., eds., *The Puerto Rican Struggle* (Maplewood, N.J.: Waterfront Press, 1984), p. 106; Angelo Falcón, "Puerto Rican Political Participation: New York City and Puerto Rico," in Jorge Heine, ed., *Time for Decision: The United States and Puerto Rico* (Lanham, Md.: North-South Publishing, 1983), pp. 29–30, 38–43.

CHAPTER THREE

1. Craig M. Pearson, "'Too Little, for Too Many' Brings Puerto Rican Migrants to the State," *Hartford Courant*, 2 May 1954, p. 4.
2. Craig M. Pearson, "'Last Migration' Brings 12,000 Puerto Ricans to Connecticut, Revives Old Problems," *Hartford Courant*, 25 April 1954, p. 1.
3. "Pablo Roman, a Puerto Rican Pioneer in City," *Hartford Times*, 8 May 1957, p. 14.
4. Daniel Gottlieb, "Puerto Ricans Like Life Here; They're Crowded but Optimistic," *Hartford Times*, 6 May 1957, p. 12.
5. "Puerto Rican Relations in Community Vary," *Hartford Times*, 10 May 1957, p. 7.
6. Gerald A. Ryan, "Need for Involvement in Community Is Seen," *Hartford Courant*, 20 November 1965, p. 1.
7. Pearson, "'Last Migration' Brings 12,000."
8. Craig M. Pearson, "Puerto Ricans Need Aid in Language, Customs," *Hartford Courant*, 23 May 1954, p. 21.
9. Dan Gottlieb, "Puerto Ricans Come by Air to Harvest Tobacco Crops," *Hartford Times*, 13 September 1958, p. 26.
10. Pearson, "'Last Migration' Brings 12,000."
11. Dan Gottlieb, "Newest Neighbors Number about 3,000," *Hartford Times*, 4 May 1957, p. 3.
12. "Puerto Rican Relations."
13. Gottlieb, "Newest Neighbors."
14. Pearson, "'Too Little, for Too Many.'"
15. Harold L. Ickes to Claude R. Wickard, 1 April 1943, quoted by Edwin Maldonado, in "Contract Labor and the Origins of Puerto Rican Communities in the United States," *International Migration Review* 13 (Spring 1979): 107.
16. Clayton Knowles, "Five Congressmen Shot in House by 3 Puerto Rican Nationalists; Bullets Spray from Gallery," *New York Times*, 2 March 1954, p. 1.
17. Peter Kihss, "Puerto Rico Head Calls It 'Lunacy,'" *New York Times*, 2 March 1954, p. 19.

18. "F.B.I. and Police Dig for Plot Roots Here," *New York Times*, 3 March 1954, p. 1.

19. "Assembly Condemns Shooting," *New York Times*, 4 March 1954, p. 10.

20. "Puerto Ricans Donate to Illinois Blood Bank," *New York Times*, 4 March 1954, p. 10.

21. "'Threatener' Indicted," *New York Times*, 3 March 1954, p. 14.

22. *Hartford Times*, 3 March 1954, p. 25.

23. Neil J. Smelser, *Theory of Collective Behavior* (New York: Free Press, 1963), p. 8.

24. Craig M. Pearson, "Connecticut's Puerto Ricans Strive with Language, Living," *Hartford Courant*, 9 May 1954, p. 1.

25. Pearson, "Connecticut's Puerto Ricans."

26. Pearson, "Connecticut's Puerto Ricans."

27. James M. Owens, "Hard Working Family Asks Only Fair Share," *Hartford Courant*, 22 March 1959, p. 1.

28. Juan "Johnny" Castillo, interview, 14 August 1992.

29. Pearson, "Connecticut's Puerto Ricans."

30. "Local Puerto Ricans."

31. James M. Owens, "Puerto Ricans Aided Here by Own Dept.," *Hartford Courant*, 19 March 1959, p. 1.

32. Manuel E. Royo to Eulalio Torres, inter-office report, 13 January 1960, Department of Puerto Rican Community Affairs, Commonwealth of Puerto Rico, New York City, Archival Collection, Box 33, Centro de Estudios Puertorriqueños, Hunter College, City University of New York.

33. "Booming Industry Attracts Puerto Ricans," *Hartford Courant*, 5 May 1957, p. B1.

34. Gottlieb, "Newest Neighbors."

35. "Puerto Rican Relations."

36. James M. Owens, "Average Migrant Found Law-Abiding Citizen," *Hartford Courant*, 16 March 1959, p. 1.

37. "Puerto Rican Relations."

38. Gottlieb, "Puerto Ricans Come by Air."

39. Gerald A. Ryan, "Newest Minority Finds Ways of City Strange," *Hartford Courant*, 14 November 1965, p. 1A.

40. Madelyn Colon, "Puerto Rican Americans," in *How the Other Half Lived*, edited by Robert E. Pawlowski (West Hartford, Conn.: n.p., 1973), p. 84.

41. Clarence Senior, *The Puerto Ricans: Strangers—Then Neighbors* (Chicago: Quadrangle Books, 1965), pp. 90–91.

42. Gerald A. Ryan, "Newest Minority Finds Ways of City Strange," *Hartford Courant*, 14 November 1965, p. 1A.

43. Owens, "Average Migrant"; Michael Lapp, "Managing Migration: The Migration Division of Puerto Rico and Puerto Ricans in New York City, 1948–1968" (Ph.D. diss., Johns Hopkins University, 1990), p. 161.

44. Gottlieb, "Newest Neighbors."

45. Gerald A. Ryan, "English Classes Opening Portals to Better Jobs," *Hartford Courant*, 16 November 1965, p. 1A.

46. Owens, "Puerto Ricans Aided."

47. Standard orientation prepared by Gilberto Camacho for newly arrived contract workers, circa 1967. Department of Puerto Rican Community Affairs, Commonwealth of Puerto Rico, New York City, Archival Collection, Box 500, Centro de Estudios Puertorriqueños, Hunter College, City University of New York.

48. Daniel J. Boorstin, *Hidden History* (New York: Vintage Books, 1989), p. 202.

49. Dan Gottlieb, "30 Puerto Ricans Reveal Housing Problems to Clark," *Hartford Times*, 26 March 1959, p. 29.

50. Dan Gottlieb, "Organizer Appointed for Puerto Ricans," *Hartford Times*, 16 October 1959, p. 4.

51. Linda Owens and James Owens, "Puerto Ricans Prepare for Rejoicing," *Hartford Courant Magazine*, 18 June 1961, p. 7. On St. John the Baptist Day, the Catholic faithful in Puerto Rico dipped themselves in the ocean to commemorate the baptism of Christ and to ward off evil spirits. In Hartford, the only place a Puerto Rican could do the traditional splash was her bathtub. In 1997, the religious significance of this celebration was all but lost in Puerto Rico. In Hartford, the celebration, sponsored by the San Juan Center, was then known as the Festival de San Juan Bautista.

52. "2,000 Puerto Ricans Due on Area Farms," *Hartford Times*, 13 March 1964, p. 17.

53. "2,000 Puerto Ricans Due."

54. "Puerto Ricans Parade to Celebrate State Day," *Hartford Courant*, 5 October 1964, p. 19.

55. "Puerto Ricans Parade."

56. Nicholas Carbone, interview, 30 July 1991.

57. Letter, Gilberto Camacho to Robert Little, 5 May 1965, Department of Puerto Rican Community Affairs, Commonwealth of Puerto Rico, New York City, Archival Collection, Box 374, Centro de Estudios Puertorriqueños, Hunter College, City University of New York.

58. "Puerto Ricans Organize Democratic Political Club," *Hartford Times*, 21 July 1965, p. 17.

59. Gerald A. Ryan, "Old Customs Still Cling as New Problems Arise," *Hartford Courant*, 19 November 1965, p. A1.

60. Gerald A. Ryan, "Need for Involvement in Community Is Seen," *Hartford Courant*, 20 November 1965, p. 1.

61. Gerald A. Ryan, "Families Are Crowded to Reduce Rent Costs," *Hartford Courant*, 17 November 1965, p. 1A.

62. Ryan, "Families Are Crowded."

63. Douglas Hill, "Puerto Ricans' Housing Found Poor and Costly," *Hartford Times*, 9 February 1966, p. 1B.

64. Federico Campbell, "Language Top Problem of Immigrant," *Hartford Courant*, 10 May 1967, p. 17.

65. Federico Campbell, "'Reluctant' to Seek Homes in Non-Spanish Area," *Hartford Courant*, 13 May 1967, p. 6.

66. Campbell, "Language Top Problem"; "Plea for Tolerance Sounded," *Hartford Courant*, 25 September 1967, p. 1.

67. "Youths Hurl Rocks, Bottles at South Green; 10 Nabbed," *Hartford Times*, 11 August 1969, p. B1. This spot became an empty lot next to the offices of Jorge Simón, the first corporation counsel of Puerto Rican background, appointed in December 1990 by Hartford's city council.

68. Antonio Soto, interview, 5 August 1991.

69. Bill Ryan, "City's Puerto Ricans Ask: Who Speaks for Us, Senor?" *Hartford Times*, 15 August 1969, p. 1.

70. Barry Wanger, "More Help Pledged for Puerto Ricans," *Hartford Times*, 13 August 1969, p. 1.

71. Soto, interview, 5 August 1991.

72. "Puerto Rican Leader, City Trying to Ease Tensions," *Hartford Times*, 14 August 1969, p. 48.

73. Bill Williams, "Success of Talks to Officials Pleases City Puerto Ricans," *Hartford Times*, 15 August 1969, p. B1.

74. Bill Ryan, "Puerto Rican Trek to Hartford Began in 1945 with Farm Jobs," *Hartford Times*, 31 August 1969, p. 1A.

75. Ryan, "Puerto Rican Trek."

76. Eugenio Caro, interview, 14 August 1992.

77. "Looting and Destruction Deplored by the NAACP," *Hartford Times*, 2 September 1969, p. 4B.

78. "Disorder Called Worst Yet in Hartford by Witnesses," *Hartford Times*, 2 September 1969, p. 7B.

79. "266 Persons Charged by Police Following Second Violent Night," *Hartford Times*, 4 September 1969, p. 4B.

80. "Curfew Lifted for Tonight; State of Emergency Stays," *Hartford Times*, 5 September 1969, p. 1.

81. "Mayor Asks Suburbs' Help," *Hartford Times*, 8 September 1969, p. 1.

82. "Looting and Destruction Deplored."

83. "Puerto Rican on City Staff Will Be Proposed Tonight," *Hartford Times*, 8 September 1969, p. 4B.

84. "Ghetto Priest: Let's Bring People Together," *Hartford Times*, 11 September 1969, p. B1.

85. "Top Puerto Rican Invited to City," *Hartford Times*, 10 September 1969, p. 4B.

86. "Coalition Loses Ally over Wire," *Hartford Times*, 11 September 1969, p. B1.

87. "Coalition Loses Ally."

88. "Coalition Loses Ally."

89. "Coalition Loses Ally."

90. "'Puerto Rican Citizens' to Be Council Subject," *Hartford Times*, 11 September 1969, p. 8B.

91. "Puerto Ricans to March," *Hartford Times*, 21 September 1969, p. 6B.

92. "Puerto Rican Ideals Said Misunderstood," *Hartford Times*, 24 September 1969, p. 4B.

93. "Puerto Ricans to Parade Today," *Hartford Times*, 28 September 1969, p. 2B.

94. "Need for an Understanding Puerto Rican Day Theme," *Hartford Times*, 29 September 1969, p. 1B.

95. "Need for an Understanding Puerto Rican Day Theme."

CHAPTER FOUR

1. See William Yancey, Eugene P. Ericksen, and Richard N. Juliani, "Emergent Ethnicity: A Review and a Reformulation," *American Sociological Review* 41 (June 1976): 392.

2. Sylvia Vargas, interview, 1 August 1991.

3. "Parade Queen Chosen," *Hartford Times*, 19 September 1969, p. 4B.

4. Gerardo "Jerry" Zayas, interview, 10 August 1992.

5. Olga Mele, interview, 6 August 1992.

6. Juan "Johnny" Castillo, interview, 14 August 1992.

7. Juan Fuentes, interview, 1 August 1991.

8. Juan Daniel Brito, "Cumplió Años La Casa de Puerto Rico," *Qué Pasa*, [Hartford] June 1986, p. 5.

9. Gilberto Camacho to Francisca Bou, letter, 25 August 1969, and Francisca Bou to Gilberto Camacho, letter, 28 August 1969, Department of Puerto Rican Community Affairs, Commonwealth of Puerto Rico, New York City, Archival Collection, Box 10, Centro de Estudios Puertorriqueños, Hunter College, City University of New York.

10. Gilberto Camacho to Thomas J. Meskill, letter, 5 December 1970. Department of Puerto Rican Community Affairs, Commonwealth of Puerto Rico, New York City, Archival Collection, Box 10, Centro de Estudios Puertorriqueños, Hunter College, City University of New York.

11. Mele, interview, 6 August 1992.

12. Morton Coleman, "Interest Intermediation and Local Urban Development," (Ph.D. diss., University of Pittsburgh, 1983), p. 210.

13. Elwyn Nicholas Kernstock, "How New Migrants Behave Politically: The Puerto Rican in Hartford, 1970" (Ph.D. diss., University of Connecticut, 1972), p. 121.

14. Kernstock, "How New Migrants Behave," pp. 120–25.

15. U.S. Department of Commerce, Bureau of the Census, *Census of Population: 1970*, vol. 1, *Characteristics of the Population, Part 8, Connecticut* (Washington, D.C.: U.S. Government Printing Office, 1973).

16. *Census of Population: 1970*, vol. 1.

17. Nicholas Carbone, interview, 30 July 1991.

18. Castillo, interview, 14 August 1992. Populares were the members of Puerto Rico's Partido Popular Democrático.

19. Charles J. Quinn to Peter K. Orne, letter, 19 February 1977. Courtesy of Olga Mele.

20. Mele, interview, 6 August 1992.

21. Janet Anderson, "Ethnic Need: Political Muscle," *Hartford Courant*, 19 March 1970, p. 1

22. See "Vecinos Denuncian Desalojan Puertorriqueños," p. 1; "Inseguridad Para los Puertorriqueños," p. 3; and "La Destrucción de Las Areas Hispanas," p. 5, *Qué Pasa* [Hartford], September 1978.

23. Juan Fuentes, interview, 1 August 1991.

24. Max Fernández, interview, 6 August 1991.

25. "Puerto Ricans Hold Meeting," *Hartford Courant*, 9 July 1970, p. 49.

26. Jackie Ross, "City Community Center Opened by People's Liberation Party," *Hartford Courant*, 16 December 1970, p. 38.

27. Kernstock, "How New Migrants Behave," pp. 201–2.

28. Kernstock, "How New Migrants Behave," p. 208.

29. See Anderson, "Ethnic Need." Kernstock offers an estimate of about eighteen thousand by multiplying the Puerto Rican school population in September 1969 (4,441 children) by four, the size of an average Puerto Rican family. "How New Migrants Behave," p. 106.

30. Clara Rodríguez, *Puerto Ricans: Born in the U.S.A.* (Boston: Unwin Hyman, 1989), pp. 3–4.

31. Madelyn Colon, "Puerto Rican Americans," in *How the Other Half Lived*, edited by Robert B. Pawlowski (West Hartford, Conn.: n.p., 1973), p. 86.

32. Janet Anderson, "Jobs, Friends Draw Puerto Ricans to 'Desirable' Hartford," *Hartford Courant*, 15 March 1970, p. 1.

33. Gilberto Camacho to Carmen Cortés, letter, 30 August 1971, Department of Puerto Rican Community Affairs, Commonwealth of Puerto Rico, New York City, Archival Collection, Box 10, Centro de Estudios Puertorriqueños, Hunter College, City University of New York.

34. Kernstock, "How New Migrants Behave," pp. 162–63.

35. Carbone, interview, 30 July 1991.

36. Carbone, interview, 30 July 1991.

37. Eugenio Caro, interview, 14 August 1992.

38. Two important studies of this phenomenon are by Lloyd Rogler, *Migrant in the City: The Life of a Puerto Rican Action Group* (New York: Basic Books, 1972), and James Jennings, *Puerto Rican Politics in New York City* (Washington, D.C.: University Press of America, 1977).

39. Kernstock, "How New Migrants Behave," p. 146.

40. Yasha Escalera, interview, 21 February 1993.

41. Gilberto Camacho to Manuel A. Casiano, Jr., memo, 21 May 1970, section 8, p. 5, Department of Puerto Rican Community Affairs, Commonwealth of Puerto Rico, New York City, Archival Collection, Box 10, Centro de Estudios Puertorriqueños, Hunter College, City University of New York.

42. For an in-depth examination of how these issues developed within the community, see Andrés Torres and José Velázquez, eds., *The Puerto Rican Movement: Voices from the Diaspora* (Philadelphia: Temple University Press, 1998).

43. Kernstock, "How New Migrants Behave," pp. 220–21.

44. The Concilio organized registration drives and legal clinics and interviewed political candidates and lobbied city, state, and federal officials. Yet it was a neocorporatist instrument of the commonwealth's office. See Michael Lapp,

"Managing Migration: The Migration Division of Puerto Rico and Puerto Ricans in New York City, 1948–1968" (Ph.D. diss., Johns Hopkins University, 1990), pp. 275–83.

45. Camacho to Casiano, memo, 21 May 1970, section 4, p. 4. Recall that the division's service area included Connecticut and other states.

46. John Sherman, "Spanish Action Coalition Plans Information and Social Center," *Hartford Courant*, 31 January 1969, p. 27.

47. Antonio Soto, interview, 5 August 1991.

48. Soto, interview, 5 August 1991.

49. Kernstock, "How New Migrants Behave," pp. 147–48.

50. José Cruz, interview, 27 January 1993.

51. Castillo, interview, 14 August 1992.

52. Escalera, interview, 21 February 1993.

53. William J. Pérez, interview, 30 January 1993.

54. Camacho to Casiano, memo, 21 May 1970, section 2, pp. 17–18.

55. Camacho to Casiano, memo, 21 May 1970, section 4, p. 4.

56. This description of the PLP is based on my interview with José Claudio, 30 September 1995.

57. For background information on the Young Lords party, see Hilda Vazquez Ignatin, "Young Lords: Serve and Protect," in Clayborne Carson, ed., *The Movement, 1964–1970* (Westport, Conn.: Greenwood Press, 1993), p. 196. Vazquez describes the development of the group from its origins as a gang in Chicago in 1959 to its adoption of a revolutionary program in the spring of 1969. The politicization of the Young Lords was prompted by the threat to Puerto Ricans of urban renewal, by its integration into a network of politically active groups, and by police harassment and repression. By 1969, the leaders of the organization decided that the key to effective political action was political education and grassroots organization. For an account of the group's origins and development in New York City, see two interviews with Pablo "Yoruba" Guzmán in Carson, *The Movement*, pp. 739, 744, 805–6, and 818, and his recent accounts in "La Vida Pura: A Lord of the Barrio," *Village Voice*, 21 March 1995, pp. 24–31, and in "The Party," in Roberto Santiago, ed., *Boricuas* (New York: Ballantine Books, 1995), pp. 52–60. For a recent assessment of the theory and practice of the group, see Agustín Lao, "Resources of Hope: Imagining the Young Lords and the Politics of Memory," *Centro* 8 (1995): 34–49.

58. *Mete Mano* 1(1), MPI, Hartford, Department of Puerto Rican Community Affairs, Commonwealth of Puerto Rico, New York City, Archival Collection, Box 10, Centro de Estudios Puertorriqueños, Hunter College, City University of New York.

59. Gilberto Camacho to Nick Lugo, Jr., letter, 12 November 1971, Department of Puerto Rican Community Affairs, Commonwealth of Puerto Rico, New York City, Archival Collection, Box 10, Centro de Estudios Puertorriqueños, Hunter College, City University of New York.

60. "Here We Stand," *Claridad* [New York], 19 March 1972, p. 2-S. See also "Desde Las Entrañas: Political Declaration of the United States Branch of the Puerto Rican Socialist Party," 1 April 1973, appendix A, p. 27.

61. Mildred Torres, interview, 1 August 1991.

62. Andrés Vázquez, interview, 3 March 1993.
63. Carbone, interview, 30 July 1991.
64. José Cruz to Ann Ucello, letter, 20 April 1970, quoted in Kernstock, "How New Migrants Behave," p. 150.
65. Soto, interview, 5 August 1991.
66. Escalera, interview, 21 February 1993.
67. Sydney Schulman, interview, 15 January 1993.
68. José Cruz, interview, 27 January 1993.
69. Cruz, interview, 27 January 1993.
70. Jack Zaiman, "GOP Headquarters Active Despite Election Policy," *Hartford Courant*, 1 November 1955, p. 11.
71. Jack Zaiman, "Bailey Urges Democrats to Work for Election of Six," *Hartford Courant*, 2 November 1955, p. 8; Jack Zaiman, "Cronin Wins Smashing Victory; Charter Committee Elects Five," *Hartford Courant*, 9 November 1955, p. 1.
72. Mele, interview, 6 August 1992.
73. Jack Zaiman, "Kinsella Swept in as Mayor Democrats Take Council 6–3," *Hartford Courant*, 6 November 1957, p. 1.
74. Mele, interview, 6 August 1992.
75. Soto, interview, 5 August 1991.
76. Soto, interview, 5 August 1991.
77. José Garay, interview, 25 January 1993.
78. Cruz, interview, 27 January 1993.
79. Cruz, interview, 27 January 1993.
80. Jack Zaiman, "Show of Unity by City Party Carries Democrats to Victory," *Hartford Courant*, 3 November 1971, p. 18.
81. *Hartford Courant*, 3 November 1971, p. 45.
82. "City Election Sees 17 Candidates Vying for 11 Posts," *Hartford Courant*, 5 November 1973, p. 38; David S. Barrett, "Democrats Expected to Retain Majority on Council," *Hartford Courant*, 5 November 1973, p. 38.
83. "GOP Takes Bridgeport amid Upsets; Athanson, Council Re-Elected in Sweep," *Hartford Courant*, 7 November 1973, p. 1.
84. Barrett, "Democrats Expected."
85. Sánchez advertised her business as "Maria's Newsstand" in the premier edition of the community newspaper *El Observador-The Observer*, dated 16 July 1976.
86. Soto, interview, 5 August 1991. I was unable to interview Sánchez before her untimely death in 1989.
87. Edna Negrón, interview, 29 January 1993.
88. Laurence Cohen, "Race for Board of Education Appears to Be a Question of Personalities," *Hartford Courant*, 3 November 1973, p. 23.
89. "Campaign Task Force Spent $910. for Sanchez," *Hartford Courant*, 22 December 1973, p. 33.
90. Elmer E. Cornwell, Jr., "Bosses, Machines, and Ethnic Groups," in Lawrence H. Fuchs, ed., *American Ethnic Politics* (New York: Harper Torch Books, 1968), p. 199.
91. Gerardo "Jerry" Zayas, interview, 10 August 1992.

92. Mary Ellen Flynn, interview, 12 August 1992.

93. Torres, interview, 1 August 1991.

94. Carbone, interview, 30 July 1991.

95. Flynn, interview, 12 August 1992.

96. Rufus P. Browning, Dale Rogers Marshall, and David H. Tabb, *Protest Is Not Enough: The Struggle of Blacks and Hispanics for Equality in Urban Politics* (Berkeley: University of California Press, 1984), p. 90.

97. Browning, Marshall, and Tabb, *Protest Is Not Enough*, p. 78.

98. Edward Rudd, "Angry Meeting Airs Complaints on Police Tactics in Disorders," *Hartford Courant*, 20 August 1969, p. 35.

99. Mele, interview, 6 August 1992.

100. Boricua is a nickname for a Puerto Rican.

101. Soto, interview, 5 August 1991. This pattern was not exceptional, and it applies to the relationship between blacks and other Latinos. When Martin Luther King proposed broadening the scope of the 1968 Poor People's Campaign, some within the Southern Christian Leadership Conference were less than enthusiastic. One aide told a staff meeting: "I do not think I am at the point where a Mexican can sit in and call strategy on a Steering Committee." Another declared that the Chicano leader Reies López Tijerina "didn't understand that we were the parents and he was the child." Quoted in David J. Garrow, *Bearing the Cross* (New York: Vintage Books, 1988), p. 607.

102. Janet Anderson, "Foundations to Seek Methods to Aid Puerto Rican Students," *Hartford Courant*, 2 November 1971, p. 25.

103. Kernstock, "How New Migrants Behave," p. 155.

CHAPTER FIVE

1. "It's About Time!" *La Prensa Gráfica* [Hartford], 31 January 1975, p. 2.

2. David S. Barrett, "Puerto Rican Lawyer Pushed for Council Seat," *Hartford Courant*, 23 January 1975, p. 68.

3. Transcript of WSFB-TV Channel 3 editorial, 20–21 March 1975, Department of Puerto Rican Community Affairs, Commonwealth of Puerto Rico, New York City, Archival Collection, Box 429, Centro de Estudios Puertorriqueños, Hunter College, City University of New York.

4. "A Feminist-Humanist Organization," *MUJER Newsletter*, 13 July 1975.

5. "Mujeres Unidas for Justice, Equality and Reform," *MUJER Newsletter*, c. July 1976, p. 2.

6. Diana Alverio, interview, 8 June 1993.

7. "Lideres Negros Buscan Alianza?," *La Prensa Gráfica* [Hartford], 1 August 1975, p. 1.

8. Yasha Escalera, interview, 21 February 1993. Like María Sánchez, Wilber Smith passed away before I was able to interview him.

9. Neal R. Peirce, *The New England States* (New York: Norton, 1976), pp. 217–20, and E. S. Grant and Marion Hepburn Grant, *The City of Hartford, 1784–1984* (Hartford: Connecticut Historical Society, 1986), p. 21.

10. Pierre Clavel, *The Progressive City* (New Brunswick, N.J.: Rutgers University Press, 1986), pp. 25–26.

11. Memo, 20 November 1974, reprinted in *La Prensa Gráfica* [Hartford], 31 January 1975, p. 7.

12. Edna Negrón Smith to Olcott Smith, open letter, printed in *La Prensa Gráfica* [Hartford], 31 January 1975, pp. 5–6.

13. Eugenio Caro, interview, 14 August 1992.

14. Calixto Torres, "Protestan Manifestaciones de Process," *La Prensa Gráfica* [Hartford], 31 January 1975, p. 1.

15. "Statement from NAACP" and "Senator Smith's Statement," *La Prensa Gráfica* [Hartford], 31 January 1975, pp. 3, 6.

16. Rafael Torregrosa, "Our People Are Here to Stay," *La Prensa Gráfica* [Hartford], 10 February 1975, p. 8.

17. Juan Fuentes, "Gracias NAACP," *La Prensa Gráfica* [Hartford], 31 January 1975, p. 2.

18. José La Luz, "Racism, Hartford Process, La Historia de Una Conspiración," *La Prensa Gráfica* [Hartford], 17 February 1975, p. 2.

19. Negrón Smith to Olcott Smith, open letter.

20. Morton Coleman, "Interest Intermediation and Local Urban Development" (Ph.D. diss., University of Pittsburgh, 1983), p. 191; "Councilman, Process, and CRCOG, Indicted by Feds.," *La Prensa Gráfica* [Hartford], 10 February 1975, p. 1.

21. "Devco Proposed 'Lease-Back Arrangement' to the City," *La Prensa Gráfica* [Hartford], 31 January 1975, p. 1.

22. "Devco Sirve a Intereses Privados," *La Prensa Gráfica* [Hartford], 10 February 1975, p. 1.

23. Maggie W. Alston, open letter, printed in *La Prensa Gráfica* [Hartford], 31 January 1975, p. 2.

24. La Luz, "Racism, Hartford Process."

25. "Councilman, Process and CRCOG Indicted."

26. "Process Presented Tory Award for Racist Practices," *La Prensa Gráfica* [Hartford], 24 February 1975, p. 1.

27. "Process Memo Affront to Hartford-BHCA," *La Prensa Gráfica* [Hartford], 7 March 1975, p. 1.

28. Kenneth J. Neubeck and Richard E. Ratcliff, "Urban Democracy and the Power of Corporate Capital: Struggles over Downtown Growth and Neighborhood Stagnation in Hartford, Connecticut," in Scott Cummings, ed., *Business Elites and Urban Development: Case Studies and Critical Perspectives* (Albany: State University of New York Press, 1988), p. 324.

29. Edwin Vargas, interview, 31 January 1989.

30. Nicholas Carbone, interview, 30 July 1991. In 1976, a federal judge issued a permanent injunction barring the suburbs from using CDBG monies until their housing plans incorporated the needs of low-income residents. In 1977, this decision was reversed and Hartford's suit was dismissed by a U.S. court of appeals. See Neubeck and Ratcliff, "Urban Democracy," pp. 324–26. UDAGs are Urban Development Action Grants. The UDAG program was approved by Congress in 1977 during Carter's administration. Funds were granted by application for the purposes of particular projects. Because of Carter's emphasis on public-private partnerships, these grants were designed to leverage private investments.

31. Video recording of forum held in Spanish at Immaculate Conception Church, Hartford, 7 January 1979.

32. La Luz, interview, 6 July 1989.

33. In 1962, the Students for a Democratic Society drafted a platform, known as the Port Huron statement, stating reform goals that conservative political scientist Samuel P. Huntington considered "well within the broad limits of the American radical tradition." In 1969, SDS was transformed into a pro-communist, revolutionary group, and it went underground by the end of the year. In March 1970, three members, now known as Weathermen, blew themselves up by accident while making bombs in a New York City brownstone. In 1969, the *New York Times* revealed that the United States was "secretly" bombing Cambodia, and the following year college campuses across the nation created, according to President Richard Nixon, a security problem of "critical proportions," as protestors raged over the bombings. See Samuel P. Huntington, *American Politics: The Promise of Disharmony* (Cambridge: Harvard University Press, Belknap Press, 1982), p. 186; Arthur M. Schlesinger, Jr., *The Imperial Presidency* (Boston: Houghton Mifflin, 1973), pp. 256–58.

34. La Luz, interview, 6 July 1989. The Asociación de Trabajadores Agrícolas (ATA) was a splinter group of the Ministerio Ecuménico de Trabajadores Agrícolas (META). META was organized in the fall of 1972 in Vineland, New Jersey, with branches in Connecticut and Puerto Rico. META's director in New Jersey was the Reverend Wilmer Silva, and in Connecticut it was the Reverend Wilfredo Vélez. During the summer of 1973, a conflict between Silva, a member of the Partido Independentista Puertorriqueño, and Connecticut member Juan Irizarry, who was affiliated with the PSP, broke open as Silva and Irizarry traded accusations of partisanship and deviation from META's stated mission. The group divided and on 5 August 1973 the Connecticut splinter group became the Asociación de Trabajadores Agrícolas under the leadership of Juan Irizarry. By 1976, ATA disintegrated and was succeeded by the Comité de Apoyo al Trabajador Agrícola (CATA) under new leadership. See Gloria Bonilla-Santiago, *Organizing Puerto Rican Migrant Farmworkers: The Experience of Puerto Ricans in New Jersey* (New York: Peter Lang, 1988), pp. 87–88, 97, 135, 145, 177–78.

35. La Luz, interview, 6 July 1989.

36. Carol Giacomo, "Puerto Ricans Seeking Role in Politics," *Hartford Courant*, 3 August 1977, p. 35.

37. Michael Regan, "City Man Prepares for Race," *Hartford Courant*, 9 August 1977, p. 25.

38. Michael Regan, "Two Challenge City's Parties," *Hartford Courant*, 10 August 1977, p. 37.

39. Nicholas Carbone, interview, 4 March 1993.

40. Edwin Vargas, interviews, 31 January 1989, 15 June 1992, and 19 November 1992.

41. Juan Fuentes, interview, 13 February 1993; Carbone, interview, 4 March 1993.

42. "Teachers Union Picks Four," news clipping, c. 1977, courtesy of Edwin Vargas.

43. Michael Regan, "3 Mayoral, 16 City Council Candidates Running for Election," *Hartford Courant*, 30 October 1977, p. 16C.

44. "Hartford Results," *Hartford Courant*, 9 November 1977, p. 1.

45. "Inseguridad Para Los Puertorriqueños," *Qué Pasa* [Hartford], September 1978, p. 3.

46. José E. Cruz, "Puerto Rican Elected Officials in the United States," in National Puerto Rican Coalition, *1993 Directory of Puerto Rican Elected Officials*, (Washington, D.C.: NPRC, 1993), p. 6.

47. National Puerto Rican Coalition, *Assessing the Impact of Federal Cutbacks on Employment and Training Opportunities for Puerto Ricans: Summary of a Seven-City Study* (Washington, D.C.: NPRC, 1983), p. 19.

48. Elwyn Nicholas Kernstock, "How New Migrants Behave Politically: The Puerto Rican in Hartford, 1970" (Ph.D. diss., University of Connecticut, 1972), pp. 237–38.

49. Quoted in "El Insulto de Swank," *Qué Pasa* [Hartford], November 1978, p. 7.

50. Caro, interview, 14 August 1992.

51. "La Marcha de la Dignidad," *Qué Pasa* [Hartford], November 1978, p. 3.

52. Caro, interview, 14 August 1992.

53. "Nueva Coalición," *Qué Pasa* [Hartford], February 1979, p. 9.

54. "El Comite 24 un Año Despues," *Qué Pasa* [Hartford], December 1979, p. 8.

55. *Journal of the Court of Common Council*, 1977–79, vols. 1–2, p. 1432.

56. La Luz, interview, 6 July 1989.

57. Vargas, interview, 19 November 1992.

58. Carbone, interview, 4 March 1993.

59. "Posible Vacante en el Consejo Municipal," *Qué Pasa* [Hartford], June 1978, p. 1.

60. "Hispanic on City Council," *Qué Pasa* [Hartford], December 1978, p. 7.

61. Juan Fuentes, "Carbone En Espera Decisión de Líderes Puertorriqueños," *El Observador-The Observer* [Hartford], clipping, day and month missing, 1979, p. 4.

62. Press release of Oscar Nieves, c. December 1978, Department of Puerto Rican Community Affairs, Commonwealth of Puerto Rico, New York City, Archival Collection, Box 371, Centro de Estudios Puertorriqueños, Hunter College, City University of New York.

63. Andrés Vázquez, interview, 3 March 1993.

64. Mildred Torres, interview, 1 August 1991.

65. Carbone, interview, 4 March 1993.

66. Carbone, interview, 30 July 1991.

67. This and subsequent quotations are from a video recording of the forum, held at Immaculate Conception Church, Hartford, 7 January 1979.

68. David S. Barrett, "Selection Unit Backs Sánchez for Council," *Hartford Courant*, 10 January 1979, p. 41.

69. La Luz, interview, 6 July 1989.

70. Torres, interviews, 1 August 1991 and 2 March 1993.

71. Calixto Torres, interview, 7 August 1991.
72. Carbone, interview, 4 March 1993.
73. Transcript of "News Highlights," Radio Station WTIC-AM/FM, 8 January 1979.
74. Juan Fuentes, "Concilio Tiene Ultima Palabra," *El Observador-The Observer* [Hartford], 20–30 January 1979, p. 6.
75. Karlynn Carrington, "Puerto Rican Unit Endorses Torres for Council Seat," *Hartford Courant*, 11 January 1979, p. 38.
76. Barrett, "Selection Unit Backs Sanchez."
77. Vargas, interview, 31 July 1991.
78. "El Comite 24 un Año Despues," *Qué Pasa* [Hartford], December 1979, p. 8.
79. Roberto Laboy, "Nosotros, Puertorriqueños," *Qué Pasa* [Hartford], December 1978, p. 6.
80. For an example of this attitude from city and business officials, see "Confrontan Cámara," *Qué Pasa* [Hartford], December 1978, p. 3.

Chapter Six

1. Cecilia La Luz, "Apuntes Políticos," *Qué Pasa* [Hartford], June 1979, p. 5.
2. Eugenio Caro, interview, 14 August 1992.
3. Peter Ayala, interview, 7 August 1991.
4. Kenneth J. Neubeck and Richard E. Ratcliff, "Urban Democracy and the Power of Corporate Capital: Struggles over Downtown Growth and Neighborhood Stagnation in Hartford, Connecticut," in Scott Cummings, ed., *Business Elites and Urban Development: Case Studies and Critical Perspectives* (Albany: State University of New York Press, 1988), p. 308.
5. Antoinette Leone Ruzzier, interview, 12 August 1992; José Garay, interview, 14 August 1992; Juan Fuentes, interview, 1 February 1993.
6. José Garay, interview, 14 August 1992.
7. Olga Mele, interview, 6 August 1992; Mary Ellen Flynn, interview, 12 August 1992; Ruzzier, interview, 12 August 1992; Jerry Zayas, interview, 10 August 1992.
8. "Acusan de Bigamia a Concejal Hispano," *Qué Pasa* [Hartford], July 1980, p. 1.
9. Ruzzier, interview, 12 August 1992; Garay, interview, 14 August 1992.
10. See Juan Daniel Brito, "Primarias Demócratas,"*Qué Pasa* [Hartford], 8 September 1983, p. 11.
11. "Comité de la Ciudad Endosa Candidatos," *Qué Pasa* [Hartford], July–August 1981, p. 8.
12. "Las Posibilidades de Trabajo Conjunto entre la Comunidad Negra e Hispana," *Qué Pasa* [Hartford], November 1981, p. 7.
13. "Historico Triunfo de Milner," *Qué Pasa* [Hartford], November 1981, p. 1.
14. Juan Brito and Pedro Espinoza, "Hotel Hilton ¿Solucion o Burla?" *Qué Pasa* [Hartford], November-December 1981, p. 3; C. L. Smith Muniz, "Ludgin

Calls for Probe of San Juan Center," *Hartford Courant*, 15 December 1980, p. C1; Max Fernández, interview, 6 August 1991.

15. Mike Borrero, "A Propósito de las Pasadas Elecciones," *Qué Pasa* [Hartford], January 1982, p. 15.

16. Carlos Piñeiro, "Mis Felicitaciones," *Qué Pasa* [Hartford], January 1982, p. 15.

17. In 1989, the pay was raised to $15,000 a year, still a negligible amount.

18. Zayas, interview, 10 August 1992.

19. Yasha Escalera, interview, 21 February 1993.

20. Escalera, interview, 21 February 1993

21. Tony Hernández, "Edwin Vargas: Lider Sindical y Activista Puertorriqueño,"*Qué Pasa* [Hartford], 24 February–18 March 1984, p. 3.

22. "Mildred Soto y Ramón Pacheco Nominados a Posiciones en el Gobierno Municipal," *Qué Pasa* [Hartford], 15 April–1 May 1984, p. 1.

23. Escalera, interview, 21 February 1993.

24. Escalera, interview, 21 February 1993.

25. Edwin Vargas, Jr., interview, 30 July 1991; see also "Nancy Meléndez Va a la Reelección," *Qué Pasa* [Hartford], July 1985, p. 3; Juan Daniel Brito, "Comité de la Ciudad Apoya Candidatura de Meléndez," *Qué Pasa*[Hartford], July 1985, p. 16.

26. Euripides Rios, "Líderes Boricuas Htfd Ofrecen Señal de Unidad," *El Periodico* [Hartford], March 1985, p. 1.

27. "Apoyo a Nancy Meléndez," *Qué Pasa* [Hartford], April 1985, p. 1.

28. Edwin Vargas, Jr., and José La Luz, "The People of Hartford Address the Visiting Mayors," *Hartford Courant*, 18 April 1985, p. D9.

29. Mark Pazniokas, "Hartford's Hispanic Community Begins Flexing Political Muscle," *Hartford Courant*, 7 May 1985, p. A1.

30. Edwin Vargas, Jr., photocopy of talking points.

31. "Getting Out Vote Means Doing It All," photocopy of news clipping, 1985.

32. Peter Ayala, interview, 7 August 1991; see also "Solidaridad con Puerto Rico," *Qué Pasa* [Hartford], October 1985, p. 20.

33. "María González-Borrero Elegida a Junta de Educación," *Qué Pasa* [Hartford], February 1986, p. 1.

34. Torres, interview, 1 August 1991; Peter Ayala, interview, 7 August 1991; Caro, interview, 14 August 1992; Vargas, interview, 3 March 1993.

35. Arthur Brouillet, interview, 8 August 1991.

36. William Hagan, interview, 30 July 1991.

37. Danny Pérez, interview, 2 August 1991.

38. Juan Figueroa, interview, 9 August 1991.

39. Ayala, interview, 7 August 1991.

40. Juan D. Brito, "El Triunfo de los Vecindarios," *Qué Pasa* [Hartford], December 1987, p. 3, and "Necesitamos Cambios en Hartford," *Qué Pasa* [Hartford], December 1987, p. 4.

41. Brouillet, interview, 8 August 1991.

42. Edwin Vargas, Jr., "Chronology of the Puerto Rican PAC, Inc.," photocopy, c. 1988.

43. Abe Giles, interview, 3 August 1991.

44. Mark Pazniokas and Bill Keveney, "Puerto Ricans Show Power in City Primaries," *Hartford Courant*, 16 September 1988, p. 1.

45. Hagan, interview, 30 July 1991, and Frances Sánchez, interview, 6 August 1991.

46. This paragraph and the next two are based on my interview with Edna Negrón and Jack Cullin, 28 July 1991.

47. Born of a mixed Cuban-Puerto Rican marriage, Simón considered himself Puerto Rican. Many Puerto Ricans, especially those who disagreed with Simón's legal decisions, questioned the authenticity of his ethnic identity. This paragraph and the next are based on my interview with Vargas, 30 July 1991.

48. Vargas's reference to a "second" Puerto Rican on the council is confusing because in 1991 there were two Puerto Rican councilpersons. He was referring to a second *Democratic* councilperson. Recall that Eugenio Caro was PFC's representative, at least nominally. I was unable to interview Charles Mathews to confirm Vargas's rendition of this incident.

49. This became apparent to me from participant observation at various meetings and strategy sessions I attended during the primary campaign; it was also acknowledged by William Hagan, a founder and key PFC member, in a post-election conversation.

50. Don Noel, "Mayor Perry Pledged Open Government, but She Hasn't Delivered," *Hartford Courant*, 3 February 1992, p. C13; Brett Deutsch, "Council Members Form Majority to Control City Government," *Hartford News*, 5–12 August 1992, p. 1; Steve Walsh, "Mayor Brought Down Her Own House?" *Hartford News*, 26 August–2 September 1992, p. 1.

51. See Louis Freedberg, "Political Godmother," *Vista* magazine, Fall 1988, pp. 9–10; Bill Keveney, "Maria C. Sánchez Dies; City Puerto Rican Leader," *Hartford Courant*, 26 November 1989, p. A1.

52. Vargas, interview, 3 March 1993.

53. Caro, interview, 14 August 1992.

54. Steve Walsh, "Vargas Leads Puerto Rican Political Emergence," *Hartford News*, 10–24 April 1991, p. 1. Quotes from Figueroa, Soto, and Negrón are from this article.

55. Jorge Simón, interview, 30 July 1991.

56. Juan Figueroa, interview, 9 August 1991.

57. Figueroa, interview, 9 August 1991.

58. A. James Reichley, *The Life of the Parties* (New York: Free Press, 1992), p. 144.

59. John D. Buenker, *Urban Liberalism and Progressive Reform* (New York: Scribner's, 1973), p. 208.

60. Rebecca Brito, interview, 10 August 1992.

61. City of Hartford, Department of Planning and Economic Development, *State of the City, 1995*.

CHAPTER SEVEN

1. Jonathan Rabinovitz, "'Insurance Capital' Hartford Finds Itself without Its Net," *New York Times*, 4 December 1995, p. A1.

2. Michael Omi and Howard Winant refer to these explanations as the "Bootstraps" and "They All Look Alike" approaches of ethnicity paradigms to the problem of racial incorporation. See *Racial Formation in the United States* (New York: Routledge, 1994), pp. 20–23.

3. Robert H. Salisbury, *Interests and Institutions: Substance and Structure in American Politics* (Pittsburgh: University of Pittsburgh Press, 1992), p. 268.

4. A similar point concerning the function of historic buildings in cities is made by Lewis Mumford. These, he argues, provide a "structural link" with the past that enriches the future. Lewis Mumford, *The Urban Prospect* (New York: Harcourt, Brace, 1968), p. 120.

5. Morton Coleman, "Interest Intermediation and Local Urban Development" (Ph.D. diss., University of Pittsburgh, 1983), p. 156; Kenneth J. Neubeck and Richard E. Ratcliff, "Urban Democracy and the Power of Corporate Capital: Struggles over Downtown Growth and Neighborhood Stagnation in Hartford, Connecticut," in Scott Cummings, ed., *Business Elites and Urban Development: Case Studies and Critical Perspectives* (Albany: State University of New York Press, 1988), p. 326.

6. On this ambivalence, see Frank Bonilla, "Migrants, Citizens, and Social Pacts," in Edwin Meléndez and Edgardo Meléndez, eds., *Colonial Dilemma* (Boston: South End Press, 1993), pp. 181–88; Anthony Downs, "The Future of Industrial Cities," in Paul E. Peterson, ed., *The New Urban Reality* (Washington, D.C.: Brookings Institution, 1985), pp. 281–94; David Harvey *The Urban Experience* (Baltimore: Johns Hopkins University Press, 1989), pp. 274–78 and passim; and Frances Fox Piven and Richard A. Cloward, *Poor People's Movements* (New York: Pantheon Books, 1977), pp. xii, xiii, 359.

7. Felix M. Padilla, *Puerto Rican Chicago* (Notre Dame, Ind.: University of Notre Dame Press, 1987), pp. 196–97.

8. Francisco L. Rivera-Batiz and Carlos Santiago, *Puerto Ricans in the United States: A Changing Reality* (Washington, D.C.: National Puerto Rican Coalition, 1994), p. 35.

9. Research on Mexican-Americans cited by Peter Skerry confirms this point. See Peter Skerry, *Mexican-Americans: The Ambivalent Minority* (New York: Free Press, 1993), especially chapter 4.

10. Expressiveness has been singled out as characteristic of identity-oriented social movements. Instrumental rationality has been associated with social movements based on resource mobilization. For a discussion that highlights the differences and commonalities between the two, see Jean L. Cohen, "Strategy or Identity: New Theoretical Paradigms and Contemporary Social Movements," *Social Research* 52 (Winter 1985): 663–716.

11. David Ward, *Poverty, Ethnicity, and the American City, 1840–1925* (Cambridge: Cambridge University Press, 1989), p. 177.

12. For the claim that ethnicity is a cover for economic interests, see Richard D.

Alba, "The Twilight of Ethnicity among Catholics of European Ancestry," *Annals of the American Academy of Political and Social Science* 454 (1981): 86–97; Irving Howe, "The Limits of Ethnicity," *New Republic*, June 25, 1977, pp. 17–19; Stephen Steinberg, *The Ethnic Myth: Race, Ethnicity, and Class in America* (Boston: Beacon Press, 1989); and Pierre Van Den Berghe, *The Ethnic Phenomenon* (New York: Elsevier-North Holland, 1981). For the argument that ethnicity reflects social stratification, see Douglas S. Massey, "Social Class and Ethnic Segregation: A Reconsideration of Methods and Conclusions," *American Sociological Review* 46 (1981): 641–50; Ceri Peach, "Conflicting Interpretations of Segregation," in Peter Jackson and Susan J. Smith, eds., *Social Interaction and Ethnic Segregation* (London: Academic Press, 1981), pp. 19–33; and Roger Waldinger, "When the Melting Pot Boils Over: The Irish, Jews, Blacks, and Koreans of New York," in Michael Peter Smith and Joe R. Feagin, eds., *The Bubbling Cauldron: Race, Ethnicity, and the Urban Crisis* (Minneapolis: University of Minnesota Press, 1995), pp. 265–81.

13. Douglas Gurak and Mary M. Kritz, "The Caribbean Communities in the United States," *Migration Today* 12 (1985): 6–12; Lloyd H. Rogler, Rosemary Santana Cooney, and Vilma Ortiz, "Intergenerational Change in Ethnic Identity in the Puerto Rican Family," *International Migration Review*, 14 (Summer 1980): 193–214.

14. According to Herbert Gans, these polarities describe authentic and symbolic ethnicity, respectively. The former refers to group membership and cultural values and practices, while the latter involves a degree of identity and feeling that is secondary and that can easily be satisfied privately. See Herbert Gans, *The Urban Villagers* (New York: Free Press, 1982), pp. 235–36.

15. Such is the claim made by James Jennings. He writes that efforts in this arena were "sporadic and inconsistent." See James Jennings, "Introduction: The Emergence of Puerto Rican Electoral Activism in Urban America" in James Jennings and Monte Rivera, eds., *Puerto Rican Politics in Urban America* (Westport, Conn.: Greenwood Press, 1984), p. 3.

16. The same is true of older communities. For example, Virginia Sánchez Korrol has shown that during the 1920s, when the New York *colonias* were *the* Puerto Rican community in the United States, Puerto Rican electoral efforts were significant. She writes: "Surely, political awareness and participation among Puerto Ricans in New York was far greater than previously assumed. . . . By the twenties, an awareness of the importance of functioning within a North American political orbit intensified. . . . Aligned with dominant and minority party politics, Puerto Rican groups attempted to exchange the vote for social welfare benefits." Virginia Sánchez Korrol, *From Colonia to Community: The History of Puerto Ricans in New York City* (Berkeley: University of California, 1994), p. 199.

17. Calixto Torres, interview, 7 August 1991.

18. For documentation on the process and the issues raised during this particular plebiscite drill, see Meléndez and Meléndez, "Introduction," in Meléndez and Meléndez, eds., *Colonial Dilemma*, pp. 1–16; Angelo Falcón, "A Divided Nation: The Puerto Rican Diaspora in the United States and the Proposed Referendum," in Meléndez and Meléndez, eds., *Colonial Dilemma*, pp. 173–80; Gordon

Jonathan Lewis, ed., *The Plebiscite and the Diaspora: Policy Forum Proceedings* (New York: Institute for Puerto Rican Policy, 1993).

19. Gilberto Camacho to Eulalio Torres, interoffice report, 15 November 1960, Department of Puerto Rican Community Affairs, Commonwealth of Puerto Rico, New York City, Archival Collection, Box 32, Centro de Estudios Puertorriqueños, Hunter College, City University of New York.

20. Gilberto Camacho to Nick Lugo, Jr., letter, 24 August 1972, Department of Puerto Rican Community Affairs, Commonwealth of Puerto Rico, New York City, Archival Collection, Box 371, Centro de Estudios Puertorriqueños, Hunter College, City University of New York.

21. Angel Viera Martínez to Julia Rivera de Vincenti, letter, 10 February 1972. Department of Puerto Rican Community Affairs, Commonwealth of Puerto Rico, New York City, Archival Collection, Box 371, Centro de Estudios Puertorriqueños, Hunter College, City University of New York. This is no longer the case. Ten categories of people, including contract laborers working on U.S. farms, are allowed to cast absentee ballots under current regulations.

22. The recruitment program initiated in 1944 by the Office of the War Manpower Commission in San Juan was considered a failure because only 15 percent of the workers returned to Puerto Rico. See Edwin Maldonado, "Contract Labor and the Origins of Puerto Rican Communities in the United States," *International Migration Review* 13 (Spring 1979): 111.

23. See monthly report memo from Arnaldo Nieves to the office director, 24 September 1975, Department of Puerto Rican Community Affairs, Commonwealth of Puerto Rico, New York City, Archival Collection, Box 377, Centro de Estudios Puertorriqueños, Hunter College, City University of New York.

24. Press release, Commonwealth of Puerto Rico, Department of Labor, Migration Division, Hartford Office, 24 August 1976. Department of Puerto Rican Community Affairs, Commonwealth of Puerto Rico, New York City, Archival Collection, Box 412, Centro de Estudios Puertorriqueños, Hunter College, City University of New York.

25. The archival evidence supporting this point is extensive. See, e.g., Voto Boricua, open letter, 7 April 1975, Department of Puerto Rican Community Affairs, Commonwealth of Puerto Rico, New York City, Archival Collection, Box 429, Centro de Estudios Puertorriqueños, Hunter College, City University of New York; Notice to Community Leaders from Voto Boricua, 18 July 1975, Department of Puerto Rican Community Affairs, Commonwealth of Puerto Rico, New York City Archival Collection, Box 429, Centro de Estudios Puertorriqueños, Hunter College, City University of New York; Comité Voto Boricua, open letter, 8 August 1975, Department of Puerto Rican Community Affairs, Commonwealth of Puerto Rico, New York City Archival Collection, Box 429, Centro de Estudios Puertorriqueños, Hunter College, City University of New York; Mary Blevins, press release, 10 May 1976, Department of Puerto Rican Community Affairs, Commonwealth of Puerto Rico, New York City, Archival Collection, Box 372, Centro de Estudios Puertorriqueños, Hunter College, City University of New York; Peter G. Kelly to Lionel De Jesus, letter, 20 May 1976, Department of Puerto Rican Community Affairs, Commonwealth of Puerto Rico, New York City,

Archival Collection, Box 429, Centro de Estudios Puertorriqueños, Hunter College, City University of New York; Lionel De Jesus to Peter G. Kelly, letter, 9 June 1976, Department of Puerto Rican Community Affairs, Commonwealth of Puerto Rico, New York City, Archival Collection, Box 429, Centro de Estudios Puertorriqueños, Hunter College, City University of New York; this particular letter lists eighteen community leaders who participated in Connecticut's first presidential preference primary in support of Jimmy Carter; Meg Bassett to Stanley Weinberg, Jr., letter, 14 June 1976, Department of Puerto Rican Community Affairs, Commonwealth of Puerto Rico, New York City, Archival Collection, Box 429, Centro de Estudios Puertorriqueños, Hunter College, City University of New York; memo, Bruce Young-Candelaria to members of executive committee, New England Hispanics for Jimmy Carter, 9 July 1976, Department of Puerto Rican Community Affairs, Commonwealth of Puerto Rico, New York City, Archival Collection, Box 429, Centro de Estudios Puertorriqueños, Hunter College, City University of New York; Bruce Young-Candelaria, circular-letter, 30 November 1976, Department of Puerto Rican Community Affairs, Commonwealth of Puerto Rico, New York City, Archival Collection, Box 429, Centro de Estudios Puertorriqueños, Hunter College, City University of New York; New England Hispanics for Jimmy Carter, a group of mostly Puerto Ricans, was created specifically to (1) elect Carter, (2) insure Hispanic policy input, and (3) promote Hispanic political participation at all levels of the political process.

26. La Luz's exhortation is mentioned in a letter from Gilberto Camacho to Edwin Jorge, 3 March 1971, Department of Puerto Rican Community Affairs, Commonwealth of Puerto Rico, New York City, Archival Collection, Box 10, Centro de Estudios Puertorriqueños, Hunter College, City University of New York; PSP calls for absentee balloting and poll watching in Puerto Rico are documented in "PSP Begins US Voter Registration Drive," *Claridad* [New York], 20 July 1975, p. 8-S; Milton García, "In the Elections in P.R., You Can Be a Volunteer for PSP," *Claridad* [New York], 10 October 1976, p. 10-S; Information about the proceedings of the 1982 convention is based on my interview with Wilfredo Matos, 29 January 1993; a chronicle of the Wells Fargo robbery is provided by Ronald Fernandez, *Los Macheteros* (New York: Prentice Hall, 1987).

27. Louise Simmons, interview, 28 August 1995. See also, "Regional March to Free Puerto Rican Political Prisoners," "Marcha Nacional Pro Justicia y Derechos Civiles Para los 15 Presos Políticos Boricuas," and "Libertad para los Presos Políticos Puertorriqueños," flyers of the Connecticut Committee against Repression and Hartford Committee against Repression, c. August 1986; also, "Sáb., 24 de Sept. de 1988, ¡De Lares a Hartford La Lucha Continúa!" and "¡Defendamos los Derechos de los Boricuas! ¡Libertad Para los 15 Independentistas!," flyers of the Hartford Committee against Repression, 1988.

28. Simmons, interview, 28 August 1995.

29. Lewis, *The Plebiscite and the Diaspora*, p. 23.

30. Sherrie Baver, "Puerto Rican Politics in New York City: The Post-World War II Period," in Jennings and Rivera, eds., *Puerto Rican Politics*, p. 46–47, 55.

31. See Gilberto Camacho to Nick Lugo, Jr., letter, 22 September 1971, Department of Puerto Rican Community Affairs, Commonwealth of Puerto Rico,

New York City, Archival Collection, Box 10, Centro de Estudios Puertorriqueños, Hunter College, City University of New York; Gilberto Camacho to Ralph Muñiz, letter, 6 October 1971, Department of Puerto Rican Community Affairs, Commonwealth of Puerto Rico, New York City, Archival Collection, Box 360, Centro de Estudios Puertorriqueños, Hunter College, City University of New York; Gilberto Camacho to Nick Lugo, Jr., letter, 24 May 1972, Department of Puerto Rican Community Affairs, Commonwealth of Puerto Rico, New York City, Archival Collection, Box 10, Centro de Estudios Puertorriqueños, Hunter College, City University of New York.

32. Patricia Snyder Weiburst, Gennaro Capobianco, and Sally Innis Gould, *The Italians* (Storrs: University of Connecticut, 1978), pp. 93, 107–8.

33. Daniel Bell and Virginia Held, "The Community Revolution," *Public Interest* 16 (Summer 1969): 144; Jeffrey Berry, *The Interest Group Society* (Boston: Little, Brown, 1984), p. 26.

34. The War on Poverty, an initiative undertaken during the presidency of Lyndon Johnson, began with the enactment of the Economic Opportunity Act of 1964 and was followed by the food stamps program, also established in 1964, and by the Medicare Act of 1965, which established Medicare, a health program for the elderly, and Medicaid, a program of medical care for the poor. Neighborhood organization and mobilization were encouraged by the Community Action Program (CAP), which funded organizations such as the Community Renewal Team in Hartford. The civil rights movement began in 1955 in Montgomery, Alabama. After Rosa Parks was arrested for refusing to move to the back of a bus, as blacks were required to do in the presence of white passengers, black leaders formed the Montgomery Improvement Association, led by Martin Luther King, Jr., to boycott the bus system. In 1963, when King delivered his "I Have a Dream" speech to more than two hundred thousand citizens at the March on Washington, the movement was at its peak.

35. Elwyn Nicholas Kernstock, "How New Migrants Behave Politically: The Puerto Rican in Hartford, 1970 (Ph.D. diss., University of Connecticut, 1972), p. 171.

36. Morton Coleman, "Interest Intermediation and Local Urban Development" (Ph.D. diss., University of Pittsburgh, 1983), p. 221.

37. Madelyn Colon, "Puerto Rican Americans," in Robert E. Pawlowski, ed., *How the Other Half Lived* (West Hartford, Conn., n.p., 1973), p. 86.

38. Kernstock, "How New Migrants Behave," p. 131.

39. Kernstock, "How New Migrants Behave," p. 258.

40. Kernstock, "How New Migrants Behave," pp. 196, 256.

41. Harry A. Bailey, Jr., and Ellis Katz, "Ethnic Groups and Political Behavior," in Harry A. Bailey, Jr., and Ellis Katz, eds., *Ethnic Group Politics* (Columbus, Ohio: Merrill, 1969), p. 60; Judith Herbstein, "The Politicization of Puerto Rican Ethnicity in New York: 1955–1975," *Ethnic Groups* 5 (July 1983): 33, 34, 36.

42. Kirk Johnson, "Hartford, Its Boom Over, Sees Downtown Decaying," *New York Times*, 22 August 1990, p. 1.

43. See Pierre Clavel, *The Progressive City* (New Brunswick, N.J.: Rutgers University Press, 1986), for details.

44. This is a key point in John Mollenkopf's "On the Causes and Conse-quences of Political Mobilization," paper presented at the meetings of the Ameri-can Political Science Association, New Orleans, 4–8 September 1973, pp. 4, 9. Here I have borrowed John Walton's phrasing in "Theoretical Methods in Comparative Urban Politics," in John R. Logan and Todd Swanstrom, eds., *Beyond the City Limits: Urban Policy and Economic Restructuring in Comparative Perspective* (Philadelphia: Temple University Press, 1990), pp. 253, 255.

45. Olga Mele, interview, 6 August 1992.

46. Paul Peterson, *City Limits* (Chicago: University of Chicago Press, 1981), pp. 116–28.

47. Peterson, *City Limits*, pp. 3–4.

48. Peterson, *City Limits*, p. 41. According to Peterson (pp. 41–44), develop-ment policies are those that enhance the economic position of the city; redistribu-tive policies shift resources from the better off to the less well off segments of the community, and allocational policies are neutral, providing for housekeeping functions that benefit all citizens.

49. Rufus P. Browning, Dale Rogers Marshall, and David H. Tabb, *Protest Is Not Enough;: The Struggle of Blacks and Hispanics for Equality in Urban Politics* (Berkeley: University of California Press), pp. 250, 252, 255.

50. John R. Logan and Todd Swanstrom, "Urban Restructuring: A Critical Review," in Logan and Swanstrom, *Beyond the City Limits*, pp. 5, x.

51. John H. Mollenkopf, *A Phoenix in the Ashes* (Princeton: Princeton Uni-versity Press, 1992), p. 200.

52. John H. Mollenkopf, *The Contested City* (Princeton: Princeton University Press, 1983).

53. Michael Parkinson "Political Responses to Urban Restructuring: The Brit-ish Experience under Thatcherism," in Logan and Swanstrom, *Beyond the City Limits*, pp. 86–116.

54. Susan Fainstein, "Economics, Politics, and Development Policy: The Con-vergence of New York and London," in Logan and Swanstrom, *Beyond the City Limits*, pp. 119–49.

55. Saskia Sassen, "Beyond the City Limits: A Commentary," in Logan and Swanstrom, *Beyond the City Limits*, p. 242.

56. Walton, "Theoretical Methods," p. 255.

57. Louise Simmons, "Dilemmas of Progressives in Government: Playing Solo-mon in an Age of Austerity," *Economic Development Quarterly* 10 (May 1996): 159–71; Claus Offe, *Contradictions of the Welfare State*, John Keane, ed. (Cam-bridge: MIT Press, 1984); James O'Connor, *The Fiscal Crisis of the State* (New York: St. Martin's Press, 1973).

58. Simmons, "Dilemmas of Progressives," pp. 164.

59. Simmons, "Dilemmas of Progressives," p. 169.

60. Simmons, "Dilemmas of Progressives," p. 169.

61. Simmons, "Dilemmas of Progressives," p. 167.

62. James Madison, *The Federalist Papers* (New York: Mentor Books, 1961), p. 322.

63. Simmons, "Dilemmas of Progressives," p. 167.

64. Niccoló Machiavelli, *The Prince* (New York: Mentor Books, 1980), p. 84.

65. Machiavelli, *The Prince*, p. 64.

66. Machiavelli, *The Prince*, pp. 84, 64.

67. Steve Walsh, "Political New Day Dawns for South End, Puerto Ricans," *Hartford News*, 12–25 September 1991, p. 1.

68. Steve Walsh, "Council Removes Shipman, Appoints Interim Manager," *Hartford News*, 18 December 1991–8 January 1992, p. 1.

69. Steve Walsh, "Town Committee Races Rip Mayor's Coalition," *Hartford News*, 12–19 February 1992, p. 3.

70. Edward Ericson, "Power Plays," *Hartford Advocate*, 6–12 August 1992, p. 4.

71. Steve Walsh, "Council Factions Do Battle on Chamber Floor," *Hartford News*, 16–23 September 1992, p. 1.

72. Steve Walsh, "Perry Slate Divided over Next City Manager Appointment," *Hartford News*, 20 November–4 December 1991, p. 1.

73. Walsh, "Council Removes Shipman."

74. See "The North Hartford Alliance," *Hartford News*, 12–19 February 1992, p. 3.

75. Salisbury, *Interests and Institutions*; Edward C. Banfield, *Political Influence* (Glencoe, Ill.: Free Press, 1961), pp. 4–6; W. Douglas Costain and Anne N. Costain, "Interest Groups as Policy Aggregators in the Legislative Process," *Polity* 14 (Winter 1981): 259.

76. "Objetivos Estratégicos del Comité de Acción Política Puertorriqueño," 20 November 1986, photocopy, author's collection.

77. Author's participant-observation, summer 1992. See also "Amenazan con Privatizar Servicios de Apoyo, *El Extra News* [Hartford], 20 July 1992, p. 1. In November 1994, Hartford's board of education hired Education Alternatives, Inc., to manage the school system in the first privatization decision of its kind in the country. In March 1996, the board rescinded the contract, and in May the city council passed a resolution declaring a state of emergency in the schools and requesting more state involvement in addressing the problems of the school system. On 16 April 1997, the General Assembly dissolved the city's board of education effective 1 June, replacing it with a seven-member panel appointed by the governor and top legislative leaders.

78. Edna Negrón and Jack Cullin, interview, 28 July 1991.

79. Max Fernández, interview, 6 August 1991.

80. All quotations from Juan Figueroa in this and the following section are from my interview of 9 August 1991.

81. This paragraph is based on my interview with Edna Negrón, 28 July 1991. All direct citations are from this interview.

82. Negrón's variation on the phrase "It's Greek to me."

83. Norman Krumholz and Pierre Clavel, *Reinventing Cities: Equity Planners Tell Their Stories* (Philadelphia: Temple University Press, 1994), p. 182.

84. Simmons, "Dilemmas of Progressives," pp. 166–67.

85. Tom Puleo, "Park Street Blues," *Northeast*, 5 January 1997, pp. 8–11, 14–16.

86. Minutes, PRPAC meeting, 17 April 1986, author's collection.

87. Edwin Vargas, Jr., to Alfred Gatta, letter, 21 May 1986, and Alfred Gatta to Edwin Vargas, Jr., letter, 27 May 1986, author's collection.

88. Marie Kirkley-Bey, interview, 6 August 1991.

89. This paragraph is based on interviews with William Hagan, 30 July 1991, and with Marie Kirkley-Bey and Frances Sánchez, 6 August 1991.

90. Browning, Marshall, and Tabb discuss a similar finding but note how differences were "deemphasized" rather than unknown. See *Protest Is Not Enough*, p. 259.

91. I arrived at this judgment after reflecting on my interviews with William Hagan, 30 July 1991, and John Bonelli, 7 August 1991.

92. Jack L. Walker, Jr., *Mobilizing Interest Groups in America* (Ann Arbor: University of Michigan Press, 1991); Laura R. Woliver, *From Outrage to Action: The Politics of Grassroots Dissent* (Urbana: University of Illinois Press, 1993).

93. Browning, Marshall, and Tabb, *Protest Is Not Enough*; Rosa Estades, *Patterns of Political Participation of Puerto Ricans in New York City* (Rio Piedras, PR: Editorial Universitaria, University of Puerto Rico, 1978) and "Symbolic Unity: The Puerto Rican Day Parade," in Clara Rodríguez, Virginia Sánchez Korrol, and José Oscar Alers, eds., *The Puerto Rican Struggle* (Maplewood, N.J.: Waterfront Press, 1984), pp. 82–89; Susan A. MacManus and Charles S. Bullock III, "Electing Women to Local Office," in Judith A. Garber and Robyne S. Turner, eds., *Gender in Urban Research* (Thousand Oaks, Calif.: Sage, 1995), pp. 155–77; Steven P. Erie, *Rainbow's End: Irish-Americans and the Dilemmas of Urban Machine Politics, 1840–1985* (Berkeley: University of California Press, 1988), pp. 72–85.

94. Jorge A. Simón, interview, 30 July 1991.

95. *Santa v. Cimiano*, complaint, U.S. District Court, District of Connecticut, 30 October 1991; Exhibit C, Statement of Allan J. Lichtman, Ph.D., 31 October 1991, p. 5.

96. Yuri Slezkine argues that the Soviet Union dug its own grave by nurturing the centrifugal tendencies inherent in ethnicity. See Yuri Slezkine, "The USSR as a Communal Apartment, or How a Socialist State Promoted Ethnic Particularism," *Slavic Review* 53 (1994): 414–52, and Katherine Verdery, "Beyond the Nation in Eastern Europe," *Social Text* 38 (Spring 1994): 12–23. Dominic Lieven and John McGarry, by contrast, argue that dissolution was an effect of the bankruptcy of Marxism-Leninism and the emergence of democratic forces. See Dominic Lieven and John McGarry, "Ethnic Conflict in the Soviet Union and Its Successor States," in John McGarry and Brendan O'Leary, eds., *The Politics of Ethnic Conflict Regulation* (London: Routledge, 1993), p. 63.

97. David A. Hollinger, *Postethnic America: Beyond Multiculturalism* (New York: Basic Books, 1995), p. 165.

98. U.S. Bureau of the Census, *Statistical Abstract of the United States 1995* (Washington, D.C.: 1995), table 61, p. 55.

99. Talcott Parsons, "Some Theoretical Considerations on the Nature and Trends of Change of Ethnicity," in Nathan Glazer and Daniel P. Moynihan, eds., *Ethnicity: Theory and Experience* (Cambridge: Harvard University Press, 1975), p. 64.

100. Steven A. Holmes, "Census Sees a Profound Ethnic Shift in the U.S.," *New York Times* 14 March 1996, p. A16.

101. Hollinger, *Postethnic America*, pp. 15–16.

102. Celia W. Dugger, "Immigrant Voters Reshape Politics," *New York Times*, 10 March 1996, p. A1; Rodolfo O. de la Garza et al., *Latino Voices* (Boulder, Colo.: Westview Press, 1992); Harry Pachon and Louis DeSipio, *New Americans by Choice: Political Perspectives of Latino Immigrants* (Boulder, Colo.: Westview Press, 1994).

103. Hollinger, *Postethnic America*, p. 153.

104. Jeanne M. Wolfe and Grace Stracham, "Practical Idealism: Women in Urban Reform, Julia Drummond and the Montreal Park and Playground Association," in Caroline Andrew and Beth Moore Milroy, eds., *Life Spaces: Gender, Household, Employment* (Vancouver: University of British Columbia Press, 1988), pp. 65–80.

105. Ronald Lawson and Stephen E. Barton, "Sex Roles in Social Movements: A Case Study of the Tenant Movement in New York City," in Guida West and Rhoda Lois Blumberg, eds., *Women and Social Protest* (New York: Oxford University Press, 1990), pp. 41–56.

106. Martha A. Ackelsberg, "Communities, Resistance, and Women's Activism: Some Implications for a Democratic Polity," in Ann Bookman and Sandra Morgen, eds., *Women and the Politics of Empowerment* (Philadelphia: Temple University Press, 1988), pp. 297–313.

107. Ida Susser, "Working-Class Women, Social Protest, and Changing Ideologies," in Bookman and Morgen, eds., *Women and the Politics of Empowerment*, p. 267.

108. Sánchez Korrol, *From Colonia to Community*, pp. 90–91.

109. Gordana Rabrenovic, "Women and Collective Action in Urban Neighborhoods," in Judith A. Garber and Robyne S. Turner, eds., *Gender in Urban Research* (Thousand Oaks, Calif.: Sage, 1995), pp. 92–93.

110. Carol Hardy-Fanta, *Latina Politics, Latino Politics* (Philadelphia: Temple University Press, 1993).

111. Hilda Vazquez Ignatin, "Young Lords, Serve and Protect," *The Movement*, May 1969, p. 4; reprinted in Claiborne Carson, ed., *The Movement: 1964–1970* (Westport, Conn.: Greenwood Press, 1993), p. 196.

112. "Tengo Puerto Rico en mi Corazon," in Carson, *The Movement*, p. 805.

113. Joseph R. Conlin, ed., *The American Radical Press, 1880–1960*, vol. 1. (Westport, Conn.: Greenwood Press, 1974).

114. Bruce Miroff, *Icons of Democracy* (New York: Basic Books, 1993), p. 231.

115. J. David Gillespie, *Politics at the Periphery: Third Parties in Two-Party America* (Columbia: University of South Carolina Press, 1993).

CHAPTER EIGHT

1. Don Noel, "Unity of Blacks, Latinos Comes at the Price of Schism with Whites," *Hartford Courant*, 21 December 1990, p. C15.

2. Todd Swanstrom, "Beyond Economism: Urban Political Economy and the Postmodern Challenge," *Journal of Urban Affairs* 15 (1993): 56.

3. Edwin Vargas, Jr., conversation with author, 3 June 1993 and 2 July 1993.

4. Statement by Councilman Eugenio Caro, Sr., People for Change, 22 June 1989, photocopy.

5. Daniel Bell, "Ethnicity and Social Change," in Nathan Glazer and Daniel P. Moynihan, eds., *Ethnicity: Theory and Experience* (Cambridge: Harvard University Press, 1975), p. 169.

6. Connecticut Department of Labor statistics assembled by Louise Simmons.

7. Department of Planning, *Hartford: The State of the City* (Hartford: September 1983).

8. Department of Planning and Economic Development, *Hartford, Connecticut: State of the City 1995.*

9. For an account of labor and community struggles in the context of economic restructuring, see Louise Simmons, *Organizing in Hard Times* (Philadelphia: Temple University Press, 1994).

10. The Puerto Ricans in Boston are another example of this. Miren Uriarte argues that Puerto Ricans arrived with a "sense of peoplehood" that was reinforced by the circumstances they encountered. See "Organizing for Survival: The Emergence of a Puerto Rican Community" (Ph.D. diss., Boston University, 1988), p. 301.

11. Representatives of this school of thought include Donald G. Baker, *Race, Ethnicity, and Power* (London: Routledge, 1983); Stephen Steinberg, *The Ethnic Myth: Race, Ethnicity, and Class in America* (New York: Beacon Press, 1989); Richard H. Thompson, *Theories of Ethnicity: A Critical Appraisal* (Westport, Conn.: Greenwood Press, 1989); an excellent counterpoint to these critiques is Joseph Rothschild, *Ethnopolitics* (New York: Columbia University Press, 1981).

12. Nathan Glazer, *Ethnic Dilemmas, 1964–1982* (Cambridge: Harvard University Press, 1983), pp. 331–34.

13. Glazer, *Ethnic Dilemmas*, pp. 335–36.

14. Glazer, *Ethnic Dilemmas*, p. 124; John Higham, *Send These to Me: Jews and Other Immigrants in Urban America* (New York: Atheneum, 1975), pp. 242–43.

15. The statement in which one of GM's executives conflated the company's and the national interest is well known. In 1979, the federal government guaranteed up to $1.5 billion in loans to the Chrysler Corporation to prevent the economic disaster that a potential bankruptcy was likely to cause. Chrysler repaid all its loans within four years, seven years ahead of schedule. Affirmative action, a policy that took into consideration race, gender, and ethnicity in employment and higher education enrollment, was much maligned not only because it used the resources of the general community to promote particular interests but because it condoned the use of suspect categories in decisionmaking. This is one case in which blanket condemnations of discrimination were rooted in the inability to distinguish between invidious and remedial purposes.

16. Milton J. Esman, *Ethnic Politics* (Ithaca: Cornell University Press, 1994), pp. 40, 46–47.

17. Esman, *Ethnic Politics*, p. 48; Glazer and Moynihan write: "We do not celebrate ethnicity as a basic attribute of man, which when suppressed will always rise again. . . . Nor do we dismiss ethnicity as an aberration on the road to a rational society in which all such heritages of the past will become irrelevant to social and political action." See *Ethnicity: Theory and Experience*, p. 20.

18. Arthur M. Schlesinger, Jr., *The Disuniting of America* (New York: Norton, 1992), pp. 110, 112.

19. Donald Rothchild and Alexander J. Groth, "Pathological Dimensions of Domestic and International Ethnicity," *Political Science Quarterly* 110 (Spring 1995): p. 69; cf. Rita Jalali and Seymour Martin Lipset, "Racial and Ethnic Conflicts: A Global Perspective," in Demetrios Caraley and Cerentha Harris, eds., *New World Politics: Power, Ethnicity, and Democracy* (New York: Academy of Political Science, 1993).

20. This is consonant with David Carroll Cochran's argument about the relationship between ethnic diversity and democratic stability in "Ethnic Diversity and Democratic Stability: The Case of Irish Americans," *Political Science Quarterly* 110 (Winter 1995–96), pp. 587–604. The Puerto Rican case helps answer key questions left unexplored in Cochran's article: is the politicization of nonwhite, non-European ethnicity a threat to democratic stability, and, what are the conditions that help politicized ethnicity produce responsiveness?

21. See Michael Banton, *Racial and Ethnic Competition* (Cambridge: Cambridge University Press, 1983), pp. 130–31.

22. Steven P. Erie, *Rainbow's End: Irish-Americans and the Dilemmas of Urban Machine Politics, 1840–1985* (Berkeley: University of California Press, 1988), p. 237.

23. Erie, *Rainbow's End*, p. 256.

24. Erie, *Rainbow's End*, pp. 262–63.

25. Browning, Marshall, and Tabb found evidence of progress along similar lines in cities where biracial coalitions gained control of municipal government. See Rufus P. Browning, Dale Rogers Marshall, and David H. Tabb, *Protest Is not Enough: The Struggle of Blacks and Hispanics for Equality in Urban Politics* (Berkeley: University of California Press, 1984), p. 250.

26. Louis DeSipio and Gregory Rocha, "Latino Influence on National Elections: The Case of 1988," in Rodolfo O. de la Garza and Louis DeSipio, eds., *From Rhetoric to Reality: Latino Politics in the 1988 Elections* (Boulder, Colo.: Westview Press, 1992), pp. 17, 19–20; Rodolfo O. de la Garza and Louis DeSipio, "Overview: The Link between Individuals and Electoral Institutions in Five Latino Neighborhoods," in Rodolfo O. de la Garza, Martha Menchaca, and Louis De-Sipio, eds., *Barrio Ballots: Latino Politics in the 1990 Elections* (Boulder, Colo.: Westview Press, 1994), p. 27.

27. *Cuchifrito* is the generic term for deep-fried food in Puerto Rico.

28. Don Noel, "Latino Community's Political Clout," *Hartford Courant*, 25 November 1991.

29. Edwin Vargas, Jr., interview, 20 February 1993.

30. Juan Figueroa, interview, 9 August 1991; Jan Howard, "State Forces a Regional Approach to Housing," *Weekly Star* [Newtown, Conn.], 10 August

1991, p. 1; Jan Howard, "State Legislation Seeks to Encourage 'Inclusionary' Zoning," *Weekly Star* [Newton, Conn.], 17 August 1991, p. 26.

31. Francisco L. Rivera-Batiz and Carlos Santiago, *Puerto Ricans in the United States: A Changing Reality* (Washington, D.C.: National Puerto Rican Coalition, 1994), pp. 41, 48.

32. *State of the City 1995*, pp. 19, 27.

33. Ira Katznelson, "The Crisis of the Capitalist City: Urban Politics and Social Control," in Willis D. Hawley et al., *Theoretical Perspectives on Urban Politics* (Englewood Cliffs, N.J.: Prentice Hall, 1976), pp. 214–29; Peter K. Eisinger, "Black Employment in Municipal Jobs: The Impact of Black Political Power," *American Political Science Review* 76 (June 1982): 380–92.

34. Rivera-Batiz and Santiago, *Puerto Ricans in the United States*, pp. 48, 50.

35. Erie, *Rainbow's End*, p. 266.

36. *State of the City 1995*, pp. 11, 23, 24, 37.

37. See Talcott Parsons, "Some Theoretical Considerations on the Nature and Trends of Change of Ethnicity," in Glazer and Moynihan, *Ethnicity: Theory and Experience*, p. 78.

38. Suzanne Oboler contends that a focus on ethnicity "obscures the class and racial dynamics of the interaction both within each group and between them and the society at large." See *Ethnic Labels, Latino Lives: Identity and the Politics of (Re)Presentation in the United States* (Minneapolis: University of Minnesota Press, 1995), p. 86 and passim. Her claim is true, yet individuals do respond to ethnic appeals. In some cases ethnicity stands by itself, and at other times it subsumes race and class. This is important only to the extent that the hierarchy of interactions between categories has an impact on outcomes. If by obscuring racial and class cleavages, ethnicity promotes political representation, such focus is worth emphasizing.

39. Niccolò Machiavelli, *The Prince* (New York: Mentor Books, 1980), p. 34.

Select Bibliography

Books

Abramson, Harold J. *Ethnic Pluralism in the Connecticut Central City*. Storrs: Institute of Urban Research, University of Connecticut, 1970.

Akulicz de Santiago, Anne. *The Puerto Rican Community of Milwaukee: A Study of Geographic Mobility*. Milwaukee: Spanish Speaking Outreach Institute, University of Wisconsin-Milwaukee, 1980.

Andrews, Charles McLean. *The River Towns of Connecticut*. Baltimore: Johns Hopkins University, 1889.

Arnold, Robert H. *Hartford: Yesterday and Today*. Glastonbury, Conn.: Farmcliff Press, 1985.

Bailey, Harry A., Jr., and Ellis Katz, eds. *Ethnic Group Politics*. Columbus, Ohio: Merill, 1969.

Baker, Donald G. *Race, Ethnicity, and Power*. London: Routledge, 1983.

Baney, Terry Alan. *Yankees and the City: Struggling over Urban Representation in Connecticut: 1880 to World War I* (New York: Garland, 1993).

Banfield, Edward C. *Political Influence*. Glencoe, Ill.: Free Press, 1961.

Banfield, Edward C., and James Q. Wilson. *City Politics*. Cambridge: Harvard University Press, 1967.

Banton, Michael. *Racial and Ethnic Competition*. Cambridge: Cambridge University Press, 1983.

Berry, Jeffrey. *The Interest Group Society*. Boston: Little, Brown, 1984.

Bonilla-Santiago, Gloria. *Organizing Puerto Rican Migrant Farmworkers: The Experience of Puerto Ricans in New Jersey*. New York: Peter Lang, 1988.

Boorstin, Daniel J. *Hidden History*. New York: Vintage Books, 1989.

Boyte, Harry C. *The Backyard Revolution: Understanding the New Citizen Movement*. Philadelphia: Temple University Press, 1980.

Browning, Rufus P., Dale Rogers Marshall, and David H. Tabb. *Protest Is Not Enough: The Struggle of Blacks and Hispanics for Equality in Urban Politics*. Berkeley: University of California Press, 1984.

Buenker, John D. *Urban Liberalism and Progressive Reform*. New York: Scribner's, 1973.

Buitrago Ortiz, Carlos. *Los Orígenes Históricos de la Sociedad Pre-capitalista en Puerto Rico*. San Juan: Ediciones Huracán, 1976.

Bullard, Robert D. *Dumping in Dixie: Race, Class, and Environmental Quality*. Boulder, Colo.: Westview Press, 1990.

Centro de Estudios Puertorriqueños, ed. *Labor Migration under Capitalism: The Puerto Rican Experience*. New York: Monthly Review Press, 1979.

255

Chenault, Lawrence. *The Puerto Rican Migrant in New York City*. 1938. Reprint. New York: Russell & Russell, 1970.

Cigler, Allan J., and Burdett A. Loomis, eds. *Interest Group Politics*. Washington, D.C.: Congressional Quarterly Press, 1986.

Clavel, Pierre. *The Progressive City*. New Brunswick, NJ: Rutgers University Press, 1986.

Collier, Christopher. *Connecticut in the Continental Congress*. Chester, Conn.: Pequot Press, 1973.

Conlin, Joseph R. ed. *The American Radical Press, 1880–1960,* vol. 1. Westport, Conn.: Greenwood Press, 1974.

Connecticut Advisory Committee. U.S. Commission on Civil Rights. *El Boricua: The Puerto Rican Community in Bridgeport and New Haven*. Washington, D.C.: U.S. Commission on Civil Rights, 1973.

Connecticut Public Expenditure Council. *The Structure of Connecticut's State Government*. Hartford, 1973.

Connecticut. Committee on the Structure of State Government. *Better Organization for Better Government*. Hartford: Committee on the Structure of State Government, 1976.

Conzen, Kathleen Neils. *Immigrant Milwaukee, 1836–1860*. Cambridge: Harvard University Press, 1976.

Cummings, Scott. *Immigrant Minorities and the Urban Working Class*. Port Washington, N.Y.: National University Publications, 1983.

Cruz Monclova, Lidio. *Historia de Puerto Rico (Siglo XIX)*, vol. III, *Segunda Parte (1885–1898)*. Rio Piedras, PR: Editorial Universitaria, 1979.

Daggett, David. *Steady Habits Vindicated: A Serious Remonstrance to the People of Connecticut, against Changing Their Government*. Hartford: Hudson & Goodwin, 1805.

Dahl, Robert A. *Who Governs?* New Haven: Yale University Press, 1961.

Daniels, Bruce C. *Connecticut's First Family: William Pitkin and His Connections*. Chester, Conn.: Pequot Press, 1975.

de la Garza, Rodolfo O., et al. *Latino Voices*. Boulder, Colo.: Westview Press, 1992.

Domhoff, G. William. *Who Really Rules?* Santa Monica: Goodyear, 1978.

Erie, Steven P. *Rainbow's End: Irish-Americans and the Dilemmas of Urban Machine Politics, 1840–1985*. Berkeley: University of California Press, 1988.

Esman, Milton J. *Ethnic Politics*. Ithaca: Cornell University Press, 1994.

Estades, Rosa. *Patterns of Political Participation of Puerto Ricans in New York City*. Rio Piedras, PR: Editorial Universitaria, University of Puerto Rico, 1978.

The Federalist Papers. Introduction by Clinton Rossiter. New York.: Mentor Books, 1961

Fernandez, Ronald. *Los Macheteros*. New York: Prentice Hall, 1987.

Fitzpatrick, Joseph P. *Puerto Rican Americans: The Meaning of Migration to the Mainland*. Englewood Cliffs, N.J.: Prentice Hall, 1971.

Flores, Juan. *Divided Borders: Essays on Puerto Rican Identity*. Houston: Arte Público Press, 1993.

Friedland, Joan W., and Wilson H. Faude. *Birthplace of Democracy*. Chester, Conn.: Globe Pequot Press, 1979.

Fuchs, Lawrence H. *The American Kaleidoscope: Race, Ethnicity, and the Civic Culture*. Hanover, N.H.: University Press of New England, 1990.

Gans, Herbert J. *The Urban Villagers*. New York: Free Press, 1982.

Garber, Judith A., and Robyne S. Turner, eds. *Gender in Urban Research*. Thousand Oaks, Calif.: Sage, 1995.

Garrow, David J. *Bearing the Cross*. New York: Vintage Books, 1988.

Gillespie, J. David. *Politics at the Periphery: Third Parties in Two-Party America*. Columbia: University of South Carolina Press, 1993.

Glasser, Ruth. *Aquí me Quedo: Puerto Ricans in Connecticut*. Connecticut Humanities Council, 1992.

Glazer, Nathan. *Ethnic Dilemmas*. Cambridge: Harvard University Press, 1983.

Glazer, Nathan and Daniel P. Moynihan. *Beyond the Melting Pot: The Negroes, Puerto Ricans, Jews, Italians, and Irish of New York City*. Cambridge: MIT Press, 1970.

———, eds. *Ethnicity: Theory, and Experience*. Cambridge: Harvard University Press, 1975.

Gleason, Philip. *Speaking of Diversity: Language and Ethnicity in Twentieth-Century America*. Baltimore: Johns Hopkins University Press, 1992.

Grant, E. S., and Marion Hepburn Grant. *The City of Hartford, 1784–1984*. Hartford: Connecticut Historical Society, 1986.

Grant, Marion Hepburn. *In and about Hartford*. Hartford: Connecticut Historical Society, 1978.

Handlin, Oscar. *The Newcomers: Negroes and Puerto Ricans in a Changing Metropolis*. Cambridge: Harvard University Press, 1959.

Hardy-Fanta, Carol. *Latina Politics, Latino Politics*. Philadelphia: Temple University Press, 1993.

Harvey, David. *Social Justice and the City*. Baltimore: Johns Hopkins University Press, 1973.

———. *The Urban Experience*. Baltimore: Johns Hopkins University Press, 1989.

Hero, Rodney. *Latinos and the U.S. Political System: Two-Tiered Pluralism*. Philadelphia: Temple University Press, 1992.

Higham, John. *Send These to Me: Jews and Other Immigrants in Urban America*. New York: Atheneum, 1975.

Hollinger, David A. *Postethnic America: Beyond Multiculturalism*. New York: Basic Books, 1995.

Hubbard, William. *A General History of New England, from the Discovery to MDCLXXX*. New York: Arno Press, 1972.

Hunter, Floyd. *Community Power Structure*. Chapel Hill: University of North Carolina Press, 1953.

———. *Community Power Succession: Atlanta's Policy-Makers Revisited*. Chapel Hill: University of North Carolina Press, 1980.

Huntington, Samuel P. *American Politics: The Promise of Disharmony*. Cambridge: Harvard University Press, Belknap Press, 1982.

Janick, Herbert F., Jr. *A Diverse People: Connecticut 1914 to the Present*. Chester, Conn.: Pequot Press, 1975.

Jeffries, John W. *Testing the Roosevelt Coalition: Connecticut Society and Politics in the Era of World War II*. Knoxville: University of Tennessee Press, 1979.

Jennings, James. *Puerto Rican Politics in New York City*. Washington, D.C.: University Press of America, 1977.

Jennings, James, and Monte Rivera, eds. *Puerto Rican Politics in Urban America*. Westport, Conn.: Greenwood Press, 1984.

Key, V. O. *Politics, Parties, and Pressure Groups*. New York: Crowell, 1958.

Koenig, Samuel. *Immigrant Settlements in Connecticut: Their Growth and Characteristics*. Hartford: Connecticut State Department of Education, 1938.

Krumholz, Norman, and Pierre Clavel. *Reinventing Cities: Equity Planners Tell Their Stories*. Philadelphia: Temple University Press, 1994.

Ladd, Everett C. *Ideology in America*. Lanham, Md.: University Press of America, 1986.

Levenson, Rosaline. *County Government in Connecticut: Its History and Demise*. Storrs: Institute of Public Service, University of Connecticut, 1966.

Lieberman, Joseph. *The Power Broker*. Boston: Houghton Mifflin, 1966.

Lissak, Rivka Shpak. *Pluralism and Progressives: Hull House and the New Immigrants, 1890–1919*. Chicago: University of Chicago Press, 1989.

Litt, Edgar. *Ethnic Politics in America*. Glenview, Ill.: Scott, Foresman, 1970.

Logan, John R., and Todd Swanstrom, eds. *Beyond the City Limits: Urban Policy and Economic Restructuring in Comparative Perspective*. Philadelphia: Temple University Press, 1990.

Love, William DeLoss. *The Colonial History of Hartford*. Chester, Conn.: Centinel Hill Press, 1974.

Omi, Michael, and Howard Winant. *Racial Formation in the United States*. New York: Routledge, 1994.

Machiavelli, Niccolò. *The Prince*. Introduction by Christian Gauss. New York: Mentor Books, 1980.

Martin, George E. *Ethnic Political Leadership: The Case of the Puerto Ricans*. San Francisco: R & E Research Associates, 1977.

Michel, Henri. *The Second World War*. New York: Praeger, 1975.

Mills, C. Wright. *The Power Elite*. New York: Oxford University Press, 1956.

Mills, C. Wright, Clarence Senior, and Rose Kohn Goldsen. *The Puerto Rican Journey: New York's Newest Migrants*. New York: Russell & Russell, 1967.

Miroff, Bruce. *Icons of Democracy*. New York: Basic Books, 1993.

Miyares, Marcelino. *Models of Political Participation of Hispanic-Americans*. New York: Arno Press, 1980.

Moe, Terry. *The Organization of Interests: Incentives and the Internal Dynamics of Political Interest Groups*. Chicago: University of Chicago Press, 1980.

Mollenkopf, John. *The Contested City*. Princeton: Princeton University Press, 1983.

———. *A Phoenix in the Ashes*. Princeton: Princeton University Press, 1992.

Morales, Julio. *Puerto Rican Poverty and Migration: We Just Had to Try Elsewhere*. New York: Praeger, 1986.

Mumford, Lewis. *The City in History*. New York: Harcourt, Brace, 1961.

———. *The Urban Prospect*. New York: Harcourt, Brace, 1968.

Novak, Michael. *The Rise of the Unmeltable Ethnics*. New York: Macmillan, 1971.

Oboler, Suzanne. *Ethnic Labels, Latino Lives: Identity and the Politics of (Re)Presentation in the United States*. Minneapolis: University of Minnesota Press, 1995.

O'Connor, James. *The Fiscal Crisis of the State*. New York: St. Martin's, 1973.

Offe, Claus. *Contradictions of the Welfare State*. Edited by John Keane. Cambridge: MIT Press, 1984.

Pachon, Harry, and Louis DeSipio. *New Americans by Choice: Political Perspectives of Latino Immigrants*. Boulder, Colo.: Westview Press, 1994.

Padilla, Felix M. *Latino Ethnic Consciousness, The Case of Mexican Americans and Puerto Ricans in Chicago*. Notre Dame, Ind.: University of Notre Dame Press, 1985.

———. *Puerto Rican Chicago*. Notre Dame, Ind: University of Notre Dame Press, 1987.

Pawlowski, Robert E. *La Gente La Casa: the Development of Hartford's Puerto Rican Community*. Hartford: La Casa de Puerto Rico, c. 1991.

Peirce, Neal R. *The New England States*. New York: Norton, 1976.

Peterson, Paul E. *City Limits*. Chicago: University of Chicago Press, 1981.

Piven, Frances Fox, and Richard Cloward. *Poor People's Movements: Why They Succeed, How They Fail*. New York: Vintage Books, 1977.

Polsby, Nelson. *Community Power and Political Theory*. New Haven: Yale University Press, 1963.

Portes, Alejandro, and Robert L. Bach. *Latin Journey: Cuban and Mexican Immigrants in the United States*. Berkeley: University of California Press, 1985.

Reichley, A. James. *The Life of the Parties*. New York: Free Press, 1992.

Rivera-Batiz, Francisco L., and Carlos Santiago. *Puerto Ricans in the United States: A Changing Reality*. Washington, D.C.: National Puerto Rican Coalition, 1994.

Rodríguez, Clara. *Puerto Ricans Born in the U.S.A.* Boston: Unwin Hyman, 1989.

Rodríguez, Clara, Virginia Sánchez Korrol, and José Oscar Alers, eds. *The Puerto Rican Struggle*. Maplewood, N.J.: Waterfront Press, 1984.

Rogler, Lloyd. *Migrant in the City: The Life of a Puerto Rican Action Group*. New York: Basic Books, 1972.

Rose, Arnold M. *The Power Structure*. New York: Oxford University Press, 1967.

Rose, Gary L. *Connecticut Politics at the Crossroads*. Lanham, Md.: University Press of America, 1992.

Roth, David. *Connecticut*. New York: Norton, 1979.

Rothschild, Joseph. *Ethnopolitics*. New York: Columbia University Press, 1981.

Rusk, David. *Cities without Suburbs*. Washington, D.C.: Woodrow Wilson Center Press, 1993.

Salisbury, Robert H. *Interests and Institutions: Substance and Structure in American Politics*. Pittsburgh: University of Pittsburgh Press, 1992.

Sánchez Korrol, Virginia E. *From Colonia to Community: The History of Puerto Ricans in New York City.* Berkeley: University of California Press, 1994.

Sandberg, Neil C. *Ethnic Identity and Assimilation: The Polish-American Community.* New York: Praeger, 1974.

Schattschneider, E.E. *The Semi-Sovereign People.* Hinsdale, Ill.: Dryden Press, 1960.

Schlesinger, Arthur M., Jr. *The Disuniting of America.* New York: Norton, 1992.

———. *The Imperial Presidency.* Boston: Houghton Mifflin, 1973.

Schnare, Robert E. *Local Historical Resources in Connecticut: A Guide to Their Use.* Darien, Conn.: Connecticut League of Historical Societies, 1975.

Senior, Clarence. *The Puerto Ricans: Strangers—Then Neighbors.* Chicago: Quadrangle Books, 1965.

Shuffelton, Frank. *Thomas Hooker, 1586–1647.* Princeton: Princeton University Press, 1977.

Silverman, Morris. *Hartford Jews, 1659–1970.* Hartford: Connecticut Historical Society, 1970.

Simmons, Louise. *Organizing in Hard Times.* Philadelphia: Temple University Press, 1994.

Skerry, Peter. *Mexican-Americans: The Ambivalent Minority.* New York: Free Press, 1993.

Smelser, Neil J. *Theory of Collective Behavior.* New York: Free Press, 1963.

Smith, James E. *One Hundred Years of Hartford's "Courant."* New Haven: Yale University Press, 1949.

Steinberg, Stephen. *The Ethnic Myth: Race, Ethnicity, and Class in America.* Boston: Beacon Press, 1989.

Stone, Clarence N. *Economic Growth and Neighborhood Discontent.* Chapel Hill: University of North Carolina Press, 1976.

———. *Regime Politics: Governing Atlanta, 1964–1988.* Lawrence: University Press of Kansas, 1989.

Stuart, Patricia. *Summary of Charter Provisions in Connecticut Local Government.* Storrs, Conn.: Institute of Public Service, University of Connecticut, 1984.

Taylor, Robert J. *Colonial Connecticut.* Millwood, N.Y.: KTO Press, 1979.

Thompson, Richard H. *Theories of Ethnicity: A Critical Appraisal.* Westport, Conn.: Greenwood Press, 1989.

Torres, Andrés. *Between Melting Pot and Mosaic: African Americans and Puerto Ricans in the New York Political Economy.* Philadelphia: Temple University Press, 1995.

Trumbull, J. Hammond. *The Memorial History of Hartford County.* Boston: Edward L. Osgood, 1886.

Tucker, Robert C., ed. *The Marx Engels Reader.* New York: Norton, 1972.

Ture, Kwame, and Charles V. Hamilton. *Black Power: The Politics of Liberation in America.* New York: Vintage Books, 1992.

Van Den Berghe, Pierre. *The Ethnic Phenomenon.* New York: Elsevier-North Holland, 1981.

Van Dusen, Albert E. *Connecticut.* New York: Random House, 1961.

Wagenheim, Kal. *A Survey of Puerto Ricans on the U.S. Mainland in the 1970s.* New York: Praeger, 1975.

Walker, Jr., Jack L. *Mobilizing Interest Groups in America.* Ann Arbor: University of Michigan Press, 1991.

Ward, David. *Poverty, Ethnicity, and the American City, 1840–1925.* Cambridge: Cambridge University Press, 1989.

Waste, Robert J. *Power and Pluralism in American Cities.* New York: Greenwood Press, 1987.

Waters, Mary C. *Ethnic Options: Choosing Identities in America.* Berkeley: University of California Press, 1990.

Weaver, Glenn. *Hartford: An Illustrated History of Connecticut's Capital.* Woodland Hills, Calif.: Windsor Publications/Connecticut Historical Society, 1982.

Weiburst, Patricia Snyder, Gennaro Capobianco, and Sally Innis Gould. *The Italians.* Storrs: University of Connecticut, 1978.

Welling, James C. *Connecticut Federalism, or Aristocratic Politics in a Social Democracy.* New York: New York Historical Society, 1890.

Wolfinger, Raymond E. *The Politics of Progress.* Englewood Cliffs, N.J.: Prentice Hall, 1974.

Woliver, Laura R. *From Outrage to Action: The Politics of Grassroots Dissent.* Urbana: University of Illinois Press, 1993.

BOOK CHAPTERS

Ackelsberg, Martha A. "Communities, Resistance, and Women's Activism: Some Implications for a Democratic Polity." In *Women and the Politics of Empowerment,* edited by Ann Bookman and Sandra Morgen, pp. 297–313. Philadelphia: Temple University Press, 1988.

Amit-Talai, Vered. "The Minority Circuit: Identity Politics and the Professionalization of Ethnic Activism." In *Re-situating Identities: The Politics of Race, Ethnicity, and Culture,* edited by Vered Amit-Talai and Caroline Knowles, pp. 89–114. Peterborough, Canada: broadview press, 1996.

Baver, Sherrie. "Puerto Rican Politics in New York City: The Post–World War II Period." In *Puerto Rican Politics in Urban America,* edited by James Jennings and Monte Rivera, pp. 43–59. Westport, Conn.: Greenwood Press, 1984.

Bell, Daniel. "Ethnicity and Social Change." In *Ethnicity: Theory, and Experience,* edited by Nathan Glazer and Daniel P. Moynihan, pp. 141–74. Cambridge: Harvard University Press, 1975.

Bonilla, Frank. "Migrants, Citizens, and Social Pacts." In *Colonial Dilemma,* edited by Edwin Meléndez and Edgardo Meléndez, pp. 181–88. Boston: South End Press, 1993.

Carbone, Nicholas R. "The General Assembly's Failure to Help Its Capital City." In *Perspectives of a State Legislature,* 2d ed., edited by Clyde D. McKee, Jr., pp. 213–22. Hartford: n.p., 1980.

———. "The Inner City." In *Hartford: The City and the Region,* edited by Sondra Astor Stave, pp. 59–63. West Hartford: University of Hartford, 1979.

Colon, Madelyn. "Puerto Rican Americans." In *How the Other Half Lived*, edited by Robert E. Pawlowski, pp. 80–87. West Hartford, n.p. 1973.

Cornwell, Elmer E., Jr. "Bosses, Machines, and Ethnic Groups." In *American Ethnic Politics*, edited by Lawrence H. Fuchs, pp. 194–216. New York: Harper Torch Books, 1968.

Cruz, José E. "Puerto Rican Elected Officials in the United States." In *1993 Directory of Puerto Rican Elected Officials*, pp. 3–22. Washington, D.C.: National Puerto Rican Coalition, 1993.

de la Garza, Rodolfo O., and Louis DeSipio. "Overview: The Link between Individuals and Electoral Institutions in Five Latino Neighborhoods." In *Barrio Ballots: Latino Politics in the 1990 Elections*, edited by Rodolfo O. de la Garza, Martha Menchaca, and Louis DeSipio, pp. 1–41. Boulder, Colo.: Westview Press, 1994.

de la Garza, Rodolfo O., Robert D. Wrinkle, and Jerry L. Polinard. "Ethnicity and Policy: The Mexican-American Perspective." In *Latinos and the Political System*, edited by F. Chris Garcia, pp. 426–40. Notre Dame, Ind: University of Notre Dame Press, 1988.

DeSipio, Louis, and Gregory Rocha. "Latino Influence on National Elections: The Case of 1988." In *From Rhetoric to Reality: Latino Politics in the 1988 Elections*, edited by Rodolfo O. de la Garza and Louis DeSipio, pp. 3–22. Boulder, Colo: Westview Press, 1992.

Downs, Anthony. "The Future of Industrial Cities." In *The New Urban Reality*, edited by Paul E. Peterson, pp. 281–94. Washington, D.C.: Brookings Institution, 1985.

Falcón, Angelo. "A Divided Nation: The Puerto Rican Diaspora in the United States and the Proposed Referendum." In *Colonial Dilemma*, edited by Edwin Meléndez and Edgardo Meléndez, pp. 173–180. Boston: South End Press, 1993.

———. "A History of Puerto Rican Politics in New York City: 1860s to 1945." In *Puerto Rican Politics in Urban America*, edited by James Jennings and Monte Rivera, pp. 15–42. Westport, Conn.: Greenwood Press, 1984.

———. "Puerto Rican Political Participation: New York City and Puerto Rico." In *Time for Decision: The United States and Puerto Rico*, edited by Jorge Heine, pp. 27–53. Lanham, Md.: North-South Publishing, 1983.

———. "Puerto Rican Politics in Postliberal New York: The 1992 Presidential Election." In *Ethnic Ironies: Latino Politics in the 1992 Elections*, edited by Rodolfo O. de la Garza and Louis DeSipio, pp. 185–210. Boulder, Colo.: Westview Press, 1996.

Fuchs, Lawrence H. "Introduction." In *American Ethnic Politics*, edited by Lawrence H. Fuchs, pp. 1–9. New York: Harper Torch Books, 1968.

Guzmán, Pablo. "The Party." In *Boricuas*, edited by Roberto Santiago, pp. 52–60. New York: Ballantine Books, 1995.

Higham, John. "Introduction: The Forms of Ethnic Leadership." In *Ethnic Leadership in America*, edited by John Higham, pp. 1–18. Baltimore: Johns Hopkins University Press, 1978.

Hilferding, Rudolf. "The Materialist Conception of History." In *Modern Interpre-*

tations of Marx, edited by Tom Bottomore, pp. 125–37. Oxford: Basil Blackwell, 1981.

Horowitz, Donald L. "Ethnic Identity." In *Ethnicity: Theory, and Experience,* edited by Nathan Glazer and Daniel P. Moynihan, pp. 111–40. Cambridge: Harvard University Press, 1975.

Hyde, William Waldo. "Our City Government." In *Hartford in History,* edited by Willis I. Twitchell, pp. 235–49. Hartford: Press of the Plimpton Mfg. Co., 1899.

Jalali, Rita, and Seymour Martin Lipset. "Racial and Ethnic Conflicts: A Global Perspective." In *New World Politics: Power, Ethnicity, and Democracy,* edited by Demetrios Caraley and Cerentha Harris, pp. 55–76. New York: Academy of Political Science, 1993.

Jennings, James. "Future Directions for Puerto Rican Politics in the U.S. and Puerto Rico." In *Latinos and the Political System,* edited by F. Chris Garcia, pp. 480–97. Notre Dame, Ind.: University of Notre Dame Press, 1988.

———. "Introduction: The Emergence of Puerto Rican Electoral Activism in Urban America." In *Puerto Rican Politics in Urban America,* edited by James Jennings and Monte Rivera, pp. 3–12. Westport, Conn.: Greenwood Press, 1984.

Johnson, Charles F. "The Dutch in Hartford." In *Hartford in History,* edited by Willis I. Twitchell, pp. 39–48. Hartford: Press of the Plimpton Mfg. Co., 1899.

Katznelson, Ira. "The Crisis of the Capitalist City: Urban Politics and Social Control." In *Theoretical Perspectives on Urban Politics,* edited by Willis D. Hawley et al., pp. 214–29. Englewood Cliffs, N.J.: Prentice Hall, 1976.

Lane, Robert E. "The Way of the Ethnic in Politics." In *Ethnic Group Politics,* edited by Harry A. Bailey, Jr., and Ellis Katz, pp. 85–109. Columbus, Ohio: Charles E. Merrill, 1969.

Lawson, Ronald, and Stephen E. Barton. "Sex Roles in Social Movements: A Case Study of the Tenant Movement in New York City." In *Women and Social Protest,* edited by Guida West and Rhoda Lois Blumberg, pp. 41–56. New York: Oxford University Press, 1990.

Leinenweber, Charles. "The Class and Ethnic Bases of New York City Socialism, 1905–1915." In *Immigrant Radicals: The View from the Left,* edited by George E. Pozetta, pp. 293–318. New York: Garland, 1991.

Lieven, Dominic, and John McGarry. "Ethnic Conflict in the Soviet Union and Its Successor States." In *The Politics of Ethnic Conflict Regulation,* edited by John McGarry and Brendan O'Leary, pp. 62–83. London: Routledge, 1993.

Marable, Manning. "Building Coalitions among Communities of Color: Beyond Racial Identity Politics." In *Blacks, Latinos, and Asians in Urban America,* edited by James Jennings, pp. 29–43. Westport, Conn.: Praeger, 1994.

Meléndez, Edwin, and Edgardo Meléndez. "Introduction." In *Colonial Dilemma,* edited by Edwin Meléndez and Edgardo Meléndez, pp. 1–16. Boston: South End Press, 1993.

Meyer, David R. "Image and the Physical Environment." In *Hartford: The City and the Region,* edited by Sondra Astor Stave, pp. 13–17. West Hartford: University of Hartford, 1979.

Mintz, Sidney. "Ethnicity and Leadership." In *Ethnic Leadership in America,* edited by John Higham, pp. 198–205. Baltimore: Johns Hopkins University Press, 1978.

Nelson, Dale. "The Political Behavior of New York Puerto Ricans: Assimilation or Survival?" In *The Puerto Rican Struggle,* edited by Clara Rodríguez, Virgina Sánchez Korrol, and José Oscar Alers, pp. 90–110. Maplewood, N.J.: Waterfront Press, 1984.

Neubeck, Kenneth J., and Richard E. Ratcliff. "Urban Democracy and the Power of Corporate Capital: Struggles over Downtown Growth and Neighborhood Stagnation in Hartford, Connecticut." In *Business Elites and Urban Development: Case Studies and Critical Perspectives,* edited by Scott Cummings, pp. 299–332. Albany: State University of New York Press, 1988.

Parker, Edwin P. "Social Life and Customs." In *Hartford in History,* edited by Willis I. Twitchell, pp. 82–98. Hartford: Press of the Plimpton Mfg. Co., 1899.

Parsons, Talcott. "Some Theoretical Considerations on the Nature and Trends of Change of Ethnicity." In *Ethnicity: Theory and Experience,* edited by Nathan Glazer and Daniel P. Moynihan, pp. 53–83. Cambridge: Harvard University Press, 1975.

Pawlowski, Robert E. "Introduction." In *How the Other Half Lived,* edited by Robert E. Pawlowski, pp. 6–10. West Hartford, Conn., n.p., 1973.

Peach, Ceri. "Conflicting Interpretations of Segregation." In *Social Interaction and Ethnic Segregation,* edited by Peter Jackson and Susan J. Smith, pp. 19–33. London: Academic Press, 1981.

Rabrenovic, Gordana. "Women and Collective Action in Urban Neighborhoods." In *Gender in Urban Research,* edited by Judith A. Garber and Robyne S. Turner, pp. 77–96. Thousand Oaks, Calif.: Sage, 1995.

Rodríguez, Néstor P. "The Globalization of Racial and Ethnic Relations in the Late Twentieth Century." In *The Bubbling Cauldron: Race, Ethnicity, and the Urban Crisis,* edited by Michael Peter Smith and Joe R. Feagin, pp. 211–25. Minneapolis: University of Minnesota Press, 1995.

Rogers, John. "Foreword." In *How the Other Half Lived,* edited by Robert E. Pawlowski, p. 3. West Hartford, Conn., n.p. 1973.

Smith, Michael Peter, and Joe R. Feagin. "Putting 'Race' in Its Place." In *The Bubbling Cauldron: Race, Ethnicity, and the Urban Crisis,* edited by Michael Peter Smith and Joe R. Feagin, pp. 3–27. Minneapolis: University of Minnesota Press, 1995.

Stave, Sondra Astor, and Bruce Stave. "Making Hartford Home: An Oral History of Twentieth Century Ethnic Development in Connecticut's Capitol City." In *Hartford: The City and the Region,* edited by Sondra Astor Stave, pp. 31–49. West Hartford, Conn.: University of Hartford, 1979.

Stone, Clarence N. "Power and Social Complexity." In *Community Power: Directions for Future Research,* edited by Robert J. Waste, pp. 77–113. Beverly Hills, Calif.: 1986.

Stone, Clarence N., and Heywood T. Sanders. "Reexamining a Classic Case of Development Politics: New Haven, Connecticut." In *The Politics of Urban*

Development, edited by Clarence N. Stone and Heywood T. Sanders, pp. 159–81. Lawrence: University Press of Kansas, 1987.

———. "The Study of the Politics of Urban Development." In *The Politics of Urban Development,* edited by Clarence N. Stone and Heywood T. Sanders, pp. 3–22. Lawrence: University Press of Kansas, 1987.

———. "Summing Up: Urban Regimes, Development Policy, and Political Arrangements." In *The Politics of Urban Development,* edited by Clarence N. Stone and Heywood T. Sanders, pp. 269–90. Lawrence: University Press of Kansas, 1987.

Susser, Ida. "Working-Class Women, Social Protest, and Changing Ideologies." In *Women and the Politics of Empowerment,* edited by Ann Bookman and Sandra Morgen, pp. 257–71. Philadelphia: Temple University Press, 1988.

"Tengo Puerto Rico en mi Corazon." In *The Movement, 1964–1970,* edited by Claiborne Carson, p. 805. Westport, Conn.: Greenwood Press, 1993.

Twitchell, Joseph H. "Hartford: The Birthplace of the Written Constitution." In *Hartford in History,* edited by Willis I. Twitchell, pp. 66–81. Hartford: Press of the Plimpton Mfg. Co., 1899.

Vazquez Ignatin, Hilda. "Young Lords, Serve and Protect." In *The Movement, 1964–1970,* edited by Claiborne Carson, p. 196. Westport, Conn.: Greenwood Press, 1993.

Waldinger, Roger. "When the Melting Pot Boils Over: The Irish, Jews, Blacks, and Koreans of New York." In *The Bubbling Cauldron: Race, Ethnicity, and the Urban Crisis,* edited by Michael Peter Smith and Joe R. Feagin, pp. 265–81. Minneapolis: University of Minnesota Press, 1995.

Wolfe, Jeanne M., and Grace Stracham. "Practical Idealism: Women in Urban Reform, Julia Drummond and the Montreal Park and Playground Association." In *Life Spaces: Gender, Household, Employment,* edited by Caroline Andrew and Beth Moore Milroy, pp. 65–80. Vancouver: University of British Columbia Press, 1988.

Woodward, Henry P. "Manufactures in Hartford." In *Hartford in History,* edited by Willis I. Twitchell, pp. 170–83. Hartford: Press of the Plimpton Mfg. Co., 1899.

JOURNAL ARTICLES

Abney, Glenn, and Thomas P. Lauth. "Interest Group Influence in City Policy Making: The Views of Administrators." *Western Political Quarterly* 38 (March 1985): 148–61.

Adrian, Charles R. "Some General Characteristics of Nonpartisan Elections." *American Political Science Review* 47 (September 1952): 766–76.

Alba, Richard D. "The Twilight of Ethnicity among Catholics of European Ancestry." *Annals of the American Academy of Political and Social Science* 454 (1981): 86–97.

Austen-Smith, David, and Jeffrey Banks. "Elections, Coalitions, and Legislative Outcomes." *American Political Science Review* 82 (1988): 405–23.

Bach, Eve, Nicholas R. Carbone, and Pierre Clavel. "Running the City for the People." *Social Policy* 12 (Winter 1982): 15–23.

Backstand, Jeffrey R., and Stephen Schensul. "Co-evolution in an Outlying Ethnic Community: The Puerto Ricans of Hartford, Connecticut." *Urban Anthropology* 11 (Spring 1982): 9–37.

Barkan, Elliott R. "Race, Religion, and Nationality in American Society: A Model of Ethnicity—From Contact to Assimilation." *Journal of American Ethnic History* 14 (Winter 1995): 38–75.

Beauregard, Robert A. "Civic Culture and Urban Discourse: A Rejoinder." *Journal of Urban Affairs* 18 (1996): 241–44.

———. "Why Passion for the City Has Been Lost." *Journal of Urban Affairs* 18 (1996): 217–31.

Bell, Daniel, and Virginia Held. "The Community Revolution." *Public Interest* 16 (Summer 1969): 142–77.

Bonacich, Edna. "A Theory of Ethnic Antagonism: The Split Labor Market." *American Sociological Review* 37 (October 1972): 547–59.

Buenker, John D. "Progressivism in Connecticut." *Connecticut Historical Society Bulletin* 35 (October 1970): 97–109.

Cochran, David Carroll. "Ethnic Diversity and Democratic Stability: The Case of Irish-Americans." *Political Science Quarterly* 110 (Winter 1995–96): 587–604.

Cohen, Jean L. "Strategy or Identity: New Theoretical Paradigms and Contemporary Social Movements." *Social Research* 52 (Winter 1985): 663–716.

Conzen, Kathleen Neils, et al. "The Invention of Ethnicity: A Perspective from the U.S.A." *Journal of American Ethnic History* 12 (Fall 1992): 3–41.

Cornwell, Jr., Elmer E. "Ethnic Group Representation: The Case of the Portuguese." *Polity* 13 (Fall 1980): 5–20.

Costain, W. Douglas, and Anne N. Costain. "Interest Groups as Policy Aggregators in the Legislative Process." *Polity* 14 (Winter 1981): 249–72.

Eisinger, Peter K. "Black Employment in Municipal Jobs: The Impact of Black Political Power." *American Political Science Review* 76 (June 1982): 380–92.

Fitzpatrick, Joseph P., and Lourdes Travieso-Parker. "Hispanic Americans in the Eastern United States." *Annals of the American Academy of Political and Social Science* 454 (March 1981): 98–110.

Fuchs, Lawrence H. "Comment: 'The Invention of Ethnicity': The Amen Corner." *Journal of American Ethnic History* 12 (Fall 1992): 53–58.

Gans, Herbert J. "Symbolic Ethnicity: The Future of Ethnic Groups and Cultures in America." *Ethnic and Racial Studies* 2 (January 1979): 1–20.

Gitlin, Todd. "From Universality to Difference: Notes on the Fragmentation of the Idea of the Left." *Contention* 2 (Winter 1993): 15–40.

Glasser, Ruth. "En Casa en Connecticut: Towards a Historiography of Puerto Ricans outside of New York City." *Centro* 7 (1995): 51–59.

Glazer, Nathan. "A New Look at the Melting Pot." *Public Interest* 16 (Summer 1969): 180–87.

Grofman, Bernard, and Lisa Handley. "Minority Population Proportion and Black and Hispanic Congressional Success in the 1970s and 1980s." *American Politics Quarterly* 17 (October 1989): 436–45.

Gross, Bertram M., and Jeffrey F. Kraus. "The Political Machine Is Alive and Well." *Social Policy* 12 (Winter 1982): 38–45.

Gurak, Douglas, and May M. Kritz. "The Caribbean Communities in the United States." *Migration Today* 12 (1985): 6–12.

Herbstein, Judith. "The Politicization of Puerto Rican Ethnicity in New York: 1955–1975." *Ethnic Groups* 5 (July 1983): 31–54.

Hogan, Neil. "The Actual Enumeration: New Haven and the U.S. Census." *Journal* (New Haven Colony Historical Society), 1991.

Lao, Agustín. "Resources of Hope: Imagining the Young Lords and the Politics of Memory." *Centro* 8 (1995): 34–49.

Maldonado, Edwin. "Contract Labor and the Origins of Puerto Rican Communities in the United States." *International Migration Review* 13 (Spring 1979): 103–21.

Manley, John F. "Neo-Pluralism: A Class Analysis of Pluralism I and Pluralism II." *American Political Science Review* 77 (June 1983): 368–83.

Massey, Douglas S. "Social Class and Ethnic Segregation: A Reconsideration of Methods and Conclusions." *American Sociological Review* 46 (1981): 641–50.

Moe, Terry. "Toward a Broader View of Interest Groups." *Journal of Politics* 43 (May 1981): 531–43.

Mohl, Raymond A. "Ethnic Transformations in Late-Twentieth Century Florida." *Journal of American Ethnic History* 15 (Winter 1996): 60–78.

Moynihan, Daniel P. "Patterns of Ethnic Succession: Blacks and Hispanics in New York City." *Political Science Quarterly* 94 (Spring 1979): 1–14.

Panitch, Leo. "Recent Theorizations of Corporatism: Reflections on a Growth Industry." *British Journal of Sociology* 31 (June 1980): 159–87.

Parenti, Michael. "Ethnic Politics and the Persistence of Ethnic Identification." *American Political Science Review* 61 (September 1967): 717–26.

Piven, Frances Fox. "Globalizing Capitalism and the Rise of Identity Politics." *Socialist Register 1995*: 102–16.

Rogler, Lloyd H., Rosemary Cooney Santana, and Vilma Ortiz. "Intergenerational Change in Ethnic Identity in the Puerto Rican Family." *International Migration Review* 14 (Summer 1980): 193–214.

Rothchild, Donald, and Alexander J. Groth. "Pathological Dimensions of Domestic and International Ethnicity." *Political Science Quarterly* 110 (Spring 1995): 69–82.

Senior, Clarence. "Puerto Rican Dispersion in the United States." *Social Problems* 2 (October 1954): 93–99.

Schmitter, Philippe C. "Modes of Interest Intermediation and Models of Social Change in Western Europe." *Comparative Political Studies* 10 (April 1977): 7–38.

———. "Still the Century of Corporatism?" *Review of Politics* 36 (January 1974): 85–131.

Simmons, Louise. "Dilemmas of Progressives in Government: Playing Solomon in an Age of Austerity." *Economic Development Quarterly* 10 (May 1996: 159–71.

Slezkine, Yuri. "The USSR as a Communal Apartment, or How a Socialist State Promoted Ethnic Particularism." *Slavic Review* 53 (1994): 414–52.

Swanstrom, Todd. "Beyond Economism: Urban Political Economy and the Postmodern Challenge." *Journal of Urban Affairs* 15 (1993): 55–78.

Tiebout, Charles. "A Pure Theory of Local Expenditures." *Journal of Political Economy* 64 (1956): 416–24.

Verdery, Katherine. "Beyond the Nation in Eastern Europe." *Social Text* 38 (Spring 1994): 12–23.

Wallerstein, Immanuel. "Ethnicity and National Integration in West Africa." *Cahiers d'Etudes Africaines* 1 (July 1960): 129–39.

Warner, Sam Bass, Jr. "Urban Discourse: A Reply to Robert A. Beauregard." *Journal of Urban Affairs* 18 (1996): 237–36.

Warren, Robert. "Alternatives to Celebrity in the Rescue of the City: A Reply to Robert A. Beauregard." *Journal of Urban Affairs* 18 (1996): 237–40.

Wernette, D. R., and L. A. Nieves. "Breathing Polluted Air." *EPA Journal* (March/April 1992): 16–17.

Wiggins, Charles W., and William P. Browne. "Interest Groups and Public Policy within a State Legislative Setting." *Polity* 14 (Spring 1982): 548–58.

Williams, Oliver P., and Charles R. Adrian. "The Insulation of Local Politics under the Nonpartisan Ballot." *American Political Science Review* 53 (December 1959): 1052–63.

Wolfinger, Raymond E. "The Development and Persistence of Ethnic Voting." *American Political Science Review* 59 (December 1965): 896–908.

Wrinkle, Robert D., et al. "Ethnicity and Nonelectoral Political Participation." *Hispanic Journal of Behavioral Sciences* 18 (May 1996): 142–53.

Yancey, William L., Eugene P. Ericksen, and Richard N. Juliani. "Emergent Ethnicity: A Review and a Reformulation." *American Sociological Review* 41 (June 1976): 391–403.

DOCTORAL DISSERTATIONS

Coleman, Morton. "Interest Intermediation and Local Urban Development." University of Pittsburgh, 1983.

Kernstock, Elwyn Nicholas. "How New Migrants Behave Politically: The Puerto Rican in Hartford, 1970." University of Connecticut, 1972.

Koss, Joan Dee. "Puerto Ricans in Philadelphia: Migration and Accommodation." University of Pennsylvania, 1965.

Lapp, Michael. "Managing Migration: The Migration Division of Puerto Rico and Puerto Ricans in New York City, 1948–1968." Johns Hopkins University, 1990.

McDonough, Edward Francis. "A Cost-Benefit Analysis of a Hartford, Connecticut Urban Renewal Project." University of Massachusetts, 1968.

Uriarte-Gaston, Miren. "Organizing for Survival: The Emergence of a Puerto Rican Community." Boston University, 1988.

Watson, Franklin Jordan. "An Analysis of Selected Demographic and Social Differences among the Suburbs of the Metropolitan Community of Hartford, Connecticut: 1960." University of Connecticut, 1966.

PAPERS

Markham, Walter Gray. "Chromatic Justice: Color as an Element of the Offense." Paper presented at the meetings of the American Political Science Association, Chicago, 29 August-2 September 1974.
Mollenkopf, John H. "On the Causes and Consequences of Political Mobilization." Paper presented at the meetings of the American Political Science Association, New Orleans, 4–8 September 1973.
Valocchi, Stephen. "Hartford Voices: Race, Ethnicity and Neighborhood during the Great Depression." September 1993. Unpublished manuscript.

GOVERNMENT DOCUMENTS

City of Hartford, Department of Planning. *Hartford Plan of Development, 1985–2000.* 1986.
Comprehensive Planning Unit, Hartford Department of Planning. *Hartford: State of the City.* September 1983.
Hartford Department of Planning and Economic Development. *Hartford, Connecticut: State of the City 1995.*
Journal of the Court of Common Council, 1977–79. 2 vols.
Senior, Clarence, and Donald O. Watkins. "Toward a Balance Sheet of Puerto Rican Migration." In *Status of Puerto Rico: Selected Background Studies Prepared for the United States-Puerto Rico Commission on the Status of Puerto Rico,* pp. 689–795. Washington, D.C., 1966.
U.S. Department of Commerce, Bureau of the Census. *Census of Population: 1970,* vol. I, *Characteristics of the Population, Part 8: Connecticut.* Washington, D.C.: U.S. Government Printing Office, 1973.

ARCHIVAL AND PRIVATE COLLECTIONS

Department of Puerto Rican Community Affairs, Commonwealth of Puerto Rico, New York City, Archival Collection (currently housed at the Centro de Estudios Puertorriqueños, Hunter College, City University of New York)
Legislative Electoral Action Program Collection, Hartford.
New England Farmworkers Council Collection, Hartford.
Juan Brito Collection, Hartford.
Juan Fuentes Collection, Hartford.
Edwin Vargas, Jr. Collection, Hartford.

INTERVIEWS

(* = conducted in Spanish, translated by the author)
Diana Alverio, 8 June 1993, Hartford.
Ramón Arroyo, 29 July 1991, Hartford.
Peter Ayala, 7 August 1991, Hartford.
César Batalla, 15 January 1993, Bridgeport, Conn.
John Bonelli, 7 August 1991, Hartford.
Rebecca Brito, 10 August 1992, Hartford.
Arthur Brouillet, 8 August 1991, Hartford.
Nicholas Carbone, 30 July 1991 and 4 March 1993, Hartford.
* Eugenio Caro, 14 August 1992, Hartford.
* Juan "Johnny" Castillo, 14 August 1992, Hartford.
James Crowley, 20 July 1994, Hartford.
* José Cruz, 27 January 1993, Puerto Rico.
Jack Cullin, 28 July 1991, Hartford.
Yasha Escalera, 21 February 1993, Hartford.
Max Fernández, 6 August 1991, Hartford.
Juan Figueroa, 9 August 1991, Hartford, CT.
Mary Ellen Flynn, 12 August 1992, Hartford.
* Juan Fuentes, 1 August 1991, 1 February 1993, and 13 February 1993, Hartford.
* José Garay, 14 August 1992 and 26 January 1993, Hartford.
Abe Giles, 3 August 1991, Hartford.
William Hagan, 30 July 1991 and 26 September 1991, Hartford.
Juan Hernández, 21 June 1997, Worcester, Mass.
Robert Killian, 20 July 1994, Hartford.
George Kinsella, 20 July 1994, Hartford.
Marie Kirkley-Bey, 7 August 1991, Hartford.
* José La Luz, 6 July 1989, New York City.
* Wilfredo Matos, 29 January 1993, Bridgeport, Conn.; 22 July 1994, Hartford.
* Olga Mele, 6 August 1992 and 21 February 1993, Hartford.
Edna Negrón, 28 July 1991 and 29 January 1993, Hartford.
Ramón Pacheco, 3 August 1991, Hartford.
Danny Pérez, 2 August 1991, Hartford.
Eddie Pérez, 6 August 1991, Hartford.
William J. Pérez, 30 January 1993, Puerto Rico.
Carrie Saxon Perry, 20 July 1994, Hartford.
George Ritter, 22 July 1994, Hartford.
Thomas Ritter, 21 July 1994, Hartford.
Alfredo Rodríguez, 5 March 1993, Hartford.
Carmen Rodríguez, 6 August 1991, Hartford.
Ethan Rome, 1 August 1991, Hartford.
Antoinette Leone Ruzzier, 12 August 1992, Hartford.
* Frances Sánchez, 7 August 1991, Hartford.
Sydney Schulman, 15 January 1993, Hartford.
Jorge Simón, 30 July 1991 and 6 August 1991, Hartford.

Antonio Soto, 5 August 1991, Hartford.
Calixto Torres, 7 August 1991, Hartford.
Mildred Torres, 1 August 1991 and 2 March 1993, Hartford.
Edwin Vargas, Jr., 31 January 1989, 22 June 1989, 30–31 July 1991, 7 August
   1991, 23 May 1992, 15 June 1992, 14 January 1993, 20 February 1993,
   2 March 1993, 3 June 1993, 2 July 1993, 17 September 1993, Hartford;
   19 November 1992, Washington, D.C.
Sylvia Vargas, 1 August 1991, Hartford.
* Andrés Vázquez, 3 March 1993, Hartford.
* Gerardo "Jerry" Zayas, 10 August 1992, Hartford.

OTHER SOURCES

American City Corporation. "Hartford Process Underway." In *Urban Life in New
   and Renewing Communities* 13. June-July 1972.
Berman, Paul. "In Defense of Reason." *New Yorker,* 4 September 1995, 93–94.
City of Philadelphia, Commission on Human Relations. *Philadelphia's Puerto Ri-
   can Population with 1960 Census Data.* March 1964.
Donchian, Daniel. "A Survey of New Haven's Newcomers: The Puerto Ricans."
   Human Relations Council of Greater New Haven. May 1959.
Friedan, Betty. "Children's Crusade." *New Yorker,* 3 June 1996, 5–6.
Golob, Fred. "The Puerto Rican Worker in Perth Amboy, New Jersey." Occasional
   Studies no. 2. Institute of Management and Labor Relations, Rutgers Univer-
   sity. March 1956.
Gourevitch, Philip. "Misfortune Tellers." *New Yorker,* 8 April 1996, 96–100.
Guzmán, Pablo. "La Vida Pura: A Lord of the Barrio." *Village Voice,* 21
   March 1995, 24–31.
Heartney, Eleanor. "Identity Politics at the Whitney." *Art in America,* May 1993,
   42–47.
Howe, Irving. "The Limits of Ethnicity." *New Republic,* June 25, 1977, 17–19.
Imse, Thomas P. "Puerto Ricans in Buffalo." City of Buffalo, Board of Community
   Relations. 1961.
Jones, Isham B. "The Puerto Rican in New Jersey: His Present Status." New Jersey
   State Department of Education, Division against Discrimination. July 1955.
Koch, J. E. "Puerto Ricans Come to Youngstown." *Commonweal,* 8 Octo-
   ber 1953, 9–11.
Lemann, Nicholas. "Black Nationalism on Campus." *The Atlantic,* January 1993,
   pp. 31–47.
McLane, Daisann. "The Cuban-American Princess." *New York Times Magazine,*
   26 February 1995, p. 42.
National Puerto Rican Coalition. *Assessing the Impact of Federal Cutbacks on
   Employment and Training Opportunities for Puerto Ricans: Summary of a
   Seven-City Study.* Washington, D.C., September 1983.
———. *A Demographic Profile of Puerto Ricans in the United States.* Prepared by
   Jeffrey S. Passel. Washington, D.C., 1992.
Puelo, Tom. "Park Street Blues." *Northeast,* 5 January 1997, pp. 8–11, 14–16.

Puerto Rican Socialist Party. "Desde Las Entrañas: Political Declaration of the United States Branch of the Puerto Rican Socialist Party." Photocopy. 1 April 1973.

String, Alvin. "Puerto Ricans in New Jersey." *Public Health News*, August 1962.

Traub, James. "The Hearts and Minds of City College." *New Yorker*, 7 June 1993, pp. 42–53.

Index

Abreu, Santiago Polanco, 56
absentee ballots, 166–167
acculturation: and names, 51
Act of Consolidation of 1896, 90
Adult Counseling Service, 72
Aetna Life and Casualty Company: sale of divisions to Travelers Group, Inc., 155
affirmative action, 76, 205
African American Alliance. *See* North Hartford Alliance
African Americans: and alliance with Italians, 146; and alliance with Puerto Ricans, 74, 98, 102, 106, 131, 173, 182–183, 201, 204, 207; civil rights movement, 6; compared/contrasted to Puerto Ricans, 9, 55, 60, 71, 76, 81, 95–97, 127, 169–170; and competing interest with Puerto Ricans, 156, 182; and containment of Puerto Ricans, 146–147; slavery, 9; and suburban flight, 25; and tension between Puerto Ricans, 135–137, 142, 151–152, 182–183, 201, 204, 212
Alverio, Diana, 101. *See also* Voto Boricua
Americanism: decline of, 6
Americanization, 74. *See also* Kernstock, Elwyn Nicholas
Athanson, George (city council, mayor), 57, 113, 121, 126–128, 130
Atrévete campaign: and voter registration, 175
Ayala, Peter, 126, 139, 140

Bailey, John M., 102; and takeover of Democratic party organization, 23
Barlow, Boce W., Jr., 91, 97
Barnard-Brown school: and language instruction, 51
barriers. *See* cultural barriers; language barriers
baseball, 77–78, 83, 98, 113, 151, 160, 161. *See also* Julián Vargas League

Bennett, Collin (city council), 60, 73
bilingual education, 51, 92, 161, 194, 203
Billington, Dorothy, 111
Bithorn, María (Dr.), 129
Black Political Leadership of North Hartford, 103
board of education: and privatization, 184, 186, 190
Borges, Frank (city council), 133, 135, 136
Borrero, Mike, 125, 130–132
Brito, Rebecca (Becky) Delgado, 126, 154
brokered representation, 89–99, 121
Brouillet, Arthur, 80, 140–142
Bureau of Adult Education of the Hartford Board of Education, 41–42

Camacho, Gilberto, 52, 54, 62, 65, 69, 80, 82, 84, 165–166, 168
Caminemos Adult Learning Center, 92
Campaign Committee of the Bilingual Task Force, 93
Campos, Pedro Albizu, 44, 166–167
capitalism: in relation to migration, 3
Capitol Region Council of Governments (CRCOG), 105
Caraballo, Zoilo, 37, 39, 41–42
Carbone, Nicholas (deputy mayor), 2, 30–32, 53–54, 57, 70–71, 76, 80, 84, 86, 92–95, 98–100, 106–107, 110–111, 115–117, 120–123, 126–127, 155, 158, 173, 175, 194; and defeat of, 189
Carmona, Cesar, 110
Caro, Eugenio, 97, 102–103, 110, 114, 118, 120, 122, 125–126, 136, 139, 140–144, 147, 151–153, 168–169, 170, 186–187, 192, 202, 212
Castillo, Juan (Johnny), 48, 68, 71–72, 77–78, 83, 148
Castillo, Yolanda (city council, daughter of Juan Castillo), 71, 80, 148, 169, 186
CAUSA. *See* Connecticut Association of United Spanish Administrators

CCC. *See* Citizens Charter Commission
CCLUF. *See* Connecticut Civil Liberties Union Foundation
CETA. *See* Comprehensive Employment Training Act
Citizens Charter Commission (CCC), 23–24
Citizens Lobby, 17; and exclusion of Puerto Ricans, 35
citizenship: and Jones Act, 3
Civil Rights Act of 1964, 105
civil rights violations, 105, 167
Clark, John, Jr. (city council), 26
Claudio, José, 73, 168
Clay Hill Mothers Club, 83
Colón, Juan, 136
colonialism: in relation to migration, 3; and Puerto Ricans in Chicago, 11; in Puerto Rico, 81
Columbia University: study of Puerto Ricans in New York, 49
Comanchero incident, 56–58, 63, 67–69, 96. *See also* rioting
Comerieños Ausentes, 61
Comité Vargas Para Consejal, 111
Committee of 24, 114–115, 118, 120, 122–123, 125, 176
Community Renewal Team (CRT), 43, 68, 76, 97
Comprehensive Employment Training Act (CETA), 112
Comulada, Fernando (city council), 147–148, 187
Concilio Latinoamericano Para el Avance Laboral (Labor Council for Latin American Advancement), 130
Connecticut Association of United Spanish Administrators (CAUSA), 78, 81
Connecticut Civil Liberties Union Foundation (CCLUF), 195–196, 211
Constitution Plaza: and suburban flight, 27; and urban redevelopment, 173
containment: compared to Nazism, 105
contingency theory of power: defined, 17–18, 178
Cooney, Andrew (Father), 50, 89, 176
Córdova Díaz, Jorge Luis, 60, 64
CRCOG. *See* Capitol Region Council of Governments
Crowley, James, 135, 145, 151
CRT. *See* Community Renewal Team

Cruz, José, 54–55, 76, 83, 87–88, 90, 97, 163, 170
cuchifrito politics, 209
Cullin, Jack, 144, 185, 190
cultural barriers, 43–44

D'Esopo, Salvator, 169
Debbs, Eugene, 199
DeLucco, Dominick J. (mayor), 169
Department of Labor of Puerto Rico, 4, 50
Devco. *See* Greater Hartford Community Development Corporation
Dignity March, 114
DiPentima, Anthony, 187
Direct Mail Voter Registration Bill, 140
discrimination, 11, 70, 111; banned in housing, 27; in housing, 52, 55
dominant political coalition approach: defined, 16–17

education. *See* bilingual education
Emeterio Betances, Ramón, 139
employment: and city residents, 32–33; and financial, insurance, and real estate sector (FIRE), 29–30; and layoffs, 155
empowerment, 12
Escalera, Yasha, 78, 80, 87, 113, 130, 133, 135, 144, 170
ethnic awareness: defined, 11
ethnicity, 11; and political capability, 35, 162; the challenge of, 213–215; in the political process, 14–15, 202–208
Eurocentric values, 15

factionalism, 81, 88, 123, 132
Fair Employment Practices Act, 26
farmworkers, 88, 109, 161; and absentee ballot voting, 165
Figueroa, Juan, 140–142, 152–154, 186, 188, 190, 195, 201, 211
FIRE (financial, insurance, and real estate sector). *See* employment
Flynn, Mary Ellen, 93–94, 116
Forum for Participation, 81
Freedman, Elisha (city manager), 56–57
Fuentes, Juan, 73, 104

Gang of Five, 148, 182, 186–187, 212
Garay, José, 90, 127
García, Edwin, 145, 210
García, Robert (congress), 96, 131

Gatta, Alfred (city manager), 135, 191
Gerena, Víctor: and Wells Fargo robbery, 167
GHP. *See* Hartford Process
Giles, Abe, 80, 89, 96, 142
González, Antonio, 127–128, 130, 133, 149, 170
González, María B. (also González, María), 116, 140, 141, 143, 149
González-Borrero, María, 139
Goodrich, Samuel, 20
Grand Central Station metaphor, 15
Grasso, Ella (Governor), 17, 70, 86, 99, 113–114, 118, 124, 130
Greater Hartford Community Council, 62, 69
Greater Hartford Community Development Corporation (Devco), 102
Greater Hartford Corporation, 102. *See also* Hartford Process
Greater Hartford Council of Churches, 49–51
Greater Hartford Labor Council, 96, 111
Greater Hartford Process, Inc. (GHP). *See* Hartford Process

Hartford Board of Education, 105, 159
Hartford Democratic Town Committee, 1, 130
Hartford Federation of Teachers, 111, 138, 151, 152, 184
Hartford Foundation for Public Giving, 69, 83, 97
Hartford Process, 102–106, 112, 122, 133, 145, 175; and controversial memo, 103–106, 170, 171
Heslin, Mary (deputy mayor), 99–101, 121
Hispanic Democratic Reform Club, 111, 121
Hispanic Health Council, 82–83, 87, 107, 168, 185
Hispanic Leadership Caucus, 134, 136, 138, 139, 141, 149, 209. *See also* Puerto Rican Political Action Committee of Connecticut (PRPAC)
Hooker, Thomas (Hartford's founder), 8, 9
housing, 55, 64, 105, 118, 120, 122, 132, 161, 174, 203, 211, 214; and displacement, 73, 122. *See also* public housing

I Vote Puerto Rican. *See* Voto Boricua
Ibargüen, Alberto, 117, 130

identity politics: defined, 10; and expressiveness and rationality, 156, 160–162; and interest articulation, 162–169; salutary effects of, 209–211; and urban power, 193–196
incorporation: defined, 10
independence: of Puerto Rico from U.S., 108–109, 166–167
insurance industry: and city redevelopment, 173
interests vs. interest groups, 10
Internet: and seders in rock clubs, 14
interracial marriage, 197
Italian American Democrats of Hartford, 169

Jiménez, Esther, 76, 170
Johnson Act, 3
Jones Act, 3
Julián Vargas League, 77

Kennelly, Barbara (city council, secretary of state, U.S. representative), 102, 115–117, 120, 124, 191
Kernstock, Elwyn Nicholas: 1970 survey of Puerto Ricans, 74, 81, 98, 171
Kinsella, James (city council, mayor), 89, 163
Kinsella, Pete (city treasurer), 135
Kinsella School, and renaming of, 139
Kirkley-Bey, Marie, 141, 192

La Casa de Puerto Rico, 73, 81–83, 93, 98, 103–104, 107, 110, 139, 140, 151, 168, 176, 185, 186
La Luz, Alejandro, 58; and Comancheros incident, 60, 72, 166, 168
La Luz, José, 107–110, 115–117, 119, 121, 123, 125–126, 134, 136–141, 151, 152, 161, 168, 200
La Oficina del Commonwealth. *See* Department of Labor of Puerto Rico
La Popular, Bodega Hispana, 42, 160
Laubach system of English language instruction, 51
Labor Day riots, 28, 58, 67–69, 96
language barriers, 43–44, 55, 60, 72, 92; and voting, 65
Latin American Action Project, 54–55, 64
LEAP. *See* Legislative Electoral Action Program

Legislative Electoral Action Program (LEAP), 142, 190
Libassi, Peter, 103–104, 106, 176
Los Macheteros: and Wells Fargo robbery, 167
Ludgin, Robert (city council), 114–115, 122, 126–127, 129, 132
Lugo, José, 140

Mahon, John J., 91–92
Martínez, Angel Viera (speaker, Puerto Rican House of Representatives): and absentee ballot voting, 165
Martínez, Jesús ("Wito"), 89–90, 161
Martorell, Feliciano, 62, 64–65
Mathews, Charles (city council, deputy mayor), 135, 138, 145, 147, 149, 151, 187
Mele, Olga, 43, 46–47, 68, 70, 72, 77, 89, 93, 96–97, 160, 163, 170, 176
Meléndez, Nancy (city council), 126, 134–139, 151, 161, 209
migration: intercity, 5; of Puerto Ricans to New England, 3; revolving-door, 75
military service: and absentee ballot voting, 165–166
Milner, Thirman, 130, 131, 132, 138
Milward, Henrietta (deputy mayor), 183, 187
Monserrat, Joseph, 55–56
Morales, Florencio, 43, 76
Movimiento Pro Independencia (MPI), 84–85, 108. See also Puerto Rican Socialist Party
MPI. See Movimiento Pro Independencia
MUJER. See Mujeres Unidas for Justice, Equality, and Reform
Mujeres Unidas for Justice, Equality, and Reform (MUJER), 101, 121, 168

NAACP, 26, 96–97, 103–104
names: and acculturation, 51
National Puerto Rican Coalition (NPRC), 191
National Puerto Rican Forum, 125, 140
Negrón, Edna (also Edna Negrón Smith), 79, 92, 104–105, 139, 144–145, 152–153, 185, 188, 190
neocorporatism: defined, 16
New Deal: and liberalism, 8
New England Farm Workers Council, 134

Nieves, Oscar, 116–117
North Hartford Alliance, 183
NPRC. See National Puerto Rican Coalition

O'Brien, Henry J. (archbishop), 51
Ocasio, Angel, 83, 110
OEO. See Office of Equal Opportunity
Office of Equal Opportunity (OEO): and civil rights violations, 105
Ortíz, Félix, 116
otherness: and closing of ranks, 10

Pacheco, Ramón, 134
parades: Connecticut Puerto Rican Day Parade, 52–53, 65, 82, 98, 113, 124, 130, 160, 161, 163; New York City, 14; of September 28, 1969, 62–63
People for Change (PFC), 140–142, 146, 148, 178, 187, 190, 212
People for Vargas, 111. See also Comité Vargas Para Consejal
People's Liberation Party (PLP), 73, 84, 88, 107, 168, 175
Pérez, Danny, 141, 147
Pérez, William J., 84, 91–92
Permanent Commission on the Status of Women (Connecticut), 101
Perry, Carrie Saxon (mayor), 145, 146, 178, 209, 212
Peters, Mike (mayor), 161
PFC. See People for Change
PFC-Perry-South End coalition, 147, 181
Pickett, Charles (Reverend), 60–61
Piñero, Carlos, 132, 166
piropos (complimenting women), 58
PLP. See People's Liberation Party
pluralism: defined, 16
political equality: and political participation/representation, 160
political inequality, 158–159
political mobilization: and demographic growth, 76; and ethnicity, 156–157; and identity politics, 10; and integration, 10
population: and Aetna/Travelers purchase, 155; of Puerto Ricans in Hartford, 4, 74–75; of Puerto Ricans in New York, 4; of Puerto Ricans in the U.S., 3
poverty, 154, 172, 174, 212
power awareness: defined, 11
power elite: defined, 16

PRPAC. *See* Puerto Rican Political Action
    Committee of Connecticut; Hispanic
    Leadership Caucus
PRPAC-Perry coalition, 147, 181, 183
PSP. *See* Puerto Rican Socialist Party
Public Act 91-392, 211
public assistance. *See* public housing; welfare
public housing, 48, 52, 55, 103, 136
Puerto Rican Action for Progress, 60–61, 83
Puerto Rican Democratic Club, 86
Puerto Rican Democratic Club (of Greater
    Hartford), 125
Puerto Rican Democrats of Hartford, 54–
    55, 83, 86, 88
Puerto Rican Families Association, 83
Puerto Rican Federation for Self-Help, 83
Puerto Rican Historical Society, 83
Puerto Rican Nationalist Party: and shoot-
    ing of U.S. representatives, 44–45
Puerto Rican Parade Committee, 62, 82
Puerto Rican Political Action Club of
    Greater Hartford, 136
Puerto Rican Political Action Committee
    of Connecticut (PRPAC), 1, 6, 79, 123–
    126, 134, 138, 139–149, 151–154, 184–
    193, 195–196, 201–203, 209, 211–212;
    and PFC-PRPAC coalition, 192; and
    PRPAC-Perry coalition, 178–183
Puerto Rican Socialist Party (PSP), 73, 85,
    88–89, 104, 105, 107–109, 114, 118–
    119, 151, 167, 175, 176, 199
Puerto Rican Vote. *See* Voto Boricua
Puerto Ricans: and alliance with African
    Americans, 74, 98, 102, 106, 131, 173,
    182–183, 201, 204, 207; compared/con-
    trasted to African Americans, 9, 55, 60,
    71, 76, 81, 95–97, 127, 169–170; and
    competing interest with African Ameri-
    cans, 156, 182; and containment by Afri-
    can Americans, 146–147; and tension
    between African Americans, 135–137,
    142, 151–152, 182–183, 201, 204, 212
Puerto Ricans and Hispanics for Political
    Progress, 125, 131

Quiroz, Ramón: and Comancheros inci-
    dent, 58

Rainbow Myth, 13
Rincón de Gautier, Felisa (mayor of San
    Juan), 48, 52

rioting: assassination of Martin Luther
    King, Jr., 28; Comancheros incident, 56–
    58, 63, 67–69, 96; Labor Day riots of
    1969, 28, 58, 67–69, 96; riots of 1969,
    107, 121, 127, 163, 207
Rivera de Vincenti, Julia (secretary of labor,
    Puerto Rico): and absentee ballot voting,
    165
Rodríguez, Alfredo: and voter registration,
    130
Rodríguez, Carmen, 126, 143, 209
Roldán, Doris, 101
Romany, Sarah, 104
Roraback, J. Henry, 20
Rosario Cantado, 160, 176
Rosazza, Peter (Bishop), 113, 116
Royal Typewriter, 72; and on-the-job train-
    ing, 41
Ryan, Bill (reporter, *Hartford Times*): and
    Comancheros incident, 57–58

SAC. *See* Spanish Action Coalition
San Juan (Catholic) Center, 51, 55, 65, 73,
    78–82, 113, 132, 168, 176
Sánchez, Dolores (state senate), 90, 97, 195
Sánchez, Frances, 139, 143–146, 149, 153,
    187, 192–193
Sánchez, María, 53–57, 68, 70–73, 76–79,
    83, 89–94, 96, 98, 107, 108, 111, 115–
    116, 118–121, 123, 126–127, 130, 133–
    134, 139, 151, 159, 161, 168, 169, 170,
    176; death of, 143–144
Sánchez, Pedro Orozco: and shooting of
    U.S. representatives, 45
SAND. *See* South Arsenal Neighborhood
    Development Corporation
Scott, Tom (senator): and English-only pro-
    posal, 140
SDS. *See* Students for a Democratic Society
Shade Tobacco Growers Agricultural Asso-
    ciation (STGAA), 43, 49
shooting: of U.S. representatives, 44–45
Simmons, Louise (city council), 178–179,
    180, 189
Simón, Jorge (city corporation counsel),
    145, 152, 181–184, 192, 195–196, 201
Smith, Wilber, 101, 115, 121, 170
socioeconomics: and mid-sized vs. big cit-
    ies, 159
Soto, Antonio, 56, 62, 76, 83, 87, 89–90,
    92–93, 97, 152, 161

South Arsenal Neighborhood Development Corporation (SAND), 60

Spanish Action Coalition (SAC), 60–61, 73, 82–83, 96, 98

Spanish American Association of Hartford, 54

Spanish American Center, 78, 80, 130

Spanish American Civic League, 83

Spanish Democratic Club, 125

Spellacy, Thomas J. (mayor), 22–23

St. John the Baptist Day, 52, 98

Stanback, Howard (city manager), 189

State Interracial Commission: established, 25

Statewide Puerto Rican Convention: and independence from U.S., 166

STGAA. See Shade Tobacco Growers Agricultural Association

structuralism: defined, 16

Students for a Democratic Society (SDS), 108, 109

suburban flight, 25–27, 103

Suisman, Richard (city council): and Heslin vacancy, 100

Swank magazine incident, 112–115, 121–123, 160, 175, 176

TAINO Housing Development, 73, 82–83, 87, 168, 185

teachers: recruitment from Puerto Rico, 76–77. See also Teachers Corps

Teachers Corps, 77, 92; as source of community leaders, 79

Three Kings Day, 203

Torres, Calixto, 79, 118

Torres, Felipe N.: and resolution condemning shooting of U.S. representatives, 44–45

Torres, Mildred, 78, 85, 93–94, 110, 116–121, 124–127, 130–134, 138–139, 151–152, 168

Torres, Olga, 125, 127, 133–136

Tory award, 106, 176

Travelers Group, Inc.: and purchase from Aetna, 155

Trumbull, John H. (governor): and policy ignoring plight of cities, 21

unemployment, 154, 172, 174, 191, 203, 212

United Church Women of Greater Hartford, 51

University of Hartford: and Teachers Corps, 77

urban decay, 102. See also suburban flight

urban power: and access to, 169–176; and exercise of, 176–193; understanding of; 15–18

urban redevelopment, 29–32, 102, 173

Vargas, Edwin, Jr., 1, 79, 94, 96, 106–111, 115–121, 123–126, 130–132, 134, 136–138, 140–141, 143, 145–147, 151, 152, 156, 161, 167–169, 181–183, 185, 187, 190–191, 200–201, 211

Vargas, Julián, 37, 42, 54, 76–77, 160, 163, 170

Vaughan, Thomas (police chief): and hiring of Spanish interpreters, 57

Vázquez, Andrés, 86, 110, 113, 116–121, 124, 125

Vecinos Unidos, 122

Vietnam War, 6

violent protests: and shooting of U.S. representatives, 44–45

voter registration, 47, 53, 62, 65, 101, 111, 115, 132, 166, 169, 171, 175, 185, 191, 196, 211; and English-only proposal, 140; and literacy requirements, 173

voting: and absentee ballots, 165–166

Voto Boricua, 100–101, 121, 166, 168, 175

welfare, 48, 71, 174, 212

Wells Fargo robbery, 167

Young Lords Organization (Young Lords party), 84, 199

Young Turks, 136, 168

Zayas, Gerardo (Jerry) (city council), 68, 78, 80, 93, 104, 113, 125, 127, 130, 133, 136, 149

Zirkel, Perry Alan, 77, 79